Catastrophe AND Meaning

Catastrophe

THE

HOLOCAUST

AND THE

TWENTIETH

CENTURY

AND Meaning

*Edited by Moishe Postone
and Eric Santner*

THE UNIVERSITY OF CHICAGO PRESS
CHICAGO & LONDON

MOISHE POSTONE is associate professor of modern European history, sits on the Committee on Jewish Studies, and also teaches in the College at the University of Chicago. He has written *Time, Labor, and Social Domination: A Reinterpretation of Marx's Critical Theory* (1993), as well as numerous articles on critical theory, anti-Semitism and National Socialism, and postwar Germany. ERIC SANTNER is chair of the Department of Germanic Studies, sits on the Committee on Jewish Studies, and also teaches in the College at the University of Chicago. He is the author, most recently, of *On the Psychotheology of Everyday Life: Reflections on Freud and Rosenzweig* (2001).

The University of Chicago Press, Chicago 60637
The University of Chicago Press, Ltd., London
© 2003 by The University of Chicago
All rights reserved. Published 2003
Printed in the United States of America
12 11 10 09 08 07 06 05 04 03   1 2 3 4 5

ISBN: 0-226-67610-2 (cloth)
ISBN: 0-226-67611-0 (paper)

Library of Congress Cataloging-in-Publication Data

Catastrophe and meaning : the Holocaust and the twentieth century / edited by Moishe Postone and Eric Santner.
    p. cm.
Includes bibliographical references and index.
   ISBN 0-226-67610-2 (hardcover : alk. paper) — ISBN 0-226-67611-0 (pbk. : alk. paper)
   1. Holocaust, Jewish (1939–1945)—Influence. 2. Holocaust, Jewish (1939–1945)—
Historiography. 3. Memory. I. Postone, Moishe. II. Santner, Eric L., 1955–
D804.3 .C376 2003
940.53'18—dc21

                                                                        2003000209

♾ The paper used in this publication meets the minimum requirements of the American National Standard for Information Sciences—Permanence of Paper for Printed Library Materials, ANSI Z39.48–1992.

To the lost members of our families

Contents

Introduction

CATASTROPHE AND MEANING

Moishe Postone and Eric Santner

At the beginning of a new century the attempted extermination of European Jewry persists as an impasse to understanding and as a claim on our moral imagination. Though we no longer inhabit the century that produced the Holocaust, it is quite clear that citizens of the twenty-first century continue to dwell in the shadow of this event. If anything, the shadow seems, in recent years, to have taken on new life, to haunt the imagination with increasing force. There are no doubt a number of contingent reasons for this. The approach of a time when the last survivors of the Holocaust will have died has generated a sense of urgency regarding the disappearance of firsthand witnesses and the need to gather the testimony of these individuals. The children and grandchildren of survivors have, moreover, come increasingly to recognize not only the obligations of memory but also the profound and often unconscious ways in which the trauma of their family members has been passed on to them; the members of the second and third generation have come to realize that the catastrophe undergone by their elders has left traces in their minds and bodies, traces that call for elaboration and interpretation.

The need for such elaboration and interpretation has been strongly reinforced by recent historical changes, especially the collapse of the Soviet Union and

European Communism in the last decade of the twentieth century. This collapse has had great historiographic as well as historical significance. It has impelled historians to rethink the course of the century, now grasped as a whole, and to delineate its important phases which, in turn, also has generated reconsiderations of the relation of the Holocaust to its larger historical context.

The demise of Soviet socialism in Europe and, above all, the unification of the two Germanies have also created a radically new geopolitical context for the construction of national histories and identities, for the ways in which the crimes of the Nazi period come to be integrated into the history of Germany and modern Europe more generally. One of the more concentrated sites for such concerns has been the debate about the construction of a Holocaust memorial in the center of Berlin. For the first time a nation will erect, in the middle of its capital, an installation (designed by Peter Eisenman, an American Jew) commemorating the most horrific crimes of its history. Nevertheless, the history of public responses to the Holocaust in the second half of the twentieth century—that is, the production of historiography, literature, film, art, memorials, video archives, public debate (not to mention trials, tribunals, lawsuits)—has by no means been a linear one of the gradual expansion of knowledge and understanding. Neither, however, has it been one of initial, or even delayed, preoccupation followed by a steady loss of interest and engagement. Instead it has followed a more fitful, nonlinear rhythm determined by a number of different factors.

This history has, of course, been shaped by the temporal distance an individual (or a generation) has to the events in question. A memoir by a survivor is worlds apart from a memoir by a child of the same survivor. A generation that learns of the events from contemporary eyewitnesses will have a different sort of access to them than one that learns primarily through books, television, film, and movies which are themselves produced by individuals at a temporal remove from the "object." One's response is thus to a large degree constrained by generational imperatives.

Geography and national identity also, quite obviously, play a crucial role. In spite of all claims to scientific and professional objectivity, a work of historiography by a German historian about the Holocaust will be unavoidably informed by the specific ways in which the historian has had to struggle with the legacies of the crimes in his or her own life and society. (And clearly this holds for Jewish or Israeli historians as well.) The Holocaust Museum in Washington, D.C., has a different purpose and meaning than Yad Vashem in Jerusalem. A Holocaust memorial in Berlin will be informed by different cultural and political imperatives than similar constructions elsewhere.

These temporal and spatial constraints are obviously always intermingled. Recent debates about the construction of the Berlin memorial have, for example, taken place in the context of a newly unified Germany eager to reclaim its place as not only an economic but also a political, cultural, moral, and, most recently, military force in Europe and the world. Responses to the Holocaust are, in other words, always framed by specific contexts of production and reception which inform and inflect them, color them with the needs, desires, and concerns of the "local" constellation of their emergence. As already indicated, these constellations have undergone numerous shifts and transformations since 1945.

Here it might be noted that a great deal of new work on the Holocaust makes a self-conscious effort to inscribe these contexts and situational constraints into the work's composition itself. Paradigmatic for this procedure has been Art Spiegelman's *Maus*, in which the author, the son of a survivor, reconstructs (in utterly unique ways) not only the story of his father's life during the Holocaust but also the troubled and conflictual story of the impact of the father's experience on the author's life and identity as a member of the so-called second generation. Furthermore, Spiegelman's work very carefully thematizes the process and sites of historical transmission itself, the explicit and implicit ways in which knowledge of the Holocaust is passed across a generational divide.

Interest in and attention to the Holocaust in the public sphere has often clustered around significant events, crises, debates, and what we might call paradigm shifts or breakthroughs in modes of representation and response. Certainly the major trials pertaining to the Holocaust have had an enormous impact on the imagination and the discourse about it. Indeed, it might be said that sustained historiographic work on the Holocaust only began in earnest after the Eichmann trial in 1961 which was itself staged, in part, as an effort to disseminate knowledge and awareness of the Nazis' "Final Solution" in Israel and the world more generally. But as indicated, major works of historiography can themselves assume the status of an "event," one that creates a new framework for comprehension, a new way of symbolizing or integrating the object of research into a broader understanding of history and society. Such works have a certain "performative" dimension; they open up possibilities of thought that were in some sense simply not there before but rather enter the world with their initial articulation. This was certainly the case with Raul Hilberg's *Destruction of the European Jews*, which appeared the same year as the Eichmann trial. This unsurpassed work explores in enormous detail the administrative and technical aspects of the killing operations. Hilberg's central metaphor of "the machinery of destruction" was in its turn crucial for Hannah Arendt's account of the Eichmann trial and her now famous characterization of the killing operations as manifesting a "banality of evil." (Arendt also depended on Hilberg for her controversial reflections on the role of the Jewish Councils in the ghettos.)

Political and cultural developments not directly linked to the Holocaust have played a crucial role in shifts in modes of representation and response, in the rhythms of memory and forgetting, attraction and repulsion. For the most part, the Holocaust was very much marginalized in general historical discourse and in public discourse during the Cold War decades of the late 1940s, the 1950s, and the early 1960s, or it was subsumed by purportedly more universalistic motifs. So, for example, monuments to murdered civilians in Eastern Europe and the Soviet Union identified Jewish victims as Polish, Russian, Lithuanian, or Ukrainian—but not as Jews. In the West, *The Diary of Anne Frank* was framed by a universalistic message that downplayed the Jewish dimension of that tragic story. This marginalization began to change in the course of the international "thaw" of the 1960s in the United States, France, Germany, Israel, and even the Soviet Union with the publication of studies on anti-Semitism and Nazism by scholars such as George Mosse, as well as with important novels written against the background of the Holocaust, such as Jerzy Kozinski's *Painted Bird* and André Schwartz-Bart's *Last of the Just.*

In Germany, the growing concern with the Holocaust was expressed politically as well. The student revolts of the 1960s are generally held to be a crucial breakthrough in the history of responses to the Holocaust in the Federal Republic of Germany. For this was a moment when a new generation of Germans was struggling—often violently, often self-destructively—to distance itself, to *disidentify* with its parents and the institutions of the Federal Republic (this was largely a West German phenomenon) that were seen as being continuous with the Nazi period. The strong focus on the Holocaust among West German students became much more complicated and fraught after 1967 as a result of the strong left-wing identification with the Palestinian cause. During the early 1970s, public discussion of the Holocaust ebbed, only to grow strong once again toward the end of that decade.

The curiosity about Nazism and the Holocaust that emerged in the wake of the student revolts often took shape within the framework of critiques of capitalism and its role in fascism. This curiosity would, in the late seventies and eighties, assume a more "subjective" aspect with the publication of numerous works of autobiographical fiction and nonfiction in which members of the second generation attempted to come to terms with their parents—above all with fathers directly or indirectly implicated in Nazi crimes—and with the psychic legacies of Nazism and the Holocaust. The most intimate spheres of life were seen to have been touched and, not rarely, irreparably poisoned by a sense of belonging to families and communities that created "that." The most recent instance of this literary trend is Bernhard Schlink's novel *The Reader.*

These (often impossible) efforts to come to terms with the past not only intellectually but also at the level of affect and emotion came to include a new "openness" to the dimension of fascination, to the ways in which Hitler and Nazism captured the imagination of millions of Germans during the Third Reich. Triggered in part by the publication of Albert Speer's memoirs and a series of Hitler biographies (one thinks above all of Joachim Fest's work), writers and especially filmmakers tried to stage this dimension of "fascinating fascism" for the purposes of analysis, critique, and what Freud referred to as the "work of mourning." Certainly the most ambitious of these efforts was Hans Jürgen Syberberg's 7–hour film, *Our Hitler,* in which the fantasmatic—and, so the film's argument goes, in some sense cinematic—kernel of Nazi ideology was explored with a disturbing combination of sorrow, irony, and nostalgia. (It was above all this seeming nostalgia that made more than a few viewers wonder about the ultimate goals of the film.) Syberberg's film seemed, at least for some, to have taken on the tasks of mourning, the failure of which, according to the psychoanalysts Margarete and Alexander Mitscherlich, had so profoundly marked the immediate postwar period. Only by working through the deep narcissistic attachment to the grandiosity of the National Socialist movement, the Mitscherlichs argued, could Germans begin to reinvest their passions in a new democratic political culture. This attempt to explore the deep psychic attachments to Nazi ideology would, of course, become central to the work of the German painter Anselm Kiefer, perhaps the most celebrated German artist of the postwar generation and certainly the one most identified with efforts to explore the legacies of Nazism.

With regard to "media events," the one that has often been held to have had the greatest impact on the greatest number of people is the NBC miniseries *Holocaust.* Above all in West Germany, the impact of this broadcast in 1979 was hailed as a major turning point in the "integration" of the Holocaust into the historical consciousness and conscience of the public. It was, it appeared, the very sentimental, even "kitsch," aesthetic of the series that allowed broad sections of the public to identify and empathize with the (middle-class German-Jewish) victims portrayed in the film. Not since the performance of the Anne Frank story in theaters across the country in the 1950s had so many been so emotionally engaged with the fate of the Jews in the Third Reich. In this case as in so many others, one can never be certain about the depth of the response, about the place such events might ultimately occupy in the rhythms of forgetting and remembering. One certainty that did emerge from the debates surrounding the effectiveness of *Holocaust,* however, was that knowledge of the attempted extermination of the Jews would, in the future, be largely disseminated through film and television and that aesthetic decisions about representation would shoulder an ever greater burden of responsibility for the future of memory. It was for this reason that the vast aesthetic differences between two later films, Claude Lanzmann's *Shoah* and

Steven Spielberg's *Schindler's List,* would assume such enormous proportions for those who were deeply engaged with this history.

Perhaps the most famous political event in the history of responses to the Holocaust was the public debate unleashed by the ceremony marking the fortieth anniversary of the end of World War II at the cemetery at Bitburg, Germany, in 1985. It was President Ronald Reagan's remarks in defense of his visit to a military cemetery in which former SS members were also buried that best captures the stakes of the debate: "there's nothing wrong with visiting that cemetery where those young men are victims of Nazism also. . . . They were victims, just as surely as the victims in the concentration camps." The question of the claim to "victimhood" would also, in the years that followed, occupy a central place in what became known as the "Historians' Debate" in Germany.

This debate, played out in large measure in newspapers and journals in Germany, focused on the question of "revisionism" in the writing of the history of the Holocaust. Central to revisionist trends was the effort to balance the crimes of Nazism with those of Stalinism and to suggest that the Nazi terror might become more understandable in light of the threats represented by Bolshevism. Most important, once the Holocaust was placed on the same level with the Stalinist terror, it became, as it were, another national atrocity, another example of mass violence in the twentieth century; it ceased to be an event that uniquely challenges the Germans in their right to or capacity for a "normal" national identity.

It is worth noting that attempts to downplay the uniqueness of the Holocaust were discursively more powerful during the first Cold War period (the late 1940s, the 1950s, the early 1960s) and the second (the early 1980s). The period between the two Cold Wars was characterized by growing public discussion, especially in Germany, of the specificity of Nazi crimes and the Holocaust. In that sense, the "Historians' Debate" of the 1980s represented a clash between fundamentally different forms of contemporary German self-understanding that were dominant at different moments of postwar history.

Running parallel to these politically charged debates in the German press were more scholarly discussions concerning the question of the historicization of the Holocaust. One focus of these debates was the question about the centrality of the Holocaust not only in the ideology and policies of the Nazi regime but also in the daily lives of "normal" German citizens during the Third Reich. To what degree was daily life affected by the "Final Solution"? What were the ways in which Germans showed themselves to stand apart from Nazi ideology and goals, to "resist" without necessarily becoming a part of any organized political resistance? The pursuit of such questions was contested, in part, by those who argued that the focus on everyday life tended to dissolve the specificity of the National Socialist regime and had unintended legitimating consequences.

The question of the possibility of something like "normal" life standing along-side a murderous project of the dimensions of the "Final Solution" belongs, at least in part, within the much larger debates that have preoccupied historians working on the Holocaust almost since the beginning of such research. These debates—abbreviated as one between "intentionalists" and "functionalists"— revolve, as is well known, around the question of decision-bearing agency and its proper locus in the complex process/series of events that we call the Holocaust, that is, whether the extermination of the Jews unfolded according to the logic of a criminal conspiracy with Hitler calling the shots (on the basis of long-held be-liefs and plans) or, rather, whether the extermination project emerged in more haphazard fashion according to a ramifying pattern of radicalization influenced by often contingent factors.

Though both intentionalists and functionalists largely concern themselves with matters of policy and operational responsibility, on a certain reading the functionalist approach might seem to mitigate against any notion of a "normal life" side by side with the Holocaust. For the functionalist argument is ultimately one that *disperses* the responsibility for the extermination across a wide spectrum of large and small actors who, in piecemeal fashion and often without a sense of the whole project and its scope, produced and sustained the machinery of de-struction. At the root of the huge success of and massive controversy around Daniel Goldhagen's book, *Hitler's Willing Executioners,* in 1996, was the way in which he combined this picture of dispersed operational responsibility with a rather straightforward intentionalism. There was indeed a criminal conspiracy bent on extermination from the start—with the Nazi rise to power—but it was one in which an entire society willingly, even zealously, participated (a willing-ness which Goldhagen traces to an especially malignant form of anti-Semitism that permeated German culture at least since the early nineteenth century).

The debates on the Holocaust have far-reaching implications for understand-ing other horrific crimes and, more generally, for grappling with the historical emergence of such crimes, which have become all too common in the recent past. The eruption of genocidal passions and projects in such places as Cambo-dia, Rwanda, Bosnia, and Kosovo has contributed to the sense that possibilities unleashed in the Holocaust have continued, in some fashion, to circulate in the life of nations. One feels that perhaps with the Holocaust something new entered the world, that this event was not simply an actualization of already existing human potential but a shift in the space of possibilities itself, a space we all now inhabit. Thus the urgency of further and ever more refined analyses of the emergence of this shift, of the "birth" of this mutation of human possibilities, and of its relation to general historical processes in the twentieth century. As Jürgen Habermas has put it, "There [in Auschwitz] something happened, that up to now nobody considered as even possible. There one touched on something which represents the deep layer of solidarity among all that wears a human face; notwithstanding all the usual acts of beastliness of human history, the integrity of this common layer had been taken for granted . . . Auschwitz has changed the basis for the continuity of conditions of life within history."[1]

II

The essays in this volume take up the challenge of this urgency. They engage and carry forward a number of central debates concerning the catastrophe: its enabling conditions, its place in larger twentieth-century histories, the responsibilities of memory, the possibilities of new futures.

The first cluster of issues pertains to the place and nature of anti-Semitism in the unfolding of the event we variously call the Holocaust, the "Final Solution," the Shoah, or simply the destruction of the Jews *(Judenvernichtung)*. The publication in 1996 of Goldhagen's *Hitler's Willing Executioners* forms, at some level, the backdrop for the two essays of this first cluster, both of which, in their own way, reject Goldhagen's thesis of an "eliminationist anti-Semitism" at the heart of German political culture dating to the early modern period.

In his essay, Saul Friedländer emphasizes the importance of the interplay between immediate circumstance on the Russian front during World War II and three major historical processes: the anti-Jewish tradition embedded in the evolution of Christianity; the so-called Age of Ideology, which characterized late nineteenth- and early twentieth-century Europe; and the tendencies toward rationalization, bureaucratization, and instrumentalization characteristic of modernity. Nevertheless, Friedländer shows that neither consideration of immediate historical processes nor of the overarching history of Christian anti-Semitism nor of modernity can account for the specificity of the Holocaust. Consequently, he argues for the critical importance of the apocalyptic, all-encompassing, "redemptive" anti-Semitic ideology of Hitler and the hard core of the Nazi Party. Characterizing redemptive anti-Semitism as an ideology based on a vision of an apocalyptic struggle to the death between the Jews and "Aryan humanity," Friedländer focuses on Hitler's statements regarding the Jews in October and December 1941, and argues that the conditions of World War II in those months allowed this ideology to come to fruition. He maintains, more generally, that the changes in the extent and nature of Hitler's anti-Semitic utterances and policies between 1919 and 1941 must be understood in political-instrumental terms. Although Friedländer does not argue that extermination had always been Hitler's goal, he does maintain that the Holocaust cannot be understood adequately without reference to redemptive anti-Semitism. In contrast with Goldhagen, he differentiates between the anti-Semitism of Hitler, the inner core of the party and its associated agencies, and the more traditional anti-Semitism of other German elites and of the German population at large. In all of this Friedländer emphasizes, however, that traditional anti-Semitism was a *necessary* condition for the execution of the radical ideology.

Shulamit Volkov, too, distinguishes among a variety of anti-Semitisms but takes a more critical view of the place of anti-Semitic ideology in the perpetration of the Holocaust. Her essay offers a critical reflection on the relation of ideology to practice, arguing that the former is never simply translated into the latter; rather, ideology and practice are always intermingled and co-constitutive. Indeed, ideology is in some cases posited as the "cause" of actions retroactively. She notes that Nazi Germany had already been carrying out the mass murders and deportations of Jews prior to Hitler's genocidal remarks in October and December 1941, to which Friedländer refers. The programmatic extermination of the Jews, in other words, cannot be explained only with reference to the anti-Semitic ideology of Hitler and his inner circle. According to Volkov, only narratives that examine the detailed course of events and substitute the question *how* for that of *why* can come near to an explanation of the Holocaust.

One of the abiding questions of concern to anyone trying to understand the Holocaust is its relation to general historical narratives that structure the span of the twentieth century in Europe. What place does the Holocaust occupy in the history of capitalism and Western modernity, in the so-called dialectic of enlightenment, the history of instrumental reason? Where does the Holocaust fit in the field of forces constituting the international civil war between Bolshevism and anti-Bolshevism? What is its place in the history of racism and colonialism, the history of eugenics, or the larger history of what Foucault called *biopower,* the entrance of bare life into the calculations of states? Is there a singular historical narrative of the twentieth century in Europe that could comprehend all these other developments? How can the Holocaust be posited as a singular event that nevertheless in some sense condenses and stands for the violence of the century? How, finally, does one integrate contingency into these grand narrative schemes? Anson Rabinbach, Dan Diner, and Moishe Postone each struggle with this problem of the narrative contextualization of an event that seems to break the frame of narrative comprehension.

Rabinbach revisits the debates between those who understood Nazism primarily with reference to the pathologies of modernity, and those who did so with reference to the unique pathologies of modern German historical development. Focusing on Theodor Adorno and Max Horkheimer, he argues that only an analysis of modernity as a dialectic of enlightenment and counterenlightenment can account for the possibility of the Holocaust as well as the ongoing potential for genocidal politics in the contemporary world, for example in Rwanda and Bosnia. This approach illuminates aspects of modernity at its greatest stress points, where the dialectic of enlightenment generates the temptation of "redemptive" violence.

Diner presents two possible general axes of interpretation of the history of the twentieth century. One axis (which is continuous with the dominant narrative of the nineteenth century) is focused on struggles for hegemony among states and nations. The other axis focuses on issues of class, political values, and ideology, and is organized around the international civil war of 1917–89 between Bolshevism and anti-Bolshevism. Diner argues that the Holocaust cannot easily be explained by or integrated into either axis of interpretation of the century. Anti-Semitism, he maintains, explains why the Jews were chosen as victims, but other, more general factors explain the *form* of the killing. In this way, Diner attempts to relate the Holocaust to more general historical phenomena while suggesting that the links among those phenomena remain contingent.

Postone attempts to relate the Holocaust and its aftermath more closely to general historical patterns of the twentieth century by developing further the theory of commodity fetishism as a social theory of ideology. Criticizing interpretations of National Socialism either as antimodern or as a logical end point of modernity, he analyzes modern anti-Semitism as a revolt against the massive ongoing changes resulting from the intangible, abstract domination of capital— misrecognized as a Jewish conspiracy. Within this ideological framework, the Jews came to be seen as a dangerous threat to life itself that had to be completely extirpated in order to save humanity. According to Postone, then, the crime of extermination, and not only the choice of victims, can be grounded in an analysis of modern anti-Semitism. Extending his analysis of capital to postwar issues of history and memory, he calls into question recent interpretations that characterize the immediate postwar decades as forward-directed, driven by a universalistic project. Such interpretations contrast this historical project with the subsequent particularism of the politics of identity and with the growing importance of Holocaust discourse in the public sphere. Instead, Postone proposes distinguishing critically between a form of universality that negates difference and one that can encompass difference, and relates that distinction to two very different forms of future orientation: one based on appropriating the past, and one that remains driven by it.

In the third cluster of essays, questions of history, memory, identity, agency, and victimhood enter the foreground. For Omer Bartov, the experience of war, mass death, and defeat in World War I was the crucible out of which emerged an ideology of former front-line soldiers—call them proto-Nazis—profoundly alienated from civilian life and values. The notion of the community of battle

(Kampfgemeinschaft) that emerged from the war served as the basis for the Nazi conception of the ethnic community *(Volksgemeinschaft)*. Crucial to the self-understanding of this "community" was a rhetoric of victimization mingled with a glorification of war, a mixture that fueled convictions pertaining to threats from a diabolical enemy set upon the destruction of the German people. Wehrmacht soldiers, according to Bartov, were very much driven by such ideological convictions, which allowed genocide to be coded as a grimly glorious, redemptive act. The rhetoric of suffering and victimhood, which obscured the Wehrmacht's complicity in criminal actions, persisted, Bartov argues, into the postwar period in the underground bitterness of veterans who felt that their glorious sacrifices were not given sufficient public recognition.

The identification of oneself as victim is also at the center of Frank Trommler's discussion of the trajectory of public discourse in postwar Germany on the Holocaust. Before 1945, he argues, Germans were deeply drawn into a culture of mourning, which was focused originally on World War I and then generalized by the Nazi cult of the dead. This sense of mourning, ironically, began to dissipate after Stalingrad, and was replaced by a culture of self-pity, in which all Germans were victims. The subsequent absence of a culture of mourning made it easier, according to Trommler, to suppress feelings of guilt and responsibility after the war. During the first two postwar decades, the period of "collective silence," legal language was hegemonic as the public code for dealing with the Holocaust. This allowed for a strong separation of public and private responses to the past, for a mode of addressing the past while avoiding it. This mode of responding to the past was challenged and partially superseded in the 1970s and 1980s by what Trommler refers to as the triumph of the therapeutic, borne primarily by the children of the war generation. This transition from shame and evasion to an emphasis on the Holocaust as a wound in the national body politic did not, however, signal a deepening of mourning, according to Trommler. On the contrary, he claims, referring to Freud, it represented a new form of acting out rather than any form of working through the past. That is to say, the identification of self as victim was perpetuated. Any final closure, Trommler says, is precluded by the very nature of the crime of genocide.

The question of agency has typically been analyzed with respect to the perpetrators. What were the constraints on action, on the making of choices? What forces and combination of events mobilized and shaped the energies of the murderers? What is the measure of individual responsibility in the context of mass murder? In her essay, Debórah Dwork turns to the question of agency on the part of the victims. In a discussion of a mysterious massacre of ninety French Jewish women by female German *kapos* at Budy, Dwork shows how assumptions about the capacity for agency on the part of the victims shaped the extant narratives of the massacre. For Dwork, an understanding of this agency—of the capacity for resistance, even radical political activism—can only be recuperated by attending to the individual characteristics of the victims, by resisting the temptation to view the victims as the Nazis did: simply as "Jews."

Certainly one of the central issues when thinking about the Holocaust from a distance of more than half a century is the nature of the *afterlife* of historical trauma, the ways in which disaster inscribes itself not only in human memory but also in the very texture of cultural, social, and political life across generations. The difficulties of taking the measure of this afterlife are exacerbated by the fact that traumatic events make their impact largely in the form of *gaps* in understanding rather than a legacy with a clear and stable representational content. The point is not that we don't have access to vast resources of accurate information and sound knowledge about the events in question; that our problem pertains to a lack of knowledge or faulty information is, of course, the claim made by many Holocaust deniers. The point is rather that the very substantial knowledge we possess seems to heighten an awareness of the insufficiency of cognition in the encounter with the reality of what happened. This paradox is no doubt one of the hidden sources of much Holocaust denial: knowledge itself produces gaps in understanding, opens onto the unimaginable. As noted by Primo Levi, the survivor-witness who has told us more about life in the camps than any other figure, in his first great chronicle of the concentrationary universe, "Today, at this very moment as I sit writing at a table, I myself am not convinced that these things really happened."[2]

In a recent essay on these and related matters, Giorgio Agamben has put this aporia of testimony as it figures, above all, in the lives of survivors, in the following terms:

> The discrepancy in question concerns the very structure of testimony. On the one hand, what happened in the camps appears to the survivors as the only true thing and, as such, absolutely unforgettable; on the other hand, this truth is to the same degree unimaginable, that is, *irreducible to the real elements that constitute it.* Facts so real that, by comparison, nothing is truer; a reality that necessarily exceeds its factual elements—such is the aporia of Auschwitz.[3]

Our dilemma is that the facts that make up the events in question open onto a radical breach in the world of shared human meanings and values, onto what Levi described as "the anguish inscribed in everyone of the 'tohu-bohu,' of a deserted and empty universe crushed under the spirit of God but from which the spirit of man is absent: not yet born or already extinguished."[4] What is at stake in the Holocaust is, in a word, a disaster of such proportions that it seems to have produced in our universe not simply delimited or circumscribed losses, losses that can, in principle, be narrated and made available to common knowledge, that can be collectively and individually mourned; the difficulty is rather that these very losses generate or, at the very least, resonate with a kind of ontological absence that would seem to escape the efficacy of social and psychic practices of integration, representation, signification, any kind of repair, *Trauerarbeit,* or "redemption."

The essays in the final section of this volume constitute an extended meditation on and exploration of what might be called the "virtual archives" of the Holocaust, archives, that is, in which the traces of the "aporia of Auschwitz," so easily missed by normal historical research, are still legible. These archives assume various forms. They can be found, as Froma Zeitlin suggests in her reading of recent literary responses to the transgenerational "life" of the Holocaust, in the dreams and disorientations, the somatic disturbances and sense memories, in sum, in the various forms of hauntedness that disturb the peace of those who have been touched—and sometimes only in indirect fashion—by the "Final Solution." In one of the works Zeitlin discusses, Binjamin Wilkomirksi's *Fragments,* this hauntedness appears to have assumed sufficient transferential force to produce a kind of "vicarious traumatization" culminating in a sort of faux memoir. In his contribution, Geoffrey Hartman emphasizes that it is language itself, precisely as tainted, as corrupted by political power and ideology, that registers a persistence of the catastrophe that can, in turn, only be worked through, if at all, by an enormous linguistic effort. One thinks here of the poetry of Paul Celan, who, as Hartman writes, "passes his words through an inorganic region of stone and star, to recover some kind of semantic and phonic *matière première.*" In Dominick LaCapra's work it is above all in *affect,* in the ways in which trauma permeates the rhythms of speech and behavior, the repetitions and distortions that inflect posttraumatic life, where we come upon the virtual archives of the Shoah. For LaCapra, these archives preserve, in part, the memory traces of "impossible" situations, situations in which in some fundamental way the very space of human possibilities collapsed. We might say, then, that virtual archives register not just this or that injury to a human being or collectivity but rather an assault on human agency itself.

In his closing remarks, Paul Mendes-Flohr suggests that the gap between hope and optimism and the concomitant irreducibility of mourning to any sort of explanation or cultural achievement is itself a sort of virtual archive in which "the scandal of Auschwitz" is preserved not merely as an object of mournful contemplation but also as an occasion of "unmitigated outrage" against the social and political *structures* that continue to cause human suffering. That is, if the Holocaust continues in some sense to defy representation and integration, then it does so, perhaps, not simply because of its radical otherness or utter uniqueness, but rather because of a kind of overproximity, that is, because we are still in some ways caught up in the forms of life—and social fantasies—that made it possible. It is, finally, in this sense that the virtual archives that register the *persistence* of a traumatic past—its failure to be put to rest as a "past"—may also be our best indices of an ongoing endangerment of our future.

NOTES

1. Jürgen Habermas, cited in Saul Friedländer's introduction to his edited volume, *Probing the Limits of Representation. Nazism and the "Final Solution"* (Cambridge, Mass.: Harvard University Press, 1992), 3.

2. Primo Levi, *Survival in Auschwitz,* trans. Stuart Wolf (New York: Touchstone, 1996), 103.

3. Giorgio Agamben, *Remnants of Auschwitz. The Witness and the Archive,* trans. Daniel Heller-Roazen (New York: Zone Books, 1999), 12; our emphasis.

4. Primo Levi, *The Drowned and the Saved,* trans. Raymond Rosenthal (New York: Random House, 1989), 85.

Part One

**HISTORY,
ANTI-SEMITISM,
AND THE
HOLOCAUST**

One

IDEOLOGY AND EXTERMINATION: THE IMMEDIATE ORIGINS OF THE "FINAL SOLUTION"

Saul Friedländer

On October 2, 1941, Operation Typhoon, the final German assault on Moscow, was launched. In his order of the day to the millions of soldiers poised for what was supposed to be "the last of the great decisive battles of the year . . . the last powerful blow that will shatter this enemy before the onset of the winter," Hitler made quite clear who was the "horrendous, beast-like" enemy intent on "annihilating not only Germany, but the whole of Europe." The carriers of the system in which Bolshevism was but the other face of the vilest capitalism, he proclaimed, were in both cases the same: "Jews and only Jews!" [Juden und nur Juden][1]

As a new phase of the war started with the German attack against the Soviet Union, a radical escalation of "the war against the Jews" unfolded on Russian territory. In this new phase, early or mid-October 1941 appears as another fateful turning point. It was probably between mid-October and mid-December 1941 that the final decision regarding the murder of the whole of European Jewry was taken.

As we consider these events from a distance of six decades, their historical place still remains undetermined. Was this the horrendous finale of an anti-Jewish tradition embedded in the evolution of Christianity and that of the Western world? Was it the murderous end phase of the age of ideology? Does it demonstrate the deadly potential of modernity? Or, could one define the annihilation of European Jewry as the result of an entirely unforeseeable convergence of these three historical developments within a specific German context?

This text will mainly concentrate on the fall months of 1941; they have probably been more systematically scrutinized than any other phase of these events, and no new facts will be uncovered here. Rather, I wish to reemphasize, against the grain of present-day historiography, the importance of Hitler's initiatives and of his ideology in the context of the anti-Jewish crusade. I shall stress the pseudoreligious dimensions of this ideology—redemptive anti-Semitism—and its integrative and mobilizing function within a system including Party, State, and society. More generally, I shall attempt to point to the place of this ideology in the conflation of the three historical processes mentioned above with the immediate circumstances that triggered the onset of the most extreme enterprise of sustained, systematic mass extermination in modern history.

"REDEMPTIVE ANTI-SEMITISM"

"Redemptive anti-Semitism" is the most radical form of anti-Jewish hatred. It is the convergence of racial anti-Semitism on the one hand and of a religious or pseudoreligious ideology of redemption (or perdition) on the other.[2] Whereas racial anti-Semitism in general was but one element within a wider racial worldview, redemptive anti-Semitism constituted an all-encompassing belief system in which race rationalized the struggle against the Jews but was not the only foundation of it. Moreover, in redemptive anti-Semitism the struggle against the Jews took on an apocalyptic dimension. The redemption of the *Volk,* the race or Aryan humanity, would be achieved only by the elimination of the Jews. The victory of the Jews remained a possibility: it would mean the end of the Volk, the race or Aryan humanity.

In *Nazi Germany and the Jews* I made a clear distinction between this extreme brand of anti-Semitism and "ordinary" *völkisch* anti-Jewish ideology. It seemed to me that the convergence of the racial anti-Semitic themes and of the redemption of an Aryan Christian humanity by the struggle against and the victory over the Jews found its ideological underpinnings in late nineteenth-century Germany, particularly in the "Bayreuth Circle." As the historian of the Circle expressed it: "It is in the nature of anti-Semitic ideology to use a more or less prominent friend-foe model. What nonetheless gives Bayreuth's anti-Semitism an unmistakably particular aspect is the resoluteness with which the opposition between Germandom and Jewry is raised to the position of the central theme of world history. In Chamberlain's *Foundation [of the Nineteenth Century]* this dualistic image of history finds its tersest formulation."[3] In end-of-the-century Bayreuth and later,

Houston Stewart Chamberlain's thought was indeed dominant; it strongly influenced the Munich anti-Jewish ranter and Bayreuth devotee Dietrich Eckart, who in turn became Hitler's early and most influential ideological mentor.

Shortly after the beginning of his political career, Hitler came to see himself as the messianic figure chosen by Providence to lead Germany in this fateful battle. According to his own words in *Mein Kampf,* in defending himself against the Jew he was fighting for the work of the Lord.

Very tentatively and only a priori at this stage, one could suggest the following link between "redemptive anti-Semitism," the Christian tradition, the era of ideology, and modernity. In the final stage of the era of ideology, the two hegemonically oriented worldviews of the century, Nazism and Communism, surged on the world scene as pseudoscientific constructs and as millenarian utopias. These political religions mobilized the deepest fears and hopes of the Christian tradition, particularly its apocalyptic dimension: the vision of a struggle against a demonic force that, in Nazism, became "the Jew." But, whereas a concept such as "redemptive anti-Semitism" is easily included in a synthesis of twentieth-century ideology and deep-rooted millenarianism, it seems ill suited to an approach that identifies Nazism with modernity. Are we thus facing two incompatible and basically opposed interpretive approaches?

According to the leading thesis which links Nazi exterminations and modernity, the "Final Solution" was born from "the spirit of science" as an aspect of rationally pursued "social therapies" generated at the end of the nineteenth century, which led to more extreme corollaries in the 1920s, in the wake of war and crisis, and assumed their most radical form under the Nazi regime. From this perspective, the anti-Jewish measures of the Nazis become part of a general biological-racial selection plan. After the beginning of the war, these policies were integrated by various, often competing Nazi agencies in a systematic program of ethnic population relocation and elimination embracing the whole of eastern Europe, in order to strengthen the Germanic racial core. According to this interpretation, the extermination of the Jews was mainly the outcome of biological and demographic-economic planning, similarly directed against the mentally ill, the gypsies, and, potentially, other groups defined as "asocials" or racially inferior by Nazi criteria. In the longer run, this kind of rationality could have led to the mass transfer and killing of entire populations all over eastern Europe, as outlined in the Generalplan Ost. Thus explicated, Nazi exterminations were essentially the product of a pitiless instrumental rationality, in terms of racial-demographic plans or, for that matter, in line with more immediate military needs.

Thus, for example, the extermination of the Jews on Soviet territory did possibly accelerate as a result of the Wehrmacht's food supply problems; the annihilation in the Warthegau may have been triggered by the overfilling of the ghettoes and the need to resettle incoming ethnic Germans; the general concept of mass liquidation of Jews in the Eastern territories may have been indirectly influenced by some Nazi demographic-economic planning for the entire area. Yet, neither these explanations nor any other schemes based on the same type of "instrumental rationality" apply to the deportations of the Jews from western Europe immediately after total extermination in the East began, or to the deportations from Norway, Saloniki, or the island of Rhodes.

It has also become common to equate Nazism and its crimes with basic utopias of modernity beyond "the spirit of science" as such. More specifically, the goal supposedly pursued by the Nazis was "the utopian aim of transforming society in the image of perfection," or, in other terms, the realization of "a social homogeneity and social identity endemic to the Western ideal of a rational society."[4] This identification of Nazi goals with quintessential visions of modernity is highly questionable. By definition these goals should have applied to the domain of the *Volksgemeinschaft* only. And, indeed, no attempt was made to kill the mentally ill or to jail the "asocials" in the occupied countries. This racial "sanitation" was concentrated in Germany only and in the areas annexed to Germany. Only one group was hounded all over the continent, to the very last individual, to the very last day of German presence: the Jews. These diverging policies against various groups of victims suffice to indicate that the war against the Jews was only indirectly related to the transformation of the *Volksgemeinschaft* in the image of racial perfection.

Finally, the equation of Nazism and modernity is based on an ongoing confusion between the "modernist" utopias of middle range Nazi racial theorists, scientists, bureaucrats, and intellectuals of various brands and a political religion identifying the Jews as the enemy of humankind, preached by the ultimate bearer of all authority: Adolf Hitler. His message may not have been shared by all, but his were the guidelines for the policies of total extermination.

Thus we are brought back to a peculiar brand of apocalyptic anti-Semitism, the extraordinary virulence of which remains the only way of explaining both the physical onslaught against all Jews living within German reach and against any part of human culture created by Jews or showing any trace of the Jewish spirit.

Physically separating Jews from Aryans may have fitted into a racial-biological vision of humanity, but separating Jewish authors from Aryan ones, or Jewish from Aryan science, Jewish from Aryan music, and so on, belongs to a different kind of obsession. The evolution of Nazi euthanasia may explain how the methods and the "specialized" personnel for the killing of the mentally ill were utilized in the extermination of the Jews, but the connection between these logistics of mass murder and the elimination of libretti by Jewish authors from operas performed in the Reich or the identification of Heinrich Heine as an "unknown poet" demands a different historical framework. What is ultimately so difficult to grasp in National-Socialism is precisely the fact that the Jewish issue was its ideological core. The Jewish diarist Victor Klemperer expressed this unequivocally on April 16, 1941: "Once I would have said: I do not judge as a Jew. . . . Now: Yes, I judge as a Jew, because as such I am particularly affected by the Jewish business in Hitlerism, and because it is central to the whole structure, to the whole character of National Socialism and is uncharacteristic of everything else."[5]

In other words, Hitler's goals, mainly his vision of an apocalyptic final struggle against the Jews, were metapolitical. This vision invested the core of his movement with the fervor of a crusading sect. But, as we shall see, the Nazi leader knew how to "translate" his metapolitical aims into modern politics, modern organization, modern concepts. Far more than in Communism, this peculiar fusion of seemingly distinct worlds gave to the regime both its fanaticism and its deadly efficiency.

HITLER'S RHETORIC AND THE ONSET OF THE "FINAL SOLUTION"

When Operation Typhoon started, Hitler was convinced that the Soviet capital would fall before the onset of winter. By mid-October, however, Goebbels's diaries expressed growing pessimism. At that very same time, the United States Congress had agreed to the arming of American vessels. This, in Goebbels's (and Hitler's) eyes, meant "a further [American] step towards war."[6] And yet another threat was lurking: On October 20, the German commander of the French city of Nantes was shot. Armed internal resistance was beginning even in occupied western Europe. The German situation grew worse as weeks went by. And, in early December as the United States was pulled into the war, the Red Army counterattacked in front of Moscow.

During the same period the murder of the Jews on Soviet territory had expanded rapidly. Throughout the first six weeks of the campaign, the victims were mainly Jewish men. From early August the extermination gradually engulfed the entire Jewish population. In mid-September the wearing of the "Jewish Star" was imposed upon the Jews of the Reich. A few days later, Hitler ordered the deportation of most of the Jews of Germany and the Protectorate to the ghettos of the East. From October 17 onward, the first transports of Jews left for Lodz, Kovno, Riga, and Minsk. In Kovno and Riga, thousands of Jews were shot on arrival. On October 18, all Jewish emigration from Europe was forbidden, "in view of the forthcoming final solution of the Jewish question." During that same month, some seven thousand Jews were executed by the Wehrmacht in Serbia and mass killings of Jews also took place in Eastern Galicia. On November 1, the construction of Belzec, the first extermination camp, started near Lublin. In early December, a killing site became operational in Chelmno, near Lodz.

Most historians who study the origins of the "Final Solution" agree that the immediate process leading to the total extermination of European Jewry started at some point between the launching of the German attack on the Soviet Union and the end of 1941. Some scholars have argued that a decision—indirectly expressed in Goering's letter to Heydrich of July 31, 1941, ordering him to start the preparations for the "Final Solution of the Jewish Question in Europe"—was taken early on, in the euphoria of German victories; the order for concrete implementation may have been issued a few months later, sometime in the fall, probably in October. Others, pointing to the absence of any new plan regarding the Jews in Hitler's comments during the summer months, except for his hypothetical plans to deport them to northern Russia after the end of the campaign, have located the sole decision for total extermination also in October of 1941, in view of the initiatives just mentioned. Yet others have emphasized the chaotic aspects of the Nazi anti-Jewish measures during this entire period and argued against the notion of a single order regarding the extermination; instead they have stressed the unfolding of increasingly more radical measures at various local levels; step by step, these measures coalesced into a general extermination plan by the beginning of 1942.

Finally, the discovery of Himmler's appointments calendar in the ex-Soviet archives in Moscow and in it the entry of December 18, 1941, and the related interpretation of Hitler's address to the Gauleiters on December 12 as recorded by Goebbels, to both of which I shall return, have bolstered the argument that Hitler ordered the total extermination of the Jews following the entry of the United States into the war. It is in the context of these events that we shall now place Hitler's declarations about the Jews and interpret their possible significance, first in relation to the onset of the "Final Solution," then in terms of the wider ideological framework that was previously outlined.

—

Hitler's apocalyptic anti-Jewish faith was not instrumental, but he was a master at transforming his obsessions into an effective political instrument. Thus, an analysis of the varying intensity of his anti-Jewish declarations and of the changing emphasis placed on specific anti-Jewish themes in a particular context may shed light, as we shall see, on intentions and policies otherwise not clearly apparent.

On the Bavarian scene of his political beginnings and during the reconstruction period of the National Socialist Party after 1925, anti-Semitic fury was a perfect propaganda tool. It became less functional after 1930, once Hitler had to don a statesmanly garb; moreover, it could have been a liability during the first years of the Nazi regime. Thus, in public at least, between 1930 and 1935, Hitler maintained a measure of restraint in regard to the Jews. That restraint disappeared in the atmosphere of ideological confrontation and mobilization which dominated Nazi propaganda and engulfed Europe between 1936 and the beginning of the war. Hitler's murderous anti-Jewish Reichstag speech of January 1939 was both an outburst of rage at foreign reactions to the pogrom of the previous November and an attempt to frighten the "Jewish warmongers" in Paris, London, and Washington, who, he believed, dictated the policies of the Western democracies.

After the beginning of the war, from September 1939 to the victory over France in June 1940, public anti-Jewish pronouncements were more subdued, as befitted the Nazi leader's hope of reaching a compromise peace with Great Britain. However, once it became clear that the British would continue fighting and once the decision to attack the Soviet Union had been made, the threatening anti-Jewish prophecy of January 1939 resounded again in the Reichstag speech of January 1941. The ensuing rhetorical lull that lasted until the fall of that year, notwithstanding the onset of the Russian campaign, is more difficult to explain.

Hitler's "proclamation to the German people" on June 22, 1941, the day of the attack against the Soviet Union, used only such consecrated formulas as a plot between "Jews, Democrats and Reactionaries" or "the Judeo-Bolshevik power center in Moscow."[7] The speeches or proclamations that followed, until early October, either contained no references to the Jews or merely reiterated those standard formulas (on September 12 and 27). The only significant nonpublic exception is the conversation between Hitler and Goebbels on August 18 in which the Nazi leader declared that the Jews of Europe would be deported to Russia after the end of the campaign and also allowed his minister to impose the Jewish badge in the Reich. A month beforehand, in his conversation with the Croat Marshall Sladko Kvarternik, Hitler had mentioned the possibility of deporting the Jews of Europe to some isolated area such as Madagascar (used as an example) or northern Russia.[8]

In line with the relative paucity of anti-Jewish statements, the Jews are hardly mentioned in Hitler's "Table Talk" between early July (when its recording first started) and mid-October of 1941. The one exception is a tirade against Christianity on the night of July 11 in which, together with Bolshevism, it is defined as a monstrous product of Judaism.[9] Given the all-out ideological nature of the Eastern campaign, such "silence" is puzzling. It may be that during the first months of the campaign, Hitler was so sure of an imminent victory that he did not see the need to evoke the sinister power of the Jews. In October, however, a sudden change occurred. In Hitler's private and public repertory, the Jews moved to center stage.

The beginning of Hitler's rhetorical shift appeared on October 2, in what must have been the strangest "order of the day" read to any army in modern times. The next day, in his Sportpalast speech to launch the "Winter Relief," he designated the Jews as "the world enemy."[10] Some three weeks later, on October 21, Hitler unleashed his first massive attack against the Jews, in his "Table Talk": Jesus was not a Jew; the Jew Paul falsified Jesus' teaching in order to undermine the Roman Empire. . . . The Jew's aim was to destroy the nations by destroying their racial core. In Russia, he argued, the Jews deported hundreds of thousands of men in order to leave the abandoned women to males imported from other regions. They organized miscegenation on a huge scale. The Jews continued to torture people in the name of Bolshevism, just as Christianity, the offshoot of Judaism, had tortured its opponents in the Middle Ages. "Saul became Saint Paul; Mordechai became Karl Marx." Then came the notorious finale: "By exterminating this pest, we shall do humanity a service of which our soldiers can have no idea."[11] The most rabid themes of the early speeches, of the dialogue with Dietrich Eckart and especially of *Mein Kampf* had returned, sometimes in almost identical words.

On October 25, in the presence of Himmler and Heydrich, Hitler was even more explicit, reminding his guests—as if they needed to be reminded—of his notorious "prophecy": "I prophesized to Jewry," Hitler declared, "that the Jew would disappear from Europe if the war could not be avoided. This race of criminals carries the guilt of the two millions of dead of the World War and now already that of hundreds of thousands. Nobody should come and tell me that one cannot drive them into the marshes in the East! Who thinks of our men? It is not bad, moreover, that public rumor attributes to us the intention of exterminating the Jews. Terror is a salutary thing."[12]

At the beginning of the following month, another long historical-political tirade against the Jews took place in the presence of two other SS guests, commanders Blaschke and Richter. Once the Europeans discovered the nature of the Jew, Hitler stated, they would also understand the solidarity that tied them together. The Jew was the obstacle to this solidarity. He lived only because European solidarity did not exist. At the outset of his disquisition Hitler prophesied to his guests that the end of the war would witness the "crash" [Himmelssturz] of the Jews and then launched into a long tirade describing the Jews as inveterate liars and cheaters.[13]

The first of Hitler's two major public anti-Jewish speeches of those weeks was the address to the Party "old fighters" on November 8, 1941, the annual commemoration date of the aborted Munich putsch of 1923. A year before, on the same occasion, the Jews had not been mentioned at all. This time, the Nazi leader launched into one of the most vicious and massive anti-Jewish tirades of his career. Hitler pointed to "the international Jew" as "the one behind this war" and

called him "world arsonist" [Weltbrandstifter]. "I wouldn't be a National Socialist any more," he yelled, "if I distanced myself from this finding." After attacking
Jewish exploitation of the war, he turned to the Jews' enslavement of the Soviet
Union: "The man who is temporarily the master of that state [Stalin] is nothing
else but an instrument in the hands of omnipotent Jewry. . . . When Stalin is on
the scene, in front of the curtain, Kaganowitch [Stalin's Jewish son-in-law] stands
behind him". . . and so on. In between these insults and threats, the Nazi leader
gave clear expression to the apocalyptic dimension of the ongoing struggle: "This
struggle, my old Party comrades, has really become not only a struggle for Germany, but for the whole of Europe, a struggle [that will decide] between existence and annihilation!"[14] In this same speech Hitler again reminded his audience
that he had often been a prophet in his life, but this time the prophecy did not relate to the extermination of the Jews, implicit in his entire speech, but to a closely
related theme: November 1918, when Germany was stabbed in the back, would
never occur again. "Everything is imaginable," he exclaimed, "except one thing,
that Germany will ever capitulate!"[15]

In a notorious article in *Das Reich* entitled "Die Juden sind schuld" (The Jews
are guilty), Goebbels echoed his master's voice. He reminded his readers of Hitler's prophecy that the Jews would be exterminated in case of war and added: "We
are experiencing now the consummation of this prophecy; the fate of the Jews
that is being fulfilled is harsh, but no more than deserved. Pity or regret is completely out of place here."[16] The Propaganda Minister was clearly alluding to the
mass exterminations in Russia and to the deportation of the Jews from Germany.

Within the limits imposed by the occasion, Hitler returned to his anti-Jewish
tirades, when, on November 28, he received the Great Mufti of Jerusalem. After explaining to his visitor that although British capitalism and Soviet Communism appear to be opposites, "in both countries Jewry was pursuing identical
aims." The present struggle had to be understood as a confrontation of two ideological forces: "On the political level," Hitler declared, "[this struggle] appeared
in essence to be a confrontation between Germany and England, but in terms of
ideology, it was a struggle between National Socialism and Jewry."[17]

In his circle of intimates, where Hitler's nightlong disquisitions were the common fare, the Nazi leader could let his anti-Jewish fantasies run wild. He was
back at his favored theme on the night of December 1 to 2. Prodded by one of
the guests about the issue of racial instinct, Hitler declared that some Jews were
not necessarily intent on harming Germany, but even so they would never distance themselves from the long-term interests of their own race. Why were Jews
destroying other nations? The Führer admitted that he did know the fundamental natural-historical laws of this phenomenon. But by dint of their destructive
activity the Jews created the necessary defense mechanisms among the nations.

Hitler told his night audience that Dietrich Eckart had once mentioned to him that he had known one upright Jew, Otto Weininger, who took his own life once he discovered the destructive nature of his race. Strangely, the Nazi leader concluded, Jewish mixed breeds of a second or third generation would often come together again with Jews. But, he added, ultimately nature eliminates the destructive elements: in the seventh, eighth, or ninth generation the Jewish part is "out-mendeled" [ausgemendelt]—a pun on the name of the Czech monk, Gregor Mendel, who discovered the heredity laws—and "racial purity, re-established."[18]

On December 11, in the wake of Japan's attack on Pearl Harbor, Hitler announced to the Reichstag that Germany was declaring war on the United States. From the outset, the messianic theme was present: "If Providence wanted that this struggle should not spare the German people, then I am grateful that [Providence] entrusted me with the leadership of this historical confrontation, a confrontation that will decisively mold not only the history of our Germany but that of Europe, actually that of the entire world for the next five hundred or one thousand years."[19] Then he turned his fury against Roosevelt and the Jews. The Jews, according to the Nazi leader, were planning to use the American tool in order to prepare "a second Purim for the European nations which were becoming increasingly anti-Semitic. . . . It was the Jew, in his full satanic vileness who gathered around this man [Roosevelt], but also to whom this man reached out."[20] This was total, uncontrolled rage: for Hitler, America and Roosevelt were completely in the hands of the Jews. It may explain the otherwise puzzling German declaration of war on the United States. Hitler would not wait for the initiative to come from Roosevelt and the Jews.

The next day, Hitler addressed the Reichsleiter and Gauleiter in a secret speech summed up by Goebbels in his diary: "In regard to the Jewish question the Führer is determined to wipe the slate clean [reinen Tisch zu machen]. He prophesied to the Jews that if they once more brought about a world war, they would be annihilated. It was not a mere declaration. The world war is here, the extermination of the Jews must be its necessary consequence. This matter has to be envisaged without any sentimentality. We are not here to have compassion for the Jews, but to have compassion for our German people. As the German people has once again sacrificed some 160,000 dead in the Eastern campaign, those responsible for this bloody conflict will have to pay for it with their lives."[21]

According to the aforementioned entry in Himmler's appointment calendar, in a meeting with Himmler, on December 18, Hitler gave the following instruction: "Jewish question | exterminate as partisans."[22] The vertical line in this entry remains unexplained. The identification of the Jews as "partisans" obviously did not refer to the Jews on Soviet territory who were being exterminated for the last six months, but rather to the deadly internal enemy who, by treasonously plotting in Germany and German-occupied Europe, could, as in November 1918, stab the Reich in the back.

On the eve of the meeting with Himmler on December 17, Hitler had once more raised the Jewish issue with Goebbels. According to the Propaganda Minister, "the Führer is determined to proceed consistently in this matter [the Jewish question] and not be stopped by bourgeois sentimentality." Hitler and his minister discussed the evacuation of the Jews from the Reich, but it seems that subsequently the Jewish issue in general was addressed: "All the Jews have to be transferred to the East. What happens to them there cannot be of great interest to us. They have asked for this fate; they brought about the war, now they must also pay the bill." Then Goebbels added: "It is comforting that despite the burden of military responsibility the Führer still finds the time . . . for these matters and mainly has a clear view about them. He alone is in the position to solve this problem definitively, with the necessary hardness."[23]

Thus, after ten months of relative public silence regarding the Jewish issue, Hitler suddenly addressed it with unusual frequency and growing fury between mid-October and mid-December 1941. In the course of these two months the Nazi leader explicitly mentioned the extermination of the Jews on October 19, October 25, December 12, December 17, and December 18 and was indirectly quoted to that effect by Goebbels, Alfred Rosenberg, and Hans Frank between December 12 and 16. Nothing of the kind ever happened before in Hitler's declarations; it was a radical change. Indeed, the fact that five out of seven of these exterminatory statements were made within a few days, after December 11, could be seen as an explicitly ominous message conveying that some sort of decision had probably been reached as a result of the U.S. entry into the war. On the night of December 28 to 29, Hitler came to speak of the arch anti-Semite, Julius Streicher: "What Streicher did in 'Der Stürmer' was to draw an idealized portrait of the Jews. The Jew is much meaner, much more blood thirsty than Streicher described him."[24]

The major difficulty in evaluating the significance of Hitler's declarations lies in the fact that he used the extermination threats on occasions prior to any extermination plans, that is, before June 1941. The main problem, however, is Hitler's linkage of the exterminations to a general war context that could apply to any time after June 1941 and to October of that year as compellingly as to the December 1941–January 1942 period. As previously mentioned, the only plausible answer is the considerable intensification of the threats after an event that indeed turned what could still be considered a European war into a world war in its fullest sense: the entry of the United States into the conflict. It is only then, it should be added, that in terms of Hitler's worldview, the battle included all the forces that were the mortal enemies of the new Germany: all the "plutocratic" forces allied with world Bolshevism. Behind this satanic coalition stood the Jew.

All the themes that surfaced in Hitler's anti-Jewish diatribes between October 1941 and early 1942 were elements of an ideological repertory that had not varied in any significant way since the early 1920s. These themes were shared by the Nazi hard core and applied over two decades to changing circumstances by way of minor adaptations. The sinister presence of "the Jew" behind both plutocracy and Bolshevism appeared in almost identical terms in Hitler's earliest anti-Semitic speeches: "capitalism" or "Wall Street" were used rather than "plutocracy"; "Marxism" appeared as frequently as "Bolshevism." The Jewish undermining of the Ancient World by Paul's falsification of the teaching of an Aryan Christ into a doctrine akin to Bolshevism was a staple of Dietrich Eckart's interpretation of history and of Hitler's subsequent harangues (it was one of the major themes of nineteenth-century German and European anti-Semitism). The "Jewish stab-in-the back" theme as an interpretation of Germany's defeat in World War I reappeared in full force in the fall of 1941, in its reversed form: such internal enemies would be eliminated. Simultaneously—and that may have been Hitler's only innovation in relation to his own past ideological rhetoric—the Nazi leader increasingly spoke of "Europe" from June 1941 on. The Jew was a general factor of subversion but, more specifically, he was an obstacle to European unity (by engineering the war between two racially kindred European nations: Germany and England) when such unity was vital for the struggle against the two gigantic threats to European civilization: "America" on the one hand, Russia on the other. The Jew had to disappear from Europe.

Were Hitler's increasingly frequent and ever more threatening anti-Jewish outbursts merely expressions of growing rage and frustration, or are we faced once more with an element of instrumentality in this outpouring of the vilest insults and the most vicious intimations of a murderous revenge? Most probably, some of the anti-Jewish measures and public declarations were aimed at Roosevelt and at the Jews who, so Hitler undoubtedly believed, stood behind the American president. Yet this would not suffice to explain the growing fury of the "Table Talk" or of the murderous address to the Gauleiters. It seems that apart from a crazed urge for revenge and retribution and also apart from the belief that in order to avoid another defeat the internal foes (Partisanen), those ready to stab Germany in the back, had to be eliminated, Hitler wanted to make his intentions unmistakably clear to his acolytes without having to give an explicit order. At the moment of decision, he wished to strengthen the belief of his minions: the Jew was the mortal foe of Germany, of Europe, of civilization; the Jew started the war; the moment of retribution had come. Finally, by showing the way without entering into the details of what had to be done, he clearly conveyed that although Jews had to disappear, as stated to Himmler on December 18, he left it to his henchmen to find the appropriate methods. This general "mandate" for extermination finds an echo in one of Hitler's strangest utterances. On January 25, 1942, five days after the Wannsee conference, Hitler had two guests who were both well informed about the situation and in whose presence the Jewish question could be addressed without too many detours: Lammers and Himmler. "It must be done rapidly," Hitler explained, regarding the deportation of the Jews to the East. "The Jew must be expelled from Europe. Otherwise we will have no European unity; he [the Jew] incites everywhere. In the end, I don't know, I am so immensely human . . . I say only: he must be expelled. If he is destroyed in the process, I can't help it. I see only one thing: absolute eradication, if they don't leave on their own."[25]

IDEOLOGY, SOCIETY, AND MASS MURDER UNDER NATIONAL SOCIALISM

The hard core of the Nazi Party probably shared Hitler's redemptive anti-Semitism. What is certain is that the anti-Jewish campaign was carried out under the responsibility of Hitler's ideological guard: the Party. In his closing speech at the 1935 Party rally, in which he proclaimed the anti-Jewish racial laws, Hitler had declared that if the Jewish problem "should yet again prove insoluble [it] would have to be assigned by law to the National Socialist Party for a definitive solution."[26] Since 1938, the Jewish issue had been mainly in the hands of the Party; at the end of 1941, the Party was put in charge of the "Final Solution."

The ideologically motivated plans of various Party agencies and the power struggles that they reflected were not determined only by anti-Jewish goals; however, they tied in with the anti-Jewish policies once decisions were made, and this not only at the general "racial" or "European" levels. Mass resettlement of ethnic Germans, for example, demanded, in Nazi eyes, the expulsion and, eventually, the extermination of part of eastern European Jewry; such partial plans could easily become part of a general plan of total extermination. In other terms, sectorial Party interests were always subordinated to Hitler's goals. Once the decision about the fate of European Jewry had been reached, all Nazi agencies became the support and implementation system which, from the end of 1941, made the anti-Jewish extermination crusade its absolute priority. The enormous amount of loot that fell into the hands of Party members, high and low, certainly bolstered their ideological commitment.

It is difficult to estimate how deeply Hitler's brand of anti-Semitism penetrated non-Party agencies and particularly the Wehrmacht. The extreme anti-Jewish proclamations of Field Marshalls Walter von Reichenau, Erich von Manstein, and some others among the highest ranking officers do not seem typical. Yet the "barbarization of warfare" and the "ideologization of warfare," mainly on the Eastern Front and in the Balkans, are hard to disentangle. After the invasion of Poland, General Johannes Blaskowitz had sent a complaint about the murder operations of the SS; but after the invasion of the Soviet Union, the Wehrmacht became an active auxiliary in many of these anti-Jewish operations. In western Europe, it even initiated some of the anti-Jewish measures during the second half of 1940 and almost always cooperated in their implementation.[27] In his order of the day of October 2, 1941, Hitler would probably not have declared that behind all of Germany's enemies stood "the Jews and only the Jews" if he had not known or sensed that among hundreds of thousands of soldiers such a radical anti-Semitic outburst would find some echo. At officer rank in any case, traditional conservative anti-Semitism and violent anti-Bolshevism were the ready ideological ground for the anti-Jewish crusade. The same is true for other state agencies and for the economic sector. Here, too, the substantial material advantages resulting from the persecution and the extermination of the Jews bolstered the readiness to accept the most radical measures.

There remains the much debated issue of the attitudes and reactions of the wider German population to Hitler's anti-Jewish diatribes and to the anti-Jewish policies of the Nazi regime. Recent inquiries indicate that there was more day-to-day anti-Jewish violence among the German populace than previously assumed, and that later possibly up to one-third of the population was aware that mass killings of Jews were taking place in the East, although the full extent and details of the "Final Solution" may not have been known to most Germans.

In August 1941, outrage among the population and the churches had deflected the murder of the mentally ill, at least in part; later, the "Aryan" wives of a group of Jewish men about to be deported from Berlin forced their release. Thus, at times, popular reactions were taken into account by the regime. But the Berlin demonstration—and it was a very limited and peculiar one—was the only popular protest regarding the fate of the Jews. In general terms, the population's indifference to persecution of the Jews during the 1930s continued as indifference to mass murder during the war. Churches often expelled Christian members who wore the Jewish star, and intellectuals in various domains (including future luminaries of West German historiography) enthusiastically joined the anti-Semitic campaign, adding studies and theories of their own. Even opposition circles adhered to their traditional anti-Jewish stances, notwithstanding their knowledge of the extermination. Moreover, as Frank Bajohr has shown, tens of thousands of Germans were purchasing for next to nothing belongings transported from all over occupied Europe to the *"Judenmärkte"* of major German cities,[28] and tens of thousands of *Volksgenossen* were now living in Jewish homes.

From 1933 to 1939, widespread indifference to the fate of the Jews may have been fueled by traditional anti-Semitism as well as by the primacy of the "Führer cult" and the enthusiasm for "national revival." In 1940 and early 1941, the immense surge of nationalist pride triggered by German victories may have bolstered even further the support for the regime and its measures. From June 1941 onward and even more so after the entry of the United States into the war, many Germans may have come to believe the slogans identifying the Jews as the ultimate enemy behind Stalin, Roosevelt, and Churchill, behind Bolshevism and plutocracy alike. Mainly, the vast majority continued to believe in Adolf Hitler and the regime. Even if his brand of anti-Jewish obsession was not shared by the majority of Germans, the faith in his leadership was such that his decisions were accepted with all their consequences.

As for the tens of thousands of killers, Germans and non-Germans alike, they were probably motivated by orders, by pack behavior, by constant and ever more ferocious anti-Jewish incitement, sometimes by prevalent and deep-seated anti-Semitic stereotypes and probably more often than not by ordinary human sadism, the kind of sadism that incites to the worst cruelty against the weakest of the weak.

In summation, the killers were not essentially motivated by some kind of rabid "eliminationist anti-Semitism" that, according to Daniel Goldhagen's interpretation, was supposedly present in most of the German population. Rather, the population, the elites, the state agencies, and the Wehrmacht were suffused by a traditional religious and social anti-Semitism that, in and of itself, paralyzed any countervailing attitudes and proved to be a ready ground for the most extreme anti-Jewish steps. No less significant for the acceptance and often the active support of the regime's policies against the Jews was, as we mentioned, some measure of belief in official propaganda, nationalism, and "Führer cult" on the one hand, along with material interests and opportunism on the other.

But, in the absence of a powerful, endemic, anti-Jewish drive from within the population and therefore from within the Wehrmacht and the other state agencies, the murder campaign against the Jews could not have been systematically carried out and sustained for almost four years in the face of constant organizational and bureaucratic problems and especially in the face of the growing constraints imposed by the war, had there not existed another driving force. This essential impetus came from the political leadership: from Hitler, the hard core of the party, and its main terror agencies, where, as recent studies about the SD have shown, extreme anti-Semitism was prevalent.[29]

In Nazi Germany, murder on a large scale was easily implemented and rationalized by various groups. But—and allow me to repeat this decisive point—initiating the total extermination of millions of people and transporting them to killing sites from the furthest corners of the continent in the midst of an increasingly desperate general war, demanded the fanatical drive of a pitiless ideological faith. This faith itself, Hitler's redemptive anti-Semitism, had its root in German history and in the Christian tradition. It also fed upon the potentially murderous instrumentalism inherent to modernity.

~

How unconscious the victims were of the oncoming events, as the "Final Solution" started, clearly appears from Victor Klemperer's diary entry of December 31, 1941: "Heads up for the painful last five minutes!"[30]

NOTES

1. For the text of Hitler's "order of the day" of October 2, 1941, see Max Domarus, *Hitler. Reden und Proklamationen*, pt. 2, vol. 4 (Munich: Süddeutscher Verlag, 1965), 1756–57.

2. For a detailed discussion of this concept, see Saul Friedländer, *Nazi Germany and the Jews*, vol. 1, *The Years of Persecution, 1933–1939* (New York: HarperCollins, 1997).

3. Winfried Schüler, *Der Bayreuther Kreis von seiner Entstehung bis zum Ausgang der Wilhelminischen Ära* (Münster: Aschendorff, 1971), 256.

4. Anson Rabinbach, *In the Shadow of Catastrophe: German Intellectuals between Apocalypse and Enlightenment* (Berkeley and Los Angeles: University of California Press, 1997), 14.

5. Victor Klemperer, *I Will Bear Witness*, vol. 1, *1933–1941* (New York: Random House, 1998), 382.

6. Joseph Goebbels, *Tagebücher*, pt. 2, vol. 1, July-September, 1941, ed. Elke Froehlich (Munich: K. G. Saur, 1996), 262.

7. Domarus, *Hitler*, pt. 2, 4:1726–32.

8. Andreas Hillgruber, ed., *Staatsmänner und Diplomaten bei Hitler* (Frankfurt am Main: Bernard und Graefe, 1967), 613 ff.

9. Adolf Hitler, *Monologe im Führerhauptquartier, 1941–1944*, ed. Werner Jochmann (Hamburg: A. Knaus, 1980, 41).

10. Domarus, *Hitler*, pt. 2, 4:1759.

11. Hitler, *Monologe*, 96 ff.

12. Ibid., 106.

13. Ibid., 130–31.

14. Domarus, *Hitler*, pt. 2, 4:1772–74.

15. Ibid., 1778.

16. Ralf Georg Reuth, *Goebbels* (New York: Harcourt Brace, 1993), 200.

17. *Memorandum of an Official of the Foreign Minister's Secretariat, November 30, 1941*, Documents on German Foreign Policy, ser. D, vol. 13 (Washington, D.C.: U.S. Government Printing Office, 1964), 883.

18. Hitler, *Monologe*, 147–48.

19. Domarus, *Hitler*, pt. 2, 4:1794.

20. Ibid., 1804.

21. Goebbels, *Tagebücher*, pt. 2, 2:498 ff.

22. Christian Gerlach, "Die Wannsee-Konferenz, das Schiksal der deutchen Juden und Hitlers

politische Grundsatzentscheidung, alle Juden Europas zu ermorden," in *Krieg, Ernährung, Völkermord* (Hamburg: Hamburger Edition, 1998), 121.

23. Goebbels, *Tagebücher,* pt. 2, 2:533–34.

24. Hitler, *Monologe,* 158.

25. Ibid., 228–29.

26. For an analysis of Hitler's speech see Friedländer, *Nazi Germany,* 142 ff.

27. Ulrich Herbert, "Die deutsche Militärverwaltung in Paris und die Deportation der französischen Juden," in *Von der Aufgabe der Freiheit,* by Christian Jansen et al. (Berlin: Akademie Verlag, 1995), 431 (it seems that in Belgium the Wehrmacht command was more reticent in implementing the anti-Jewish measures; they were implemented nonetheless).

28. Frank Bajohr, *Arisierung in Hamburg. die Verdrängung der Jüdischen Unternehmen, 1933–1945* (Hamburg: Christians, 1997), 328 ff.

29. Michael Wildt, ed., *Die Judenpolitik des SD, 1935–1938: Eine Dokumentation* (Munich: R. Oldenbourg, 1995), 48.

30. Klemperer, *I Will Bear Witness,* 436.

Two

ANTI-SEMITISM AS EXPLANATION: FOR AND AGAINST

Shulamit Volkov

The historiography dealing with the Holocaust has long been a field of contesting and competing views. One thing, however, seems to have remained constant in all its ups and downs—the reliance upon anti-Semitism as rationale for the National Socialists' "Final Solution." Various protestations notwithstanding, almost all historians finally make use of anti-Semitism as the single most important element in analyzing the road to Auschwitz—twisted or direct. Clearly, along the main divide characteristic of this historiography, it is the "intentionalists" who place a greater emphasis on anti-Semitism. But even the most persistent "functionalists" find it necessary to come back to it in one way or another. Some have tried to relativize its centrality as far as the presumably "regular" Nazi voters were concerned.[1] Others have tried to show that even the chief bureaucrats directing the Nazi extermination machinery were only marginally concerned with it.[2] But at least in viewing the main protagonists—Hitler himself and his closest associates—anti-Semitism always reemerges as the main explanatory mode.

While all this may indeed be indisputable, the relevant arguments often remain rather blurred. Considered self-evident, the pros and cons of this prevailing paradigm are only rarely reexamined. In this essay I would like to try and do just that: rethink the role of Nazi anti-Semitism as an ideology leading to the

"Final Solution," guiding the hands of the murderers. This is no slight matter, of course. The quantity and the quality of existing historiography are immense. As I do not intend to bring into the discussion any new facts, nor present any new documents, I would have to rely on this literature, subjecting it—yet again—to close critical reading, examining it from my own point of view.

I wish to start by pointing out one of the ambiguities that has plagued the use of the term *anti-Semitism* for years. Both colloquially and in professional usage *anti-Semitism* normally refers to at least two different, though of course not unrelated, phenomena. To begin with, it indicates the deeply entrenched traditional hatred of the Jews; that ever-present antipathy towards them, based upon centuries of vilification, going back to pre-Christian times. The term itself, introduced into common parlance in Germany during the early 1870s, was not initially conceived as a simple synonym for the age-old hatred.[3] From the outset it was meant to denote a *new* phenomenon, or at the very least a new *version* of the old one. For the anti-Jewish propagandists of the Berliner *Gründerjahre,* and the anti-Dreifusards in fin-de-siècle Paris, *anti-Semitism* meant more than the familiar, rather naive, rejection of Jewish presence. Instead, it was applied as the proper name of a full-fledged new ideology, a complete worldview, grounded in what was then considered a new scientific theory, proving once and for all the spiritual and racial inferiority of the Jews and the imminent danger they posed to humankind in general and to the unique cultures of Germany or France—as the case may be—in particular. The early *historiography* of anti-Semitism, written before World War I, only rarely applied the term. It was mainly concerned with traditional Jew hatred. Anti-Semitism conceived as a full-fledged ideology began to attract scholarly attention only later. Well into the second half of the twentieth century, so it seems, even Nazi policies towards the Jews were still frequently explained by that common, traditional Jew hating, often carelessly mixed with the new ideological mode to a greater or lesser extent.

Daniel Goldhagen's much discussed book is a case in point.[4] Despite the author's repeated claims to originality, his overriding thesis on the primacy of anti-Semitism—"eliminationist" or otherwise—goes back, with a vengeance, one must add, to the initial paradigm. It offers, in fact, yet another version of that single most common explanation of National Socialism based on Jew hating. This, for Goldhagen, is the alpha and omega of the entire tragic affair. It was out of sheer hatred, runs the argument, that Hitler and his accomplices first decided and then carried out their "Final Solution." It is the old hatred, dressed, to be sure, in various modern forms, that set the whole machinery in motion, exploiting for its own murderous schemes the ancient and all-pervasive animosity against the Jews.[5] Here anti-Semitism turns out to be—more through the repetitive rhetorics of the book than through the force of its argument—not only a necessary but also a sufficient condition for the Holocaust; the only factor needed for explaining it. The author apparently believes that his thesis is so amply supported by the evidence and so indisputably manifest, that the burden of disproving it lies flatly upon his opponents.[6] He repeats the old formulas, supporting it with some new evidence and communicating it with a new jargon. Thus—it seems—he has taken the entire scholarly community by surprise.

Historians—busy reevaluating the sources, engaged in that prolonged debate between "intentionalists" and "functionalists" and, some would also say, fighting their own petty ideological or even political battles—normally tended to think that that old familiar paradigm, long since proven inconclusive and in any case far too simple for the task at hand, was by now altogether superseded. It had been for long, no doubt, the most prevalent approach, adopted by many independent and fair-minded researchers. It was practically indisputable among Jewish historians—by no means only by Zionists.[7] In fact, establishing anti-Semitism as a permanent factor of Jewish history and as an explanation for much of its turbulence had already been a common historical practice by the time Zionist thinkers began to formulate their own worldview. Since Heinrich Graetz, generations of *liberal* Jewish historians trusted, indeed, that with sociocultural integration on the Jewish side and the enactment of legal emancipation on the non-Jewish side, a new era finally dawned and in it anti-Semitism was bound to disappear. But at the same time, they continued to accord great significance to the tradition of Jew hating and to the powerful effects of hostility and discrimination upon their history. They invariably saw in anti-Semitism a major constitutive element in the formation and transformation of Jewish life throughout the ages.

Zionists, to be sure, took an even more extreme position. They not only insisted on the centrality of anti-Semitism in Jewish history but also were more skeptical concerning the plausibility of its future disappearance. In the aftermath of the pogroms in Russia during the early 1880s, but also in view of the recurring waves of anti-Semitism in the presumably enlightened new German *Kaiserreich,* the promise of emancipation lost much of its splendor while the constancy of Jew hating seemed to be compellingly reaffirmed. As in so many other matters, it was Ahad Ha'am again who gave the most fitting expression to this mixed historical lesson. In his essay "Two Masters," published 1902, he stated that modern society could in fact manage to preserve "pockets of reaction and barbarism" even in an age of "general progress and enlightenment." "It is not impossible," he wrote, "that with time humanism would spread and would indeed include all mankind. . . . The world will be filled with justice, honesty and mercy . . . only 'except the Jews.'"[8] Thus, the paradigm for understanding all present and future anti-Jewish verbiage or policies, even under the veil of progress and modernity, has been formulated: eternal hatred of the Jews was accepted as a historical constant. In itself it required little elaboration. Its very antiquity was its rationale; *its origins served as an explanation.*[9]

Jewish historiography then developed two parallel models for dealing with anti-Semitism: the cyclical and the spiral. The cyclical version saw in anti-Semitism a kind of permanent obsession, a pathological antagonism towards Jews, reappearing anew in slightly changing forms "in every generation." Such, for instance, was Leo Pinsker's attitude in his *Autoemancipation,* as well as Nachum Sokolov's in his *Eternal Hatred toward an Eternal People*—both books almost simultaneously published in 1882.[10] The ideological pioneers of Zionism managed to apply, even at that early stage, a rather elementary version of social pathology-*cum*-social psychology to account for the permanence of anti-Semitism in all known non-Jewish societies—past and present. More recent examples are likewise easy to come by. The late Shmuel Ettinger, for instance, followed a similar line.[11] For him it was the stereotype of the contemptible Jew, ever present in Western civilization, that provided the clue for the permanence of anti-Semitism. Jew-hating could only fade away temporarily, according to his scheme, reemerging anew through the reemployment of old familiar images. No fundamental change needed to be explained within this scheme. Anti-Semitism, to use Daniel Goldhagen's argument again, was always there—threatening, violent, and "eliminationist."

The spiral version, in turn, stresses dynamism and escalation instead of permanence and repetition. It argues for a *process* in which anti-Semitism has been continuously radicalized, especially during the modern period. From a certain point onward, it contends—be it the early restructuring of the modern European state, to use Hannah Arendt's familiar prototype, or since the emergence of racism, according to Jacob Katz—anti-Semitism underwent a process of radical change, becoming ever more aggressive in tone and intention, reaching its final consummation in Auschwitz.[12]

Naturally, the distinctions between the two models are often blurred. The proponents of both place great emphasis on traditional anti-Semitism and vary primarily in the significance they attach to its latter-day transformations and the new types of its legitimation. It is, moreover, often difficult to separate the two approaches. The tension is quite apparent in Goldhagen's book. On the one hand, he repeatedly emphasizes the traditional anti-Jewish animus—presumably typical of German society from times immemorial. On the other, he is determined to show its "evolution": it was "a story of continuity and change *par excellence,*" he writes.[13] Nevertheless, Goldhagen's own exposition leaves no doubt as to what is central for him and what he considers no more than an elaboration: it is that pervasive and permanent hatred that explains everything, he reasserts, the original, deep-seated antipathy towards the Jews. The rest is only variations on a theme.

Goldhagen, after all, mainly deals with *personal* animosity, with fear and aversion, with malice and vindictiveness. He wishes to explain the acts of individuals—the behavior of Hitler's "willing executioners." It is not their ideology that interests him but their drive; not their Weltanschauung but their passion.

It is instructive to remember that in the immediate postwar years, it was common among historians to deny the very *existence* of a Nazi ideology. It was fashionable then, even more than now, to compare Nazism with Communism, and the poverty of Nazi ideology therefore appeared blatant indeed. "National Socialism has no political theory of its own," wrote Franz Neumann as early as 1944, "and . . . the ideologies it uses or discards are mere *arcana dominationis,* techniques of dominations." "[T]he German Leadership," he added, "is the only group in present German society that does not take its ideological pronouncements seriously and is well aware of their purely propagandistic nature."[14] At that time, emphasis usually fell—as in some of the prewar narratives, too—on the National Socialists' "state of mind," on their instincts and passions rather than on their ideas. Fear of the "other" or the collective force of a common hatred, shared by so many Germans for so long towards the Jews—these, above all, were deemed relevant for explaining the Holocaust. Only since the late 1960s, in fact, with the new interest in nineteenth-century anti-Semitism, in *völkisch* ideology, and in racism, and then with the appearance of Ernst Nolte's *Three Faces of Fascism* and Eberhard Jäckel's *Hitler's Weltanschauung* did the historiography of Nazism seem to have finally matured.[15] It now plunged into a far more sophisticated and better-informed search for causation. It was, in short, seeking new explanations.

Goldhagen's single-minded stress on anti-Semitism as an "animus" seemed questionable at the very outset. Indeed, when his book first appeared, it was at first challenged by historians—of various schools—who felt that his argument was simply one that had been long discarded. Other shortcomings in his approach also seemed familiar enough. To begin with, his insistence on not comparing German anti-Semitism with its many other manifestations elsewhere across the European continent was rightly deemed unacceptable. Decades of research have, after all, established beyond any doubt that anti-Jewish attitudes were not unique to Germany and that during the pre–World War I years, though such attitudes had by no means disappeared from the German public sphere, they were not particularly pronounced in that country. Furthermore, Goldhagen's cursory treatment of the complex historical evidence concerning the relationships between Germans and Jews from the early nineteenth century up to the Nazi era—also a thoroughly studied theme in recent years—is likewise inadmissible. Jews were perhaps never as well integrated in German bourgeois society of the *Kaiserreich* as they themselves often wished to believe. They surely encountered anti-Semitism often enough, at both the private and the public level.

But the prewar years as such could be considered a "rehearsal for destruction" only in hindsight.[16] At the time, despite the clouds on the horizon, these were years of hope and of real and conspicuous progress.

Goldhagen's claims concerning the omnipresence of the eliminationist rage in Nazi Germany have indeed been contested by intentionalists and functionalists alike. Historians from both camps protested the universality of his claims as well as his almost principled lack of differentiation.[17] The controversy soon made it evident that the argument, in fact, did not concern the role of Jew hating as *a background* to the Holocaust. Functionalists, too, usually agree that a pervasive anti-Jewish attitude was a *sine qua non* for the "Final Solution."[18] The historiographic debate lies elsewhere. It revolves around the role of *ideology,* not around questions of love or hate. One argues about the importance of the anti-Semites' Weltanschauung and about its absolute and relative impact upon the policies leading to extermination. *Nobody* really denies that there has been (more or less) widespread animosity towards Jews in Germany—before, during, and indeed even after the Nazi era. Despite Goldhagen's combative mood, no one doubts the fact that such a general hostility towards them was a basic *precondition* for the initiation and for the "success" of the "Final Solution." The argument lies elsewhere.

Moreover, the critical edge of this historiographic debate seems to have been somewhat blunted with the ebbing of the controversy between functionalists and intentionalists. As early as 1992, Christopher Browning listed a number of "modified intentionalists" like himself, and one occasionally encounters in the literature even some "moderate functionalists."[19] In a reprinting of an article dealing with the debate between what he prefers to call Hitlerists and structuralists, Ian Kershaw has announced that all things considered, "one would have to conclude that neither model offers a wholly satisfactory explanation, and that some room for compromise is obvious."[20] Finally, in the introduction to his book *Nazi Germany and the Jews,* Saul Friedländer summarizes his present position by stating that "[t]he crimes committed by the Nazi regime were neither a mere outcome of some haphazard, involuntary, imperceptible, and chaotic onrush of unrelated events nor a predetermined enactment of a demonic script; they were the result of converging factors, of the interaction between intentions and contingencies, between discernible causes and chance."[21] This, no doubt, is an admiringly balanced view. According to Friedländer, too, it is not vague intentions or a diffuse "animus" with which we are dealing, but an ideology—a more or less systematic set of ideas that eventually led to the Holocaust. Here the *meaning and place* of anti-Semitism along the road to Auschwitz is being debated—a far more complex matter. Still, the tendency to oversimplify, perhaps also the urge to follow our intuition and draw a direct line between ideology and action, seems irresistible. After all, *anti-Semitism as an ideology* is easily transformed into the functional equivalent of *anti-Semitism as an animus,* and both can thus be treated as self-evident, straightforward explanations. Neither, I believe, is really fit for the task.

In a scholarly reevaluation of the relevant historiographic scene, published in 1985, Dov Kulka stated that only through anti-Semitism—as an *ideology,* to be sure—was it at all possible "to explain the inexplainable."[22] More recently, in a polemical article in one of Israel's most widely-read dailies, Yehuda Bauer and Ysrael Gutman reassert that despite all the arguments, "the Archimedean point is the ideology."[23] Here lies, according to them, not only the uniqueness of the Holocaust but also the uniqueness of the National Socialist system as a whole. Accordingly, one does not need to *explain* much beyond it. It is, once again, "the origins that explain," to return to Marc Bloch's critical formulation. It is the very existence of the anti-Semitic ideology—in a rather intensified form and with some particular and peculiar details—that seems to reduce the mystery of the Holocaust. In his much-quoted speech in Berlin, "50 Years After," the Swiss philosopher-historian Walter Hofer proclaimed that it was "simply incomprehensible how the claim can be made that the National Socialist racial policy was not the realization of Hitler's *Weltanschauung.*"[24] But, after all, is it not precisely this link—between Weltanschauung and policy—that we ought to explain? Is it not that process of "realization"—apparently so unrelenting and so ruthless—that is the extraordinary fact about the Nazis and their accomplices?

But when dealing with this matter, it is apparently all too easy to forget that long-established historical lesson, namely that ideologies are never simply *realized;* that they are never just *put into practice.* The common model of background and events, preparation and performance—this familiar two-tier structure, in which the first always explains the second—has repeatedly proven flawed. Turning theory into the cause of praxis, moving between ideas and action on some sort of a one-way road, has never been a satisfactory exercise. It is a fine construct of our narrational skill but a dubious historiographic practice. In fact, no full-fledged utopian ideology (anti-Semitism—eliminationist, redemptive, or otherwise—all included) has ever been available "in advance," so to speak, as simply a program for political, economic, or social action.

Examples are easy to come by. The locus classicus of this methodological issue is, no doubt, the controversy over the relationships between the philosophy of the Enlightenment and the French Revolution. The issue received some highly sophisticated treatment in recent literature, but Alfred Cobban's brilliant essay of 1965 is always a pleasure to quote from.[25] It opens with a memorable passage from Taine: "When we see a man . . . apparently sound and of peaceful habits, drink eagerly of a new liquor, then suddenly fall to the ground, foaming at the mouth . . . we have no hesitation in supposing that in the pleasant draught there was some dangerous ingredient."[26] Cobban then recalls the testimony of Edmund Burke, who believed that the revolution was caused by the spread of enlightened ideas, and ends with Michelet and Lamartine, who saw in the philosophy of the eighteenth century "the code civil and religious liberty *put into action* in the Revolution by the People." Even Louis Blanc, "for all his socialist ideology," still saw the "revolutionary struggle as one of conflicting principles," and so finally did most of the later socialist historians.[27] Nevertheless, Cobban is not intimidated. He goes on to demolish the entire edifice, mercilessly probing the presumably self-evident link between ideas and praxis, exposing its problematic nature and closing with a characteristically frank indecision: "The influence of the Enlightenment cannot be disregarded in any history of the French Revolution . . . but the revolutionaries did not set their course by its light in the beginning, nor did they steer the ship of state into the haven of the Enlightenment in the end."[28]

Among the many examples demonstrating the intermingling of ideology and practice, the case of nationalism is singularly fitting. It is particularly pertinent as an analogy for anti-Semitism, not only because of the imminent historical link between the two[29] but also because in both cases one could distinguish between a widespread *sensibility,* an "animus," to be sure, and a mature *ideology.* It is generally agreed that some form of initial national awareness as well as few budding political institutions relying upon it were present in a number of European societies long before the French Revolution. Clearly, a vague national consciousness preceded the formulation of a national worldview and full-fledged modern national ideologies. The history of both England and France abound with examples of that prolonged interaction between theory and practice, characteristic of the development of modern nationalism. It is, however, usually argued that Germany represented a different model, one in which nationalism *as an idea* much preceded its realization; one in which a clear ideology has more or less simply been put into practice.[30]

But though an embryonic national consciousness can surely be detected at least among members of certain social strata even in pre-Napoleonic Germany, and though a national discourse gradually evolved there during the first half of the nineteenth century—this, too, I believe, never reached the stage of containing a clear blueprint for action. Fichte's *Reden an die deutsche Nation,* often quoted with great aplomb, is a good example of this argument. In fact, the *Reden* contain no clear ideological design and are instead suffused with universal ideals as much as with some early sense of nationalism. They were later used for a variety of often contradictory political purposes, but at the time they mainly gave voice to the frustration of the occupied and contained no orderly draft for solving any immediate or general problem. The political ambitions of the early nineteenth-century

Burschenschaften, likewise, were drowned in a romantic rhetorical idiom—a far cry from any well-conceived Weltanschauung. And the revolutionaries of 1848 clearly had no clue as to what kind of national unity they were aiming at.

Neither, of course, did Otto von Bismarck when he finally took office as the Prussian Chancellor in September 1862. Bismarck's policy making is, indeed, a prime example for the complex nature of the relationships between political intentions and performance. The fact that he had repeatedly been credited with fulfilling the dreams of the German national movement at the time neither means that he *intended* to do so, nor that his *Kaiserreich* had ever been the true realization of these dreams. The quick ideological adjustment eventually made by the German liberals, moving from a vocal opposition to his policies to a warm support of all his vagaries, was only a fitting counterpart to his own equivocation. It was only later on, with the actual establishment of the new Reich, its scope and its particular type of regime, that Bismarck's solution seemed to many—though never to all—the realization of their previous national vision. But, in any case, this only happened *in retrospect.* The German national ideology took its *concrete* shape—and a temporary one at that—not prior to or in preparation of the consolidation of the Reich but *in parallel* to this process and perhaps only *after* it had been achieved.[31]

This, to be sure, is *not* an attempt to resurrect a simplified, reductionist Marxism, according to which material circumstances explain any form of consciousness. What we are forced, yet again, to confront—in all available examples, but in a most convincing way, finally, in the case of National Socialism—is the *tangled web of interaction between ideology and praxis.* It is not some kind of "ideological falsehood," to use Bauer and Gutman's phrase, that can explain the "Final Solution," even if the hopes of "getting rid" of the Jews did in fact constitute a powerful motive force for its realization. Neither was an anti-Semitic blueprint suddenly drawn and executed following some concrete events in occupied Poland and in Russia between 1939 and 1942—as has sometimes been suggested. *Anti-Semitism—both as a general sentiment and as a vague but powerful ideology had been there before, but its effectiveness came from the chances of implementation, and these became evident only with the onset of the military campaign in the east.* It was not the prevalent anti-Jewish sentiment as such, nor the grand redemptive schemes that so captured the imagination of anti-Semites since the days of the Bayreuth Circle, which finally directed the hands of the executioners. It was rather a version of it all that suddenly became *feasible,* almost "easy" to carry out then and there, under the particular conditions at the Russian front in the fall and winter of 1941. Against the background of the systematic terror and discrimination practiced by the Nazis against the Jews for some eight years, plans of extermination were now finally turned into reality, bolstered by a virulent anti-Semitism that had acquired a dynamic of its own and became yet another major force to be reckoned with in those days.

This argument is, of course, not mine and is by no means unknown in the literature, but for some reason it normally remains unacknowledged. Observe, for instance, Eberhard Jäckel's essay, written over twelve years ago: "Der Weg zum Mord an den Juden" (The path toward the murder of the Jews). Despite his protestations concerning the preeminence of Hitler's deep-seated racism, the constant interaction between ideology and practice clearly emerges from his day-to-day review of Nazi policies during the critical moments just before and just after the beginning of Barbarossa. At that time, Hitler himself "probably did not yet know how it should all continue."[32] He still hesitated, according to Jäckel, as late as August 1941, while Heydrich and Goebbels, who were apparently pushing forward at that time, did so "in an effort to win favor and gain power more than out of sheer hatred."[33] In any case, the fortunes of war and the circumstances surrounding it were most intimately linked to the decisions concerning the "Final Solution."

Another example of ostensibly stressing the primacy of ideology while in fact describing a much more complex interaction between theory and practice can be found in Omer Bartov's two books on Hitler's army.[34] Bartov labors to show the deep impact of that peculiar blend of anti-Bolshevism and racism upon the soldiers on the Eastern Front. At the same time, however, he describes the far more complex situation that existed. Bartov repeatedly stresses the effectiveness of Nazi indoctrination, but what emerges from his overall description is the *interplay* of ideological indoctrination and inhuman conditions at the front—not the primacy of one over the other. Finally, this is also apparent in Saul Friedländer's latest book. While the author opens by proclaiming that his main explanatory tool would be the "redemptive anti-Semitism" typical of the Nazi leadership, the strength of his argument lies—to my mind—elsewhere.[35] It lies in the *complex, incremental* character of his narrative concerning the treatment of the Jews under National-Socialism; in the way in which he so pertinently describes their gradual exclusion from German society, their debasement and dehumanization supported by a mixture of emotions, ideology, opportunism, and political circumstances.

Let us once again quickly review the arguments concerning the fateful months between October and December 1941.[36] Hitler was relatively silent concerning the Jews, as indeed Friedländer clearly shows, since about January 1941. His diatribes against them vigorously recur from about mid–October, and by mid-December he was daily concerned with the logic of their extermination. His generally biting and combative oratorical style during these months may perhaps be explained by the overall military situation both at the Eastern Front and elsewhere upon the global theater of war. It was by then quite obvious that victory against the Russians could not be achieved before winter, and a counter-offensive on the Moscow front could not be avoided. In addition, the American entry into the war was imminent, and resistance was becoming daily more violent in the west.

But the context of Hitler's anti-Jewish outbursts surely included other factors, too. It was during these very weeks that action against the Jews everywhere in Europe escalated to new heights. The first "Table Talk" entry against them is indeed dated October 21, followed by further outbursts on October 25 and November 5, and by speeches and private utterances during the rest of November and throughout December. Organized extermination, however, began either at the same time or perhaps even somewhat earlier.[37] Following Heydrich's briefing of the higher SS and police officers on July 2, 1941, sporadic killings by the *Einsatzgruppen* occurred along the entire front. They seem to have escalated during August and September. On 29–30 September over thirty-three thousand Jewish men, women, and children were killed at Babi-Yar near Kiev. By that time "full-scale genocide had already been embarked upon by the *Einsatzgruppen* in the Soviet Union,"[38] and active preparations for full-scale extermination were taking place elsewhere. The expulsion of Jews from Berlin began on October 1, 1941. Between October 16 and November 2, nine trains from various towns in Germany arrived at Lodz. Twenty-one other "transports" came from Prague, Vienna, and Luxembourg. Additional trains were intended to reach Riga but finally arrived at Kovno, where Jews were immediately murdered at a nearby site on the twenty-fifth and twenty-ninth of November. Somewhat earlier, killing of the ghetto inhabitants in Minsk was already taking place at the beginning of November; by the end of the month it was occurring in Riga too. The first experiments in gassing were also performed at that time.

Hitler's anti-Semitic rhetoric, then, did not precede these events but occurred simultaneously with them. Clearly, the Nazi leadership made sure that the Führer's basic attitude regarding the "Jewish Question" was known to all involved. Hitler's own outbursts obviously encouraged them and drove them on. But his own ideological obsessions were fed by the increasing tempo of the killing—not only the other way around. The web of causes and effects in this case is probably impossible to disentangle. But seen in this light and regardless of its explanatory power, Nazi anti-Semitism can no longer be treated as only a *cause* for other events, an omnipresent *motivation* at the background of the Holocaust. After all, it, too, needs explaining: anti-Semitism is *part of the enigma*. Beyond its vague animus and wild, redemptive, utopian visions, anti-Semitism—like other ideologies—was not only shaping events but also affected by them, intensified or watered down in response to them, reformulated and redirected in relation to them.

In view of this complexity, only those narratives that manage to substitute the question *how* for that of *why* seem to get at least *near* an explanation of the Holocaust—the ones that endeavor to reconstruct the devilish interplay of action and ideas, that linger on the particulars, that insist on giving us even the most minute details. Nine out of Friedländer's ten chapters in his new book deal with the actual course of events, with *how* the Germans behaved and *how* the Jews suffered; with the daily interaction between the thoughts and actions of both victims and perpetrators.[39] And in reading these chapters, one does feel indeed that the mystery begins to unravel. The transition between mere anti-Semitic verbiage and *"die Tat,"* to use Hitler's own phraseology—that is, between that famous anti-Jewish animus and/or ideology on the one hand and the actual praxis of discrimination and ever-increasing abuse on the other—begins to make sense. A similar sensation of an almost unexpected insight is solicited by the detailed description of events during the period between 1939 and 1941 provided, for instance, by Christopher Browning in his studies of Nazi resettlement policies and the ghettoization of the Jews in Poland.[40] The chapter on German Jewry between 1938 and 1943 in the newly published two-volume collection of Yad Vashem written by Yehoyakim Cochavi achieves equally impressive results.[41] Moreover, even Goldhagen's horrifically descriptive chapters on the camps and the death marches occasionally provide such rare moments of cognition.[42]

"The degree of influence to be attributed to ideas is an unresolved question in respect of all great historical movements," writes Alfred Cobban.[43] Marx's effort to dispose of this difficulty by treating ideas as mere reflections of social-class interests has long been tremendously attractive—mainly for its simplicity and its inner coherence. But it clearly won't do. No case demonstrates the weakness of this approach more than that of Nazism. Weber's converse thesis, giving priority to doctrine and belief, ultimately has proven equally reductionist. And, alas, all the variations and combinations of these two approaches have failed to produce theoretically satisfying solutions. Historians, luckily perhaps, are not really expected to overcome such fundamental theoretical hurdles. It is as part of the practice of our craft that we must come to terms with them, each time anew. We should therefore—so I believe—loyally stick to our minute narration, continue to put our trust in the details, and beware of too easily crossing the line between explanation and that which must be explained. Doing just *that* still constitutes a major challenge.

NOTES

1. See mainly Ian Kershaw, *Popular Opinion and Political Dissent in the Third Reich* (Oxford: Clarendon Press, 1983).

2. See the various publications of Götz Aly and Susanne Heim, especially: "Die Ökonomie der 'Endlösung': Menschenvernichtung und wissenschaftliche Neuordnung," in *Sozialpolitik und Judenvernichtung: Gibt es eine Ökonomie der 'Endlösung?* (Berlin: Rotbuch Verlag, 1987), 7–90. The controversy surrounding this issue is well represented in Wolfgang Schneider, ed., *Vernichtungspolitik: Eine Debatte über den Zusammenhang von Sozialpolitik und Genozid im nationalsozialistischen Deutschland* (Hamburg: Junius, 1991). It is raging again now as a result of new discoveries about the bureaucratic involvement of a number of historians in this process.

3. On the person who apparently "invented" the term, see M. Zimmermann, *Wilhelm Marr: The Patriarch of Antisemitism* (New York: Oxford University Press, 1986). Compare also S. Volkov, "Antisemitism as a Cultural Code—Reflections on the History and Historiography of Antisemitism in Imperial Germany," *Leo Baeck Institute Yearbook* 23 (1978): 25–45; and "The Written and the Spoken Word: Continuity and Discontinuity of Antisemitism in Germany 1870–1945," in *Unanswered Questions: Nazi Germany and the Genocide of the Jews,* ed. F. Furet (New York: Schocken Books, 1989).

4. Daniel Jonah Goldhagen, *Hitler's Willing Executioners: Ordinary Germans and the Holocaust* (New York: Knopf, 1996).

5. Ibid., 34–45.

6. See Goldhagen's rhetorical argument, for instance in chap. 1: "So why is the burden of proof not on those who maintain that German society had indeed undergone a transformation and had jettisoned its culturally borne antisemitism?" Ibid., 31.

7. For a more extensive discussion see S. Volkov, "German Antisemitism and Jewish National Thought," *Jerusalem Quarterly* 15 (spring 1980): 53–69.

8. Ahad Ha'am, *Selected Essays,* trans. Leon Simon (Philadelphia: Jewish Publication Society of America, 1936), 105–6.

9. Taking as my point of departure Marc Bloch's discussion of the "Idol of Origins" in his book *The Historian's Craft* (1st English ed. [New York: Knopf, 1953], 29—35), I have more fully developed a critique of this approach to the study of anti-Semitism in my essay "The Written and the Spoken Word."

10. See Leo Pinsker's anonymously published *Autoemanzipation: Mahnruf an seine Stammengenossen von einem russischen Jude* (Berlin: W. Issleib in Komm, 1882); and Nahum Sokolov, *Sin'at Olam le'am Olam* (Eternal hatred toward an eternal people) (Warsaw: Y. Galdman, 1882).

11. For Shmuel Ettinger's position see especially his *Modern Anti-Semitism: Studies and Essays* (in Hebrew) (Tel Aviv: Sifriat Ha' Poulim, 1978). For an English version of the opening, programmatic article, see "The Roots of Modern Anti-Semitism," *Dispersion and Unity* 9 (1969): 17–37.

12. See Hannah Arendt, *The Origins of Totalitarianism* (New York: Meridian Books, 1958), especially chap. 2, "The Jews, the Nation-State, and the Birth of Antisemitism," 11–53; Jacob Katz, *From Prejudice to Destruction: Anti-Semitism 1700–1933* (Cambridge, Mass.: Harvard University Press, 1980); and clearly stating the view of Antisemitism as being gradually radicalized during the nineteenth century, Ya'akov Talmon, *The Unique and the Universal: Some Historical Reflections* (London: Secker & Warbury, 1965), 288–99.

13. Goldhagen, *Hitler's Willing Executioners,* 53.

14. Franz Neumann, *Behemoth: The Structure and Practice of National Socialism 1933–1944* (New York: Oxford University Press, 1942; reprint, New York: Octagon Books, 1963), 467.

15. Ernst Nolte's *Der Faschismus in seiner Epoche: Die Action française, Der italienische Faschismus, Der Nationalsozialismus* was first published in Munich (Piper & Co. Verlag, 1963), and its English translation appeared in 1966 (New York: Holt, Reinhardt and Winston, 1965). Compare also Eberhart Jäckel, *Hitlers Weltanschauung: Entwurf einer Herrschaft* (Tübingen: Deutsche Verlags-Anstalt, 1969), and in English, *Hitler's Weltanschauung: A Blueprint for Power* (Middleton, Conn.: Wesleyan University Press, 1972).

16. Paul W. Massing, *Rehearsal for Destruction: A Study of Political Anti-Semitism in Imperial Germany* (New York: Harper, 1949).

17. For a collection of responses, see Franklin Jamlin Littell, ed., *Hyping the Holocaust: Scholars Answer Goldhagen* (East Rockaway, N.Y.: Cummings and Hathaway, 1997).

18. Despite what seems to me a gross understatement of the extent of Antisemitic sentiment within the general German population, a close reading, even of Hans Mommsen's most outspokenly functionalist articles, reveals this to be the case. See, above all, his "Die Realisierung des Utopischen: Die 'Endlösung der Judenfrage' im 'Dritten Reich,'" in *Geschichte und Gesellschaft* (9. Jahrgang 1983/4): 421–52.

19. Christopher Browning, "Beyond 'Intentionalism' and 'Functionalism': The Decision for the Final Solution Reconsidered," in *The Path to Genocide: Essays on Launching the Final Solution* (Cambridge: Cambridge University Press, 1992), 86.

20. Ian Kershaw, "Hitler and the Holocaust," in *The Nazi Dictatorship: Problems and Perspectives of Interpretation,* 3d ed. (New York: E. Arnold; distributed in the United States by Routledge, Chapman and Hall, 1993), 105.

21. Saul Friedländer, *Nazi Germany and the Jews,* vol. 1, *The Years of Persecution, 1933–1939* (New York: HarperCollins, 1997), 5.

22. Otto D. Kulka, "Major Trends and Tendencies in German Historiography on National Socialism and the 'Jewish Question' (1924–1984)," *Leo Baeck Institute Yearbook* 30 (1985): 234.

23. Yehuda Bauer and Ysrael Gutman, "The Archemedean Point Is the Ideology," *Ha'Aretz,* April 16, 1998.

24. Walter Hofer, "50 Jahre danach. Über den wissenschaftlichen Umgang mit dem Dritten Reich," in *Geschihchte in Wissenschaft und Unterricht* 34 (1983): 14, cited and translated by Kershaw, *The Nazi Dictatorship,* 84.

25. Alfred Cobban, "The Enlightenment and the French Revolution," in *Aspects of the French Revolution* (London: Cape, 1968), 18–28. From among the more recent literature on this issue, see Keith Baker, "On the Problem of the Ideological Origins of the French Revolution," in *Modern European Intellectual History: Reappraisals and New Perspectives,* ed. Dominick LaCapra and Steven L. Kaplan (Ithaca, N.Y.: Cornell University Press, 1982), 197–219; and Roger Chartier, "Enlightenment and Revolution, Revolution and Enlightenment," in *The Cultural Origins of the French Revolution* (Durham, N.C.: Duke University Press, 1991), 3–20.

26. Cobban, "The Enlightenment and the French Revolution," 18.

27. Ibid., 19–20.

28. Ibid., 28.

29. For the historians' neglect of this link, see S. Volkov, "Nationalismus, Antisemitismus und die deutsche Geschichtsschreibung," in *Nation und Gesellschaft in Deutschland. Historische Essays. Hans Ulrich Wehler zum 65. Geburtstag,* ed. M. Hettling and P. Nolte (Munich: C. H. Beck, 1996).

30. The literature on this issue is immense and has been rapidly growing in recent years. The classic argument, however, was formulated by Friedrich Meinecke in his *Weltbürgertum und Nationalstaat* (Munich: R. Oldenbourg, 1908).

31. For years after its establishment the *Kaiserreich,* split from Austria, was far from being internally unified—politically, socially, and religiously. See, for instance, David Blackbourn, *Class, Religion and Local Politics in Wilhelmine Germany* (New Haven, Conn.: Yale University Press, 1980); Helmut W. Smith, *German Nationalism and Religious Conflict* (Princeton, N.J.: Princeton University Press, 1995); and Alon Confino, *The Nation as a Local Metaphor* (Chapel Hill: University of North Carolina Press, 1997).

32. Eberhard Jäckel, "Der Weg zum Mord an den Juden," in *Hitler's Herrschaft: Vollzug einer Weltanschauung* (Stuttgart: Deutsche Verlags-Anstalt, 1986), 112.

33. Ibid., 120.

34. Omer Bartov, *The Eastern Front 1941–1945, German Troops and the Barbarisation of Warfare* (New York: St. Martin's Press, 1986), and *Hitler's Army: Soldiers, Nazis, and War in the Third Reich* (Oxford: Oxford University Press, 1992).

35. Friedländer, introduction to *Nazi Germany and the Jews*, 3.

36. See S. Friedländer's essay, "Ideology and Extermination: The Immediate Origins of the Final Solution," in this volume. I rely on his summary of the situation here, but the significance of these months in the context of the "Final Solution" is by now generally accepted. Compare the essays by Jäckel, Browning, and Kershaw quoted above.

37. See the chronology in Kershaw, *The Nazi Dictatorship*, 100–104; and in Yehoyakim Cochavi, "The Last Stage in the History of German Jewry," in *The History of the Shoah: Germany* (in Hebrew), vol. 1 (Jerusalem: Yad Vashem, 1998), 348–400.

38. Kershaw, *The Nazi Dictatorship*, 103.

39. The only exception is chap. 3, "Redemptive Anti-Semitism," 73–112.

40. Browning, *The Path to Genocide*, chaps. 1 and 2, pp. 3–56.

41. See Cochavi, *The History of the Shoah*, 235–400.

42. See Goldhagen, *Hitler's Willing Executioners*, pt. 4. on the camps and pt. 5 on the death marches.

43. Cobban, "The Enlightenment and the French Revolution," 20.

Part Two

**THE HOLOCAUST
AND THE
TWENTIETH
CENTURY**

Three

"THE ABYSS THAT OPENED UP BEFORE US": THINKING ABOUT AUSCHWITZ AND MODERNITY

Anson Rabinbach

The post-Holocaust experience of mass murder has shown that the administrative, bureaucratic, and technical accoutrements of totalitarian regimes are not necessarily a prerequisite for genocide. As events in Rwanda, Bosnia, and Kosovo amply demonstrate, mass murder and "ethnic cleansing" can and have been accomplished without the complex ideological, technological, and political apparatuses that seemed to define the Nazi or the Stalinist killing fields during the 1930s and 1940s. Contemporary genocides are also apparently characterized by a far higher degree of passionate hatred and enthusiastic participation than was evident under the totalitarian regimes. To be sure, radio and television play a role in spreading rumor and the desire for retribution. But, as Hans Magnus Enzensberger writes, "today's protagonists have no need for rituals, marches and uniforms, nor for agendas and oaths of loyalties. They can survive without a Führer. Hatred on its own is enough."[1] This fact enjoins us to be somewhat skeptical of the sociologist Zygmunt Bauman's contention that "without modern civilization and its most central essential achievements, there would be no Holocaust."[2]

Yet it is precisely this assertion that characterized the thinking of an entire generation of German Jewish exiles. Even more important, when we consider the fact that it was the German Jewish exiles who most emphatically saw the Holocaust in the context of a much larger picture of a destructive modernity spun out of control, we are faced with a dilemma. If the connection between a pathological modernity and genocide is no longer self-evident, then should we not reconsider the thesis that the crimes of Nazism, as well as those perpetrated in the Soviet Union during the 1930s, required a certain level of modernity or even of "progress"? We might also ask what investment these refugee intellectuals had in the thesis that there is an intimate connection between modernity and Holocaust, why this trope has played a decisive role in the last half century since the catastrophe?

In light of these considerations it may be useful to first briefly reexamine the intellectual history of the theme of Holocaust as an event embedded in a certain kind of modernity. To be sure, *modernity* is an ambiguous and elusive term. The classical concept of modernity, grounded in the social theories of Marx, Weber, and Durkheim, held that the "cultural program of modernity"—secularization, technical rationality, and moral uncertainty—was of European origin and would be universalized as the world inevitably "westernized." Today, by contrast, this concept seems out of date: scholars have recognized that there is no single trajectory; that in both Western and non-Western societies, there are multiple patterns of cultural, political, and intellectual development; and that it is more appropriate to speak of "multiple modernities."[3]

Still, as recently as a decade ago, it was considered almost beyond dispute that the Holocaust with its administrative bureaucracy, its faceless "desk killers," and above all, mass, factorylike death camps, amounted to what Bauman calls "an exercise in social engineering on a grandiose scale."[4] Nazi mass murder was the by-product of the modern drive to technical mastery and control, substituting technology, administration, and organization for moral responsibility. The very success of modern industrial society in substituting pragmatic and rational criteria for transcendental values, so the argument goes, leads inescapably to the subordination of ends to means and a generalized erosion and paralysis of judgment. For this reason, the crimes of Nazism can be situated well within the mainstream of European modernity and its ideal of the healthy body. Nazi ideology promoted eugenics, demographic planning, public hygiene, and social welfare institutions to garnish support for its radical policies of euthanasia and racial hygiene on behalf of the *Volk* community. As one historian has observed, the emergence of the German racial welfare state was "in so many ways the apotheosis of very widespread trends in European social thought."[5]

One aspect of the provocation produced by Daniel Goldhagen's *Hitler's Willing Executioners* was that he utterly rejects this account, dismissing (as a "stock phrase") the widespread perception of the Holocaust as an essentially modern event characterized by "assembly-line killing."[6] Indeed, Goldhagen's book, as Raul Hilberg among others has pointed out, contains relatively little mention of either Auschwitz or the bureaucratic apparatus of professional functionaries who, at varying degrees of remove from the killing, were responsible for the countless laws, decrees, and decisions that fueled the genocide.[7]

Goldhagen's work does not systematically pursue the argument, choosing instead to provide a massive counterexample of the face-to face brutality, murderous anti-Semitic hatred, and outright sadism that characterized the Nazi murder of the Jews. But his footnotes leave no doubt as to his refusal to adopt this line of investigation. His interpretation ultimately leads, as Hilberg notes, to a depiction of the Holocaust as an orgiastic "super-pogrom in the hands of the shooters and guards."[8] Goldhagen offers a version of German history as a long preamble to murder, an approach that dismisses the Holocaust as a "modern" event; instead it is represented as a passionate crime of ethnic hatred deeply rooted in Germany's long history of anti-Semitism. As a corollary, Goldhagen also dismisses much social science theorizing about moral indifference in the Nazi killing fields. Despite his insistence on the "singularity" of the Holocaust and its "German" character, Goldhagen's book ultimately gives us an "ordinary genocide."

Of course, no genocide can be "ordinary." But the Goldhagen controversy implicitly raised from yet another perspective the question of the role of modernity in the Holocaust, even if that theme did not play a superordinate role in the discussion of his work. Why was it, one may ask, that so many German Jewish intellectuals insisted on the modernity of the Nazi Judeocide from the very outset? Why did they emphatically reject the version of German history promoted by so many German writers and thinkers after World War II as fundamentally "deviating" from the norms of the West? Why did they refuse to accept the judgment that the Germans might become a "Pariah" nation, a theme put forward at the time by such responsible German intellectuals as Thomas Mann, Karl Jaspers, or Friedrich Meinecke? In short, wasn't the excessive focus on the modernity of the killing a means by which they could hold on to their own most cherished cultural traditions and shift attention away from the German context of the genocide? Did the emphasis on the modernity of the Nazi regime and its methods of mass destruction shift the explanation to the universality of evil only to exonerate those elements of German culture that manifested themselves in barbarism? Were the émigré intellectuals, as the exiled biographer Emil Ludwig charged in 1942, still defending the German culture that had driven them out of Germany by other, very largely German means?

The idea of an exceptional German path, or *Sonderweg,* can be traced back to any number of nineteenth-century thinkers who extolled the virtues of the German *Kulturnation* as opposed to French civilization. In its original formulation, the idea of a German cultural nation had both cosmopolitan and nationalist versions. But in the decade before World War I this version of German history was dominated by nationalist writers, and even during the Weimar Republic historians like Friedrich Meinecke, Gerhard Ritter, Hans Rothfels, and Hans Delbruck still wrote German history as the story of how an exclusive culture bearing "German spirit" emanated from Lutheranism, from the Thirty Years' War, and from Germany's "inalterable" geopolitical pressures. After World War II a significant number of influential German scholars and writers (including some of these historians) simply reversed this trope, subscribing to a "radical inversion of the perception of the past." They turned the nineteenth-century glorification of Germany's superior development into its mirror opposite, an account of the diabolical course of German history culminating in the Third Reich. Liberals, Catholics, Marxists, and conservatives created "a new vulgate," documenting Germany's deviation from the "normal" course of historical development in the West: authoritarian, nationalist, romantic, irrational, and illiberal. Interpretations differed only in the specifics of their explanations: Prussian authoritarianism, Luther's submission to the German princes and the subsequent complicity of "spirit" with power, the absence of a bourgeois revolution, or the vitalistic glorification of will and power, but not in their *reductio ad Nazism* of German history.[9]

From its inception, this new negative interpretation of German cultural history as a distinctive and anti-Western German road to Nazism was largely the creation of German scholars and intellectuals as opposed to the émigrés. Among the émigrés, Thomas Mann stood virtually apart for his "negative glorification" of Germany's unique past, the post-1933 reversal of his own nationalist veneration of the melancholic, musical, and demonic creativity of German culture expressed in his 1918 *Reflections of an Unpolitical Man*. During the war Mann returned again and again to the demonic, Faustian, romantic, antirational, and apocalyptic in German thought to show that German culture was ultimately "the spiritual antithesis of Europe" and for that reason had led inexorably to the catastrophe. As Mann put it, German thought "repudiated the reason and the at once mechanistic and ideological conceptions of bygone decades; it expressed itself as an irrationalistic throwback, placing the conception *life* at the center of thought, raised on its standard the powers of the unconscious, the demonic, the darkly creative, which alone were life-giving."[10]

If Mann had once been the unpolitical German, Germany now became the "unpolitical" nation. Mann incurred the wrath of his fellow émigrés, and he in turn was contemptuous of what he called the "patriotism of the exiles," who, he complained, "hold it against me that I feel that through *this* catastrophe *everything* German, German history, German intellect, has been made complicit."[11]

During the war it was the German Jewish exiles who most emphatically challenged Mann's expiation through condemnation of his own intellectual traditions. In many respects the discourse of the modernity of the Holocaust was a counterdiscourse to the thesis of a German *Sonderweg*, the Eurocentric response of the German Jewish exiles to what they perceived to be an excessively Germanophobic discourse, which they condemned with the epithet "Vansittartism" (after Lord Vansittart, the British undersecretary of foreign affairs who famously remarked that the "other Germany has never existed save in a small and ineffective minority).["12]

Consequently, these exiles, who might have been expected to accede to Mann's critique of German culture, instead accepted the role of its most devoted custodians. Of course, the reaction of the émigrés to the theme of the German cultural *Sonderweg* is only paradoxical at first glance. It would have been more surprising if they had not regarded Mann's derogation of the German intellectual tradition as a betrayal. The German Jewish *Bildungsbürgertum*, as George Mosse observed, "more than any other single group, preserved Germany's better self across dictatorship, war, Holocaust and defeat."[13] The radical inversion of German nationalist historicism into the negative historicism of the *Sonderweg* was the continuation of an indigenous German historical discourse by other means.

During World War II, when anti-German sentiment in the United States was at its height, wholesale condemnation of German culture and German thought aided and abetted a Germanophobia of which the exiles themselves were often the victims. The majority of exiles therefore believed themselves to be representatives of what Thomas Mann's children, Klaus and Erika, called "the other Germany," the Germany that had to undertake an act of rescue of the traditions that appeared to many—including Klaus and Erika's own father—to be corrupted by National Socialism. The émigrés also feared that anti-German sentiment might even undermine their hopes for the reconstruction of a democratic and pro-Western Germany. Indeed, they were horrified by the elder Mann's support for the draconian plans (to turn Germany into several small agrarian states) put forward by Secretary of the Treasury Henry Morgenthau, and his stance provoked a fierce reaction among the émigrés who regarded it as license to chastise the whole German population for the crimes of the Hitler regime. They rejected his fusion of German regime and German *Volk* as resonant with Nazism's own racial stereotypes.

Even more provocative than Mann was the writer Emil Ludwig, whose book *The Germans: Double History of a Nation*, published in 1941, infuriated many of the exile intellectuals. Ludwig, who was the most celebrated German exile due to the immense success of his dozen biographies and his access to the White House, sketched a portrait of "the Germans" that was at once simplistic and resonant with less discerning readers. How was it, Ludwig asked, that German history "from Arminius to Hitler" had "made the name of Germany so feared"; how was it possible for the people of Goethe, Beethoven, and Kant "to be forever relapsing into barbarism."[14] Ludwig compared German history to a double-decker omnibus: "The passengers on the upper level enjoy a broader view but remain without influence on the direction of the vehicle, because the driver fails to take notice of them." Hitler, he concluded, "was a truly German phenomenon; and that all well-intentioned efforts to make a distinction between him and the German character miss their point."[15] In fact, Ludwig's cultural history (and his biographies) are all built up out of a timeless essence or spiritual core which can never be fully explained and are basically unalterable. Whether great men or nations, Ludwig reduces everything to what he called "cultural psychology": German history was the story of how *Geist* became a craven ornament of power. "Even today the Germans avail themselves of God or Honor or Country as a cloak beneath which to hide the dagger."[16] More provocative still was the chapter devoted to "Three German Jews" (Marx, Heine, Lassalle). Barely concealing his contempt for these thinkers, Ludwig accused all three of an excessive love of Germany: "They loved Germany despite the fact that, or perhaps, precisely because they were in turn suppressed, imprisoned or abroad."[17]

As if the implied comparison with the exiles of 1933 was not obvious enough, Ludwig delivered a widely reported Fourth of July address in Los Angeles in 1942 which purportedly called Germans a "warrior people" and asserted that "Hitler is Germany."[18] He expressed doubt that even anti-Nazi Germans could be relied upon to establish the principles for which the Allies were fighting. Moreover, he proposed among other things that after the German defeat, "Germany should at first be ruled in the same way that the English to great effect ruled Egypt"; in other words, be turned into a colony under benevolent foreign rule.[19]

Reaction to Ludwig's speech was both immediate and bellicose. Even before the full text appeared in print, the theologian Paul Tillich replied to Ludwig's identification of Hitler with the German people as a method drawn from the Nazis' anti-Semitic arsenal and directed against Germans: "it is an occasion for all forthright German Jews in America decisively and visibly to distance themselves from Ludwig." Writing in the German-language exile newspaper *Aufbau,* Tillich called Ludwig's speech a "dishonor" [Entehrung] to all those who opposed the Nazi regime and accused him of descending to rhetoric that could be found in any "dirty anti-Semitic pamphlet."[20] The controversy unleashed a torrent of debate, with immediate support for Tillich coming from the then relatively unknown *Aufbau* columnist Hannah Arendt, who called the quarrel a "serious and weighty matter."[21] For Arendt, Tillich was right to say that Jews should be the last to claim the right to spread the kind of thinking that had caused them to sacrifice so terribly. Arendt made it clear that she had no patience with Ludwig, whom she denounced as a one-time enthusiast of the German war machine and an admirer of Italian fascism. Ludwig's article, she charged, only proved that the fact that Jews had been driven into exile did not justify the assumption that Jews alone were or are immune from the terrible sickness unto death that had gripped the world, or exempt them from "racial madness." Speaking in the name of all "Jewish patriots," Arendt praised Tillich as a "friend of the Jews" who courageously took it upon himself to protest against "a German-Jew in a Jewish matter."[22] The debate soon spread from the exile press to the American Jewish press, and even reached the editorial pages of the *New York Times,* which condemned Ludwig's speech as the equal in its method to the methods of the anti-Semites. Even Tillich in the end had to concede that he had reacted imprudently in calling Ludwig "a Jewish writer" and appealing to "German-Jews."[23]

Ludwig's response was a blistering attack on the "German patriots in exile," as he called his German Jewish critics. He defended his argument that the "majority of Germans" approved of Hitler's chancellorship and actions, in particular the "expulsion" of the Jews. The falsifications and defamations against him, noted Ludwig, only proved his conviction that "the Germans are incapable of political conflict."[24]

Confronted with Ludwig's and Mann's versions of the German past, it is hardly surprising that the émigré intellectuals felt compelled to become the guardians of German cultural traditions. Theodor Adorno remarked in his wartime book of aphorisms, *Minima Moralia,* that the "claim that Hitler has destroyed German culture is no more than an advertising stunt."[25]

Even more emphatically, Arendt rejected any complicity of the Western intellectual tradition with Nazism. All the Nazis needed for their death factories was what she called the "atmosphere of 'scientificality'" coupled with efficient modern technique. She discounted the role of ideas in the creation of Nazi ideology and institutions, attributing its ideology to "modern mob-men who were not afraid of consistency."[26] In her "Approaches to the German Problem" published in 1945, Arendt was uncompromising: "It was not any German tradition as such," she wrote, "but the violation of all traditions which brought about Nazism." The history of ideas, she insisted, had nothing to do with the Nazis, who effected a powerful marriage between power politics and the masses: "Nazism owes nothing to any part of the Western tradition, be it German or not, Catholic or Protestant, Christian, Greek, or Roman. Whether we like Thomas Aquinas or Machiavelli or Luther or Kant or Hegel or Nietzsche—the list may be prolonged indefinitely as even a cursory glance at the literature of the 'German Problem' will reveal—they have not the least responsibility for what is happening in the extermination camps. Ideologically speaking, Nazism begins with no traditional basis at all, and it would be better to realize the danger of this radical negation of any tradition, which was the main feature of Nazism from the beginning."[27] Arendt, who elsewhere makes ideology into one of the twin pillars of totalitarianism, disavowed any attempt to make German ideas into ideology.

Ludwig expressed his disbelief and shock that his fellow German Jews, after years of exile, continued to defend the German people, and to deny that the "Jews had been forced to emigrate along with the applause of the German people." He bluntly challenged the *Aufbau* to distribute a questionnaire asking them whether it was the Nazis or the Germans who had expelled them. Those Jews, Ludwig charged, who after years of exile still stroked the hand that beat them and encouraged others to love and defend the German people, had to come to terms with their own conscience.[28]

By 1950 the divide between the "German" advocates of the *Sonderweg* and their German Jewish critics (despite the fact that Ludwig was of Jewish origin and Tillich was a Christian) was firmly established and had already discursively reified the opposition between explanations of the Third Reich centering on "the Germans" or "the Nazis," between irrational "Germany" and a perversely rational "modernity." In the historical sediment of this debate we can trace the conceptual archaeology of the Goldhagen controversy.

To be sure, these local and in some respects parochial disputes over German guilt only explain one facet of the vehemence with which the exile intellectuals tried to counter the pervasive discourse of German cultural culpability. On another level, the genocide intruded itself into their reflections on history and philosophy, demanding a retelling of the story of modernity from a perspective that recognized that the universalism and belief in progress that characterized the enlightened German middle classes were no longer plausible. For many of the exiles, the Nazis' singling out of the Jews for total annihilation made their universalism universally untrue. It was this dimension of the genocide as a concrete refutation of the philosophy of enlightenment that preoccupied many of the German Jewish thinkers, in part because it was recent German Jewish thought, for example that of Hermann Cohen and Franz Rosenzweig, that had tried to give *Bildung* a universal cast. For the exiles it was not the German counter-Enlightenment that confronted the Enlightenment of the West as a spiritual antithesis but rather the counter-Enlightenment within Western modernity itself that had to be confronted.

In his book, *L'Histoire déchirée,* Enzo Traverso demonstrates the strong affinity that existed among those thinkers—Max Horkheimer and Theodor Adorno, Günther Anders, and Jean Améry—who concurred with Arendt's characterization of Auschwitz as a "caesura" in civilization. These thinkers shared the view that if Auschwitz could not be prophesied, elements of the death camps were foreshadowed in Max Weber's warnings about the dangers inherent in a "disenchanted" world of rational procedures without transcendent values, in Franz Kafka's vision of the faceless terror of modern institutions, and in Walter Benjamin's image of history as catastrophe. Rather than condemn German thought, they refashioned a post-Auschwitz vision of history from those sources: "From that perspective," observes Traverso, "Auschwitz did not appear as an accidental departure, however serious, from the ineluctable improvement of humanity, but as the legitimate and authentic product of western civilization. Auschwitz unveiled its dark and destructive side, that instrumental rationality could be put in the service of massacre."[29] The barbarism of the Nazis was "not the antithesis of modern industrial and technological civilization, but its hidden face, its dialectical *doppelgänger.*"[30]

Was the rejection of the *Sonderweg* thesis by the German Jewish intellectuals motivated by sound political and historical judgment, or was it premised on what Gershom Scholem called the "unrequited" love between Jews and Germans? Did Arendt not put "herself in the ranks of the many intellectuals of German culture who sought to connect Nazism with Western modernity thereby deflecting blame from specifically German traditions?"[31] Or even worse, as Richard Wolin has suggested, did Arendt's need to draw a curtain over her mentor-lover Martin Heidegger's reputation lead her to the conviction that "the hallowed realm of *Kultur,* on which Arendt had hung the dreams of her youth, bore no responsibility for the German catastrophe? And to her, of course it was Heidegger who was the living embodiment of that realm and those dreams."[32] So it might seem, when we read in the aforementioned 1945 essay how easily she lets Heidegger off the hook with her offhand remark that "the scholars first put to one side by the Nazis as of relatively little use to them were old-fashioned nationalists like Heidegger, whose enthusiasm for the Third Reich was matched only by his glaring ignorance of what he was talking about."[33] Was the émigrés' insistence on the modernity of the genocide a subtle exculpation of their own "Germanness"?

These are not insubstantial charges, especially when we ask more generally whether the deep and positive transference of German Jewish exile intellectuals to the "hallowed realm of *Kultur*" did not indeed blind them to the German roots of the catastrophe and to the concrete manifestations of German anti-Semitism. Arendt's contradictory and ambivalent relationship to Heidegger cannot alone explain her loyalty to the intellectual traditions that she tried to transform into an instrument for understanding the totalitarianism which made her into a victim, and to which Heidegger had so enthusiastically subscribed. Nor was she alone in her arguments against indiscriminately enlisting the role of ideas and scholarship in explaining the Nazi regime. That Arendt considered anti-Semitism a European and not an exclusively German problem is both defensible and self-evident. More important, her vision of public space, of "the political," as articulated in *The Human Condition* was only in small part indebted to Heidegger's philosophy of *Existenz,* as was her phenomenological approach to totalitarian terror. Unlike Heidegger, she did not regard the agon of public dispute and argument as a sign of the "fallen" condition of *Dasein,* but as the space of freedom and transcendence. Her *Origins of Totalitarianism* drew on Heidegger's concept of *Dasein* not to demonstrate the inauthentic social existence of "the They" and the futility of conventional politics but to show how political tyranny results from the very attempt to deny human plurality and the political nature of human existence. Arendt identified Heidegger's contempt for "the political" as characteristic of the "unpolitical" German mandarin whose diagnosis of the condition of loneliness and atomization in effect made totalitarian domination possible.[34]

I would argue that it was not so much her loyalty to Heidegger that produced the blind spot in Arendt's account of totalitarianism, but her loyalty to what she called "the tradition" (from Plato to Nietzsche) that led her to refuse any connection between ideas and Nazism. It was that loyalty that in the end made it so difficult for Arendt to investigate with any thoroughness the revolutionary-apocalyptic dimension of Heidegger's affinity to National Socialism. Despite her brilliant analysis of the structures of totalitarian domination and the ideological "fictions" created by totalitarian regimes, Arendt avoided any investigation of how these fictions were made real for Heidegger and other Weimar thinkers of the conservative revolution in the apocalyptic-redemptive "act," in the politics of the "will," or in the moment of existential decision. In this respect, Arendt was a far more perceptive phenomenologist of the nature of totalitarian unfreedom than she was of German political culture at the end of the Weimar Republic.

The problem of *Kulturkritik* is important, though not as a sign of the émigrés' loyalty to ideas that were irredeemably linked to the politics of the irrationalist right. The German Jewish exiles believed that German cultural criticism, even where it was most corrupted by its proximity to Nazism, could still be mobilized against the power of barbarism. Their strategy was complex and sometimes even perverse. They did not simply musealize *Kulturkritik* but subverted it, turning the ideas of the conservative revolution against the revolution of the right. Just as Arendt subverted Heidegger's critique of modernity by deploying it against totalitarianism, Horkheimer and Adorno's *Dialectic of Enlightenment* also attempted to undertake a "rescue" of enlightenment, to use Horkheimer's expression. Their strategy, not unlike Arendt's, was to turn the teachings of Weimar "mythologues" like Ludwig Klages and Carl Gustav Jung into a sustained critique of the "dialectic of Enlightenment." In so doing, they tried to make German intellectual traditions "usable" or, as Horkheimer once put it, to harness the power of nihilism for their own purposes, "to positively embrace truth in the determination of meaninglessness, and by this measure, to save thought."[35] By appropriating the conservative revolution's critique of technology and instrumental rationality without embracing its discourse of the "soul" or of a return to mythical archetypes à la Klages and Jung, Horkheimer and Adorno refused to countenance any return to the modes of political discourse characteristic of the Weimar right. By self-consciously weaving elements of "counter-rationality" into their evaluations of modernity after the Holocaust, both Arendt and Horkheimer and Adorno, in entirely different ways, attempted to "demythologize" the mythologies of the Weimar conservative revolution. In other words, they sought to break up the contradiction between enlightenment and counterenlightenment in the awareness that this polarization was itself an impasse for both liberalism and conservatism in German history.

In what sense, then, can we still speak of the Holocaust as an event embedded in "modernity"? Though it would be naive to assume that genocide and modernity are as intimately linked as Bauman believes, I believe that the German Jewish response to the thesis of a German *Sonderweg* still offers a valid approach on two levels. First, it contained an important caveat to the widespread belief of the *Sonderweg* theorists that Nazism was an atavistic cult of the archaic and the primitive. It permits us to recognize that those elements in Nazism which looked backwards to a medieval or even primeval Germany could easily coexist with modern forms of technology and organization, and that Nazism was itself an effort to embrace and eliminate the contradictions inherent in a "disenchanted" world. In this respect, the exile intellectuals implicitly understood that Nazism was a cultural synthesis fusing elements from a hypermodern industrial society with a fundamentally irrationalist and unstable admixture of romantic anti-capitalist, nationalist, radical *völkisch,* and bioracial elements. Concepts like "reactionary modernism" usefully demonstrate that there was indeed a distinctive German path to modernity that emerged after World War I in circles identified with the Weimar conservative cultural revolution, and which permitted Weimar theorists to fuse technological rationality with "myth," anti-Semitism, and biosocial categories such as "degeneration."[36] National Socialism was not a "reactionary" ideology but a project of national regeneration predicated on racial hierarchy. If there is no common core or authentic cultural form of modernity, if a high level of technological and economic development is compatible with a wide range of cultural forms, then Nazism appears as an alternative form of radical modernity, just as militant Islamic fundamentalism is an alternative form of modernity today. From this perspective, the genocide is not a "normal" event inherent in a generically understood "modern society" but one whose "possibility" demonstrates the pathological potential of specific constellations of modernity in crisis and the attempt to overcome that crisis by extreme violence.

Studies of the "ideological warriors" of the Third Reich have shown that ideological passion and technical rationality were indeed both considered virtues among the elite. As Saul Friedländer has pointed out in regard to the debate over modernity versus antimodernity in Nazi ideology: "the two interpretive trends previously mentioned need not be considered as entirely separate positions; they are, in fact, dealing with two *contrary but coexisting aspects* of Nazism."[37]

Second, as George Mosse has demonstrated, Nazi culture is not an "oxymoron" but a mythologized collective "breakout" from the iron cage of modernity. It is similar to other fascisms in its emphasis on the politics of the will and on regeneration through violence while it is also unique in its exclusive claim that only the Nordic race can accomplish this aim. National Socialism enlisted enlightenment in the service of counterenlightenment. As Mosse expressed it, "the fascist ideal of the new man inherits from the hated Enlightenment the concept that a new man can be created by education and experience. The Nazis, and especially the SS, also envisaged a new man but he was to exemplify ancient Germanic virtues, a man from the past unspoilt by the present."[38] The remythologizing of race was Nazism's answer to a disenchanted world. Even when it claimed to be a revolt against the modern world in the name of traditional "values," its core myth was anticonservative in its fixation on the new man and new order that it promised to create. It was an alternate model of modernity rather than an outright rejection of it.

Because they understood this dimension of Nazism, the émigré intellectuals tapped into the narrative of German romanticism while simultaneously refusing to embrace myth as an "antidote" to rationality. Hegel, whose narrative of the French Revolution began with the rhetoric of equality and justice and ended up with the guillotine, famously observed that "the universal freedom that the Enlightenment brought into the world culminates in a 'fury of destruction.'"[39] German thinkers ever since have tried to negotiate a kind of invisible "divide" between enlightenment and counterenlightenment, creating an intellectual tradition that includes Nietzsche's dialectic of radical nihilism as well as Max Weber's tale of how "disenchantment" leaves us stranded with the polytheism of modernity's warring gods. Horkheimer and Adorno's *Dialectic of Enlightenment* tells the story of how the "cunning" of Western reason to bring myth under control elicited the "myths" that fascism perpetrated on the world, "stamping even the familiar as enemy." Confronting the experience of the genocide, Arendt and Horkheimer and Adorno replotted that story, not by crossing the divide into "counterenlightenment" but by calling into question the very terms of the divide itself. As Adorno remarked, "One of the tasks confronting thought—and not the least of those tasks—is to bring into the service of *Aufklärung* and of progress all the reactionary arguments that have been moved against Western civilization."[40]

In other words, the fact that they tried to put the critique of enlightenment in the service of enlightenment is all too often misunderstood to be a fatal contagion that implicated the anti-Nazi exiles in the very ideology that had forced them into exile.

On the contrary, their ability to sustain the tension between enlightenment and counterenlightenment distinguished the German Jewish exiles from those Weimar writers and thinkers who sought to overthrow the same antinomies by embracing a new politics of the will, most prominently Martin Heidegger and Carl Schmitt. In the 1930s Heidegger explicitly regarded Nazism as the "counter movement to nihilism" that would enact the necessary "resolve" to take a stance against the technology oriented, inauthentic, and disingenuous culture of "the They" *(Das Man)*. Schmitt considered the "valueless rationality of economic-technical thought" as the Antichrist and counterpoised to it the myth of the "political" which promised a renewal of the West's resolve to do battle with the eastern "enemy"—Russian Bolshevism. Like Heidegger, Schmitt saw in Nazism a potential vehicle of ontological renewal, the "decision" to enact a revolutionary breakthrough which not merely fuses the technical and the mythical but would do away with the opposition between them altogether. In other words, for its intellectual adherents, the National Socialist revolution was ultimately a mythical form of regeneration and an escape from the condition of modernity into a new rather than past order of human existence.

For the German Jewish exiles, the failure of those Weimar intellectuals to sustain the high tension act necessary to keep in balance the imperatives of a rational civilization and the seductive mythologies it inevitably engenders *was* the new constellation of the crisis of modernity. Even if we reject their story as somehow too "dark" or too "universal," it makes us aware that Nazism and the Holocaust can never be reduced either to an exclusively German event involving premodern Jew hatred or to a universalist "social engineering" as Bauman believes.

An exaggerated insistence on the "singularity" of the Holocaust logically elicits the predictable and legitimate response that "other" genocides should not therefore be treated as lesser events, nor should they be considered any more or less "normal" than the Holocaust. As Jean-Michel Chaumont points out in his important study of the competition for recognition among victims, "the claim for a statute of exceptionality [for the Judeocide] also imposes a statute of 'normality' on all the rest, and introduces a *de facto* division between those crimes that are unconditionally intolerable and those crimes with which one might, and even does, live."[41] The fact that such claims are sometimes put crudely forward as assaults on a purported "monopoly" of the Holocaust over the memory of mass death, as in the French debate over the *Livre noir du Communisme,* cannot simply be countered by the argument that unlike the social and political genocides of the

Stalinist or Maoist regimes, the German racial genocide was a uniquely modern event, or that it could only be perpetrated against the Jews.[42] Instead, each genocide has to be treated on its own terms and not instrumentalized by facile comparisons.

The exile intellectuals recognized that the Nazi genocide demonstrated that any attempt to break out of the dialectic of enlightenment and counterenlightenment by an act of perverse and pathological "will" has the potential for violent acts of destruction, for the politics of genocide. And such moments of political danger do not pertain only to societies that are traditionally labeled "Western," or "European" or "German," but to other points on the globe where redemptive violence threatens to erupt in the stress points engendered by the dialectic of enlightenment. Despite its excessive implication of modernity in the experience of mass murder, the story told by the German Jewish exiles in the shadow of the apocalypse of European Jewry is both particular and universal. Its universality pertains everywhere that the project of creating multiethnic, secular, and democratic societies engenders new, postmodern ideologies of reenchantment, particularly those that "racialize" or "theologize" perceived threats to the integrity of a mythologized community. The conditions for contemporary civil war and genocide are historically different from the Judeocide, but the dynamic is not entirely dissimilar. That insight may at some level be unspectacular, but it was the point that the German Jewish exiles were insisting on when they rejected the *Sonderweg* and looked into what Arendt called "the Abyss that opened up before us."[43]

NOTES

1. Hans Magnus Enzensberger, *Civil Wars: From L.A. to Bosnia* (New York: The New Press, 1994), 27.

2. Zygmunt Bauman, *Modernity and the Holocaust* (Ithaca, N.Y.: Cornell University Press, 1989), 87.

3. S. N. Eisenstadt, "Multiple Modernities," *Daedelus* 129, no. 1 (winter 2000): 1–29.

4. Bauman, *Modernity and the Holocaust*, 68.

5. Mark Mazower, *Dark Continent: Europe's Twentieth Century* (New York: Alfred A. Knopf, 1999), 100.

6. Daniel Jonah Goldhagen, *Hitler's Willing Executioners: Ordinary Germans and the Holocaust* (New York: Alfred A. Knopf, 1996), 10.

7. Raul Hilberg, "The Goldhagen Phenomenon," *Critical Inquiry* 23 (summer 1997): 721–28.

8. Ibid., 727.

9. Jean Solchany, *Comprendre le nazisme dans l'Allemagne des années zéro (1945–1949)* (Paris: PUF, 1997), 94, 95.

10. Thomas Mann, "An Appeal To Reason," in *Order of the Day: Political Essays and Speeches of Two Decades* (New York: Alfred A. Knopf, 1942), 54.

11. Klaus Harpprecht, *Thomas Mann: Eine Biographie* (Reinbek bei Hamburg: Rowohlt, 1995), 1458.

12. Lord Vansittart, *Lessons of My Life* (New York: Alfred Knopf, 1945), 146.

13. George L. Mosse, *German Jews beyond Judaism* (Bloomington: Indiana University Press, 1983), 82.

14. Emil Ludwig, *The Germans: Double History of a Nation,* trans. Heinz and Ruth Norden (Boston: Little Brown and Company, 1941), viii.

15. Ibid., ix.

16. Ibid., 15.

17. Ibid., 332.

18. Ludwig's speech was excerpted in the *New York Times,* July 6, 1942, under the title "Ludwig Asks Fight on German People." Also see Anton Kaes, "What to Do With Germany," *German Politics and Society* 13, no. 3 (fall 1995): 134.

19. The full text of Ludwig's speech appeared as "Was soll mit Deutschland geschehen?" *Aufbau,* July 24, 1942, pp. 5–6.

20. Quoting Ludwig to the effect that "[r]eligion, history, philosophy all teach principles foreign to the German character," Tillich commented: "this sentence—by just replacnig 'German' with 'Jewish'—could be printedin any dirty anti-Semitic pamphlet." Paul Tillich, "Gegen Emil Ludwig's neueste Rede," *Aufbau,* July 17, 1942, p. 7.

21. Hannah Arendt, "Für und gegen Paul Tillich," *Aufbau,* July 31, 1942, p. 6.

22. Ibid.

23. Paul Tillich, "Es geht um die Methode," *Aufbau,* August 7, 1942, p. 7.

24. Emil Ludwig, "An die Deutschen Patrioten im Exil," *Aufbau,* August 14, 1942, p. 8.

25. Theodor W. Adorno, *Minima Moralia: Reflections from a Damaged Life,* trans. E. F. N. Jephcott (London: Verso, 1974), 57.

26. Hannah Arendt, "An Image of Hell," in *Hannah Arendt, Essays in Understanding 1930—1952,* ed. Jerome Kohn (New York: Harcourt Brace and Co., 1994), 205.

27. Hannah Arendt, "Approaches to the 'German Problem,'" in *Essays in Understanding,* 108.

28. Ludwig, "An die Deutchen Patrioten."

29. Enzo Traverso, *L'histoire déchirée* (Paris: Cerf, 1997), 39.

30. Ibid.

31. Margaret Canovan, *Hannah Arendt: A Reinterpretation of Her Political Thought* (New York: Cambridge University Press, 1992), 20.

32. Richard Wolin, "Hannah and the Magician," *The New Republic,* October 9, 1995, pp. 27–37.

33. Arendt, "An Image of Hell," 202.

34. On Arendt and Heidegger see Seyla Benhabib, *The Reluctant Modernism of Hannah Arendt* (Thousand Oaks, Calif.: Sage Publications, 1996), especially 102–22; and Dana R. Vila, *Arendt and Heidegger: The Fate of the Political* (Princeton, N.J.: Princeton University Press, 1996).

35. Alfred Schmidt and Gunzelin Schmid Noerr, eds., *Max Horkheimer Gesammelte Schriften,* Bd. 12, "Nachgelassene Schriften 1931–1949" (Frankfurt am Main: Fischer Verlag, 1985), 595.

36. Jeffrey Herf, *Reactionary Modernism: Technology, Culture, Politics in Weimar and the Third Reich* (Cambridge: Cambridge University Press, 1984).

37. Saul Friedländer, "The Extermination of the European Jews in Historiography: Fifty Years Later," in *Thinking about the Holocaust after Half a Century,* ed. Alvin H. Rosenfeld (Bloomington: Indiana University Press, 1997), 6.

38. George L. Mosse, *The Fascist Revolution: Toward a General Theory of Fascism* (New York: Howard Fertig, 1999), 88.

39. James Schmidt, introduction to *What is Enlightenment? Eighteenth-Century Answers and Twentieth Century Questions,* ed. James Schmidt (Berkeley and Los Angeles: University of California Press, 1996), 21.

40. Adorno, *Minima Moralia,* 192.

41. Jean-Michel Chaumont, *La concurrence des victimes: génocide, identité, reconnaissance* (Paris: Éditions la découverte, 1997), 176.

42. See Anson Rabinbach, "Communist Crimes and French Intellectuals," *Dissent* (fall 1998): 61–66.

43. Hannah Arendt to Karl Jaspers, August 17, 1946, in *Hannah Arendt Karl Jaspers Correspondence 1926–1969,* ed. Lotte Kohler and Hans Saner and trans. Robert Kimber and Rita Kimber (New York: Harcourt Brace Jovanovich, 1992), 54.

Four

THE DESTRUCTION OF
NARRATIVITY:
THE HOLOCAUST IN
HISTORICAL DISCOURSE

Dan Diner

As the twentieth century has drawn to a close, the Holocaust appears to be assuming the character of an icon of a now-past saeculum—something like the ultimate core event of "our" time. The reasons for this are manifold and vary from culture to culture, and from country to country.[1]

Although the conspicuous presence of the Holocaust in public discourse may be easily traced from the late 1970s onwards, and its impact became particularly manifest in the 1980s, its significance for universal historical consciousness and moral standards became irrevocable only after 1989. That epochal turning point occasioned a reemergence across Europe of old historical spaces and the historical memories connected with them. To the extent this has been true, a fundamental predicament of the common European future, one that it is no longer possible to ignore, has emerged in the post-1989 period. For more than forty years Communism and the ideological antagonism between the former East and the former West neutralized the impact of World War II and its various prehistories. What has come in the wake of this is nothing short of a *return of history,* that is, an evocation of memories largely suspended. A past that seemed to have been laid *ad acta* long ago has been revived and reactivated.[2]

The consequences of such a return of history are not restricted solely to the realm of memory and cultural reconstruction. It suffices to consider in this vein the connection between memory recovered and the restoration of former property rights. When the regimes of the People's Republics in Central and East-Central Europe were dismantled after 1989, so, too, were the socializations and nationalizations of property instituted by those Communist regimes after World War II. Private property was reinstalled, bringing to light a historical stratum of former "Aryanizations" and other forms of plundering Jewish assets.[3]

Restitution for or recovery of property implies the reestablishment by legal means of formerly existing social realities. To this extent, past factualities—destroyed by Nazi occupation and mass murder, and later hidden by the neutralizing effect of later socializations—exacted their toll when legal owners, their heirs, or their legal proxies claimed ownership or demanded restitution. This toll was not confined to governments only, but left its imprint on daily life and popular consciousness in Europe as well. On a more theoretical level, this fact made the constrained anthropological interrelationship between memory and property obvious—the past became the title to the future.[4]

The reconstruction of a common European cultural space—a tendency that has become increasingly evident since the end of the Cold War—renders present the absence of European Jewry. The extermination of European Jewry is now moving into the center of a commonly molded European identity. Ultimately, all European peoples had been involved in one way or another, whether to a greater or a lesser extent, in the exterminationist project.[5] Germany, as the initiator and executor of the Nazi Weltanschauung, mobilized and enlisted other countries and peoples into a common undertaking—though strict distinctions must be maintained between countries conquered or occupied, and those otherwise integrated into German-dominated Europe. Some collaborated willfully or simply cooperated at various stages, while many that attempted to passively resist or simply preserve their neutrality were nonetheless dragged into the ferocities. The different and even antagonistic histories of the various European peoples during the short, though extremely dense, period from 1939 to 1945 serve simultaneously as a locus of memory and as a basis for common European values within a new, commonly accepted frame of reference. Today the Holocaust stands at the negative core of European self-understanding. The history of the Nazi past and of World War II are currently present and felt in a way that is without precedent in the years since 1945.

This centrality of the Holocaust to historical consciousness is not simply to be expected as a matter of course, as the opposite was the case for decades. This fact itself demands explanation. Even in written history, the Holocaust was marginal.[6] The destruction of European Jewry and the other victims of collective annihilation by the Nazis were held at arm's length in the annals of general history.

Scarcely a single major work of general history written in the 1950s and 1960s and even in the 1970s gives the Holocaust the weight and space it obviously deserves. For instance, in Gordon Craig's major European history encompassing the course of events from the Congress of Vienna in 1815 up to the present, the destruction of European Jewry is never even mentioned.[7] Paradoxically, this omission reveals a certain truth: by its very absence the Holocaust is implicitly placed beyond the realm of reconstructed history, beyond common historical narratives and systematizations.[8] The omission of the Holocaust in the twentieth century's narratives may also be the result of divergent collective perspectives, generational rifts, or individual preferences. I shall not address those possible reasons here, however, inasmuch as they are situated beyond the realm of history proper. My interest is to inquire into the specific conceptual difficulties faced by the historian in attempting to adequately integrate the event of the Holocaust into the flow of twentieth-century history.

Let me investigate first, as a precondition for the systematic integration of the Holocaust into the saeculum's narrative, two possible general axes of historical interpretation of our time. The first, based on familiar modes of historical understanding, relies fundamentally on notions of conflict and interest based on institutionalized power, whether political, diplomatic, or military.[9] The main players involved in such an intercourse of conflict and rivalry are states, peoples, and nations. In European history of the last four hundred years, large-scale conflicts and struggles are interpreted in terms of a struggle for hegemony or of a common determination to check presumptions to hegemony and restore a balance presumed to have been disturbed.[10] Conflicts based on rivalry and attempts to dominate the European system of states and powers, its means of communication as well as its codes of understanding, were generally regulated according to established forms and norms stipulated by the universal meaning of the law of nations. These were generally perceived as being in conformity with economic considerations relating to the commonly accepted understandings of how the wealth of nations ought to be accumulated. The use of force, executed by the only legitimate actors, the states, was regulated by generally accepted codes of conduct—the *guerre en forme.*[11]

Such familiar modes of interpretation are not unique to the twentieth century's predicament, and, indeed, suit the nineteenth century's proclivities of action and motivation better. And it was precisely these that were rendered deeply problematic during the "great seminal catastrophe," World War I.[12] Nevertheless, such considerations remain important for understanding the course of historical developments of the twentieth century. Even so, by themselves they are inadequate, though they still constitute a generally accepted form of historical perception, understanding, and interpretation. This axis of interpretation based on the power struggle between nation states pursuing their proper interests can be characterized as *traditional*.

The other axis of interpretation, that of value struggle and ideological contestation, suits the developments of the twentieth century better, and is of a different nature. It refers to motivations, notions, and concepts that run underneath and across the common ponderables of states and peoples while nevertheless transcending them.[13] These values draw on completely divergent loyalties—loyalties of class, political values, and ideology. They are generally universalistic—although divergent in content and orientation. Historically, they represent the introduction of philosophy into politics.

Relying on a complex of opposed values emanating from the nineteenth century—the ideal of political freedom on the one hand, and the ideal of social equality on the other—their bearers opposed each other on a visible as well as an invisible battlefield of international civil war.[14] The struggle finally culminated in the Cold War—a divided world where the values of liberalism challenged the values of Communism, and vice versa. In this respect the Cold War was a unique confrontation, reminiscent of the religious wars of early modern times, where the object of conflict is situated beyond all material desires. This modern counterpart to religious war lasted for forty years, and was rationalized in a global system of nuclear deterrence and mutual fear. This was the period in which ideological antagonism peaked and was, for reasons of technological development, converted into the logic of the threat of ultimate destruction.[15]

During an earlier, more constitutive phase of universal civil war between the protagonists of opposing worldviews, the players were of a slightly different sort. Since 1917, or to be more accurate, 1918/19, anti-Bolshevism confronted Bolshevism.[16] The civil war in Russia—evoked and instigated, like any civil war, by social conflict and opposing, incompatible, and irreconcilable beliefs and ideas—became significantly antagonistic and extremely violent in nature.[17] Compromise, resulting from bargaining and negotiations between equals, no longer was possible. The use of force, war, shed its traditional limitations so vitally important for the regulated violent intercourse among states. Inhibiting distinctions between civilian and military were obliterated. Indeed, the use of unrestricted violence and extreme cruelty were bound to the very notion of civil war, which is directed at the uncompromising extinction of the adversary.[18]

The Holocaust cannot be explained by or integrated into either axis of interpretation of the century—traditional conflict or civil war. Obviously, neither the destruction of European Jewry nor the extinction of the victims of Nazi eugenics—the so-called euthanasia program—were actions executed within the realm of warfare, whether we mean by this the traditional use of military force or the unbounded violence of civil war. Even that stage of annihilation immediately following the Nazi German invasion of the Soviet Union—when the Wehrmacht and the so-called *Einsatzgruppen,* acting under a barbarous array of orders known as the *Kommissarbefehl,* which expressed a radical and murderous "anti-Bolshevism" that explicitly identified Jews with the Communists—even that cannot convincingly confirm the contention that the Holocaust was part of a universal civil war. The same holds true for Operation Barbarossa. In fact, I argue that just the opposite seems to be the case.[19]

It is striking that in June 1941, when Nazi Germany proclaimed an ideological crusade against Bolshevism by initiating total war against the Soviet Union, its former partner in the subjugation of Europe, the liberal and democratic powers Great Britain and, later, the United States, immediately struck an alliance with the U.S.S.R., the seat of international Bolshevism these liberal democracies so despised.[20] However, the Great Alliance does not refute the axis of historical interpretation of the century, which is based on the concept of universal civil war between the protagonists of the principle of freedom on the one hand and the principle of equality on the other. The alliance of the former and future protagonists of universal civil war only confirms the fact that the historically extremely short but eminently dense period between 1941 and 1945 should be regarded as an interval of exception—an interval which, though brief, nevertheless imprints the whole century and its proper icons of representation in contemporary memory. However, measured in terms of duration and the commonly accepted proportions of historical time, the axis of interpretation based on the notion of a conflict of ideology, that is, a value conflict between Bolshevism and anti-Bolshevism, between liberalism and Communism, between East and West, is far more convincing than any other possible conceptualization of the saeculum. It is the case that the Great Alliance veiled the ideological antagonism between the values of freedom and those of a claimed and literally interpreted equality. Yet that antagonism resurfaced immediately after the cessation of hostilities, or, more accurately, already after the battle of Stalingrad in 1943, when German defeat became only a question of time.[21]

How can the universal struggle that took place between 1941 and 1945 be understood—a struggle so deeply etched into universal memory, which gave rise to a coalition of ideologically antagonistic forces against an absolute enemy, Nazi Germany? One possibility—of limited explanatory value—is to have recourse to the traditional axis of interpretation, based on the notions of hegemony and balance of power—of geopolitics, if you like. According to such an interpretation, Hitler invaded the Soviet Union as Russia, in order to eliminate the only possible suitable ally Britain may have had on the Continent.[22] Britain and Russia became natural partners again in June 1941, along the lines of the Napoleonic Wars and the alliance which was struck in 1907. The latter temporarily reversed the century-old British-Russian antagonism, allowing the two to fight as partners in the Great War side by side against German power, which obviously intended to dominate the Continent.

This mode of interpretation leads to the common, more traditional reading of the events of World War II prevalent in the 1950s and 1960s. According to such an interpretation, World War II appears as an immediate extension of the previous struggles for hegemony on the Continent, in which the great naval powers of the West sought to prevent undisputed hegemony on the Continent and to restore the balance of power. Even the numerals *One* and *Two* denominating the respective wars indicate such a mode of perception based on mere continuity. However, such an interpretation becomes obviously problematic in terms of the specificities of the German invasion of the Soviet Union and the war of extermination waged against the Soviet Union and the Slavic peoples. It grows substantively more problematic when one tries to integrate the Holocaust, an event beyond warfare, into such a reading of World War II. Nevertheless, since this interpretation was dominant in Western historiography in the first decades after 1945, the Holocaust, although a central event in the history of humankind in the twentieth century, was shunted aside and assigned a role of less than secondary importance, if it was mentioned at all.[23]

There is a convincing possibility to integrate the Holocaust into the structure of World War II. However, such an integration evokes the realm of the philosophy of history more than the level of factual reconstruction. Such an interpretation might be argued as follows: The coalition of former and future adversaries—former adversaries during the Russian civil war and future adversaries during the Cold War—the Great Alliance between Britain and the United States, on the one hand, and the Soviet Union, on the other, can be persuasively interpreted, despite their inherent antagonism, in terms of overarching ideological affinities. This interpretation moves beyond mere considerations of strategic complementarities, geopolitics, and other practical dimensions of warfare.

How is such an interpretation possible, given the ideological antagonism between freedom and equality, between Western liberalism and Soviet Communism, stretching from 1917/18 up to 1989, although articulated in different political densities? The answer points to an even more fundamental antagonism: faced with Nazism, which was based on racial warfare and whose realization was the Holocaust, the former antagonisms between Western democracy and Soviet Communism, both of which shared a universalistic social ideology, lessened in significance. While the strong ideological conflict between the Soviet Union and the Anglo-Saxon powers remained throughout the period, the fundamental ideological tension of World War II is that of the incompatibility of a universalistic, societal understanding of human history with the biologistic, racialist Nazi Weltanschauung.

Biology versus history is indeed the main opposition dividing the adversaries in World War II. Such an understanding is a conclusion reached a posteriori—a judgment in retrospect and introduced from a philosophical-historical perspective that attempts to integrate the Holocaust into a coherent narrative. Different and politically antagonistic as Western liberalism and Soviet Communism may have been, neither can ignore their common roots in the values of enlightenment, while Nazism was eager to deny those values. Both Western liberalism and Communism assume universal humankind, although both of them pursued different ways of realizing it. They confronted each other in the arena of international civil war, where the principles of freedom and of literal social equality opposed each other. This confrontation, however, had to be set aside until Nazi Germany, the standard-bearer of social and political biologism, was ultimately crushed in the war.

This war, too, although differently, bears all the ingredients of a civil war— an all-out struggle where no compromise is possible, except the complete destruction of the enemy. No wonder that in January 1943, Roosevelt and Churchill demanded in Casablanca *unconditional surrender*.[24] Roosevelt justified the necessity of this demand by invoking the commander of the Northern forces during the American Civil War, U. S. Grant, who was nicknamed "unconditional surrender Grant."[25] The implied claim, obviously, was that the war against Germany was a civil war in which anything short of total capitulation was impossible. The signification of the struggle between Western liberal democracy in alliance with Russia on one side and Nazism on the other as a universal civil war finds a parallel expression in an entry in Ernst Jünger's diary of November 10, 1942. In a note, the poet-officer interprets the disembarking of Anglo-American forces on the European theater in North Africa as a transformation of the war from a traditional continental power struggle into an ultimate universal confrontation, which Jünger terms *Weltbürgerkrieg* (world civil war).[26]

There is a definite distinction between Nazi and Western anti-Bolshevism. Western anti-Bolshevism rested on a purely political and social basis. It aimed at the destruction of a hostile system, not of its population. During the period of the Cold War, the peoples of the East were regarded by the West as silent allies in a common struggle against the repressive system of Communism. Indeed, the struggle purportedly was conducted for their liberation. The symbol of this universal and ideologically motivated struggle, actuated solely by antagonistic values and waged from 1949 to 1989, was the "dissident." This was a person identified and self-identified with the antagonistic political system beyond the frequently imperceptible line of distinction in the international civil war. Such a person could therefore easily claim acceptance and asylum. By contrast, Nazi conquest and domination in the East from 1941 to 1944 was inherently and expressly antiuniversalistic. Its objective was the subordination and eventual destruction of peoples considered, on the basis of quasi-scientific biological criteria, unworthy to live. While it shares the sense of absolute antagonism, the racial distinction involved is by definition contradictory to the concept of civil war where one party tries to convince the supporters of the other party to change sides, inasmuch as such a struggle knows the category of treason.[27] The irreconcilability of Nazi ideology, where individually based decisions concerning collective belonging were made racially impossible on principle, ultimately caused the antagonists of the international civil war of values—the liberal West and the Communist East—to strike a temporary alliance. This alliance was based on the common ground of a societal understanding of historical life-worlds, and on the principles of enlightenment. It was necessary to suspend hostilities in order to destroy the very antithesis to the concept of humankind.

The difference is obvious: Nazi anti-Bolshevism is not a possible variant of the political brand of anti-Communism exercised by liberal democracy. Just the opposite is the case. While the latter is based solely on class, the former combines and conflates class with race. Its origins can be traced back into a unique space and exceptional time in history, involving ethnic Germans and Germans from the Reich in the confrontations of the Russian civil war and its repercussions on the periphery of the former Empire. The area under focus here, the Baltics, witnessed the emergence of an ideological hybrid that first arose during the struggle from 1918 to 1920.[28] This ideological hybrid was the forerunner of Nazi anti-Bolshevism, combining characteristics of race and class.

What happened in this borderland during the Russian civil war? The Baltic-German nobility, reinforced by *Freikorps* dispatched from the Reich with the intention of settling abandoned estates in Livland and Kurland, fought in a triangular conflict, with Bolsheviks, Latvians, and Estonians. In the end, they were locked in a fierce and cruel struggle in which class and race eventually overlapped, and then melded together. Already during this brutal and uncompromising warfare with its mass killings and liquidations, all the ingredients of future Nazism were brought to the surface—its symbols, like the death's head and the swastika; its core staff, who later largely comprised most of the leading personnel of the SA; and the unbridled violence executed by the killing squads of the so-called *Baltikumer*.[29] The conclusion seems in no way exaggerated that the counterrevolutionary struggle in the Baltic countries against an enemy who was considered culturally, socially, and racially inferior, brought about the emergence of that specific brand of Nazi anti-Bolshevism in which the distinction of race finally overrode that of class. Twenty years later, during the invasion of the Soviet Union in 1941, where an ideological race war of annihilation was unleashed in all its ferocity, that unique mixture forced its way through on a secular and vast scale. The object of destruction was *Bolschewismus* (Bolshevism)—

that unique combination concocted in the eyes of the Nazis of a so-called Jewish *intelligentsia* and a supposedly Slavic *Untermenschentum.*

The destruction of European Jewry was closely related to Nazi anti-Bolshevism and its racialist vision. Indeed, the systematic killings of Jews started in the East in conjunction with Operation Barbarossa.[30] This implies a somewhat paradoxical evolution: though the anti-Jewish measures were first instituted in Nazi Germany, the murderous radicalization of those measures drew its impetus from the eastward expansion. The *Anschluss* of Austria, the first grab beyond the borders of the Reich, brought with it the first radicalization of Nazi policy towards the Jews, shifting it from enforced emigration to expulsion.[31] In Poland, a country conquered by military force, a new stage in radicalization was reached. Ghettoization in Poland replaced the policy of expulsion, previously introduced in Vienna.[32] Yet only ideological race war in the east, directed against the Soviet Union, where the so-called Bolshevist enemy combined all ingredients of enmity based on a unique aggregation of race and class, provoked that qualitative transformation involving intentional mass murder of Jews. From the eastern killing fields in 1941, the disposition for genocide moved westward, paradoxically reversing the direction of German expansion, from east to west. The story is well known: first Aktion Reinhard and its human slaughterhouses, which destroyed Polish Jewry; then Auschwitz, which annihilated Jews from western, central, and southern Europe on an industrial scale, accomplishing the "Final Solution."

What does the topography of death sketched above tell us about the modes and means of integrating the Holocaust into the saeculum's narrative? How can the different stages of the Jewish Holocaust be interpreted by linking them up with lines of general and even universal continuities, culminating in collective mass killings and collective death? In each phase of Nazi policy towards the Jews, a different element of a more general phenomenon surfaced. The policy of discrimination, dispossession, and removal inside Nazi Germany is to be understood without any reservation as strictly anti-Semitic in its motivation. Nor can any kind of discriminatory policy concerning the Jews in Europe between the two world wars be interpreted as strictly ideologically motivated, as happened in Nazi Germany. Polish anti-Jewish measures, for instance, mostly undertaken against the Jewish population in the second half of the 1930s, were particularly driven by reasons of Polonization, that is, ethnic homogenization of the country.[33] And while the Polish government wanted, for a number of social, economic, and demographic "reasons," to get rid of *part* of its three million Jews, about 10 percent of the population, the Nazi policy of discrimination and forced emigration was aimed at *all* Jews of the Reich. It was based on an objective that can be explained only according an ideological fixation—a Weltanschauung, so to speak. One cannot find any social and economic rationale for why the expulsion of German Jewry—less than 1 percent of the population—could have eased any social or demographic problems in Germany.[34]

Indeed, the story of anti-Jewish measures enforced by the Nazis in Germany and Austria can be told along the common lines of the history of anti-Semitism. Concerning the policy of ghettoization in Poland in 1939/40, the picture becomes more complicated and blurred. True, one can interpret the policy of expulsion undertaken in the annexed Polish territories of the so-called Wartheland, directed against Poles and Jews, in terms of "ethnic cleansing," a practice which often may accompany a process of national homogenization.[35] This all the more so, as the "cleansed" areas were settled by ethnic Germans from the Soviet-occupied Baltic countries. This expulsion, by the way, brought the Lodz Ghetto into being. Such a vast concentration of Jews in a city situated on German-annexed soil was not the direct outcome of an intended policy, but the result of the rivalry of the *Gauleiter* of the Wartheland Arthur Greiser, and the ruler of the Generalgouvernement, Hans Frank, who refused to accept additional Jews into his satrapy.

The expulsion of the Jews from the *annexed* Polish territories, which underwent Germanization, that is, ethnic homogenization, can be compared to similar events in the European periphery earlier—the Russian policy of devastation and expulsion directed against Turkic peoples like the Kazakhs in central Asia, for instance, in the period of the Great War; or of the Jews living in frontal border regions, where fighting took place; or the Armenian genocide committed by the Turkish government in 1915/16; or even the expulsion of the Greek Orthodox population from Asia Minor by the Turks in 1922.[36] Such cases of ethnic cleansing aimed at ethnic homogenization for reasons of warfare or of "nation building," although with different consequences. The policies ranged from mere expulsion up to total destruction and can with some effort be compared to the Nazi policy towards the Jews in Poland from 1939 to 1941: physical concentration with the intention of removal. The destination of such an intended removal, however, was left open. Only a very general orientation existed: Europe had to be cleansed of Jews. True, after the fall of France in 1940 the idea of evacuating the Jews from Poland to Madagascar was ventilated.[37] This "plan" of Jewish resettlement was from the very beginning an illusion. It could not be realized by any means, and certainly not in the middle of fighting, while Britain dominated the high seas. However, such fictitious planning exposes the illusory character of all the designs to remove the Jews from areas under Nazi control. Such vague "solutions," like the further declared intention to remove the Jews to "the east," reveal the hidden intention to annihilate the uprooted and ghettoized. This became evident when the first steps to mass killings were initiated in the east, in Russia, within the framework of total war based on racial anti-Bolshevism.

From the victims' point of view, there is little substantial difference between the mass killings in the east, executed within the framework of Barbarossa, and the industrial form of annihilation, carried on in the slaughterhouses of Aktion Reinhard, and fully realized in the ultimate death factory, Auschwitz. However, systematically and historically, a fundamental distinction has to be made in order to integrate the horrors into some sort of coherent narration, based on historical continuities as well as on contingencies relating to experiences of past events. The *form* of death carried out in the death camps was from its very beginning not directly related to the Jews as Jews. Executions on an industrial scale are rather to be traced back to the Nazi practice of euthanasia, based on the doctrines of eugenics,[38] and eugenics as such is not "scientifically" applicable to Jews as Jews. Compared to the primary victims of euthanasia, of medical murder, who were characterized in Nazi discourse as "life unworthy to live"—the Jews, who originally and in principle were not targeted for medical reasons, became in fact *secondary* victims of euthanasia, when for technical purposes the specialists of medical killing in the Reich were dispatched in the autumn of 1941 to the area of Generalgouvernement in order to establish killing centers. These would be for exterminating the Jews on Polish soil, although the Jewish victims did *not* fit into the patterns of Nazi understandings of social and racial hygiene. After all, the Nazi definition of the Jew was still related to *religious* definitions—not to a biological understanding according to supposedly objective racial criteria. And this despite the discrediting image of the Jew disseminated in Nazi propaganda.

According to the argument elaborated above, the effort undertaken to tell the story of the Holocaust properly, that is, to integrate the event into a more universalizing narrative of general history, meets with considerable difficulties. First, the prevailing mode of treating the Holocaust as part of the story of European or simply German anti-Semitism has to be considered. Such a narrative has the undisputed advantage of constructing a chronological pattern of representation, beginning with the remote past and reaching its murderous peak with Auschwitz. Compared to other readings, such an interpretation obviously relies on phenomena of *longue durée*. Extension in time constitutes the convincing emblem of what is generally understood as History. However, the narrative based on the story of anti-Semitism tells us *why Jews* in particular were singled out for collective persecution, while all other historical elements, which lead to the Holocaust in the sense of its execution, shows us *how* different practices brought about the destruction of *human beings*.

Such a distinction in questioning—the why and the how—is of primary importance. The difference in questioning is anchored in a difference of epistemological meaning. Whereas the explanation based on the impact of anti-Semitism draws heavily on theological and historical preconditions for singling out only

and *all* the Jews, the practices that brought about annihilation ought to be eluci-
dated on more general premises, on anthropological ones, so to speak. The practices of ethnic cleansing, for instance, which generally accompany the modes of
national homogenization, may explain to some degree the concentration of Jews
in ghettos as a precondition for further expulsion. Anti-Bolshevism on the other
hand shows us how the practice of indiscriminate racial and genocidal *warfare*
brought mass killings onto the Jewish population of the Soviet Union, while the
institutionalization of large-scale medical killings, *euthanasia,* was applied to the
Jews for reasons of "mere" efficiency. What makes the Holocaust so exceptional
is the fact that in a very dense period of time, three or even four different historical currents—anti-Semitism, ethnic cleansing, racial warfare, and the practices
of euthanasia, were fused and thus cumulated into an exceptional human catastrophe.

The negative culmination of different barbarous trends seems to be the very
reason the story of the Holocaust is commonly told in different versions and
evokes different periodizations. The customary periodization from 1933 to 1945,
embracing the Nazi period as a whole, leads to an interpretation of the anti-
Jewish measures and the Holocaust as its peak, as a sort of negative fulfillment
of the course of German history, indicated by the rise and the acceleration of
anti-Semitism as its universal hallmark. The periodization from 1941 to 1945
generally places the mass-murder in the realm of anti-Bolshevism and draws it
close to the notion of international civil war—of *Weltbürgerkrieg.* The culminating point of the Holocaust, from 1942 to 1944, the ultimate fabrication of death,
may lead toward a different direction as one searches for continuities in the practice of euthanasia and its prehistory in the field of eugenics. This latter course of
interpretation takes as its proper mode of explanation and examination configurations of the history of science, evaluating the Holocaust as only one, albeit the
most extreme, of the cataclysms of modernity.

The integration of the Holocaust into the course of history, the construction
of an appropriate historical narration for an event unprecedented in its brevity
and extremity, somehow disconnected from past and future, still remains an in-
surmountable task. It seems that the only serious attempt to deal with it histori-
ographically is to accept its fundamental irreconcilability with the saeculum's
core narratives.

NOTES

1. Concerning the phenomena immediately after 1944/45, see Tony Judt, "The Past Is Another
Country: Myth and Memory in Postwar Europe," in *The Politics of Retribution in Europe: World War II
and its Aftermath,* ed. Istvan Deak, Jan T. Gross, and Tony Judt (Princeton, N.J.: Princeton Univer-

sity Press, 2000), 293–324. For an interpretation of the Holocaust as a universally shared memory, see Daniel Levy and Nathan Sznaider, *Erinnerung im globalen Zeitalter: Der Holocaust* (Frankfurt am Main: Suhrkamp Verlag, 2001).

2. Surprisingly, Eric Hobsbawm in his *Age of Extremes: The Short Twentieth Century 1914–1991* (London: Michael Joseph, 1994), whose book heavily relies on a social interpretation of history, does not put any special stress on the Holocaust. Compared to this, my interpretation of the century follows by and large the concept of memory. See Dan Diner, *Das Jahrhundert verstehen: Eine Universalhistorische Deutung* (Munich: Luchterhand, 1999).

3. See for the most recent discussion Ruti Teitel, *Transitional Justice* (Oxford: Oxford University Press, 2000), 69–118; Elazar Barkan, *The Guilt of Nations: Restitution and Negotiating Historical Injustice* (New York: Norton, 2000), 3–158; and Barkan, *Restitution and Unjust Enrichment, Theoretical Inquiries in Law* 1, no. 1 (January 2000), The Cegla Institute for Comparative and Private International Law, Tel Aviv University.

4. Dan Diner, "Gedächtnis und Restitution," *Neue Züricher Zeitung,* September 8–9, 2001.

5. For a breakthrough in the realm of a renewed acceptance of the Nazi past and the unique positioning of the Poles in World War II, see the impact of Jan T. Gross, *Neighbors: The Destruction of the Jewish Community in Jedwabne, Poland* (Princeton, N.J.: Princeton University Press, 2001).

6. Peter Novick, *The Holocaust in American Life* (Boston: Houghton Mifflin, 1999).

7. Gordon A. Craig, *Europe Since 1815* (New York: Holt, Rinehart, and Winston, 1974).

8. Dan Diner, "Memory and Method: Variance in Holocaust Narrations," in *The Fate of the European Jews, 1939–1945: Continuity or Contingency? Studies in Contemporary Jewry,* an Annual, vol. 13, ed. Jonathan Frankel (Oxford: Oxford University Press, 1997): 84–99.

9. Dan Diner, "European Counterimages. Problems of Periodization and Historical Memory," *Praxis International* 10 (1990): 501–17.

10. Ludwig Dehio, *Gleichgewicht oder Hegemonie. Betrachtungen über ein Grundproblem der neueren Staatengeschichte* (Krefeld: Scherpe, 1948); Henry A. Kissinger, *A World Restored: Metternich, Castlereagh and the Problems of Peace 1812–1822* (London: Weidenfeld and Nicolson, 1957).

11. Carl Schmitt, *Der Nomos der Erde im jus publicum europaeum* (Cologne: Greuen, 1950), 215; Roman Schnur, "Weltfriedensidee und Weltbürgerkrieg 1791/92," in *Revolution und Weltbürgerkrieg: Studien zur Overtüre nach 1789* (Berlin: Duncker und Humboldt, 1983), 11–32; James M. McPherson, *Battle Cry for Freedom: The Civil War Era* (New York: Oxford University Press, 1988).

12. George F. Kennan, *Bismarks europäisches System in der Auflösung. Die französisch-russische Annäherung 1875–1890* (Frankfurt: Propyläen, 1981), 12.

13. Karl Dietrich Bracher, *Europa in der Krise: Innengeschichte und Weltpolitik seit 1917* (Frankfurt: Propyläen, 1979), 127 ff.

14. Hanno Kesting, *Geschichtsphilosophie und Weltbürgerkrieg* (Heidelberg: Winter, 1959).

15. John L. Gaddis, *We Now Know: Rethinking Cold War History* (Oxford: Clarendon, 1997).

16. Richard Ullman, *Intervention and War* (Princeton, N.J.: Princeton University Press, 1961).

17. Richard Pipes, *Russia Under the Bolshevik Regime* (New York: Knopf, 1994).

18. John Keegan and Richard Holmes, *Soldiers: A History of Men in Battle* (London: Hamilton, 1985).

19. Andreas Hillgruber, "Die 'Endlösung' und das deutsche Ostimperium als Kernstück des rassistischen Programms des Nationalsozialismus," in *Vierteljahrshefte für Zeitgeschichte* 20 (1972): 133–53; Christian Streit, "Ostkrieg, Antibolschewismus und 'Endlösung,'" in *Geschichte und Gesellschaft* 17 (1991): 241–55; Omer Bartov, *Hitler's Army: Soldiers, Nazis, and War in the Third Reich* (New York: Oxford University Press, 1991); Ludolf Herbst, *Das nationalsozialistische Deutschland 1933–1945. Die Entfesselung der Gewalt. Rassismus und Krieg* (Frankfurt am Main: Suhrkamp, 1996).

20. Amos Perlmutter, *FDR & Stalin: A Not So Grand Alliance, 1943–1945* (Columbia: University of Missouri Press, 1993).

21. Jürgen Förster, *Stalingrad: Risse im Bündnis 1942/43* (Freiburg: Rombach, 1975).

22. Gerhard L. Weinberg, *Germany and the Soviet Union, 1939–1941* (Leiden: Brill, 1954).

23. Michael Marrus, "The Holocaust at Nuremberg," *Yad Vashem Studies* 26 (1998): 5–41,

24. Alfred Vagts, "Unconditional Surrender—vor und nach 1945," *Vierteljahrshefte für Zeitgeschichte* 7 (1959): 280–309.

25. Franklin D. Roosevelt, *Complete Presidential Press Conference*, vol. 21/22 (New York: Heyden, 1972), 88.

26. Ernst Jünger, *Tagebücher*, vol. 2, in *Werke* (Stuttgart: Klett, 1962), p. 433.

27. Margret Boveri, *Der Verrat im 20. Jahrhundert* (Reinbek b. Hamburg: Rohwohlt, 1976).

28. Stanley P. Page, *The Formation of the Baltic States. A Study of the Effects of the Great Power Politics upon the Emergence of Lithuania, Latvia, and Estonia* (Cambridge: Cambridge University Press, 1959); Sigmar Stopinski, *Das Baltikum im Patt der Mächte* (Berlin: Spitz, 1997).

29. Dominik Venner, *Söldner ohne Sold* (Wien: Arndt, 1989); Ernst von Salomon, *Die Geächteten* (Berlin: Rohwohlt, 1930); Gabriele Krüger, *Die Brigade Erhard* (Hamburg: Leibnitz, 1971).

30. Peter Longerich, "Vom Massenmord zur 'Endlösung': Die Erschiessung von jüdischen Zivilisten in den ersten Monaten des Ostfeldzuges im Kontext des nationalsozialistischen Judenmordes," in *Zwei Wege nach Moskau: Vom Hitler-Stalin-Pakt zum 'Unternehmen Barbarossa,'* ed. Bernd Wegner (Munich: Piper, 1991), 251–74; Ralf Ogorreck, *Die Einsatzgruppen und die "Genesis der Endlösung"* (Berlin: Metropol, 1996).

31. Herbert Rosenkranz, *Verfolgung und Selbstbehauptung: Die Juden in Österreich, 1938–1945* (Vienna: Herold, 1978); Gerhard Botz, *Die Eingliederung Österreichs in das Deutsche Reich: Planung und Verwirklichung des politisch-administrativen Anschlusses 1938–1940* (Vienna: Europaverlag, 1972).

32. Christopher Browning, "The Nazi Ghettoization Policy in Poland, 1939–1941," in *The Path to Genocide: Essays on the Launching the Final Solution* (Cambridge: Cambridge University Press, 1992), 28–56.

33. Ezra Mendelsohn, *The Jews of East Central Europe between the Two World Wars* (Bloomington: Indiana University Press, 1983).

34. Saul Friedländer, *Nazi Germany and the Jews*, vol. 1, *The Years of Persecution 1933–1939* (New York: HarperCollins, 1997); William Hagen, "Before the 'Final Solution': Towards a Comparative Analysis of Political Anti-Semitism in Interwar Germany and Poland," *The Journal of Modern History* 68 (1996): 351–81.

35. Aly Götz, *"Endlösung": Voelkerverschiebung und der Mord an den europäischen Juden* (Frankfurt amMain: Fischer, 1995); Ian Kershaw, "Improvised Genocide? The Emergence of the Final Solution in the 'Warthegau,'" *Transactions of the Royal Society*, 6th ser. (London, 1992): 51–78.

36. Dan Brower, "Kyrgiz Nomads and Russian Pioneers: Colonization and Ethnic Conflict in the Turkestan Revolt of 1916," *Jahrbücher für die Geschichte Osteuropas* 44 (1996): 52 ff.; Robert Melson, *Revolution and Genocide: On the Origins of the Armenian Genocide and the Holocaust* (Chicago: University of Chicago Press, 1992); John A. Petropulos, "The Compulsory Exchange of Populations: Greek-Turkish Peacemaking 1922–1930," *Byzantine and Modern Greek Studies* 2 (1976): 135–60.

37. Magnus Brechtken, *'Madagaskar für die Juden': Antisemitische Idee und politische Praxis, 1885–1945* (Munich: Oldenbourg, 1997).

38. Michael Burleigh, *Death and Deliverance: "Euthanasia" in Germany, 1900–1945* (Cambridge: Cambridge University Press, 1994); Henry Friedlander, *The Origins of the Nazi Genocide: From Euthanasia to the Final Solution* (Chapel Hill: University of North Carolina Press, 1995).

Five

THE HOLOCAUST AND THE TRAJECTORY OF THE TWENTIETH CENTURY

Moishe Postone

Historians who deal with the Holocaust, as Michael Marrus has noted, are confronted by two separable tasks. One is to tell the story, to commemorate—as an obligation to the dead and as a warning to future generations. The other is "to integrate the history of the Holocaust into the general stream of historical consciousness."[1] I intend to approach the latter task—that is, the task of considering the Holocaust from the perspective of the early twenty-first century—by inquiring into the possible relation of the Holocaust and its aftermath to overarching temporal patterns of the twentieth century.

In this essay I shall explore the possibility of considering together what generally have been two very different discursive universes. On the one hand, the Holocaust is viewed as an event of deep historical significance—a rupture in the fabric of civilization and of history,[2] a crucial event in the history of this century.[3] For some, it is outside the realm of human logic and, hence, the historian's comprehension of motives and interests;[4] indeed, its significance even transcends history itself.[5] On the other hand, recent major works that try to grasp the overarching historical structuring of the twentieth century—such as Eric Hobsbawm's *Age of Extremes*[6] or Giovanni Arrighi's *Long Twentieth Century*[7]—tend to marginalize the Holocaust.[8] They either do not refer to it at all, or do not consider it with reference to the temporal structuring they present.[9]

Marginalization of the Holocaust in general historical discourse was very evident in the late 1940s and 1950s.[10] Such marginalization, it could be argued, had multiple grounds—for example, strategies of denial or avoidance,[11] or structures of psychic repression,[12] or the abstract universalistic position, which was particularly strong in left-wing and Communist discourse, that a focus on the suffering and murder of the Jews would be particularistic.[13]

Nevertheless, the difficulty of integrating Holocaust discourse and general historical discourse cannot be explained solely with reference to strategies of avoidance or abstract universalistic positions.[14] It is ultimately a theoretical problem, and is related to the question of whether the Holocaust can and should be historicized.[15] This, in turn, raises the issue of how historicization is to be understood. The fundamental question in this regard, in my view, is whether the Holocaust can also be grasped with reference to fundamental historical processes that have structured and restructured social life in the twentieth century, or whether the Holocaust—as terrible as it was—must be regarded as an event that has great meaning for the victims (and, perhaps, the perpetrators) and is of general moral importance, but has little significance on the level of deep historical structure.

In this essay I shall argue, on the basis of earlier work, that the Holocaust can and must also be analyzed with reference to historical processes on a deep structural level—that it can be illuminated by this level of consideration and, in turn, can illuminate aspects of the overarching temporal structuring of our century.

Attempting to mediate the Holocaust and fundamental historical processes of the twentieth century necessarily entails attempting to clarify both the specificity of the Holocaust as well as the salient features of those historical processes. It thereby involves problematizing the relation of history and its victims in one determinate instance. This problematic, in other words, indicates that the two historical tasks outlined by Marrus are related. And it raises the question of whether and in what ways it is still possible to think a future without betraying the past.[16]

II

A number of recent works have sought to grasp the overarching temporal structure of the twentieth century. For purposes of this paper, I shall have recourse to Eric Hobsbawm's *Age of Extremes*.[17] In attempting to conceptualize the short twentieth century, Hobsbawm discerns three basic periods. The first, from 1914 until the aftermath of World War II, was an "Age of Catastrophe," marked by two world wars, the Great Depression, the crisis of democracy, and the rise of Stalinism, Nazism, and fascism. This was followed by an unexpected "Golden Age" from about 1947 until the early 1970s, an age of rapid economic growth, expansion of welfare states, relative political stability, and a functioning international system. This "Golden Age" was superseded in the early 1970s by a new period marked by the reemergence of economic crises, mass unemployment, increasing social differentiation, the collapse of the international system, and catastrophic downturns in parts of the world.

Hobsbawm's periodization expresses a series of fundamental changes in the relation of state and (capitalist) economy. The first period can be characterized in terms of a number of different attempts to react to the world crisis of nineteenth-century liberal capitalism, whereas the second period was marked by a successful state-centric synthesis, in both East and West, which benefited large segments of metropolitan populations. The last third of the century has been characterized by the unraveling of this synthesis—the weakening of national states as economically sovereign entities, the undermining of welfare states in the West, the collapse of bureaucratic party states in the East, and the apparently triumphant reemergence of unchecked market capitalism.

The temporal patternings discerned by Hobsbawm are general and overarching, encompassing many countries and regions. They imply large-scale historical processes that cannot be adequately explained in terms of particular state policies or local contingencies.[18] Moreover, notions of historical linearity that were still thinkable in the decades following World War II, such as those associated with the discourses of modernity and modernization, have been undermined by the social and economic transformations of recent decades outlined by Hobsbawm. These transformations also have underscored the central significance of capitalism as a structuring historical category of our times—a theme to which I shall return.

III

The question, then, is whether the Holocaust and its aftermath can be historically grasped in ways that can be mediated with the sort of general historical level considered by Hobsbawm. This first requires clarifying the characterizing features of the Holocaust. This issue frequently has been framed in the language of uniqueness, which unfortunately has been understood, at times, in terms of a competition for primacy of victimhood.[19] Nevertheless, such understandings should not obscure the basic issue, which is neither a theological nor a quantitative one, whether in terms of the number of people murdered or the degree of their suffering. (There have been too many historical instances of mass murder and genocide.) Rather, the issue is one of *qualitative specificity*. Important aspects of the attempted extermination of European Jewry by the Nazis remain inexplicable so long as the Holocaust is simply subsumed under the general category of mass murder—as the result of a murderous scapegoat strategy, for example, whose victims could very well have been members of any other group.

The Holocaust was characterized by its programmatic and totalizing character: the eradication of the Jews was to be total; all Jews—including children—were to be killed. Moreover, the extermination of the Jews was marked by its apparent lack of functionality. It seems not to have been a means to another end. The Jews were not murdered for military/security reasons, for example, nor as a consequence of demographic-economic planning. Nor was Nazi policy toward the Jews similar to their policy of mass murder of Poles and Russians, which aimed to eliminate those members of the population around whom resistance might form in order to exploit the rest more easily as helots. Indeed, the Jews were not murdered for any "extrinsic" goal. Their extermination not only was to have been total, but apparently was its own goal—extermination for the sake of extermination—a goal that acquired absolute priority. Functionalist explanations of the Holocaust, accounts that seek to grasp it in terms of instrumental rationality, and conventional scapegoat theories cannot begin to explain why, in the last years of war, as the German forces were being routed by the Red Army, equipment and personnel were diverted from possible military purposes in order to transport Jews to the gas chambers from places as far away as the island of Rhodes.[20]

Any adequate interpretation of the Holocaust must be capable of grasping this qualitative specificity of the extermination of European Jewry.[21] This specificity must also be understood with reference to Nazism as a movement—which, in terms of its own self-understanding, represented a revolt. Moreover, it must be grasped by means of categories that can mediate the Holocaust and general historical developments, as expressed, for example, by the sort of historical periodization outlined above.

This sort of historical periodization, together with the specifying description of the Holocaust, suggests the need for an analytic reconsideration. Periodizing the twentieth century reminds us that history did not end with the Holocaust. This is the case not simply in the trivial sense that a half century has elapsed since the Holocaust, but also in the sense that the general structuring and texture of social life have changed several times since then, as well as in the intellectually and emotionally provocative sense that even projects of human emancipation did not end with Auschwitz. Hence the issue of historicizing the Holocaust necessarily appears differently from the perspective of the end of the twentieth century than it did in the immediate postwar decades.

IV

A wide range of explanatory approaches to the Holocaust appear in a critical light when viewed with reference to the specificity of the Holocaust as well as the problematic of mediating it and the sort of general historical framework sketched out above. From this standpoint, a number of approaches appear too historically particularistic—including those that focus only on the specificity of German history, culture, and thought,[22] or those that look only at the history of the Jews and grasp anti-Semitism transhistorically.[23]

Relatedly, the debates between so-called functionalist and intentionalist interpretations of the Holocaust shed very little light on either dimension of the problematic I have formulated. The intentionalists argue that the Holocaust was planned from the beginning; they posit a direct relation between Nazi ideology, planning, and policies, and accord Hitler's worldviews essential significance.[24] Focusing on anti-Semitic writings, intentionalists claim a linear continuity between Hitler's writings of the 1920s and the attempted extermination of European Jewry twenty years later. Functionalist arguments reject the intentionalist emphasis on will and premeditation, and downplay the significance of ideology. They claim that the course of Nazi anti-Jewish policies beginning in 1933 was erratic, rather than linear, and indicates the absence of any premeditated, preestablished plan. Rather, the Holocaust emerged contingently as a goal; it resulted from a series of bureaucratic initiatives and responses to various problems generated by the war and by the bureaucracies of a basically chaotic system.[25]

Whatever the strengths and weaknesses of these positions, neither is fully adequate to the level of consideration I am attempting to introduce. And this cannot be resolved simply by bridging the differences between them. On the one hand, functionalist positions, while attempting to do justice to the twisted road of Nazi anti-Semitic policies after 1933, and to the complexity of decision-making processes on the ground, take for granted what has to be explained—that a program of complete extermination could even become thinkable. Intentionalist positions seek to address this issue—but end up reducing issues of ideology to those of intention and motivation. This is the case both of those who explain the Holocaust by focusing on Hitler's anti-Semitism, as well as those who posit a quasi-ontological, specifically German culture of anti-Semitism.[26]

Not only does this debate recapitulate a classic modern antinomy of will versus impersonal, objective mechanisms, but neither position helps clarify any possible relation between the Holocaust and larger historical developments. Instead, both treat the Holocaust in contingent terms—the one focusing on the contingencies of decision-making processes in the Nazi state under conditions of war, the other on the contingent worldview of a dictator, or on the unique culture of one country. Such positions, as Zygmunt Bauman has noted, treat the Holocaust as comfortably uncharacteristic and sociologically inconsequential.[27]

There have, of course, also been many attempts to interpret Nazism in larger historical terms—for example, the wide variety of theories of fascism, as well as theories of totalitarianism. Nevertheless, as others, such as Saul Friedländer, have also pointed out, categories such as "fascism" or "totalitarianism" may be useful for some purposes; they do not, however, adequately help account for the planned extermination of European Jewry, which remains outside of their analytic purview.[28] The same may be said ultimately of theories—such as those of Raul Hilberg and Hannah Arendt (in *Eichmann in Jerusalem*)—that emphasize the structures of bureaucratic authority, as well as the division of labor and, hence, responsibility, that characterized the Nazi program of extermination.[29] Such approaches help illuminate how that program was and could have been executed, but do not explain the program itself.

If the debates between intentionalist and functionalist positions obscure the relation between the Holocaust and larger historical developments, most attempts to interpret Nazism and the Holocaust with reference to such developments basically subsume the Holocaust under those developments, thereby obscuring its specificity. This includes Arno Mayer's interpretation, which seeks to explain the Holocaust with reference to the Nazis' virulent anti-Bolshevism, itself only the most extreme manifestation of the hot and cold civil war that gripped Europe from 1917 to 1989.[30] Although Mayer's approach does succeed in breaking out of the narrow confines of a great deal of Holocaust discourse, it also blurs the specificity of the Holocaust. It cannot really explain the attempted extermination of *all* Jews *everywhere* (from Norway to Rhodes).

Hannah Arendt, in *The Origins of Totalitarianism,* and Max Horkheimer and Theodor Adorno, in *Dialectic of Enlightenment,* did understand that the Holocaust must be understood with reference to modern anti-Semitism, and sought to deal with that ideology as a symptom of large-scale historical transformations of European society. Although they understood those transformations in fundamentally different ways, their works share a common theme—that anti-Semitism grew as the Jews, in their old social roles, became historically superfluous.[31] Nevertheless, while the category of historical superfluousness may be able to explain widespread resentment and even mass murder, it does not provide a basis for understanding the fundamental characterizing feature of the Holocaust—that it was a planned program for the total extermination of a people.

Yet, whatever the problems with their specific approaches, Arendt and Adorno and Horkheimer correctly understood that anti-Semitism is the only category that directly addresses the issue of extermination and does so historically. Functionalist interpretations simply avoid addressing the issue. And most other explanatory approaches that do attempt to address the issue do not succeed in rendering plausible a program of complete eradication. This is clearly the case with approaches that focus on the instrumental rationality and bureaucratic-technocratic domination characteristic of modernity,[32] on the exclusions inherent in Enlightenment universalism, or on the fanaticism of virulent anti-Bolshevism. It is even the case with positions that emphasize the racist and bio-logistic thinking that swept Europe in the late nineteenth and early twentieth centuries.[33] Although such thinking obviously was a very important dimension of anti-Semitism, it alone also cannot account for the possibility of a program of total extermination.[34] For that, one must focus on modern anti-Semitism's central element—the idea of the Jews as a world historical threat to life.

Turning once again to the category of anti-Semitism does not entail necessarily returning to a position that regards the Holocaust only in terms of the specificity of German history. Moreover, it neither necessarily implies a linear, premeditated development of Nazi anti-Jewish policy, nor does it suggest that anti-Semitism alone directly explains the actions, motivations, and intentions of the actors, without further mediation. Nevertheless, focusing on anti-Semitism as an ideology is essential for any attempt to historically grasp the Nazi program of total extermination. Such an attempt also requires that anti-Semitism be understood with reference to larger historical developments.

Focusing on anti-Semitism in this way also forces us to rethink the meaning of ideology. As Dominick LaCapra also has suggested, we must distinguish ideology—as a general framework of meaning—from individual motivation and intentionality.[35] Conflating the two underlies the (unconvincing) contention that anti-Semitism, lodged deep within the psyches of German perpetrators, was directly responsible for their actions. Such a conflation, however, also underlies the contrary argument—namely, the claim that anti-Semitism was *not* of central importance because Nazi anti-Jewish policies were not implemented in a linear fashion, and many individual Germans appear not to have been motivated by a particularly powerful hatred of the Jews. By failing to distinguish ideology—as a general cultural framework, a horizon of meaning—from individual affect and motivation, this latter position is incapable of addressing the problematic of the attempted extermination of the Jews as opposed to the question of how it was effected.

In reconsidering modern anti-Semitism, I am reflecting upon an ideological form that became widespread in Europe after 1873 (the pogroms in Russia should be seen as part of this development, rather than as quasi-medieval outbursts), and reached its apex in Nazi Germany during what Hobsbawm characterized as the Age of Catastrophe. I shall not discuss why this ideology was much more powerful in some European countries than in others (although there is a relation between the degree to which capitalist modernity was mediated by the state, and the growth of modern anti-Semitism in the last third of the nineteenth century), or why it became hegemonic in Germany. Such an investigation would require levels of mediation I cannot undertake here.

Rather, I shall sketch an analysis of anti-Semitism as a general ideology and try to relate it to the general temporal structuring of the modern world I outlined earlier. Within the framework of this approach, the issue of a possible German *Sonderweg* is relevant for the question of levels of mediation; not, however, for the nature and constitution of the ideology itself. That is, my intention is not to explain *why* Nazism and modern anti-Semitism became hegemonic in Germany. Rather, I shall attempt to determine more closely *what it was* that became hegemonic by suggesting an analysis of modern anti-Semitism that indicates its intrinsic connection to National Socialism in terms that can mediate between an analysis of the Holocaust and large-scale historical processes in the twentieth century.

V

In order to approach the problematic of anti-Semitism and its relation to large-scale historical developments, I would like to draw attention to an antinomy in general interpretations of National Socialism and the Holocaust. On the one hand, many approaches, particularly those undertaken in the 1960s, have interpreted National Socialism as a revolt against modernity.[36] On the other hand, more recent approaches have interpreted the Holocaust as rooted in the Enlightenment's universalistic and rationalist notion of humanity[37] or as an inherent possibility of modernity.[38]

As I shall further elaborate in the second part of this essay, this antinomy sheds light on the self-understandings of the two postwar epochs. During the "Golden Age" of the 1950s and 1960s, the hegemony of a determinate form of modernity was also expressed by interpretations of Nazism as antimodern. Subsequently, during the intellectual reaction against the "master narratives" of modernity, Nazism increasingly became seen as quintessentially modern. In each case, Nazism was seen as the one-sided opposite of dominant discourse, as its Other. This, in turn, implicitly indicates the one-sidedness of each of the dominant discursive modes—whether modernist or postmodernist. I shall return to these themes below.

At this point I only wish to note that the interpretative antinomy of grasping Nazism as antimodern or as essentially modern is instructive: it underlines the inadequacy of the concept of modernity as a rigorous analytic concept with which National Socialism can be grasped—for Nazism both rejected some elements of modernity and emphatically affirmed others (such as modern technology and industrial capital). An approach is required, then, that can make sense of the pattern of those aspects of modernity rejected by the Nazis and those aspects accepted, and that can relate that pattern to modern exterminatory anti-Semitism.[39] By calling into question characterizations of Nazism either as anti-modern or as modern, such an approach also calls into question more generally the theoretical adequacy of categories such as "modern," "postmodern," and "antimodern."

The sort of anti-Semitism that found its most extreme expression in the Holocaust should not be confused with everyday anti-Jewish prejudice. It is an ideology that became widespread in Europe in the late nineteenth century; its emergence presupposed earlier forms of anti-Semitism that had for centuries been an integral part of Christian Western civilization. What is common to all forms of anti-Semitism is the degree of power attributed to Jews. Yet it is not only the degree but also the quality of the power attributed to the Jews that distinguishes anti-Semitism. What characterizes the power imputed to Jews in modern anti-Semitism is that it is mysteriously intangible, abstract, and universal. It is a form of power that doesn't manifest itself directly, but seeks a concrete carrier—whether political, social, or cultural—through which it can work. Because the power of the Jews, as conceived by the modern anti-Semitic imaginary, is not limited concretely, is not "rooted," it is considered enormous and extremely difficult to check. This power stands behind phenomena, but is not identical with them. It is hidden—conspiratorial.

Within the modern anti-Semitic worldview, the Jews constitute an immensely powerful, shadowy, international conspiracy, responsible for those "apparent" opposites, plutocratic capitalism and socialism, as well as for the rise of vulgar market culture and the decline of traditional values and institutions. The Jews were held responsible for economic crises and identified with the range of social restructuring and dislocation resulting from rapid capitalist industrialization, such as explosive urbanization, the decline of traditional social classes and strata, and the emergence of new strata of bankers, capitalists, and professionals along with a large, increasingly organized industrial proletariat. Modern anti-Semitism, then, claimed to explain rapid, fundamental processes of change that had become threatening for many people. Within this racialized imaginary, the Jews are not so much an *inferior race* as an *antirace,* responsible for historical processes that are profoundly dangerous and destructive to the social "health" of other peoples—a threat to life itself.[40]

This ideology has been interpreted as fundamentally antimodern. And it is certainly the case that both plutocracy and working-class movements were concomitants of capitalist modernity, of the massive social restructuring it entailed.

The problem with such interpretations, however, is that "the modern" would certainly include industrial capital. Yet, as is well known, industrial capital was *not* an object of anti-Semitic attacks, even in a period of rapid industrialization. Moreover, the attitudes of National Socialism toward many other dimensions of modernity, such as modern technology, were affirmative rather than critical.

I have argued elsewhere[41] that an approach based on the Marxian concept of fetishism can provide a more rigorous analysis of central features of anti-Semitism and, more generally, of the relation of "modern" and "antimodern" elements of Nazi ideology.[42] Unlike interpretations based on the notion of the "modern," this approach can provide the basis for an analysis of certain systematic forms of misrecognition (i.e., ideologies), for it can distinguish systematically between what is and what appears to be, between the historically specific social relations of capitalism and the way they appear. Within this framework, categories such as commodity, money, and capital are not merely economic categories, but express forms of structuring and structured practices historically specific to capitalism. As expressions of forms of practice, the categories represent an attempt to overcome the classical theoretical dichotomy of subject and object; they purport to grasp simultaneously forms of social relations and forms of thought.[43] The concept of fetishism refers to forms of thought that remain bound to the forms of appearance of capitalist social relations, thereby hypostatizing or naturalizing those social relations.[44]

By analyzing modern anti-Semitism with reference to the categories of capitalism, such an approach not only could address the theoretical antinomy outlined above regarding National Socialism and the Holocaust, but also could begin to relate exterminatory anti-Semitism to the temporal structuring of the modern world outlined above.

What distinguishes the basic social relations of capitalism (commodity, capital) as historically unique, according to this approach, is that they are mediated by labor and its products. Labor in capitalism is not only a socially productive activity ("concrete labor"), but also constitutes a historically unique, quasi-objective form of social mediation ("abstract labor") that displaces and transforms the overt social relations that characterize other forms of social life. Hence, the commodity—the most fundamental social form of capitalism—is not merely an object in which concrete labor has been objectified; it is also a form of objectified social relations. As object, the commodity both expresses and veils social relations that have no other, "independent," mode of expression.

Within this analytic framework, the fundamental relations of capitalism are dualistic: they are characterized by the opposition of an abstract, general, homogeneous dimension ("value")—including a system of abstract domination and compulsion which, although social, is impersonal and "objective"—and a concrete, particular, material dimension ("use-value"). Moreover, because they are mediated "objectively," both dimensions appear to be natural rather than social. The abstract dimension appears in the form of abstract, universal, "objective," natural laws; the concrete dimension appears as pure "thingly" nature. That is, the social relations specific to capitalism do not appear to be social and historical at all.

Against this theoretical background, it is striking that the specific characteristics of the power attributed to the Jews by modern anti-Semitism—abstractness, intangibility, universality, mobility—are all characteristics of the value dimension of the social forms fundamentally characterizing capitalism. Moreover, this dimension, like the supposed power of the Jews, does not appear as such, but always in the form of a material carrier, the commodity.

I shall begin addressing this striking similarity by briefly indicating how, within the framework of an analysis of the commodity, capitalism can appear in the form of its abstract dimension alone. This helps explain why modern anti-Semitism, which railed against so many aspects of the "modern" world, was so conspicuously silent, or was positive, with regard to industrial capital and modern technology.

The dualism of value and use-value characteristic of the commodity form of social relations is expressed by a material externalization: the "double character" of the commodity form appears "doubled" in the form of money (the manifest form of value) and of the commodity (the manifest form of use-value). Although the commodity as a social form embodies both value and use-value, the effect of this externalization is that the commodity appears only as its use-value dimension, as purely material. Money, on the other hand, appears as the sole repository of value, as the source and locus of the purely abstract, rather than as the externalized manifest form of the value dimension of the commodity form itself. Consequently, social relations historically specific to capitalism can appear, on this level of the analysis, as their abstract dimension alone (e.g., money), rather than as the dualistic structure of abstract and concrete. Their concrete dimension, in turn (e.g., the commodity as object), can appear to be simply "natural." Forms of anticapitalist thought that remain bound within the immediacy of these forms of appearance tend to perceive capitalist modernity only in terms of the manifestations of its abstract dimension, while positively embracing its concrete dimension as the "natural" or ontologically human, which presumably stands outside the specificity of capitalist society. So, for example, money is considered the "root of all evil" or, relatedly, a "radical" thinker like Proudhon opposes money to the purportedly socially "natural" dimension of labor and its products, criticizing the former if it does not immediately express labor, that is, the concrete dimension.[45]

As industrial capitalism becomes highly developed, the naturalization immanent to the commodity fetish acquires new dimensions. The capital form, like the commodity, is characterized by the antinomic relation of concrete and abstract, both of which appear to be natural. The quality of the "natural," however, changes as capitalism becomes increasingly developed. Capital is self-valorizing value; it is characterized by a continuous, ceaseless process of the self-expansion of value. Capital has no fixed, final form, but can appear in the form of money and in the form of commodities. With industrialization, this process of self-valorization underlies rapid, increasingly large-scale cycles of production and consumption, creation and destruction. Capital increasingly appears as pure process behind multiple manifest forms; its concrete dimension changes accordingly. Individual labors no longer constitute self-contained units. They increasingly become cellular components of a large, complex, dynamic system that encompasses people and machines and which is directed toward one goal, namely, production for the sake of production. The alienated social whole becomes greater than the sum of its constituting individuals and has a goal external to itself. That goal is open-ended process. The capital form of social relations has a blind, processual, quasi-organic character.

This character of the capital form allows for social and historical processes to become increasingly understood in biological terms in the course of the nineteenth century. I shall not develop this aspect of the capital fetish any further here. For our purposes what must be noted is the implications for how capital can be perceived. As indicated above, the commodity's "double character" allows the commodity to appear as a purely material entity rather than as the objectification of mediated social relations. Relatedly, it allows concrete labor to appear as a purely material, creative process, separable from capitalist social relations. On the logical level of capital, this "double character" allows industrial production to appear as a material, creative process ("labor process"), separable from capital, which, in turn, is understood only in terms of its abstract dimension as "rootless," "parasitic" finance capital.

The manifest form of the concrete is now more organic. This allows for forms of "revolt," of "anticapitalism," in which a glorification of the purportedly premodern—"material nature," blood, the soil, labor, and community *(Gemeinschaft)*—can go hand in hand with a positive affirmation of modern phenomena such as industry and technology. All are considered to be on the "thingly" side of the opposition. The notion of "fetishized anticapitalism," then, allows one to understand how all of these disparate ("modern" and "premodern") elements can be grasped in terms of an overarching commonality. They all appear to be concrete and organic, "healthy" counterprinciples to the abstract.

Biologistic and racist forms of thought in general, and modern anti-Semitism in particular, then, should not be considered as historical regressions, as atavistic. They are historically new forms of thought in the nineteenth century and do not represent the reemergence of older forms. It is because of their biological character that they appear to be atavistic; this character itself, however, should be grasped with reference to the capital fetish that gives rise to the notion that the concrete is "natural," and that increasingly presents the socially "natural" in such a way that it is perceived in biological terms.

The hypostatization of the concrete and the identification of capital with the manifest abstract underlie a form of "anticapitalism" that seeks to overcome the existing social order from a standpoint which actually remains intrinsic to that order. Inasmuch as that standpoint is the concrete dimension, this ideology tends to point toward a more overt, concrete, and organized form of capitalist social synthesis. This form of "anticapitalism," then, only *appears* to be looking backward nostalgically. As an expression of the capital fetish its real thrust is forward. It emerges in the long, rocky transition from liberal to bureaucratic capitalism and becomes virulent in an overdetermined situation of structural, political, and cultural crisis.

This form of "anticapitalism" is based on a one-sided attack on the abstract—abstract law, abstract reason, or, on another level, money and finance capital—from the standpoint of the "healthy," "rooted," "natural" concrete. In biologized modern anti-Semitism, this fetishized opposition of the abstract and the concrete, the "artificial" and the "natural," became conceptualized as the racial opposition of Jews and (in the case of Germany) Aryans. Modern anti-Semitism involves a biologization of capitalism—which itself is only understood in terms of its manifest abstract dimension—as International Jewry.

According to this interpretation, the Jews were not seen merely as capitalists, nor were they identified only with money and the sphere of circulation. Rather, they were identified with capitalism itself. Capitalism, however, did not appear to include technology and industry. Instead, capitalism appeared to be only its manifest abstract dimension, which was in turn held responsible for the economic, social, and cultural changes associated with the rapid development of modern industrial capitalism. The Jews, then, became the personifications of the intangible, destructive, immensely powerful, international domination of capital. Certain forms of anticapitalist discontent became directed against the manifest abstract dimension of capital personified in the form of the Jews, not because the Jews were consciously identified with the value dimension, but because, given the antinomy of the abstract and concrete dimensions, capitalism appeared only in its abstract guise, which was identified with the Jews. The "anticapitalist" revolt was, consequently, also the revolt against the Jews. The overcoming of capitalism and its negative social effects became associated with the "overcoming" of the Jews.

The question remains why the biological interpretation of the abstract dimension of capitalism found its focus in the Jews. This "choice" was, within the European context, by no means fortuitous. The Jews could not have been replaced by any other group. The reasons for this are manifold. The long history of anti-Semitism in Europe and the related association of Jews with money are well known. The period of rapid expansion of industrial capital in the last half of the nineteenth century coincided with the political and civil emancipation of the Jews in central Europe. The Jews rapidly became visible in civil society, particularly in spheres and professions (the universities, the liberal professions, journalism, the arts, retail) that were expanding and were associated with the newer form society was taking.

One could mention many other factors, but there is one that I wish to emphasize. Just as the commodity, understood as a social form, expresses its "double character" in the externalized opposition between the abstract (money) and the concrete (the commodity), so is bourgeois society characterized by a split between the state and civil society. For the individual, the split is expressed as between the individual as citizen and as person. As a citizen, the individual is abstract—as is expressed, for example, in the notion of equality before the (abstract) law, or in the principle of one person, one vote. As a person, an individual is concrete, embedded in real class relations that are considered to be "private," that is, pertaining to civil society, and which do not find political expression. In Europe, however, the notion of the nation as a purely political entity, abstracted from the substantiality of civil society, was never fully realized. The nation was not only a political entity; it was also concrete, determined by a common language, history, traditions, and religion. In this sense, the Jews following their political emancipation constituted the only group in Europe that fulfilled the determination of citizenship as a pure political abstraction. They were German or French citizens, but were not really considered Germans or Frenchmen. They were of the nation abstractly, but rarely concretely. They were, in addition, citizens of most European countries. The quality of abstractness, characteristic not only of the value dimension in its immediacy but also, mediately, of the bourgeois state and law, became closely identified with the Jews. In a period when the concrete became glorified over the abstract, against "capitalism" and the bourgeois state, this became a fatal association. The Jews were rootless, international, and abstract.

VII

Modern anti-Semitism, then, is a particularly pernicious fetish form. Its power and danger result from its comprehensive worldview, which explains and gives form to certain modes of anticapitalist discontent in a manner that leaves capitalism intact, by attacking personifications of its social form. Anti-Semitism so understood allows one to grasp an essential moment of Nazism as a fetishized anticapitalist movement, one characterized by a hatred of the abstract, a hypostatization of the existing concrete, and a single-minded, ruthless—but not necessarily hate-filled—mission: to rid the world of the source of all evil. Modern anti-Semitism, then, is a revolt against history as constituted by capitalism, misrecognized as a Jewish conspiracy. Within such an ideological framework, that conspiracy must be destroyed if the world is to be saved. This ideology was an absolutely necessary condition for the Holocaust, which cannot adequately be explained in terms of the historical contingencies of 1939–41. This does not mean that a plan existed in 1933 to exterminate the Jews. It does, however, delineate the ideological framework that rendered such a project conceivable.

A capitalist factory is a site of value production (valorization process), which necessarily takes the form of the production of goods, of use-values (labor process). That is, the concrete is produced as the necessary carrier of the abstract. The Nazi extermination camps do *not* represent a terrible version of such a factory, an extreme example of modernity, but, rather, should be seen as its grotesque "anticapitalist" *negation*. Auschwitz was a factory to "destroy value," that is, to destroy the personifications of the abstract. Its organization was that of a fiendishly inverted industrial process, the aim of which was to "liberate" the concrete from the abstract. The first step was to dehumanize and reveal the Jews for what they "really are"—ciphers, numbered abstractions. The second step was to then eradicate that abstractness, trying in the process to wrest away the last remnants of the concrete material "use-value": clothes, gold, hair.

Auschwitz, not the Nazi seizure of power in 1933, was the real "German Revolution," the attempted "overthrow" not merely of the political order but of the existing social formation. By this one deed the world was to be made safe from the tyranny of the abstract. In the process, the Nazis "liberated" themselves from humanity.

The approach I have outlined, then, understands a program of extermination with reference to ideology, rather than with reference to technology or complete historical contingency, and tries to ground that ideology socially and historically. Such an approach helps to explain the exterminatory project and its intrinsic ties to the "idealistic," "revolutionary" self-understanding of the Nazis. It indicates that precisely the nature of the crime of extermination, not only the choice of victims, can be grounded in an analysis of modern anti-Semitism, understood as a fetishized form of anticapitalism that emerged in the transition from liberal to state-centered capitalism.

VIII

Having sought to relate the ideological preconditions of the Holocaust to the large-scale social and cultural transformations of capitalism in the late nineteenth and early twentieth centuries, I shall now briefly extend to the second half of the twentieth century this attempt to mediate consideration of the Holocaust and overarching historical developments. Touching upon the issue of history and memory since 1945, I shall suggest that the trajectory of postwar public responses to the Holocaust illuminates, and is illuminated by, the two phases of postwar history outlined above. In this way I hope to indicate that the Holocaust is deeply intertwined with history as constituted by capital, both in terms of its ideological preconditions as well as in terms of its aftermath.

Nazi anti-Semitism, I argued, sought to overcome (misrecognized) history violently, by means of will—to assert political control over history by means of terror.[46] What characterized the first postwar decades (Hobsbawm's "Golden Age")—after an uncertain transition period marked by the suppression or marginalization of critical social movements and thought (McCarthyism in the U.S.A., show trials in Eastern Europe, the "doctors' plot" in the U.S.S.R.)—was that the key for controlling history politically, without terror, seemed to have been found.

The rapid, increasingly generalized economic growth of the 1950s and 1960s was tied to state-centered regimes of accumulation in both the Keynesian West and the post-Stalinist East. It appeared that the long crisis of liberal capitalism had finally been resolved by a successful state-centered synthesis—that people had learned to control capitalism's dynamic by means of political institutions in ways that benefited most segments of metropolitan populations. From the standpoint of this era, history no longer posed a threat, and Nazism appeared as a regression, a German aberration. That is, the wartime interest on the part of the Allies to present Germany as historically unique, and Nazism as an expression of Germany's essence, was subsequently reinforced and rendered plausible by a postwar configuration in which historical development now appeared as benign, as modern progress; Nazism, therefore, could be regarded as antimodern.

The "Golden Age" synthesis of the immediate postwar decades, characterized by the seemingly linear triumph of modernity, unraveled at the beginning of the 1970s. The historical dynamic of capitalism began to reemerge overtly, beyond the control of national state structures. A fundamentally different historical configuration began to take shape, characterized by the reemergence of socioeconomic forms thought to have been long superseded, such as the untrammeled market with its attendant increased disparities of wealth and power. This new configuration crystallized in the 1990s as neoliberal global capitalism.

These two postwar configurations and the nonlinear trajectory of Holocaust discourse can be related. As is well known, the Holocaust was discursively marginalized for several decades after 1945. This slowly changed in the course of the 1960s. Since the late 1960s and early 1970s, the Holocaust in particular, and issues of historical memory in general, have become increasingly central to public discourse. Problematizing the relation of this discursive trajectory to large-scale historical transformations since 1945 can illuminate aspects of the complex issue of history and memory in the twentieth century.

How are we to understand historically the marginalization and subsequent centrality of Holocaust discourse? And how might this discursive shift be related to, and shed light on, the character of large-scale restructurings since 1945? Charles Maier has argued that the growing centrality of historical memory in public discourse expresses a historical break that marks the end of the forward-directedness of the postwar decades: at the end of the twentieth century, Western societies have reached the end of a collective project, of the capacity to found collective institutions that rest on aspirations for the future.[47] For Maier, the new discursive centrality of historical memory expresses a "surfeit of memory"[48] and, as such, represents a retreat from universality—from transformative politics and encompassing political communities—to particularity, to the politics of ethnicity.

Maier locates this shift historically. He implicitly relates the growing importance of the politics of memory to the historical transformation that I have characterized as one from a state-centered to a neoliberal regime of accumulation. His critique suggests that a relation exists between the end of the forward-directedness of the first postwar period and increased public concern with the past.

In relating the trajectory of public discourse on the Holocaust to larger historical developments, Maier's thesis is rich and illuminating. Nevertheless, the opposition it poses between transformative politics, forward-directedness, and universality on the one hand, and particularity and the politics of memory on the other, is too one-sided. Maier does not sufficiently interrogate the postwar politics of transformation and universality which, he claims, have been recently superseded; his argument does not do full justice to the complexities of those politics, nor to those of the recently resurgent politics of memory and identity. Maier's thesis regarding the trajectory of postwar discourse on the Holocaust is, on one level, an implicit argument regarding the rise and decline of the modernizing project in the second half of the twentieth century; its analytic implicitly relies upon the category of the modern. Once again, however, this category is inadequate analytically. As we have seen, it cannot grasp the complexities of Nazi anti-Semitism; nor, however, does it adequately illuminate the two postwar configurations outlined by Hobsbawm and, relatedly, the postwar trajectory of Holocaust discourse.[49]

The history of public discourse on the Holocaust in countries such as France, Germany, and Israel indicates that the forward-directedness of the postwar decades is more complex than is allowed for by Maier's modernist critique of the politics of memory.[50] The many signs in those countries of what some commentators have characterized as processes of historical denial and repression imply that the forward-directedness to which Maier refers, the modernist projects of the "Golden Age," have multiple dimensions and cannot simply be affirmatively grasped in terms of historical progress.

I suggest that the marginalization of Holocaust discourse for two decades after the war can be related to complex historical processes that, dovetailing with possible processes of social denial and repression, generated a sort of bifurcated historical reality: a new, future-oriented present on the surface and, underneath, a past that had not been worked through. Analyzing such processes sheds light on some more general features of the periods Hobsbawm outlined and calls into question the nature of the "modernist" forward-directedness of the postwar decades as well as the subsequent "postmodern" turn to the politics of memory and identity. In order to elaborate this contention, I shall briefly discuss some well-known aspects of the complex interplay of past and present in postwar Germany and, on that basis, present some very preliminary theoretical considerations regarding the structuring of historical time and memory.

IX

I have argued elsewhere that a number of historical events and developments suggest that historical reality in Germany has existed on two levels since the war.[51] These events and developments can be read as symptomatic: they implicitly indicate that, although very important changes took place in the political culture of West Germany since 1945, especially in the late 1960s, another historical and psychic level, one related to the Nazi past, continued to exist.[52] They suggest, in other words, that the past constituted by the Nazi regime, the war, and Nazi crimes—especially the Holocaust—has continued to operate subterraneously on the present, interacting with immediate political and social reality in a complex dialectic of normality and nonnormality that has characterized postwar

German life.[53] Within the framework of such an approach, some very problematic aspects of postwar Germany's relation to its past can be understood as expressing the ways in which that past has continued to inform the present—even "behind the backs" of the social actors.[54]

This suggests that the past does not simply pass. It also indicates that, although the past may be constructed, it is not merely invented out of whole cloth. Contestations in postwar Germany over issues of history and memory have not been the ultimate sources of historical memory, but themselves are embedded as dynamic moments of much more complex patterns.

This could be inferred, for example, from the intense public discussions elicited by the American television film *Holocaust* in 1979.[55] Those discussions illuminated retrospectively the nature and extent of postwar denial, and suggested that a great deal had been buried or shunted aside psychically, even after the enormous cultural-historical breaks of the late 1960s. It suggested that historical reality had been bifurcated since the war. For the majority of the population, the goal after the war was "normalcy" at all costs.[56] Their strong identification with the Nazi past was neither reaffirmed nor worked through and overcome. Instead, it was denied. The primary moral category of the immediate postwar period was one that can exist independent of memory—work.

The intensity of public reaction to the film *Holocaust* suggests that this structure of denial had been broken through in 1979, just as it had several times earlier (for example, during the Frankfurt Auschwitz trials in 1964–65). In each case, what can be regarded as a structure of denial subsequently reasserted itself. While for some in Germany, the reemergence of the Nazi past in the late 1970s led to renewed attempts to work through that past, it also led to a kind of reaction. This reaction could be found across the entire political spectrum, but primarily went hand in hand with a conservative campaign in the 1980s to reverse many political-cultural developments that had occurred since the late 1960s, by establishing a greater degree of continuity with contested elements of the German past. This campaign included such well-known events as the Kohl-Reagan visit to the military cemetery at Bitburg in 1985,[57] and the *Historikerstreit* of 1986.[58]

At first glance, this campaign does not seem to require deeper analysis. It appears perfectly straightforward—an attempt by the Right to regain cultural and political hegemony by affirming continuity with the past. Nevertheless, aspects of this conservative campaign suggest that the issue is more complex.

I am referring to the degree to which the new conservatives presented Germany and the Germans during the Nazi period as having been a victim, or a potential one. One example is the resolution passed by the Bundestag on June 13, 1985, implicitly equating the Holocaust and the expulsions of the Germans from the east in 1944–45. This motif of Germany as victim was central to the *Histor-ikerstreit*. It was expressed most clearly by Ernst Nolte in June 1986 in the *Frank-furter Allgemeine Zeitung* when he claimed that the Holocaust was essentially de-fensive: Hitler's "Asiatic deed" was impelled by knowledge of prior atrocities committed by the Bolsheviks and by the fear that the Soviets were planning such a "deed" (i.e., extermination) against the Germans. Therefore, he exterminated the Jews.[59] Writing in the same newspaper several months later, Günther Gillessen claimed that the invasion by Nazi Germany of the Soviet Union in 1941 was defensive; it was undertaken in order to prevent an imminent Soviet invasion of Germany.[60] A variation of this theme of victimization was promoted by the of-ficial ideology of the German Democratic Republic, which presented itself as representing the real victims of Nazism.

This identification of Germans and Germany as victims entails a process of reversal. It seems plausible that associated with this reversal are deep feelings of guilt, which elicits anger against those responsible for those feelings—the Jews. As one commentator put it ironically, "Die Deutschen werden den Juden Auschwitz nie verzeihen" [The Germans will never forgive the Jews for Auschwitz].

Such processes of psychic reversal tend to reintroduce anti-Semitic images of Jewish power and destructive intentions.[61] During the Bitburg controversy, for example, some conservative German newspapers and magazines attributed great power to Jews in the United States, and suggested that the negative reactions abroad to the Bitburg visit were generated and manipulated by Jews.[62]

Symptoms of such processes of denial and repression have not come to an end with 1989. Discussions of the GDR in the early 1990s frequently expressed what in my view could be regarded as unconscious processes. For example, in the Bundestag debate of November 14, 1991, reference was made to the six million victims of the Stasi.

The processes I have described have not been confined to the German Right. The Left in postwar Germany has, of course, centrally defined itself in opposi-tion to fascism. Nevertheless, I think it is fair to assert that left-wing analyses of National Socialism tended to blur its specificity.[63] Whatever its complex grounds, this avoidance of the specificity of the Nazi past went hand in hand with a strong desire on the part of the German New Left for identification with his-torical victims. This can most clearly be seen in the attitudes of the German New Left toward Israel.

As is well known, the New Left in much of the West became anti-Zionist after the 1967 war. Nevertheless, that switch was generally more radical in Germany. No Western Left was as philo-Semitic and pro-Zionist prior to 1967; probably none subsequently identified with the Palestinian cause so strongly. Israel's vic-tory in the war of 1967 gave rise to a process of psychological inversion: the Jews, no longer victims but victors, became identified with the Nazi past, and the Palestinians became identified as "Jews." The very word *Zionism* became as negatively informed as *Nazism*.

The new anti-Zionism went far beyond a historical and political critique. Instead, it could be argued, many Germans acted out their own past on the projected stage of the Middle East. The form of anti-Zionism that became very strong after 1967 can, retrospectively, be understood as serving two functions at the same time. On the one hand, because of the identification of Zionism and Nazism, the struggle against Zionism could become the displaced expression of the struggle against the Nazi past. On the other hand, the image of Zionism that became widespread was one that recapitulated anti-Semitic images. Zionism was not simply criticized as a bad or objectionable political program but as a worldwide, very powerful, and deeply evil conspiracy.

This "doubled" function of anti-Zionism allowed anti-Semitic images to be transported into left-wing consciousness. It thereby—paradoxically—implicitly and unconsciously helped prepare the ground for a sort of reconciliation with the nation. That is, the antifascism that defined the Left, dividing it from the Right, became, through the convoluted mediation of a particular form of anti-Zionism, conflated with the anti-Semitic ideology that once had united (Nazi-fied) Germany.

I have suggested that a sign of historical repression, and of the consequent workings of the past on the present, has been the need by many in Germany to identify themselves historically as victims—whether directly, as has been the case of the new conservatives, or indirectly, as has been the case of the Left, who identify themselves with the victims of Nazism, in however convoluted a form.

These two strands began to converge in the sort of virulent anti-Zionism I have described, and came much closer together subsequently, in popular reactions to the Gulf War. What was noteworthy was not that many in the German peace movement were opposed to the war, but that they emotionally identified the bombing of Baghdad with that of Hamburg and Dresden during World War II, and expressed personal, immediate fear of the bombing (although the overwhelming majority of demonstrators were born long after the end of World War II). These reactions signaled that left-wing identification with the victims had converged with the new conservative tendency to identify Germans as victims. And this placed the peace movement very close to the bounds of a newly reimagined national community.

The phenomena I have described can be understood in terms of processes of unconscious reversals, as forms of collective acting out—which suggests that mass German identification with Nazism in general, and complicity in the Holocaust in particular, have been denied and repressed.[64] The notion that processes of historical denial and repression have given rise to a bifurcated historical reality in Germany complicates the question of the relation of future-orientation and memory. It suggests that the character of the forward-directedness of the post-war decades is more complex than is indicated by Maier's critique of memory.

In terms of what I have outlined, it could be argued that that forward-directedness in Germany also had the character of a *flight from the past*. This suggests that, instead of simply opposing future-directedness and universality to the resurgence of memory and particularity, we must differentiate both. That is, we must distinguish between a future orientation based on appropriating the past and one that, in spite of appearances, actually is driven by that very past. By the same token, we must distinguish between a relation to the past that is enabling (and, hence, future oriented) and one that remains caught within the bounds of repetition.

The significance of such a conceptual differentiation can be illuminated indirectly with reference to another—closely related—postwar shift. Maier describes the politics of memory as reflecting a new focus on narrow ethnicity, rather than encompassing communities. The communities to which Maier is alluding, however, were encompassing in a very determinate fashion in the postwar period—they were constructed on the principle of abstract equality, which represents one pole of a modern or capitalist dualism. The mode of universality they sought to achieve was abstract—it was based on a negation of difference.

In the late 1960s, many new social movements arose that criticized, in the name of qualitative specificity, abstract universality as a mode of domination. Many of those movements, to be sure, simply reproduced the antinomy of abstract equality versus particularism. Others, however, sought to get beyond that antinomy.

This opposition of abstract equality and concrete particularism parallels the opposition between a future-directedness that paves over the past and an immersion in the past that is associated with a particularistic myth of identity. In each case, the terms of the opposition are interrelated. Hence, the critique of the particularistic term of the opposition—which is at the heart of Maier's thesis of a surfeit of memory—must also entail a critique of its universalistic term; critique must be of the opposition itself, of both of its terms. What is required, then, is a historical approach that would criticize these classic dualisms and seek to discover the possibility of forms that can get beyond them—the possibility of a new form of universality that can encompass difference and of a new future-directedness that can appropriate the past.

X

I shall begin addressing this problematic by briefly considering the issue of temporality. I have described aspects of postwar German political culture in terms of denial and repression. Denial and repression, however, need not take the form of forward-directedness. That they did, in this case, suggests that the pattern of denial and repression described in this essay fed into and was reinforced by larger patterns of temporality. I shall outline an approach to those larger patterns that can relate them to issues of future-directedness and turning to the past—including issues of postwar public responses to the Holocaust. At the same time, I shall suggest that the notion of historical temporality can provide a frame for thinking together critical psychoanalytic approaches and the critical theory of capitalism.

Many theorists, such as Max Weber, have noted the peculiar temporal directionality characteristic of modern, capitalist society. This characteristic has been associated with a determinate form of time—with what Walter Benjamin called "homogenous empty time."[65] Benjamin's conception of such time expresses a paradox: although modern, capitalist society is characterized by a form of temporal directionality that does not itself lead to a qualitatively different future. (This theme has been further developed by Jacques Derrida.)[66]

I shall try to illuminate this paradox by briefly sketching an approach to capitalism and temporality, based upon the interpretation outlined above.[67] Within the framework of this interpretation, what fundamentally characterizes capitalism is a historically specific, abstract form of social mediation—a form of social relations that is unique inasmuch as it is mediated by labor—rather than primarily class relations molded by the market and private property.

Although this historically specific form of mediation is constituted by determinate forms of social practice, it becomes quasi independent of the people engaged in those practices. The result is a historically new form of social domination—one that subjects people to impersonal, increasingly rationalized, structural imperatives and constraints that cannot adequately be grasped in terms of social groupings or of institutional agencies of the state and/or the economy. This historically specific, abstract form of social mediation is bound to a historically specific, abstract form of temporality; it underlies a complex historical dynamic which is at the heart of the modern world.

This approach abandons the transhistorical notion that human history in general has a dynamic, in favor of the claim that a historical dynamic is a historically specific characteristic of capitalism. This complex historical dynamic is directional but not linear. History in capitalism is not a simple story of progress—technical or otherwise. Rather, it is bifurcated: On the one hand, the dynamic of capitalism is characterized by ongoing and even accelerating transformations of technical processes, of the social and detail division of labor and, more generally, of social life—of the nature, structure, and interrelations of social classes and other groupings, the nature of production, transportation, circulation, patterns of living, the form of the family, and so on. On the other hand, the historical dynamic entails the ongoing reconstitution of its own fundamental condition as an unchanging feature of social life—namely that social mediation ultimately is effected by labor (and, hence, that living labor remains integral to the process of production of society as a whole, regardless of the level of productivity). The accelerating rate of change and the reconstitution of the underlying structural core of the social formation are interrelated. The historical dynamic of capitalism ceaselessly generates what is "new," while regenerating what is the "same."

The historical dynamic of the modern capitalist world, within this framework, then, is not simply a linear succession of presents but entails a complex dialectic of two forms of constituted time. This dialectic involves the accumulation of the past in a form that entails the ongoing reconstruction of the fundamental features of capitalism as an apparently necessary present—even as it is hurtled forward by another form of time, which is concrete, heterogeneous, and directional. This latter movement of time is "historical time." Historical time and abstract time are interrelated; both are forms of domination.

Within this framework, people constitute historical time; they do not, however, dispose of it. Rather, historical time in capitalism is constituted in an alienated form that reinforces the necessity of the present.[68] The existence of a historical dynamic, then, is not viewed affirmatively, within the framework of such an understanding, as the positive motor of human social life. Rather, it is grasped critically, as a form of heteronomy related to the domination of abstract time, to the accumulation of the past in a form that reinforces the present. Yet, it is precisely the same accumulation of the past that comes into increasing tension with the necessity of the present and makes possible a future time. Hence the future is made possible by the *appropriation* of the past.

XI

This brief outline of capitalism's dialectic of transformation and reconstitution calls into question any straightforward opposition of forward-directedness and a repetitively compulsive "surfeit of memory"—since they can be understood as interrelated. The forward-directedness characteristic of capitalism is not based on an appropriation of the accumulated past, but expresses a structural compulsion to drive the present forward; it is driven "subterraneously" by that past in alienated form. At the same time, the present—no longer a way of life based on the past—is repetitively reconstituted, becoming increasingly "presentist." Such a historical dynamic militates against a form of life based on memory, in the sense of an appropriation of the past, and hence does not in itself point toward a qualitatively different future.

This approach to the problem of capitalism and temporality could serve as a point of departure for understanding how and why the widespread denial which characterized several countries—especially Germany—in the decades follow-ing the war took on the form of a sort of forward-directedness that flees from the past.

It also opens up the possibility of relating the supersession of that forward-directedness by a politics of memory to the large-scale historical transformation of capitalism that began in the late 1960s and early 1970s. The late 1960s were a crucial moment of this process of transformation—a moment when the neces-sity of the present became fundamentally called into question. That moment can be viewed more generally as one in which the peculiar forward-directedness of state-centered Fordist capitalism and its statist "actually existing socialist" equiv-alent ran up against historical limits. Attempts to get beyond those limits—which would have entailed breaking with the compulsive forward-directedness of capital—were, however, singularly unsuccessful, even on a conceptual level. Instead, many oppositional movements had a "double character": they sought to get beyond the abstract homogeneity of present time, but took a turn back to its antinomic opposite, to the concrete and particularistic. (Examples are the strong focus in the 1970s on concrete domination in the Communist East in ways that occluded the nature of abstract domination, as well as concretistic forms of anti-imperialism.) At the same time, the crisis of the 1970s led to a structural re-assertion of the necessity of the present, ushering in a new period when—unlike during the first postwar decades—the forward-directedness of capital increas-ingly became uncoupled from the material well-being of much of the population.

The resurgence of historical memory—including that of the Holocaust—can be understood as part of this process and, hence, as having a "double character" as well. It can be understood both as an attempt to work through the past (i.e., a turn to the past that allows for a qualitatively different future) and as a turn *back* to the past, as repetition, as a turn to the particularistic opposite of abstract equality.

This suggests that, instead of simply opposing forward-directedness and uni-versality to the resurgence of memory and particularity—as do modernist the-ory and its postmodern complementary opposites—we must differentiate both. That is, we must distinguish between a future orientation based on appropriating the past and one that, in spite of appearances, is driven by that very past and re-mains caught within the bounds of repetition. Relatedly, we must distinguish a form of universality that can encompass difference from that mode of universal-ity, hegemonic in the 1950s and 1960s, based on abstract equality and the nega-tion of difference.

I am suggesting that such distinctions could be grounded by an approach that grasps the temporal structuring of modern history with reference to the category of capital, and that such an approach can help illuminate the relation of discourse on the Holocaust to the larger structuring and restructuring of postwar capitalism.

XII

In general: I have sought to explore the possible relation of the Holocaust and its aftermath to overarching historical patterns of the twentieth century—and have done so with reference to the category of capital.

Within the framework of this interpretation the Jews became very determinate victims of history—different from those at whose cost history is constituted (such as workers or slaves), or those excluded or marginalized by history. Rather, the Jews became objects of the displaced fury generated by the far-reaching and pervasive effects of the historical dynamic of capitalism, the victims of a fetishized, perverse attempt to liberate humanity from the historical process.

That historical process, with its dualistic opposition of abstract universal and concrete particular, did not, of course, disappear with the war. I have sought to begin relating the general periods of that process after the war and the trajectory of Holocaust discourse, focusing on multiple aspects of the complex relationship of past and present. In so doing, I have had recourse to that which critical psychoanalytic approaches and the critique of political economy have in common— namely, an analysis of the present as dominated by a past that exists in veiled form. This domination, according to this analysis, results in a compulsive flight forward and/or a compulsive reenactment of the past. A qualitatively different future—a "project" that would overcome, rather than further, both the domination of the present by the alienated past and the dualistic opposition of abstract universal and concrete particular—is possible only on the basis of the appropriation of history.

Although outlined on a very abstract level of analysis, such an approach, in my view, provides an opening through which we can begin thinking a future without betraying the past.

NOTES

I thank Nicole Deqtvaal, Spencer Leonard, and Andrew Sartori for their feedback and important research assistance.

1. Michael Marrus, *The Holocaust in History* (Hanover, N.H.: University Press of New England for Brandeis University Press, 1987), xiii.

2. Dan Diner, "Between Aporia and Apology: On the Limits of Historicizing National Socialism," in *Reworking the Past: Hitler, the Holocaust, and the Historian's Debate,* ed. Peter Baldwin (Boston: Beacon Press, 1990), 144; Dan Diner, ed., *Zivilisationsbruch, Denken nach Auschwitz* (Frankfurt am Main: Fischer Taschenbuch, 1988).

3. Omer Bartov, "The Lessons of the Holocaust," *Dimensions: A Journal of Holocaust Studies* 12, no. 1 (1998): 20.

4. Isaac Deutscher, *The Non-Jewish Jew and Other Essays,* ed. Tamara Deutscher (London: Oxford University Press, 1968), 163–64.

5. Eli Wiesel, "Trivializing the Holocaust: Semi-Fact and Semi-Fiction," *New York Times,* April 16, 1978, sec. 2, p. 1.

6. Hobsbawm conceptualizes the short twentieth century with reference to three overarching periods: 1914–45, 1945–73, and 1973–91. He regards the rise and fall of the Soviet Union as central to the short twentieth century. Nevertheless, he does not consider the confrontation between capitalism and socialism to be its most fundamental feature historically. Rather, he treats the capitalist-Communist alliance against Hitler as the "hinge" of twentieth-century history, claiming that it opened the way to the postwar "Golden Age," which he regards as of fundamental world-historical importance on a global scale. See Eric Hobsbawm, *The Age of Extremes: A History of the World, 1914–1991* (New York: Pantheon Books, 1994), 6–8.

Having placed the defeat of Nazism/fascism at the center of his account, Hobsbawm characterizes fascism as a mass movement that appealed to those who considered themselves victims of society, caught between big business and rising labor movements. He notes that these sentiments found characteristic expression in a new form of anti-Semitism (117–21). Yet Hobsbawm does not then proceed to discuss the Holocaust itself. Instead, in discussing the period 1933–45, he focuses on the struggle against fascism as a struggle for a better society that led to a new era of social transformation (142–77).

Hobsbawm's account highlights the difficulties narratives of progress have in dealing with the Holocaust. Although his conception of history is not linear, he does not problematize the sort of progress that marked the postwar era of social transformation, and the relation of such "progress" to the Holocaust or, more generally, to the issue of the victims of history. Instead, Hobsbawm has recourse to an abstractly universalistic narrative that, unreflected in this regard, requires the discursive marginalization of the Holocaust.

7. In terms of the problematic raised by this essay, the issue is not simply that Arrighi does not mention the Holocaust, but that it would not be possible to grasp the Holocaust in terms of the theoretical apparatus he develops. Arrighi's account of the trajectory of the modern world is based on a description of what he terms a systemic cycle of accumulation, entailing alternating epochs of material and financial expansion that purportedly characterize historical capitalism as a world system. (See Giovanni Arrighi, *The Long Twentieth Century: Money, Power, and the Origins of Our Times* [London: Verso, 1994], x, 6.) This attempt to grasp capitalism's history in terms of a recurrent pattern (rather than, for example, in terms of the underlying forms of mediation driving that dynamic) imparts a strong descriptivist and objectivist cast to Arrighi's account. He presents capitalist development as essentially quantitative; qualitative considerations enter his account in terms of a pattern he discerns of the historical alternation of strong and loose forms of organizational regulation.

Arrighi does discuss the specificity of German industrial capitalist development (265–69, 279–92) and briefly refers to ethnic hatreds and violent feuds as reactions against the disruptions of established ways of life under the impact of intensifying world market competition (330). Nevertheless, his approach does not provide a basis for theoretically mediating forms of social objectivity and subjectivity and hence for meaningfully incorporating into his account any historical theory of ideology in general, and of the ideological bases of the Holocaust in particular.

8. Francois Furet's *Passing of an Illusion* is a partial exception. (See Francois Furet, *The Passing of*

an Illusion: The Idea of Communism in the Twentieth Century, trans. Deborah Furet [Chicago: University of Chicago Press, 1999].) Furet treats the history of the twentieth century as the history of failed radical reactions to liberal democracy (Communism, fascism), and presents modern anti-Semitism as central to one of those radical reactions, National Socialism. Nevertheless, Furet's treatment of anti-Semitism suffers from a deep ambivalence. On the one hand, Furet treats anti-Semitism as an ideological revolt against capitalism as well as Communism ("the two forms of modern materialism"), a revolt which becomes widespread at the end of the nineteenth century and virulent in Germany after World War I (46, 188–91). On the other hand, he essentially attributes exterminatory anti-Semitism and the Holocaust to Hitler (188–90), thereby undermining the possibility of treating the ideological forms he focuses on in a consistently historical manner. This theoretical ambivalence is related to Furet's reductionist understanding of a social theory of ideology as one that is based upon an analysis of interests (185). In rejecting such a social theory as inadequate, Furet treats ideology in an inconsistent manner. At times he implicitly suggests the necessity for a different social theory of ideology; at other times he treats ideology with reference to individual personalities (e.g., Hitler) in an idealist manner that, ironically, echoes the ideology of will he criticizes.

Moreover, the general theoretical framework with which Furet treats the history of the twentieth century—which is based on a partial appropriation of Ernst Nolte's treatment of fascism as a *particularistic* mimetic reaction to Bolshevism—is contravened by Furet's own treatment of Nazism. He treats that movement as exploding the limits of fascism and nationalism, as constituting a *counteruniversalistic* movement. The latter position is consistent with Furet's own brief treatment of anti-Semitism. Nevertheless, it is in tension with and suggests the weakness of his general theoretical framework.

9. Dan Diner's *Jahrhundert Verstehen* is a significant exception in this regard. (See Dan Diner, *Das Jahrhundert Verstehen: Eine universalhistorische Deutung* [München: Luchterhand, 1999].) Diner attempts to deal with the history of the twentieth century (focusing on Europe in the first half of the century) in terms of two axes—one organized around the struggle between Communism and its antagonists between 1917 and 1989, a world civil war organized around values and worldviews; the other focused on geographic and ethnic issues. By also viewing the century's history from the European periphery (the Baltic and the Black Sea / Aegean Sea), Diner sheds new light on twentieth-century developments.

Diner's discussion of the Holocaust is both central to the book and an important intervention in the functionalist / intentionalist debates. In attempting to mediate the Holocaust and general history, Diner is less concerned with the issue of periodization than the approach presented here. He implicitly suggests that the Holocaust marks the intersection of the two historical axes around which, according to him, twentieth-century history can be organized. Nevertheless, his arguments regarding the specificity of Nazi anti-Semitism and anti-Bolshevism parallel those in this essay.

10. For some (differing) treatments of the complex patterns of postwar public discourse on the Holocaust in the United States, France, Israel, and Germany, see Marrus, *The Holocaust in History;* Peter Novick, *The Holocaust in American Life* (Boston: Houghton Mifflin Co., 1999); Henry Rousso, *The Vichy Syndrome: History and Memory in France since 1944,* trans. Arthur Goldhammer (Cambridge, Mass.: Harvard University Press, 1991); Joan Wolf, "Negotiating Meaning: Narrative Politics and Memory of the Holocaust in French Public Discourse," Ph.D. diss., University of Chicago, 1997; Tom Segev, *The Seventh Million: The Israelis and the Holocaust,* trans. Haim Watzmann (New York: Hill and Wang, 1993); and Kathy Harms, Lutz R. Reuter, and Volker Dürr, eds., *Coping with the Past: Germany and Austria after 1945* (Madison: University of Wisconsin Press, 1990)—especially the following essays: Andrei S. Markovits, "Coping with the Past: The West German Labor Movement and the Left," 219–32; Wolfgang Mommsen, "The Germans and Their Past: History and Political Consciousness in the Federal Republic of Germany," 252–69; Moishe Postone, "After the

Holocaust: History and Identity in West Germany," 233–51; Anson Rabinbach, "Beyond Bitburg: The Place of the 'Jewish Question' in German History after 1945," 187–18; and Frank Trommler, "The Creation of History and the Refusal of the Past in the German Democratic Republic," 79–93.

11. See, for example, Wolfgang Benz, "Die Abwehr der Vergangenheit," in *Ist der Nationalsozialismus Geschichte? Zu Historisierung und Historikerstreit,* ed. Dan Diner (Frankfurt am Main: Fischer Taschenbuch Verlag, 1987), 17–33.

12. See Alexander Mitscherlich and Margarete Mitscherlich, *The Inability to Mourn: Principles of Collective Behavior,* trans. Beverly R. Placzek (New York: Grove Press, 1975).

13. Furet briefly discusses how widespread this attitude was in Europe, particularly in areas controlled by the Soviet Union, as well as in antifascist circles. See Furet, *The Passing of an Illusion,* 353, 381, 395.

14. For a discussion of the difficulties in bridging the general stream of history and the Holocaust, see Omer Bartov, "Intellectuals on Auschwitz: Memory, History, and Truth," *History & Memory* 5, no. 1 (spring-summer 1993): 87–129.

15. See the essays published in Diner, *Ist der Nationalsozialismus Geschichte?* especially Saul Friedländer, "Überlegungen zur Historisierung des Nationalsozialismus," 34–50; and Dan Diner, "Zwischen Aporie und Apologie: Über Grenzen der Historisierbarkeit des Nationalsozialismus," 62–73.

16. This question is at the heart of Walter Benjamin's "Theses on the Philosophy of History." Benjamin distinguishes two conceptions of the future, highlighting their opposite relations to the past. One, based on the conception of progress, is related to the notion of homogeneous empty time. This conceptual framework, according to Benjamin, expresses and reinforces what has been the actual course of history as a history of domination, in which the past is subsumed by the present and tradition by conformism—a history in which the dead are not safe from an enemy who continues to be victorious. The other conception of the future is characterized in terms of a revolutionary possibility in the fight for an oppressed past, which would entail blasting a specific era out of the homogeneous course of history. A qualitatively different future, then, is for Benjamin inextricably bound to the redemption of the past. See Walter Benjamin, "Theses on the Philosophy of History," in *Critical Theory and Society,* ed. Stephen E. Bronner and Douglas M. Kellner (New York: Routledge, 1989), 257, 260–62.

17. See Hobsbawm, *The Age of Extremes.*

18. Large-scale historical processes pose a challenge to many postmodernist and poststructuralist approaches, which were widespread in recent decades. The issues raised by overarching temporal patterns are not identical with those entailed by the question of the "reality" of the Holocaust or, more generally, of what are deemed events. For discussions of the latter issues, see Saul Friedländer, ed., *Probing the Limits of Representation: Nazism and the "Final Solution"* (Cambridge, Mass.: Harvard University Press, 1992).

19. See Novick, *The Holocaust in American Life,* 9.

20. The deportation of the Jews of Rhodes to Auschwitz in the summer of 1944 is only one example of the lengths to which the Nazis went in fulfilling their intention of eradicating European Jewry. See Martin Gilbert, *The Holocaust* (New York: Holt, Rinehart and Winston, 1985), 706–10, 722–25.

21. Steven Aschheim makes a similar point when, for example, he disagrees with Christopher Browning, who, in dealing with the mass murders, focuses on a number of prosaic psychological mechanisms such as group conformity, deference to authority, alcohol, and routinization (Christopher Browning, *Ordinary Men: Reserve Battalion 101 and the Final Solution in Poland* [New York: HarperCollins, 1992]), and George Mosse, for whom the mass murders represented a defense of bourgeois morality (George Mosse, *Nationalism and Sexuality: Respectability and Abnormal Sexuality in Modern Europe* [New York: H. Fertig, 1985]). Aschheim correctly argues that such explanations

cannot explain sufficiently a program of extermination. Even racism, he notes, has to be made genocidal. (Steven E. Aschheim, *Culture and Catastrophe: German and Jewish Confrontations with National Socialism and Other Crises* [New York: New York University Press, 1996], 79–81.)

22. See, for example, Lucy Dawidowicz, *The War Against the Jews, 1933–1945* (New York: Holt, Rinehart and Winston, 1975); Daniel Jonah Goldhagen, *Hitler's Willing Executioners: Ordinary Germans and the Holocaust* (New York: Vintage Books, 1996); Jeffrey Herf, *Reactionary Modernism: Technology, Culture, and Politics in Weimar and the Third Reich* (Cambridge: Cambridge University Press, 1984); George L. Mosse, *The Crisis of German Ideology: Intellectual Origins of the Third Reich* (New York: Grosset and Dunlap, 1964); Paul Lawrence Rose, *Revolutionary Anti-Semitism in Germany from Kant to Wagner* (Princeton, N.J.: Princeton University Press, 1990). For a critique of the *Sonderweg* thesis, see David Blackbourn and Geoff Eley, *The Peculiarities of German History: Bourgeois Society and Politics in Nineteenth-Century Germany* (Oxford: Oxford University Press, 1984).

23. See, for example, Malcolm Hay, *Europe and the Jews: The Pressure of Christendom on the People of Israel over 1900 Years* (Chicago: Academy Chicago Publishers, 1988); and Léon Poliakov, *The History of Anti-Semitism, Volume One: From the Time of Christ to the Court Jews* (New York: The Vanguard Press, 1965).

24. See, for example, Karl Dietrich Bracher, *The German Dictatorship: The Origins, Structure, and Effects of National Socialism,* trans. Jean Steinberg (New York: Praeger Publishers, 1970); Dawidowicz, *The War Against the Jews, 1933–1945*); Gerald Fleming, *Hitler and the Final Solution* (Berkeley and Los Angeles: University of California Press, 1984); Klaus Hildebrand, "Monokratie oder Polykratie? Hitlers Herrschaft und das Dritte Reich," in *Der Führerstaat, Mythos und Realität,* ed. Gerhard Hirschfeld and Lothar Kettenacker (Stuttgart: Klett-Cotta, 1981), 23–41; and Klaus Hildebrand, *The Third Reich,* trans. P.S. Falla (London and Boston: Allen and Unwin, 1984).

25. See, for example, Uwe Dietrich Adam, *Judenpolitik im Dritte Reich* (Düsseldorf: Droste Verlag, 1972); Martin Broszat, *The Hitler State,* trans. John W. Hiden (London and New York: Longman, 1981); Martin Broszat, "Soziale Motivation und Führer-Bindung des Nationalsozialismus," *Vierteljahrshefte für Zeitgeschichte* 18, no. 4 (1970); Martin Broszat, "Hitler und die Genesis der 'Endlösung': Aus Anlass der Thesen von David Irving," *Vierteljahrshefte für Zeitgeschichte* 25, no. 4 (1977); Hans Mommsen, "Die Realisierung des Utopischen: Die 'Endlösung der Judenfrage' im 'Dritte Reich,'" *Geschichte und Gesellschaft* 9, no. 3 (1985); and Karl A. Schleunes, *The Twisted Road to Auschwitz: Nazi Policy towards the Jews, 1933–1939* (Urbana: University of Illinois Press, 1970). Götz Aly and Susanne Heim, arguing within a general functionalist framework, maintain that Nazi ideology could only give rise to pogroms and massacres, not, however, to the complete extermination of European Jewry. The latter required, as its essential ingredient, the calculations of the economic and social planners of the German occupation in eastern Europe—who considered the extermination to be the means for solving the problem of overpopulation. (See Götz Aly and Susanne Heim, "Die Ökonomie der 'Endlösung': Menschliche Vernichtung und wirtschaftliche Neuordnung," *Beiträge zur Nationalsozialistichen Gesundheits- und Sozialpolitik,* vol. 4, *Sozialpolitik und Judenvernichtung: Gibt es eine Ökonomie der Endlösung?* [Berlin: Rotbuch, 1987], 7–90. See also Götz Aly, *Final Solution: Nazi Population Policy and the Murder of the European Jews,* trans. Belinda Cooper and Allison Brown [London: Arnold and Oxford University Press, 1998].) For critiques of this economistic approach, see Ulrich Herbert, "Arbeit und Vernichtung: Ökonomistisches Interesse und Primat der 'Weltanschauung' im Nationalsozialismus," in *Ist der Nazionalsozialismus Geschichte?* ed. Diner, 198–236; and Christopher R. Browning, *The Path to Genocide* (New York: Cambridge University Press, 1992), 59–76.

26. See Goldhagen, *Hitler's Willing Executioners.*

27. Zygmunt Bauman, *Modernity and the Holocaust* (Ithaca, N.Y.: Cornell University Press, 1989), 1.

28. As Friedländer put it, "the point is not that concepts such as 'totalitarianism' or 'fascism'

seem inadequate for the conceptualization of the 'Final Solution,' but obversely, that these concepts fit much better the particular phenomenon they deal with once the 'Final Solution' is not included." See Saul Friedländer, *Memory, History, and the Extermination of the Jews of Europe* (Bloomington: Indiana University Press, 1993), 56–57. See also his "From Anti-Semitism to Extermination," in *Unanswered Questions: Nazi Germany and the Genocide of the Jews,* ed. François Furet (New York: Schocken Books, 1989), 3–11.

29. Raul Hilberg, *The Destruction of the European Jews,* rev. ed. (New York: Holmes & Meier, 1985); and Hannah Arendt, *Eichmann in Jerusalem: A Report on the Banality of Evil,* rev. ed. (London: Penguin, 1994).

30. Arno Mayer, *Why Did the Heavens Not Darken? The "Final Solution" in History* (New York: Pantheon Books, 1988).

31. Arendt argues that, with what she calls the decline of the nation-state after 1873, the Jews became superfluous to the European concert of nations (*The Origins of Totalitarianism,* new ed. [New York: Harcourt Brace and World, 1966], 11–28, 50–55, 97–99). Adorno and Horkheimer understood the same period as marking the transition from liberal to state capitalism. They argue, as one aspect of their complex theory of anti-Semitism, that the Jews, who had become representatives of the market-mediated sphere of circulation, became increasingly superfluous as state capitalism superseded liberal capitalism. (Max Horkheimer and Theodor W. Adorno, *Dialectic of Enlightenment,* trans. John Cumming [New York: Seabury Press, 1972], 199, 206. See also. Horkheimer, "The Jews and Europe," in *Critical Theory and Society,* ed. Bronner and Kellner, 89–94.)

32. Goldhagen's *Hitler's Willing Executioners*—whatever its other problems—calls into question such approaches as one-sided at best.

33. See, for example, George Mosse, *Toward the Final Solution: A History of European Racism* (New York: Howard Fertig, 1978); Götz Aly, Peter Chroust, and Christian Pross, *Cleansing the Fatherland: Nazi Medicine and Racial Hygiene,* trans. Belinda Cooper (Baltimore: Johns Hopkins University Press, 1994); Michael Burleigh and Wolfgang Wippermann, *The Racial State: Germany, 1933–1945* (Cambridge: Cambridge University Press, 1991); and Paul Weindling, *Health, Race and German Politics between National Unification and Nazism, 1870–1945* (Cambridge: Cambridge University Press, 1989).

34. Steven Aschheim has also argued this. See Aschheim, *Culture and Catastrophe,* 115–35.

35. Dominick LaCapra, *Representing the Holocaust: History, Theory, Trauma* (Ithaca, N.Y.: Cornell University Press, 1994), 220. This distinction is important when psychoanalytic categories are used to illuminate social and historical phenomena. See also Mosse's treatment of racism as a worldview in *Toward the Final Solution.*

36. See Mosse, *The Crisis of German Ideology.*

37. See Berel Lang, *Act and Idea in the Nazi Genocide* (Chicago: University of Chicago Press, 1990).

38. See Bauman, *Modernity and the Holocaust.*

39. In this way the approach outlined in this essay seeks to ground theoretically the insight, shared by a range of thinkers, including Hannah Arendt and Saul Friedländer, that a radical form of modern anti-Semitism was at the ideological core of National Socialism.

40. See also Marrus, *The Holocaust in History,* 25.

41. Moishe Postone, "Anti-Semitism and National Socialism," *New German Critique,* no. 19 (Winter 1980). (A revised version also appeared as "Anti-Semitism and National Socialism," in *Germans and Jews since the Holocaust,* ed. Anson Rabinbach and Jack Zipes [New York: Holmes & Meier, 1986].)

42. Jeffrey Herf tries to thematize this relation as well. Distancing himself from the sort of analytic framework presented in this essay, Herf presents a *description* of the combination of "modern"

and "antimodern" elements in German conservative and Nazi ideology ("reactionary modernism"), rather than an *analysis* of that combination. He embeds his description within a version of the *Sonderweg* thesis that implicitly depends on a linear conception of modernity (as enlightenment plus technology). By focusing on Germany as a completely unique exception, Herf overlooks the powerful rise and spread of jingoist, racist, xenophobic, and anti-Semitic ideologies (as concomitant with a host of social and economic transformations) in late nineteenth- and early twentieth-century Europe and the United States. Bracketing these important general cultural, social, and economic transformations does not allow him to adequately engage works like *Dialectic of Enlightenment* (Adorno and Horkheimer) and *The Origins of Totalitarianism* (Arendt) that seek to embed the specificity of German development within larger historical changes. Indeed, it does not allow him to thematize the relation of that specificity to those larger changes. See Herf, *Reactionary Modernism*.

43. This approach, it should be clear, does not analyze forms of subjectivity in terms of their function for the system as a whole, nor as expressions of underlying material interests. By grasping those forms with reference to determinate forms of practice, this approach seeks to overcome what has become a theoretical dichotomy between culture and society (or culture and economy).

44. So, for example, the rise of biologistic race theory can be understood as a possibility generated by a new social order structured formally by principles of freedom and equality, in which social inequality and difference is no longer recognized as an overt structuring principle of social life. In such a society, the equality of some—of commodity owners (i.e., bourgeois subjects)—becomes considered an ontological, quasi-natural attribute of humanness (rather than as socially constituted). Conversely, systematic inequality—e.g., of women, of slaves—can also become understood ontologically and biologically.

45. See P. J. Proudhon, *System of Economic Contradictions: Or, the Philosophy of Misery,* vol. 1, trans. B. R. Tucker (Boston: B. R. Tucker, 1888), 78–128.

46. This could serve as a point of departure for grasping points of similarity between Nazism and Stalinism, as different attempts to overcome history by means of will—i.e., the party.

47. Charles S. Maier, "A Surfeit of Memory? Reflections on History, Melancholy and Denial," *History & Memory* 5, no. 2 (fall-winter 1993): 147.

48. Ibid., 138.

49. Charles Maier's opposition between universalistic, forward-directed collective projects that purportedly characterized the immediate postwar decades and a subsequent particularistic focus on the past is paralleled by Peter Novick's account of the changes in American public discourse on the Holocaust since 1945. Novick describes those changes in terms of a replacement of the integrationist ethos of the postwar years in the United States by a particularistic ethos (Novick, *The Holocaust in American Life,* 6). Like many others, he points out that the Holocaust was hardly ever spoken about publicly for several decades after World War II. Since the late 1960s, however, it has become increasingly central to American public discourse. In seeking to elucidate this temporal patterning of Holocaust discourse, Novick rejects the idea that it can be grasped with reference to issues of trauma and repression. Instead, he focuses on the politics of American Jewish organizations in promoting consciousness of the Holocaust in order to strengthen support for Israel and to shore up Jewish identity in the face of the perceived threat of assimilation.

Like Maier, Novick does not interrogate either term of the universal/particular opposition underlying his position. Moreover, the temporal patterning of Holocaust discourse Novick outlines has not been restricted to the United States but, as he acknowledges, has been the case in a number of other countries as well—notably Israel, Germany, and France. This strongly suggests that, however inflected that pattern may be locally, it cannot adequately be grasped in local terms. Novick's treatment of that pattern, however, is fundamentally local. Furthermore, even on this level, the account is incomplete; important connections Novick points to do not sustain his argument. For example, he emphasizes concern for Israel resulting from the wars in 1967 and 1973 as a primary factor in Jewish organizations' focus on the Holocaust. Yet he also notes that the Holocaust/Israel nexus begins to fall apart in the early 1980s. Nevertheless, the Holocaust has become increasingly central since that time—also in countries having no large Jewish populations and a leadership worried about assimilation.

More generally, what Novick examines is a sort of cultural shift, a shift in consciousness and forms of identity; his account deals with a strand of the complex rise of the "politics of identity" in the second half of the twentieth century. However, although he refers to such developments, he treats them only as a background for his narrative. His account does not illuminate the shifts it outlines. Those shifts elude the grasp of his instrumental/political argument, which focuses on organizational decisions. Hence, the critique of abstract universalism embodied practically in the politics of identity is *judged* negatively by Novick, but it is not really *analyzed* historically.

Ultimately, then, although Novick's book contains valuable insights and punctures a number of widely accepted positions, it does not succeed in addressing the sorts of general questions it raises regarding the temporal patterning of Holocaust discourse and the increasing centrality of that discourse in many countries, including the United States.

50. See, for example, the works cited in note 10 above.

51. See Postone, "After the Holocaust: History and Identity in West Germany."

52. See Dan Diner, "Negative Symbiose: Deutsche und Juden nach Auschwitz," *Babylon: Beiträge zur jüdischen Gegenwart* 1 (October 1986). See also Mitscherlich and Mitscherlich, *The Inability to Mourn.*

53. See Postone, "After the Holocaust."

54. The use of depth-psychological terms in trying to grasp adequately determinate historical phenomena presupposes that psychoanalytic categories are not ultimately individual but, like the category of the "individual" itself, are ultimately social and historical, however mediated on the individual level. See also Dominick LaCapra, *History and Memory after Auschwitz* (Ithaca, N.Y.: Cornell University Press, 1998), 43–73.

55. For discussion of the reception of the film *Holocaust* in the Federal Republic of Germany and the more general problems of the Holocaust and anti-Semitism, see *New German Critique* 19 (winter 1980), 20 (spring-summer 1980), and 21 (fall 1980). Many of those articles were subsequently published in Rabinbach and Zipes, eds., *Germans and Jews since the Holocaust.*

56. See, for example, Berndt Engelmann, *In Hitler's Germany: Daily Life in the Third Reich,* trans. Krishna Winston (New York: Pantheon Books, 1986), 329–33.

57. See Geoffrey Hartman, ed., *Bitburg in Moral and Political Perspective* (Bloomington: Indiana University Press, 1986); and Moishe Postone, "Bitburg und die Linke," *Pflasterstrand* 211 (June 1, 1985).

58. Many of the relevant documents of the *Historikerstreit* have been published in one volume: *Historikerstreit* (Munich: R. Piper GmbH and Co., 1987). This volume has been translated as *Forever in the Shadow of Hitler?* trans. James Knowlton and Truett Cates (Atlantic Highlands, N.J.: Humanities Press, 1993). See also Charles S. Maier, *The Unmasterable Past: History, Holocaust, and German National Identity* (Cambridge, Mass.: Harvard University Press, 1988); and Wolfgang Marienfeld, *Der Historikerstreit* (Hannover: Niedersächsische Landeszentrale für Politische Bildung, 1987). For the broader debate about whether National Socialism can be historicized, see Diner, ed., *Ist der Nationalsozialismus Geschichte?*

59. Ernst Nolte, "Vergangenheit, die nicht vergehen will," *Frankfurter Allgemeine Zeitung,* June 6, 1986. Nolte has since made explicit the implicit connection he made between Bolshevism and the Jews, which recapitulated a classic Nazi position. In accepting the Konrad Adenauer Prize for literature from the conservative Deutschland-Stiftung in June 2000, Nolte said that because Bolshevism had wide Jewish support, and Nazism was the strongest counterforce to Bolshevism, Hitler may have had rational reasons for attacking the Jews ("Hitler Apologist Wins German Honor, and a Storm Breaks Out," *New York Times,* June 21, 2000, sec. A, p. 3).

60. Günther Gillessen, *Frankfurter Allgemeine Zeitung,* August 20, 1986.

61. The images of Jewish power can also be apparently affirmative—as in Fassbinder's film, *Lili Marlene,* which portrays the Jews as fundamentally more powerful than the Nazis, as the actual victors of World War II. The film thereby reproduces the very ideology it seeks to criticize.

62. So, for example, Fritz Ullrich Fack, an editor of the *Frankfurter Allgemeine Zeitung,* wrote a barely veiled editorial (April 29, 1985) on the powerful interest groups in the United States who want to resurrect the distorted picture of the "ugly German." He then went on to accuse those opposing the Kohl-Reagan visit to Bitburg of having no qualms about sorting out the dead—an allusion to the "selection" process in the death camps which separated out those who were sent immediately to the gas chambers from those who were spared initially. Fack's editorial not only effected a psychic and moral reversal between the Nazis and Jews, but, relatedly, also did so in a manner that reflected modern anti-Semitic ideology.

63. See, for example, Markovits, "Coping with the Past," and Rabinbach, "Beyond Bitburg," in *Coping with the Past,* ed. Harms, Reuter, and Dürr.

64. See Dominick LaCapra's important discussion of the applicability to social and cultural phenomena of psychoanalytic categories such as repression and acting out in *Representing the Holocaust: History, Theory, Trauma* (Ithaca, N.Y.: Cornell University Press, 1994); and in *History and Memory after Auschwitz.*

65. Benjamin, "Theses on the Philosophy of History," 260–61.

66. Jacques Derrida, *Specters of Marx,* trans. Peggy Kamuf (New York: Routledge, 1994).

67. What follows is based on the interpretation developed in Moishe Postone, *Time, Labor, and Social Domination: A Reinterpretation of Marx's Critical Theory* (Cambridge: Cambridge University Press, 1993).

68. It is in this sense that Marx's well-known statement in *The Eighteenth Brumaire* should be understood—that the tradition of all the dead generations weighs like a nightmare on the brains of the living. See Marx, *The Eighteenth Brumaire of Louis Bonaparte,* in *Collected Works,* by Karl Marx and Frederick Engels, vol. 11, *Marx and Engels: 1851–53* (New York: International Publishers, 1979), 103.

Part Three

**ANNIHILATION,
VICTIMHOOD,
IDENTITY**

Six

"FIELDS OF GLORY": WAR, GENOCIDE, AND THE GLORIFICATION OF VIOLENCE

Omer Bartov

Thoughts of war throughout history and in many civilizations have revolved around two contradictory sets of images. The first postulated war as an elevating, heroic experience. The second described war as a site of destruction and desolation. This polarity between the portrayal of war as an occasion for humanity to express its nobility, and its perception as an opportunity for human savagery, is thus deeply embedded in culture and civilization.

During the last two centuries, however, the availability of unprecedented quantities of ever more effective weapons, the seemingly unlimited and increasingly pliable human reserves, and the growing capacity to mobilize these resources by the modern industrialized nation-state have greatly enhanced war's destructive potential. This has evoked the wildest fantasies and the most nightmarish visions. Characteristically for an age of rapid changes, the reality of total war and genocide consistently remained one step ahead of its image. For ours is an era in which human imagination has been conducting a desperate race with the practice of humanity.

The link between modern warfare and mass killing of civilian populations was most clearly manifested in World War II. And the most terrifying example of a state mobilizing significant resources for the sole aim of exterminating an entire population while simultaneously fighting a total war is the Nazi genocide of the Jews. Indeed, what makes the Holocaust into a crucial event in any examination of the link between war and genocide is that the Nazi regime perceived the extermination of the Jews as an inherent element of its war effort; that it organized the genocide as a military operation; and that it represented it to the perpetrators, to itself, and in a somewhat more indirect fashion also publicly to the German population and to the rest of the world, as a glorious undertaking worthy of comparison with the greatest military feats and moral endeavors of German history. Nevertheless, the roots of this development are to be sought several decades earlier, in World War I.

What is most crucial about Europe's first industrial war in 1914–18 is not the enthusiasm with which its outbreak was greeted in the major combatant nations. To be sure, even if the prevalence of the "spirit of 1914" has been somewhat exaggerated, it was still an extraordinary expression of devotion not merely to the nation but also to the notion of war itself as a noble, purifying, and elevating experience.[1] And yet, while World War I is remembered primarily for the continuous front of trenches that stretched from the Alps to the Atlantic, it was just as much characterized by the growing porousness of the boundaries between soldiers and civilians both as combatants and as targets of destruction. For while vast numbers of men were transformed into soldiers, all other civilians became exposed to the human, economic, and psychological cost of total war. The war invaded the most remote corners of the land, and the huge conscript armies at the front contained members of every social stratum and region of the country.

In 1914 the splendid bayonet charge over a field of flowers that so many soldiers had been taught to expect did not materialize.[2] But as the huge armies burrowed underground into a maze of trenches filled with slime and excrement, rats and rotting body parts, the soldiers began to construct their own vision of glory, distinct both from the romantic images of the past and from the discredited chauvinistic eyewash of the propagandists in the rear. This new vision, unique to the age of total war, has become part of the manner in which we imagine destruction; aestheticized and cherished, it motivated future generations of young men to fight and die in other wars, and enabled the veterans of past conflicts to make a kind of peace with their memories of massacre. Given the right political and cultural context, however, this vision became a crucial component of the twentieth century's genocidal predilections, facilitating a metamorphosis of values and perspectives in which the annihilatory energy of modern war was portrayed as generating great creative powers, and the phenomenon of industrial killing was perceived as a historical necessity of awesome beauty.[3] The Great War's new fields of glory were the breeding ground of fascism and Nazism, of human degradation and extermination. From them sprang up the storm troops of dictatorships and the demagogues of racial purity and exclusion. In a tragic process of inversion, the true comradeship and sacrifice of millions was perverted into hate and destruction. The new vision of war that emanated from the trenches of 1914–18 ensured that the twentieth century's fields of glory would be sown with the corpses of innocent victims and the distorted fragments of shattered ideals.

Contemptuous of the idealized images of war that bore no relationship to the fighting as they knew it, resentful of the staff officers' sheltered lives behind the front and the civilians in the rear, the troops developed a complex subculture all of their own making. Exemplified in frontline journals for their own consumption, a vocabulary that only they could understand, and a new kind of sarcasm and black humor, this was a state of mind that combined a good measure of self-pity with immense pride in their ability to endure inhuman conditions for the sake of a nation seemingly ignorant of and indifferent to their terrible sacrifice. This camaraderie of the combat troops was shared by soldiers on both sides of the line, and while it had some common features with the mentality of all armies in history, the crucial difference was that most of these men were conscripts who would return to civilian life as soon as the fighting ended—if they were lucky enough to survive.[4]

Thus the very camaraderie that helped the troops endure the front also created and made a virtue of the difference between them and that part of the nation that had stayed behind. Theirs was not the naive heroism extolled by the propagandists but one born of suffering and pain, horror and death. To be sure, most soldiers had but the vaguest notion of how the nation should be transformed once they returned from the front, but they increasingly felt that it was their right and duty to bring about far-reaching changes, rooted, first and foremost, in the trench experience.

By now we have become used to thinking of World War I as the moment in which innocence was forever shattered. We are haunted by the image of millions of devoted, unquestioning, patriotic young men being led to senseless slaughter, betrayed by their elders. The Western Front has come to epitomize the notion of war as a vast arena of victimhood. That all this sacrifice was in vain is underlined by the aftermath of the war. We recall the broken promises and despair, the soldiers who instead of returning to a "land fit for heroes" were abandoned to unemployment, destitution, and physical and mental decay. Hence the apathy and the extremism, the conformism and the violence that characterized the postwar era.[5] What is insufficiently understood is that the very attitudes toward violence and the perceptions of destruction, which emerged among the soldiers during the war as a means to endure it, were ultimately at the root of the even greater horror and devastation of the next war. The images of violence and fantasies of destruction that became so prevalent during the interwar period were directly linked to the reality and trauma of the front experience in 1914–18. It was these fantasies that played such a major role in the enactment of genocide two decades later. Ironically, then, the same mechanism that helped soldiers survive one war created the necessary mind-set for mass murder. A crucial component of this mechanism was the frontline notion of soldiers' glory.

Glory at the front meant enduring the most degrading, inhuman conditions under constant threat of death and while regularly killing others without losing one's good humor, composure, and humanity. It meant discovering the ability to switch between being a helpless prey and a professional killer and acting as a loving son, father, and husband, radically separating between the atrocity at the front and the normality of the rear, indeed making this very separation into a badge of honor and a key for survival. For one had to survive not only the fighting but also the homecoming. The true accomplishment of the frontline troops was not merely to tolerate this unbearable, schizophrenic condition but to glorify it, to perceive it as a higher existence rather than a horrifying state of affairs that could not be evaded. To be sure, many soldiers were incapable of this transformation of perception. But such World War I walking dead who had lost all desire to survive were doomed if they were not taken out of the line in time. To be saved from drowning, soldiers had to rely on the glory they had fabricated for themselves, whose essence was to construe atrocity as an elevating experience to be simultaneously celebrated, kept apart from personal relationships in the rear, and used as a tool to change the universe that had made it possible. And because such notions of wholesale future transformation were entertained within a context of vast devastation, they were inevitably permeated by an imagery of destruction.

When the war finally ended, the veterans felt an even greater urge to endow it with meaning. If many did not glorify the war, most seem to have glorified their own and their comrades' experience in it. This was a paradox of great import, for opposition to war shared one important element with extremism and militarism, namely the glorification of the individual soldier, whether as a ruthless fighter or as a hapless victim. And while some hoped that the shared fate of the veterans would become a formula for domestic and international peace, precisely the opposite happened, not least because what these soldiers had in common was, first and foremost, years of fear and atrocity, killing and mutilation. This was a treacherous foundation for peace.[6]

During the interwar period all political and ideological trends drew on the legacy of World War I for their own often wholly contradictory purposes, for this was a rich and highly malleable source of violent images and metaphors of destruction. But employing the memory of mass killing by such divergent interests introduced a violent dimension to postwar political discourse. The most visible and emotionally most potent form of confronting the memory of the war was the commemoration of fallen soldiers. Significantly, even when such public symbols of mourning expressed criticism or rejection of war, they simultaneously endowed the death of soldiers with a higher meaning. Sacrifice was thus glorified and its context refashioned to enhance the nobility of its victims. Indeed, since commemoration is more about instilling the past with sense and purpose than simply remembering it, the official remembrance of millions of squandered lives gave the war a retrospective meaning for the benefit of the living.[7]

The investment with meaning of death in war can be accomplished either by generalizing or by individualizing it. The fallen soldier can be presented as having sacrificed himself for a greater cause: death is glorified by its context; abstract principles and entities are valued higher than individual lives. Hence mourning will focus on the service rendered by the dead to the nation's historical mission and future; rather than being deprived of its sons, the nation is enriched by those who die for it. Conversely, by concentrating on individual devotion, suffering, and sacrifice, the fallen can be said to glorify the cause and endow it with deeper meaning by having given their lives for it. Here mourning will focus on individual qualities and example. In one case, the soldier is an extension of the nation; in the other, the nation is an extension of the soldier who embodies its very best essence.

In the wake of World War I both modes of mourning and ascribing meaning to death were common features of the vast and unprecedented wave of commemoration that swept through Europe.[8] But while public commemoration emphasized collective sacrifice for the national cause, it was also influenced by a quest for a new type of individual heroism. Within the context of mass society, vast conscript armies, and total war, there was little room for the traditional hero, whose ultimate sacrifice was inscribed on his fate and inherent to his existence. World War I ushered in the glorification of the rank and file, expressed in such countries as Britain and France in the erection of national memorials for the Unknown Soldier. Here was a figure that represented both the individual and the mass: glorified by the nation, he also stood for the multitudes sent out to die and quickly forgotten. He thus gave a face to anonymity, personifying and glorifying precisely those masses that had no place in public memory; in other words, in being remembered, the Unknown Soldier legitimized forgetting.[9]

The Unknown Soldier thus enabled a shift from the abstract nation to the individual yet presented the individual as a soldier who by definition had no specific traits and features, thereby embodying the nation after all. Through him the nation could represent itself as a site of resurrection, returning from the Valley of Death thanks to the sacrifice of its sons. It was this identification of the living nation with its anonymous but glorified fallen soldiers that provided a means to come to terms with the trauma of war, and normalized the haunting images of the dead returning from the endless cemeteries in which they now resided. For the longing for the return of one's own fallen from the dead was mixed with the desire swiftly to return to normality, to bury the dead and go on with life. The unknown soldier thus made possible both a focus on the suffering and sacrifice of the individual, and a process of distancing oneself from the particular fallen of one's family or community. The final death of the fallen was facilitated by this familiar yet unknown figure safely and irrevocably locked in a national sepulcher.

Significantly, Germany did not erect a tomb for the Unknown Soldier. Unlike France and Britain, Germany could not come to terms with the trauma of war through a symbol of final and irredeemable death.[10] Rather, many Germans hoped to overcome defeat by continuing the struggle; for this purpose, the dead could not be locked away, since they still had a role to play in urging the living to win back victory. Germany's unburied, unknown soldiers thus continued to roam the old battlefields and to march in the cities, reminding those who might have forgotten that their mission must still be accomplished. In France, the specter of the fallen warned the living from ever repeating such slaughter. In Germany, mourning was increasingly oriented to the future, and reconciliation with loss was unacceptable because of the refusal to come to terms with the past. Ultimately, it was one of those surviving unknown soldiers who would claim to embody the nation, and persuade increasing numbers of Germans that he indeed personified its fate and would mold its future.

Adolf Hitler was one of millions of unknown veterans who, unlike their fallen comrades, had urgent material and psychological needs. Glorifying the dead came more cheaply than caring for the innumerable physically and mentally mutilated survivors of the front. The massive presence of former soldiers, who often felt abandoned and misunderstood by their civilian environment, left a deep mark on interwar Europe. The difficulties of social and economic reintegration in nations still reeling from the human and material costs of total war stimulated the urge among the veterans to realize those vague but powerful aspirations they had forged at the front, to translate their discovery of comradeship and sacrifice to the realities of life after the disaster. The story of post-1918 Europe is thus largely about the cleavage between those who "had been there" and those who had not; it is a tale of rage and frustration, resentment and disillusionment.[11]

If most soldiers returning from the war wanted to pick up their lives where they had left them before they marched off to the trenches, postwar Europe had neither the resources nor the skills to deal with the needs of men exposed to the horrors of sustained industrial warfare.[12] Hence the tendency of veterans to organize their own associations, which provided them with psychological support and served as pressure groups on governments to meet the economic and political demands of those whose sacrifice for the nation endowed them with a moral weight well beyond their numbers. In contradistinction to the state's glorification of the dead, the veterans' associations glorified their war experience, which they represented both as incommunicable and as having a profound moral import for postwar society. [13]

Nevertheless, while defeated Germany ultimately came to celebrate war as an occasion for individual and collective glory, in victorious France its perception as a site of personal and national suffering only intensified. German veterans conceptualized the front as an opportunity to surpass the individual and discover the community of battle and fate *through* common sacrifice. French veterans insisted on their duty to fight *against* war following their exposure to its inhumanity. Thus the aftermath of World War I produced two kinds of (imagined) communities, whose common experience was articulated very differently, and whose glorification in their respective countries lent a great deal of weight to national perceptions of destruction. The French *community of suffering* was unified by common pain and sorrow, bound together by horror, determined to prevent such wars from ever happening again. The German *battle community* was united through sacrifice and devotion to a common cause, the comradeship of warriors, and the quest to extend its newly found values to postwar civilian society. Both creatures of war, the *community of suffering* envisioned a future without international conflict, whereas the *battle community* perceived the front as a model for posterity. For both the present was a battleground between past trauma and future hopes, but they pulled in opposite directions. Imbued with a missionary zeal, the one fought for prevention; the other, for reenactment. For the one, war was hell; for the other, it was destiny. For the French, the front equaled senseless destruction; for the Germans, the destruction of others would bring about national resurrection. The *community of suffering* glorified endurance and survival; the *battle community* ennobled comradeship and death.

Germany experienced the aftermath of World War I as an unmitigated disaster. And yet, from the midst of despair, a new notion of German glory and greatness began to emerge. Central to this process were not only the veterans' associations but also and more important the *Freikorps* formations. These paramilitary units that roamed Germany in the early years of the postwar period were composed both of former soldiers and of youngsters who had just missed service in the war. Engaged in vicious fighting against Communists at home and foreigners along the former Reich's eastern frontiers, these heirs of a long freebooter tradition attributed their despair to peacetime conditions rather than to the suffering of war, and perceived their identity as meaningful only within the context of the

Kampfgemeinschaft. On one level, this battle community was constituted only of one's direct comrades in the unit; but on a more abstract level, it included all those multitudes of men who had shared the same frontline experience and came to see the world, and their role in it, through the same prism of struggle, sacrifice, and destruction. Moreover, the *Kampfgemeinschaft* soon came to be defined in a manner that excluded from it veterans with different political views or those considered not "truly" German—namely the Jews. Conversely, the battle community increasingly included men who shared the front experience only vicariously by sheer force of conviction and imagination, racial qualities and ideological conformity. The postwar conceptualization of the *Kampfgemeinschaft* therefore became the core of the *Volksgemeinschaft,* the national, or "racial," community whose front lines were populated by the battle-hardened political soldiers of the extreme right and the fledgling Nazi movement. For these men, Germany's fields of glory led from the trenches of 1914–18 to the struggle of the Volk for its future greatness, to be waged with equal devotion and comradeship, sacrifice and ruthlessness.[14]

The notion of destruction was of course central to this worldview in its many variations. Shared in the 1920s by a relatively small but growing minority, by the 1930s it was widely disseminated as a central tenet of the Nazi regime. The terrible devastation of World War I, while it justified calls for retribution, was also perceived as clearing the way for a better future, not least because it made for the emergence of a "new man" out of the debris of the past, a warrior much better equipped for the tasks of a new Germany.[15] Intoxicated by the reality and aesthetics of destruction, these men saw war as a sure instrument to sweep away the weak and the degenerate, making room for the brave and the pure. The trenches had taught humanity that life is war, and war is life; that violence brings out the best qualities in man and that only its ruthless application propels one to the higher spheres of existence. The fact that many Germans were just as terrified and disgusted by the carnage of the war as other Europeans only served to enhance the vehemence with which such views were propagated. Moreover, this powerful undercurrent of extremism reflected a far more prevalent preoccupation with violence on both sides of the political divide, ranging from the conservatives to the Communists. Even the most explicit antiwar imagery of such artists as Otto Dix and George Grosz reveals a brutal strain, a fascination with depravity, mutilation, and inhumanity, generally absent from representations of war in France.

This is of course most evident in German World War I veteran Ernst Jünger's writings on the war, the tone and ideological import of which distinguish them from most other popular accounts of life and death in the trenches. His 1922 novel *Storm of Steel* is an acute and powerful portrayal of the emergence of the new, modern warrior from the mechanical and faceless destruction in the trenches. He does not lament his fallen comrades and feels no regret for the loss of innocence. For Jünger the individual is wholly autonomous; and it is during the war, in the midst of devastation, that he discovers his freedom, his inner strength, and "essence," and rises from the destruction whole and purified. But in Jünger's universe, World War I is only the point of departure, a necessary baptism by fire in which he acquires knowledge about himself and humanity that must then be employed by, indeed imposed on, the postwar world, as his later writings indicate.

In some respects, Jünger's new man is the embodiment of the Nazi ideal; yet his early rejection of the *Kampfgemeinschaft,* bred by his individualistic heroism and innate elitism, made him into an ambivalent and somewhat skeptical observer of the emerging *Volksgemeinschaft*'s fictions and realities. Nevertheless, Jünger relished his iconic status in Nazi imagery and rhetoric, and was in turn fascinated by the Third Reich's immense destructive energies. Indeed, his ability for detached observation of unmediated horror and his curious mix of cold reason and almost uncontrollable passion in the face of destruction was a state of mind that came to be idealized by the Wehrmacht's combat officers and even more so by the SS. Moreover, because of Jünger's fascination with naked violence and the pleasures of causing and submitting to pain, he straddles the line between nihilism, fascism, and postmodernism, articulating as he does the enormous appeal of modern industrial destruction as event and image, memory and anticipation: destruction on such a monumental scale that it fills one with awe even while being devoured by it.

As in France, Germans, too, associated traditional military glory with generals; but the circumstances of war and politics were meanwhile radically transformed. During the last two years of the war, Germany was largely controlled by Field Marshal Paul von Hindenburg and General Erich Ludendorff, whose "silent dictatorship" combined tradition and modernity.[16] Seen by the conservatives after the fall of the monarchy as an ersatz Kaiser, Hindenburg had the same predilection as Marshal Philippe Pétain to "make a gift of his person" by offering himself as Germany's savior in time of war and crisis, even if it meant returning from retirement on the brink of senility. But unlike Pétain, his paternalism was geared to conquest and expansion, not to preventing yet another slaughter. Nor was he a soldiers' general; rather, he helped launch the career of the man he derisively called the "Bohemian corporal," who personified the frontline soldier yet eventually became supreme commander of the army.

Moreover, Pétain had no Ludendorff at his side. For here was a man who was engaged in formulating the concept of total war and strove to implement it on the military, political, and economic fronts during World War I, along with such officers as General Wilhelm Groener and Colonel Max Bauer.[17] Both a relentless

technician and a political extremist, Ludendorff made up for the qualities lack-
ing in Hindenburg, behind whose stature as Prussian warlord he devised modern
warfare. It is no coincidence that Ludendorff appears again on the scene during
Hitler's Munich Beer Hall Putsch of 1923 (in which he showed more courage
than his Nazi colleagues).[18] For him, war was destiny, all-encompassing and un-
avoidable; but rather than taking the form of a mythical, chivalrous encounter, it
had to be waged by mobilizing all the energy and organizational sophistication of
the modern industrial state. Behind him was a younger generation of gifted staff
officers who emerged in the 1930s as Hitler's generals. Professional, modern in
outlook, and ruthless, these men were dedicated to making a new kind of war
that would reverse the outcome of 1914–18 and reconceptualize the relationship
between war and the state.[19] And behind them was an even younger group of
men, many of whom had missed service in the war, who became the chief or-
ganizers of the Nazi police state and the genocide of the Jews, both of which they
deemed an essential component of winning the next war.[20]

To be sure, World War I produced a whole crop of young officers in many
European countries devoted to designing a new type of modern, violent, and decisive warfare. But in Germany the notion of combining new strategies with a
total reorganization of state and society went much farther, thanks to the traditionally greater role of the army in politics and its continuing influence in the
Weimar Republic; the intellectual glorification and aestheticization of battle; the
urge to reverse the outcome of the war; and the rampant extremism and violence
of the republic's early and final years. The progression from Alfred von
Schlieffen's concept of a *Vernichtungsschlacht* (battle of annihilation) in the early
1900s to the realities of *Vernichtungskrieg* (war of extermination) in the 1940s was
neither inevitable nor entirely fortuitous.[21] The German concept of war as an exercise in total destruction emanated from a complex of ideas about the relationship between the individual and the collective, postulating the militarization of
society and the organization of the state as a tool for waging war.[22] Such ideas were
not foreign to other countries. But in the initial phases of World War II the Nazi
state employed them with unique ruthlessness. By the end of the war, however,
all major combatant nations had learned the rules of total destruction. The Third
Reich was crushed by enemies who had acquired its own methods of waging war,
and if they did not match the Nazi dedication to extermination, they could mus-
ter far greater resources of men and matériel. The devastation of Europe and the
murder of millions of citizens was testimony to the triumph of the new concept
of war.

The Nazis gave the veterans a new sense of pride in the war they had lost, and
promised those who had missed the fighting their share of glory in a future
struggle for national greatness. Much as racist and eugenicist ideas were crucial

to its ideology, Nazism must be viewed within the context of the war's traumatizing effects combined with the notion of the new man who sprouted from the trenches. All other attempts to endow the carnage of 1914–18 with a higher meaning were ultimately appropriated and put to political use by the Nazis, and no one was more adept at this than Hitler himself. For millions of Germans Hitler came to symbolize the unknown soldier of World War I. It is no coincidence that during World War II he donned a simple uniform rather than fabricating an elaborate generalissimo's costume, thereby underlining his affinity with the *Frontschweine* ("grunts") on the line. Hitler was the soldier who had come back from the dead, from anonymity and oblivion, neglect and abandonment. What men such as Field Marshal Hindenburg failed to understand was that this contemptible corporal represented for innumerable forgotten soldiers the kind of leader who knew what they had been through, spoke their language, shared their phobias and prejudices, and proved that it was possible to survive, rise to prominence, and ultimately wreak vengeance on all those foreign and domestic enemies who had brought about the inexplicable catastrophe that had deprived their sacrifice and devotion of all sense and meaning. It was the Führer who resurrected Germany's fields of glory by personifying the forgotten soldier and acting out his rage and frustration.[23]

Following Hitler's so-called seizure of power, the new German Wehrmacht began the process of binding together the old Prussian tradition represented by Hindenburg and the conservative elite; the technological, technocratic, and organizational concepts of such officers as General Erich Ludendorff and his ambitious young disciples; the veterans' ethos of the *Kampfgemeinschaft;* and Hitler's notion of the "new man," committed to the destruction of Germany's domestic and foreign, political and "biological" enemies who had allegedly stabbed Germany in the back on the brink of victory in 1918. The new leaders of the Wehrmacht had all been junior and middle-ranking officers in World War I. Devastated by the defeat, doomed to vegetate in unpromising careers in Weimar's tiny professional army, they mostly dreamed of the day of reckoning.[24] Now that their time had come, they were not about to relent. Moreover, they rapidly came to believe that as a precondition for victory they had to instill a new spirit into their fresh recruits, combining traditional patriotism with Nazi teaching, a glorification of war, and a determination to wipe out the enemy at home and abroad.[25]

The extraordinary motivation and resilience of the Wehrmacht during World War II was thus a function of its perception of war as an opportunity to rectify the errors of 1914–18 and redress the abomination of defeat. But unlike the French, who envisioned the next war as a repetition of the last, German conduct took a radically different course. For while French war plans were based on a perfectly rational—if wholly mistaken—analysis of World War I, the German tendency to take the myth of the battle community at face value contributed in no small measure to the Wehrmacht's élan.[26] And while many practical lessons from 1914–18 were applied to tactics and strategy in World War II, the emphasis on a tightly knit community of warriors, wholly dedicated to its members and to the nation, became a fundamental tenet in the organization and indoctrination of the Wehrmacht. Similarly, the prevalent belief that the army had been betrayed by the "November criminals" of 1918 introduced a unique brutality and vindictiveness to military conduct. Hitler's repeated references to himself as a front-line soldier, as well as his much-publicized obsession with annihilating real and imaginary enemies, had a tremendous influence on the motivation and ruthlessness of the troops, as manifested by their loyalty and devotion to him until very late in the war as much as by their massive participation in Germany's policies of subjugation, devastation, plunder, and extermination. For Hitler came to represent both the mythologized fathers' generation of heroic and tragic World War I warriors and the hopeless, desperate, and tough *Landser* of the Third Reich, wreaking revenge on a "world of enemies."[27]

There is an understandable reluctance to concede that German soldiers fought out of conviction, that they truly believed themselves to be part of a glorious, "world-historical" undertaking. Many prefer to view them as coerced by a dictatorial regime, united by fear of their superiors and enemies, and motivated by loyalty to their "primary group" and a sheer will to survive. All such explanations have one thing in common—they largely ignore the troops' own self-perception and understanding of their actions. For one crucial component of the reality of war was the manner in which it was perceived and interpreted by those who fought it; and the Wehrmacht's soldiers saw the world through very different eyes from our own. Our disbelief that acts of atrocity and murder, wanton destruction and ruthless plunder, could be perceived as glorious may reflect our humanistic sentiments, but it also exposes the limits of our moral universe and imagination: the troops' distorted perceptions cannot be retroactively corrected by our own.

If after World War I the reality of defeat was repressed by a great deal of talk about the community of battle, after 1945 the army's complicity in criminal actions was obscured by a rhetoric of suffering and victimhood. The conventional image that came to dominate German media and scholarship in the early postwar decades was of the simple soldier as an increasingly disillusioned victim of circumstances beyond his control, fighting a hopeless battle against unequal odds, and in no way responsible for the crimes committed "behind the army's back" by the SS. Speaking of the war as a glorious undertaking became highly unfashionable, although the fighting against the Red Army always retained a certain aura of desperate resistance to evil.[28]

Yet during the war things were very different. To be sure, not all the men who served in the Wehrmacht sympathized with the regime, and many shared the sentiment of their World War I predecessors that the ample propaganda material disseminated to their units was mere "eyewash." Yet the majority of the troops did not fight with such remarkable determination merely as cynical survivalists. Rather, as their own letters and diaries, frontline journals, and memoirs clearly indicate, they were strongly motivated by an image of battle as a site of glory precisely because it was harsh, pitiless, and deadly.[29] That their sacrifice was not given sufficient public recognition after the war embittered many of them.[30] But postwar testimonies and accounts, interviews and oral histories, public and private encounters have repeatedly demonstrated over the years that veterans still cherish their memory of the good and glorious fight and feel offended, challenged, and enraged when it is suggested that they were part of a vast criminal undertaking.[31] The longevity of this resistance to the overwhelming evidence of the Wehrmacht's crimes tells us a great deal about the efficacy of the soldiers' self-perception, their view of the enemy, and their understanding of Germany's mission in determining their conduct and molding its memory.

In trying the grasp how glory on the battlefield was conceptualized, we must understand that conventional distinctions between heroism and comradeship, and what we would normally describe as atrocities and war crimes, were not perceived in the same manner at the time (although individual soldiers occasionally did make such distinctions). Especially during the war against the Soviet Union, and in the latter phases of the war also in other parts of Europe, soldiers were told and in most cases seem to have believed that fighting enemy troops was as honorable as murdering political commissars, massacring Jews, wiping out villages in acts of collective punishment, and shooting outright or starving to death prisoners of war.[32] As early as 1939 the Wehrmacht's leadership insisted that the honor of the German officer depended on his firm National Socialist bearing *(Haltung),* and as of summer 1941 the implications of this were manifested on a vast scale. By the end of the war, Germany's fields of glory were strewn with the corpses of its political and "biological" enemies. Repeatedly exhorted to remember that this was a war of ideologies aimed at exterminating Judeo-Bolshevism, and that taking pity on seemingly innocent victims was tantamount to betraying the Volk, the troops came to view their criminal actions as the very essence of military glory, as exacting a just and necessary retribution for past defeats and humiliations and as ensuring the final victory.

It is true that as the war wore on, anything that smacked of propaganda was viewed with suspicion by the troops. But those elements of the regime's ideology and policies that coincided with the views and prejudices internalized by the troops even before their conscription were not thought of as propaganda but rather as accurate statements about, and actions relevant to, their role and mission in the war. Hence soldiers' letters to family and friends described their activities at the front in almost identical terms to those employed by the regime's propaganda. Most revealingly, the troops' perception of the enemy as diabolical led them to ascribe their own atrocities to Bolshevik savagery and Jewish criminality, and to portray mass killings of civilians as a glorious final reckoning with foes who had been poised to inflict untold barbarities on the German Volk. While the army tried to justify its actions also with conventional arguments, citing security concerns, partisan activity, and civilian resistance, one is struck by the extent to which soldiers expressed pride and satisfaction in finally being able to destroy their enemies, be they soldiers, prisoners, civilians—or, provoking the greatest glee—Jewish men, women, and children. It was at this point that massacre and glory became synonymous.[33]

In the case of the SS, the equivalence of genocide and glory was the very core of its identity. The motto of the Black Corps was SS-man, Your Honor Is Loyalty [SS-Mann, Deine Ehre heißt Treue]. The German term *Treue,* which also means "faith," crucially linked personal honor with an unflinching devotion to Hitler's person and Weltanschauung. And since the Führer was said to have ordered the extermination of the Aryan race's enemies, perpetrating mass murder was transformed into a glorious enterprise. Heinrich Himmler was well aware of the implications of this breathtaking moral inversion. Speaking to SS leaders in October 1943, he noted that the glory of the SS consisted of its ability to carry out genocide while remaining clean and decent; the task was not merely to kill efficiently but to guard against the damage that such actions may cause to the organization's moral fiber. Hence, while genocide was an honorable undertaking, its victims threatened to pollute the SS morally even as they were being massacred. In Himmler's logic, murdering women and children was virtuous, making a personal profit from such actions despicable. Precisely because both Himmler and his audience knew that in reality organized and unauthorized robbery of the victims was an institutionalized component of the "Final Solution," Himmler's rhetoric revealed an awareness of his revolutionary reconceptualization of glory well beyond its mundane manifestations. For here was a concept whose long-term polluting effects on humanity as a whole cannot be overestimated. No amount of erasing the traces by exhuming and cremating the murdered, bulldozing the death camps, and planting forests over mass graves would purge our moral universe of this redefinition of ethics and decency.[34]

If World War I had replaced the old notion of chivalry with the sustained industrial killing of nameless soldiers, Nazi Germany invented the glorification of systematic industrial killing of civilians. By now, what bound the soldiers together more than their *Kampfgemeinschaft* and its extension in an ostensible *Volksgemeinschaft* was their awareness of belonging to a *community of murder,* attested to implicitly and explicitly both by the leadership of the Reich and by many of its citizens and soldiers. With defeat looming on the horizon, the knowledge of complicity in horrendous crimes only exacerbated fears of ultimate retribution. But alongside the bonding effects of shared guilt (accompanied by frantic attempts to waive responsibility) came the construction of genocide as a liberating, redemptive act whose centrality to the salvation of humanity need only be recognized by other nations to release the perpetrators from accusations of murder: the realization that even in defeat, Germany had purged the world of the evil that had threatened its very existence.[35] When we speak of the meaning of the Holocaust at the beginning of the twenty-first century, we must not allow our horror and outrage to obscure the fact that for those who ordered, organized, and perpetrated the killing, depravity was transformed into morality, guilt into honor, atrocity into heroism, and genocide into redemption. From this perspective, it is the transformation of perceptions and values underlying the glorification of genocide that we should fear as we enter the new century.[36]

NOTES

A longer version of this chapter was published in Omer Bartov, *Mirrors of Destruction: War, Genocide, and Modern Identity* (New York: Oxford University Press, 2000). Copyright 2000 by Oxford University Press, Inc. Used by permission of Oxford University Press, Inc.

1. W. J. Mommsen, *Imperial Germany, 1867–1918: Politics, Culture, and Society in an Authoritarian State* (London: Arnold, 1995), 205–16; J.-J. Becker, *1914: Comment les Français sont entrés dans la guerre* (Paris: Presses de la Fondation Nationale des Science Politiques, 1977), 269–363; P. Fussell, *The Great War and Modern Memory* (New York: Oxford University Press, 1975), 18–29; R. Wohl, *The Generation of 1914* (Cambridge, Mass.: Harvard University Press, 1979).

2. M. Eksteins, *Rites of Spring: The Great War and the Birth of the Modern Age* (New York: Anchor Books, 1989), 300–331; J.-J. Becker, *The Great War and the French People* (Leamington Spa, England: Berg, 1985), 29–63; S. Hynes, *A War Imagined: The First World War and English Culture* (New York: Atheneum, 1991), 3–56. For pre-1914 visions of destruction, see D. Pick, *War Machine: The Rationalisation of Slaughter in the Modern Age* (New Haven, Conn.: Yale University Press, 1993).

3. J.-J. Becker et al., eds., *Guerre et cultures, 1914–1918* (Paris: Armand Colin, 1994), 133–91; G. Hirschfeld et al., eds., *Keiner fühlt sich hier mehr als Mensch . . .: Erlebnis und Wirkung des Ersten Weltkriegs* (Essen: Klartext Verlag, 1993); A. Becker, *Oubliés de la grande guerre. Humanitaire et culture de guerre, 1914–1918: Populations occupées, déportés civils, prisonniers de guerre* (Paris: Noêsis, 1998).

4. S. Audoin-Rouzeau, *Men at War, 1914–1918: National Sentiment and Trench Journalism in France during the First World War* (Providence, R.I.: Berg, 1992); F. Coetzee and M. Shevin-Coetzee, eds., *Authority, Identity and the Social History of the Great War* (Providence, R.I.: Bergholm Books, 1995), pt. 3. A good example of the British view is R. Graves' 1929 autobiography, *Good-bye to All That.*

5. R. W. Whalen, *Bitter Wounds: German Victims of the Great War, 1914–1939* (Ithaca, N.Y.: Cornell University Books, 1984); A. Prost, *In the Wake of War: "Les Anciens Combattants" and French Society, 1914–1939* (Providence, R.I.: Berg, 1992); Deborah Cohen, *The War Came Home: Disabled Veterans in Britain and Germany, 1914–1939* (Berkeley and Los Angeles: University of California Press, 2001).

6. R. Bessel, *Germany after the First World War* (Oxford: Clarendon Press, 1993), 254–84; N. Ingram, *The Politics of Dissent: Pacifism in France 1919–1939* (Oxford: Clarendon Press, 1991).

7. G. L. Mosse, *Fallen Soldiers: Reshaping the Memory of the World Wars* (New York: Oxford University Press, 1990); A. King, *Memorials of the Great War in Britain: The Symbolism and Politics of Remembrance* (Oxford: Berg, 1998); A. Becker, ed., *Les monuments aux morts: Mémoire de la Grande Guerre* (Paris: Éditions Errance, 1988).

8. J. Winter, *Sites of Memory, Sites of Mourning: The Great War in European Cultural History* (Cambridge: Cambridge University Press, 1995); D. W. Lloyd, *Battlefield Tourism: Pilgrimage and the Commemoration of the Great War in Britain, Australia and Canada, 1919–1939* (Oxford: Berg, 1998); A. Becker, "From Death to Memory: The National Ossuaries in France after the Great War," *History & Memory* 5, no. 2 (fall-winter 1993): 32–49.

9. K. S. Inglis, "Entombing Unknown Soldiers: From London to Paris to Baghdad," *History & Memory* 5, no. 2 (1993): 7–31.

10. V. Ackermann, "La vision allemande du Soldat inconnu: débats politiques, réflexion philosophique et artistique," in Becker, *Guerre et cultures*, 385–96 and more generally, part 4 of that book.

11. For two very different reactions, see A. Becker, *War and Faith: The Religious Imagination in France, 1914–1930* (New York: Berg, 1998); K. Theweleit, *Male Fantasies*, 2 vols. (Cambridge: Polity Press, 1987–89).

12. On how the war reshaped views of education, rape, gender, women's consciousness, violence, and the enemy, see S. Audoin-Rouzeau, *La guerre des enfants, 1914–1918: Essai d'histoire culturelle* (Paris: Armand Colin, 1993); Audoin-Rouzeau, *L'enfant de l'ennemi, 1914–1918: Viol, avortement, infanticide pendant la Grande Guerre* (Paris: Aubier, 1995); M. R. Higonnet et al., eds., *Behind the Lines: Gender and the Two World Wars* (New Haven, Conn.: Yale University Press, 1987), chaps. 4–5, 7–9, 14; M. L. Roberts, *Civilization without Sexes: Reconstructing Gender in Postwar France, 1917–1927* (Chicago: University of Chicago Press, 1994); C. M. Tylee, *The Great War and Women's Consciousness: Images of Militarism and Womanhood in Women's Writings, 1914–64* (Iowa City: University of Iowa Press, 1990); T. Nevin, *Ernst Jünger and Germany: Into the Abyss, 1914–1945* (Durham, N.C.: Duke University Press, 1996), chap. 2; and M. Jeismann, *Das Vaterland der Feinde: Studien zum nationalen Feindbegriff und Selbstverständnis in Deutschland und Frankreich, 1972–1918* (Stuttgart: Klett-Cotta, 1992), pt. 3.

13. B. Crim, "From *Frontgemeinschaft* to *Volsgemeinschaft:* The Role of Antisemitism within the German Military and Veteran Community, 1916–1938," (Ph.D. diss., Rutgers University, 2002), and G. A. Caplan, "Wicked Sons, German Heroes: Jewish Soldiers, Veterans, and Memories of World War I in Germany" (Ph.D. diss., Georgetown University, 2001), supersede older works such as V. R. Berghahn, *Der Stahlhelm, Bund der Frontsoldaten, 1918–1935* (Düsseldorf: Droste, 1966), and J. M. Diehl, *Paramilitary Politics in Weimar Germany* (Bloomington: Indiana University Press, 1977), and are among the first studies on Jewish veterans. For France, the major work is A. Prost, *Les Anciens Combattants et la société française, 1914–1939,* 3 vols. (Paris: Presses de la Fondation Nationale des Sciences Politiques, 1977).

14. R. Bessel, "Militarismus im innenpolitischen Leben der Weimarer Republik: Von den Freikorps zur SA," in *Militär und Militarismus in der Weimarer Republik,* ed. K.-J. Müller and E. Opitz (Düsseldorf: Droste, 1978), 193–222; H. J. Gordon Jr., *The Reichswehr and the German Republic, 1919–1926* (Princeton, N.J.: Princeton University Press, 1957); R. G. L. Waite, *Vanguard of Nazism: The Free Corps Movement in Postwar Germany, 1918–1923* (Cambridge, Mass.: Harvard University Press, 1952); H. Schulze, *Freikorps und Republik, 1918–1920* (Boppard am Rhine: H. Boldt, 1969).

15. B. Hüppauf, "Langemarck, Verdun and the Myth of a New Man in Germany after the First World War," *War and Society* 6, no. 2 (1988): 70–103.

16. M. Kitchen, *The Silent Dictatorship: The Politics of the German High Command under Hindenburg and Ludendorff, 1916–1918* (New York: Holmes & Meier, 1976).

17. G. D. Feldman, *Army, Industry and Labor in Germany, 1914–1918*, 2d ed. (Providence, R.I: Berg, 1992). On the origins of total war, see S. Förster and J. Nagler, eds., *On the Road to Total War: The American Civil War and the German Wars of Unification, 1861–1871* (Cambridge: Cambridge University Press, 1997); and Manfred F. Boemecke, Roger Chickering, and Stig Förster, eds., *Anticipating Total War: The German and American Experiences, 1871–1914* (Cambridge: Cambridge University Press, 1999).

18. A. Bullock, *Hitler: A Study in Tyranny*, rev. ed. (New York: Harper and Row, 1964), 112.

19. W. Deist, *Militär, Staat und Gesellschaft: Studien zur preussisch-deutschen Militärgeschichte* (Munich: R. Oldenbourg, 1991), 83–163, 293–338, 385–429; Deist, *The Wehrmacht and German Rearmament* (London: Macmillan, 1981); K.-J. Müller, *The Army, Politics and Society in Germany, 1933–45: Studies in the Army's Relation to Nazism* (New York: St. Martin's Press, 1987); M. Geyer, "Professionals and Junkers: German Rearmament and Politics in the Weimar Republic," in *Social Change and Political Development in the Weimar Republic,* ed. R. Bessel and E. J. Feuchtwanger (London: Croom Helm, 1981), 77–133; Geyer, "The Militarization of Europe, 1914–1945," in *The Militarization of the Western World,* ed. J. R. Gillis (New Brunswick, N.J.: Rutgers University Press, 1989), 65–102.

20. U. Herbert, *Best: Biographische Studien über Radikalismus, Weltanschauung und Vernunft, 1903–1989* (Bonn: J. H. W. Dietz, 1996), pts. 1–2; L. Hachmeister, *Der Gegnerforscher: Die Karriere des SS-Führers Franz Alfred Six* (Munich: Beck, 1998), chaps. 1–7; M. Wildt, *Das Führungskorps des Reichssicherheitshauptamtes. Versuch einer Kollektivbiographie* (manuscript, Hamburg, 1996).

21. P. Paret, ed., *Makers of Modern Strategy: From Machiavelli to the Nuclear Age* (Princeton, N.J.: Princeton University Press, 1986), pt. 4; J. L. Wallach, *The Dogma of the Battle of Annihilation: The Theories of Clausewitz and Schlieffen and Their Impact on the German Conduct of Two World Wars* (Westport, Conn.: Greenwood Press, 1986); Wallach, *Kriegstheorien: Ihre Entwicklung im 19. und 20. Jahrhundert* (Frankfurt am Main: Bernard and Graefe, 1972); M. Geyer, "Insurrectionary Warfare: The German Debate about a *Levée en Masse* in October 1918," *Journal of Modern History* 73, no. 3 (September 2001): 459–527; A. Gat, *A History of Military Thought: From the Enlightenment to the Cold War* (Oxford: Oxford University Press, 2001).

22. On the controversies surrounding the German concept of Blitzkrieg and the transition to total war, see T. Mason, *Nazism, Fascism and the Working Class,* ed. J. Caplan (Cambridge: Cambridge University Press, 1995), chaps. 1, 4, 9; R. J. Overy, *War and the Economy in the Third Reich* (Oxford: Clarendon Press, 1994), chaps 6–8, 9; and O. Bartov, "From *Blitzkrieg* to Total War: Controversial Links between Image and Reality," in *Stalinism and Nazism: Dictatorships in Comparison,* ed. I. Kershaw and M. Lewin (Cambridge: Cambridge University Press, 1997): pp. 158–84. See also *Germany and the Second World War,* ed. Militärgeschichtliches Forschungsamt, vol. 1, *The Build-up of German Aggression* (New York: Oxford University Press, 1990), pts. 2–3.

23. For Hitler's popular appeal, see I. Kershaw, *The "Hitler Myth": Image and Reality in the Third Reich* (Oxford: Oxford University Press, 1987); for his image among the Wehrmacht's soldiers and their internalization of Nazi ideas, see O. Bartov, *Hitler's Army: Soldiers, Nazis, and War in the Third Reich* (New York: Oxford University Press, 1991), chap. 4. And see now the definitive biography, I. Kershaw, *Hitler,* 2 vols. (New York: W. W. Norton, 1999–2000).

24. F. L. Carsten, *The Reichswehr in Politics, 1918–1933,* 2d ed. (Berkeley and Los Angeles: University of California Press, 1973); J. Wheeler-Bennett, *The Nemesis of Power: The German Army in Politics, 1918–1945,* 2d ed. (London: Macmillan, 1980), pt. 1.

25. J. Förster, "Operation Barbarossa as a War of Conquest and Annihilation," in *Germany and the Second World War,* ed. Militärgeschichtliches Forschungsamt, vol. 4, *The Attack on the Soviet Union* (Oxford: Oxford University Press, 1998), pp. 513–21; Förster, "The German Army and

the Ideological War against the Soviet Union," in *The Policies of Genocide: Jews and Soviet Prisoners of War in Nazi Germany,* ed. Gerhard Hirschfeld (London: Allen & Unwin, 1986), 15–29; M. Messerschmidt, *Die Wehrmacht im NS-Staat: Zeit der Indoktrination* (Hamburg: R. V. Decker, 1969); O. Bartov, *The Eastern Front, 1941–45: German Troops and the Barbarisation of Warfare* (London: Macmillan, 1985), 68–105; K.-J. Müller, *General Ludwig Beck: Studien und Dokumente zur politisch-militärischen Vorstellungswelt und Tätigkeit des Generalstabschefs des deutschen Heeres 1933–1938* (Boppard am Rhein: H. Boldt, 1980).

26. J. M. Hughes, *To the Maginot Line: The Politics of French Military Preparation in the 1920's* (Cambridge, Mass.: Harvard University Press, 1971); R. A. Doughty, *The Seeds of Disaster: The Development of French Army Doctrine, 1919–1939* (Hamden, Conn.: Archon Books, 1985); E. Kier, *Imagining War: French and British Military Doctrine between the Wars* (Princeton, N.J.: Princeton University Press, 1997), 39–88.

27. Apart from Bartov, *Hitler's Army,* see T. Schulte, *The German Army and Nazi Policies in Occupied Russia* (Oxford: Berg, 1989), 1–27, 211–76; S. G. Fritz, *Frontsoldaten: The German Soldier in World War II* (Lexington: University Press of Kentucky, 1995); and H. Heer and K. Naumann, eds., *War of Extermination: The German Military in World War II, 1941–1944* (New York: Berghahn Books, 2000).

28. See R. G. Moeller, "Remembering the War in a Nation of Victims: West German Pasts in the 1950s," in *The Miracle Years: A Cultural History of West Germany, 1949–1968,* ed. H. Schissler (Princeton, N.J.: Princeton University Press, 2001), 83–109; and "Schnappschüsse," *Mittelweg 36,* no. 5 (February-March 1996): 1–10, for examples of early postwar West German magazine-cover illustrations depicting soldiers as tough heroes. For changing models of masculinity, see F. Biess, "Survivors of Totalitarianism: Returning POWs and the Reconstruction of Masculine Citizenship in West Germany, 1945–1955," in Schissler, *The Miracle Years,* 57–82; and U. G. Poiger, "Rock 'n' Roll, Female Sexuality, and the Cold War Battle over German Identities," in *West Germany under Construction: Politics, Society, and Culture in the Adenauer Era,* ed. R. G. Moeller (Ann Arbor.: University of Michigan Press, 1997), 373–441. For a summary of the historiography, see O. Bartov, "German Soldiers and the Holocaust: Historiography, Research and Implications," *History & Memory 9,* no. 1/2 (fall 1997): 162–88.

29. See, e.g., such collections of letters as O. Buchbender and R. Sterz, eds., *Das andere Gesicht des Krieges: Deutsche Feldpostbriefe, 1919–1945* (Munich: C. H. Beck, 1982); and H. Fuchs Richardson, ed., *Sieg Heil! War Letters of Tank Gunner Karl Fuchs, 1937–1941* (Hamden, Conn.: Archon Books, 1987). Further in R-D. Müller and H-.E. Volkmann, eds., *Die Wehrmacht: Mythos und Realiät* (Munich: Oldenbourg, 1999), pts. 5–6.

30. On the integration of veterans into West German society, see J. M. Diehl, *The Thanks of the Fatherland: German Veterans after the Second World War* (Chapel Hill: University of North Carolina Press, 1993); on the memory of the war and the return of prisoners of war, see R. Moeller, *War Stories: The Search for a Usable Past in the Federal Republic of Germany* (Berkeley and Los Angeles: University of California Press, 2001); and F. Biess, "Soldiers into Citizens: The Return of the POWs to East and West Germany, 1945–1955," Ph.D. diss., Brown University, 1999.

31. K. Naumann, *Der Krieg als Text: Das Jahr 1945 im Kulturellen Gedächtnis der Presse* (Hamburg: Hamburger Edition, 1998). On the recent controversy over the exhibition Crimes of the Wehrmacht, 1941–1944 and its larger historical context, see O. Bartov, A. Grossmann, and M. Nolan, eds., *The Crimes of War: Guilt and Denial in the Twentieth Century* (New York: New Press, 2002); for a catalogue of the exhibition, see Hamburg Institute for Social Research, ed., *The German Army and Genocide: Crimes against War Prisoners, Jews, and Other Civilians, 1939–1944* (New York: New Press, 1999).

32. C. Streit, *Keine Kameraden: Die Wehrmacht und die sowjetischen Kriegsgefangenen 1941–1945,* 2d ed. (Bonn: Verlag J. H. W. Dietz Nachf., 1991).

33. Bartov, *Hitler's Army,* chap. 4; Bartov, *Eastern Front,* chap. 3; W. Manoschek, ed., *"Es gibt nur eines für das Judentum: Vernichtung": Das Judenbild in deutschen Soldatenbriefen 1939–1944* (Hamburg: Hamburger Edition, 1995); K. Latzel, *Deutsche Soldaten—nationalsozialistischer Krieg? Kriegserlebnis—Kriegserfahrung 1939–1945* (Paderborn: Ferdinand Schöninyh, 1998).

34. Extracts from Himmler's Posen speeches to SS leaders on October 4, 1943, and to a meeting of generals in Sonthofen on May 5, 1944, can be found in J. Noakes and G. Pridham, eds., *Nazism 1919–1945: A Documentary Reader,* vol. 3 (Exeter: University of Exeter Press, 1988), 1199–1200.

35. For one of numerous examples of anticipation of revenge for atrocity, see E. Klee et al., eds., *"The Good Old Days": The Holocaust as Seen by Its Perpetrators and Bystanders* (New York: Free Press, 1991), 38–43. A soldier from a motorized column who watched a massacre of Jews in Lithuania wrote: "I can only say that the mass shootings in Poneriai were quite horrific. At the time I said: 'May God grant us victory because if they get their revenge, we're in for a hard time'" (43). And see reproduction of Hitler's political testament in G. Fleming, *Hitler and the Final Solution* (Berkeley and Los Angeles: University of California Press, 1984), pp. 92–93; English translation in R. Hilberg, *The Destruction of the European Jews,* rev. ed. (New York: Holmes & Meier, 1985), 3:989.

36. This observation has gained added poignancy following the attacks of September 11, 2001, which seem in retrospect to have signaled the beginning of the twenty-first century with mass murder in the name of Islamic liberation from oppression and redemption through martyrdom.

Seven

STALINGRAD, HIROSHIMA, AUSCHWITZ: THE FADING OF THE THERAPEUTIC APPROACH

Frank Trommler

When Alexander and Margarete Mitscherlich, as practicing psychoanalysts, articulated their misgivings about the indifference of Germans towards the victims of National Socialism, they analyzed this phenomenon as an "inability to mourn," a phrase that has become commonplace. The centrality of this phrase to the discourse on German repression of guilt is closely linked to the general assumption about psychoanalysis and its focus on a hidden past. Speaking about the "inability to mourn" provided expert language in a terrain in which moral grandstanding, evasiveness, public subterfuge, and private guilt feelings intertwined. In a country that looked unfavorably upon psychoanalysis, the acceptance of this language represented a breakthrough of sorts—even if the diagnosis itself was hardly delivered according to psychoanalytic standard practices. As Tilman Moser, a student of the Mitscherlichs', concluded in a recent critical reevaluation of the book *The Inability to Mourn,*[1] the authors' approach turned out to be "a mixture of analytic-cum-therapeutic, political and pedagogical attitudes." Moser suggested that "this was largely inappropriate to the task of identifying the actual psychic condition of the 'generation of culprits' and of encouraging self-recognition and a disposition for change."[2] In other words, the Mitscherlichs, lashing out against the moral failures of Germans, vented their frustrations rather than providing room for understanding and therapy.

Reflecting on the causes and effects of therapeutic language has its problems when it involves a country that a few decades earlier had held the world in daily suspense with the bombastic rhetoric and heinous politics of its Führer. In fact, for a long time such a reflection seemed out of proportion with the needs for reorganizing and policing the Germans, punishing the Nazi perpetrators, preventing a return of nationalism, and initiating democratic reconstruction. Even the language of moral reconstruction that gained currency after 1945 and determined the proclamations of public and government officials after the founding of the Federal Republic rarely included psychological terms. This language made references to the terrible atrocities committed in the German name and included the word *guilt,* but seldom did it invite the population to confront the reality of these atrocities and engage in the clarification of specific guilt. The disconnect with the work of German psychologists and psychotherapists—a profession hardly willing to shed the tainted cloak of collaboration in the Third Reich[3]—was glaringly obvious. The term *collective silence,*[4] broadly used for this period, indicates the "psychic numbing" (Jay Lifton) that can be found on all sides after a major catastrophe, but also a willful cover-up of personal and collective responsibilities for the crimes of the Nazi regime.

ENCODING THE TOPIC OF THE PERSECUTION OF THE JEWS

When the persecution of the Jews, after a short period of frank discussion in 1945–47, was publicly debated, it occurred mostly in the language of political negotiations, as in the cases of financial restitution to survivors under the telling term *Wiedergutmachung* and the passing in 1952 of the Luxembourg Agreement, in which the Federal Republic agreed to pay compensation to the state of Israel.[5] The encoding of the topic in legal language, for which the Nuremberg Trials set the tone with the concept of crimes against humanity, gained momentum in the late 1950s, when the first major trials against concentration camp guards were prepared, culminating in the Auschwitz Trial in Frankfurt in 1963–65. The legal language reigned supreme as a public code for approaching Auschwitz for at least two decades; it was overwhelmingly beholden to the thinking of the perpetrators, their intentions or often indifference, their bureaucratic mindset and banality which Hannah Arendt so shockingly revealed in her report, *Eichmann in Jerusalem,* in 1963. The linguistic cleansing of Nazi language that Dolf Sternberger, Gerhard Storz, and W. E. Süskind undertook in the widely read and imitated articles compiled under the title *Aus dem Wörterbuch des Unmenschen* (1957) illuminated the extent to which the Nazi *Unmensch* was still present. The series is, however, equally telling in the way it circumvents the harsh realities of persecution and death that many of these words signified before 1945.

Newly emerging writers like Heinrich Böll, Siegfried Lenz, or Alfred Andersch thematized the cleansing of the language. And yet in their efforts to arrive at a message of decency and remembrance they rarely left the confines of the existing public code of moral intentions. Their heroes were meant to symbolize the spirit of decency; their stories were meant to mirror a collective experience rather than to challenge it. The "taboo against aggressiveness and criticism,"[6] against polemic and combative discourse which characterized all cultural and aesthetic ventures—except those directed against Communism—represented a kind of collective convalescence. Its flipside was a *Berührungsangst,* a fear to touch on the facts of mass killings, of the elimination of the Jews from everyday life in the most brutal way, of living together with murderers. It might be mentioned, though, that in the 1950s these writers did not encounter many Jews in Germany who would have shared their experiences for the purpose of literary publication. The language of moral reconciliation that Andersch explored without much success in the Jewish figure of Judith in his novel, *Sansibar oder der letzte Grund* (1957), prevented the confrontation with the brutal details of Jewish existence. Even Jean Améry, the Jewish critic whose reflections on persecution and life in a concentration camp later became most influential for Andersch and other writers, spoke of twenty years of deliberate silence when he published *Jenseits von Schuld und Sühne* in 1966.[7]

In view of the many forms of silence, both on the side of the victims and that of the perpetrators, one might generate more insights by studying how much effort went into *preventing* the wrong encoding of the Jewish fate in this period. The most obvious issue on the German side is the case of anti-Semitism, which used to be the favorite code of dealing with Jews and now, though still rampant, was to be avoided at all cost.[8] How much this amounted to a conscious policy became apparent when, in 1959, the newly dedicated synagogue in Cologne was desecrated, followed by a wave of similar incidents which led to a public outcry and the commitment of schoolchildren and youth groups to clean up desecrated cemeteries. The image of German youth erasing the signs of the still-existing anti-Semitism is a telling symbol of the state of *Vergangenheitsbewälti-gung,* as the coming to terms with the Nazi past was labeled in the 1950s. Intent upon mollifying the harshness of the human cataclysm by building bridges to Jews and Israel, groups of students, educators, and journalists learned to make the turn to the younger generation itself a medium of addressing the issues of guilt and shame.[9] The language of reconciliation through youth did not unsettle the reigning paradigms, but it manifested, often in existential or religious terms, a general disclosure of guilt.[10] It took another decade before the public encoding of youth meant rebellion against the perpetuation of what was then called fascist mentalities.

I might mention another effort at preventing the wrong encoding of the Jewish fate: Theodor Adorno's famous verdict of 1949 against writing poetry after Auschwitz.[11] His was only one expression of the taboo against the aesthetic encoding of the mass killings that was widely accepted by the literary elites before Adorno's rather intimidating formulation gained broader attention in the 1960s. It is neither surprising that it was an outsider of the literary scene who broke through this taboo nor that Adorno attacked him in an open letter for choosing the wrong form of mediation. The outsider was Rolf Hochhuth, who put Auschwitz on the stage in the fifth act of his widely debated play, *The Deputy* (1963), about the failure of Pope Pius XII to protest the mass murder of Jews. Hochhuth made a point of acting out this world event with a number of stage heroes which Adorno criticized as inappropriate in the *Frankfurter Allgemeine*.[12] Only one year later, another outsider of the German literary scene, the German Jewish writer Peter Weiss, chose to present the proceedings of the Auschwitz Trial in slightly formalized language onstage. With the documentary style of *The Investigation* (1965), Weiss managed to strike a balance between aesthetization and authenticity, which made for an impressive simultaneous premiere in eighteen theaters in West and East Germany. Being experienced less as theater than a commemorative event about Auschwitz, this form of artistic encoding raised less objection and stimulated more attempts to open the topic for literary representation.

APPLYING THE THERAPEUTIC CODE TO GERMANY

The 1970s and 1980s were the decades when the separation of the public and the private dissolved; in the case of Germany, these boundaries had kept the discourse on National Socialism and Auschwitz within the confines of a collective biography. This development became the ferment for what Adorno postulated in 1967: that a change in the approach toward Auschwitz could only be expected from a "turn to the subject," since the chances to change the political and social structures were extremely slim.[13] However, although Adorno invoked the help of psychoanalysis for the study of the causes of genocidal behavior, his educational agenda revolved solely around cognition, neglecting the simultaneous noncognitive mode of articulation and expression.[14] It was this mode that increasingly mediated the encounter with Auschwitz and its memory. Applying the term *therapeutic* in this connection reflects Philip Rieff's notion of the *Triumph of the Therapeutic*[15] in the conflict between moral and aesthetic attitudes toward experience, to which Richard Sennett added important insights about the increasing dominance of the private over the public, transforming politics into a mode of therapeutic indulgence.[16] This transformation was carried out in Germany mainly by the sons and daughters of the war generation. They are in the center of what I call the therapeutic approach to the Holocaust, as the Nazi genocide against the Jews was called after the airing of the TV series *Holocaust* in 1979.[17]

The fading of this approach occurred with increasing distance to the events, leading to a new cultivation of memory. Due to the fact that a third generation after 1945 does not have any direct contact with the fateful involvement in the exclusion and persecution of Jews, the understanding of memory has changed from remembering experiences under and after Nazism, during and after the war,[18] to a mental agenda for those who do not remember. This does not make their approach to Auschwitz less serious or less a reflection of German responsibilities. On the contrary, after the unification of the two German states in 1990, memorialization of the Holocaust has been recognized as an official part of the new all-German *(gesamtdeutsch)* identity. The transition of this issue, however, from a subject of shame and evasion to an almost proudly demonstrated wound in the national body politic hardly signals the deepening of mourning. As shown by the willingness of audiences to accept the devastating charge of eliminationist anti-Semitism that Daniel Goldhagen presented in 1996/97,[19] it takes three generations to embrace collective guilt, yet it is the embrace of something outside of one's own biography.[20]

It is ironic that at a time when Freud's influence on psychiatry and intellectual and academic life steadily declined since the high-water mark in the 1950s,[21] his presence in Holocaust studies tremendously expanded. His texts "Remembering, Repeating, and Working-Through" of 1914 and "Mourning and Melancholia" of 1917 achieved nearly iconic status for the study of survivors, perpetrators, and their children. It might not be without significance that Freud's stock came to rank higher among literary scholars and cultural critics than among psychoanalysts and psychologists. The clinical work with patients requires a set of data and practices that relegates the exegesis of such texts to the level of mere exam questions, whereas the texts begin to shine in the hands of the literary scholar who operates within discourses of representation that assign to the individual both particular and symbolic value. The distinction between "working through" and "acting out" as crucial factors in coming to terms with the repressed past became an imaginative tool for the study of the representation of the Holocaust which includes personal testimonies as well as aesthetic artifacts.

Although the Mitscherlichs complained that their book, *The Inability to Mourn,* failed to awaken the Germans to a more trenchant encounter with the repressed past, their impact on the public discourse was enormous. Elevating "mourning" and "working through" to maxims of collective responsibility, they injected Freudian formulas into the national discourse that still carried weight when the psychological costs of unification were counted in 1990. Instrumentalizing the code of collective repression and working-through, an influential meeting between East and West German scholars in Berlin in 1992 left no doubt that the coming together of two Germanies would have to go through another round of working through the past. Under the title *Erinnern, Wiederholen, Durcharbeiten: Zur Psycho-Analyse deutscher Wenden,*[22] the conference volume documents the Freudian impact on the unification discourse. Omnipresent is the experience of guilt, resonating with Günter Grass's much-criticized plea against unification on account of the crimes of Auschwitz. In 1990, Grass transferred the code of repression onto the relationship between West and East Germany: "Do we want to repress now, too (being masters at repressing) how the smaller German state was weighed down, far more than is just, with the burden of a lost war?"[23] The therapeutic approach to national issues led to harsh reactions in many political quarters. While the language of the new unification could hardly be compared with that of Bismarck's unification in 1871, its permeation with therapeutic concerns made it completely incompatible and infuriated the conservative Right. These concerns still resonated in the debates about a national memorial for the victims of the Holocaust in Berlin. The return of the German government to the former capital in 1999 added urgency to this official marker of national shame and historical remembrance. The criticism that the issue of a memorial had become a compensatory measure had itself a therapeutic ring.

Foreign reactions to the developments in Germany, especially around the issue of unification, projected their own versions of the therapeutic code. They helped formulate the misgivings about Germany's uneven, often disconcerting treatment of the Holocaust in a simple language of individualization of crime, remorse, and rehabilitation. In the United States, earlier versions had opened the interventionist discourse on Nazi Germany toward a psychological, even psychoanalytical approach. After Germany had been personified in the crude rhetoric of World War I as the villain of civilization, the therapeutic code came into a new, more medically charged usage before and during World War II when National Socialism was referred to as a self-inflicted infection and Richard Brickner's study, *Is Germany Incurable?* (1943), initiated numerous public discussions. Brickner asserted that Germany's paranoia "is not used here as an epithet, but as a responsible medical diagnosis."[24] Pondering the "German Enigma,"[25] scholars like Erich Fromm, Erik Erikson, and Kurt Lewin pursued hidden causes for the barbaric crimes in family structures, social attitudes, child rearing, and lifestyle. While the reference to mourning and working through belongs to a later phase, Freudian concepts entered the discussion of Germany as a "case" long before 1945. Though it raised the suspicion of the politicians, therapeutic strategies for the "treatment" of Germany represent a continuity by themselves, a long-standing feature of international discourse.

INSTRUMENTALIZING AUSCHWITZ
AGAINST THE NUCLEAR HOLOCAUST

Although the Mitscherlichs affected the public discourse mainly by their so-ciopsychological agenda in which Germans appear as a collective,[26] they built their arguments on the reflection of individual cases (as few as they actually in-cluded in their book). In fact, much of their frustration about the inability to mourn stemmed from their perception of the missing pressure and articulation of psychic pain *(Leidensdruck)* on the part of individuals in the country of the per-petrators. If there was a potential for therapeutic engagement with the older gen-eration in the two decades after the war, neither they nor other psychoanalysts seemed to have found the key. Later observers had legitimate doubts whether the German members of the profession would have been adequately equipped to handle these cases.[27]

The most predisposed group of patients belonged to the generation that followed the war generation. In her study, *Nationalsozialismus in der "zweiten Gen-eration"* (1989), Anita Eckstaedt has documented the extent to which the psy-chological dependencies on National Socialism have afflicted the "second gen-eration." A more comprehensive study would have to account for the various constellations in which memories of and references to the persecution of Jews reappear in reports about childhood and family by members of this generation, often combined with an overuse of the term *trauma.*[28] This terrain is much less researched than the psychological recovery of the second generation of Holo-caust survivors.[29] Within the German context, the discussion tends to lead to questions about the usefulness of psychoanalysis and psychotherapy or, more of-ten, to debates about the generational afflictions and upheavals which have pro-duced an uneasy transfer between individual and collective arguments. It is in this connection that the reference to Auschwitz—the Holocaust—became a catalyst for expressing special moral obligations that neither the language of fam-ily histories nor that of war memories evoked. Associated with the experience of victimization and horror, Auschwitz produced emotional scenarios which, with the appropriate stimulation from present concerns, were acted out in the public arena.

What happened in the late 1970s and early 1980s resembles the slow focus-ing of a camera on an object that had been known but not clearly seen in its threatening details.[30] The breakthrough came with the American TV series *Holo-caust,* which was aired in Germany in 1979 and provoked a tremendous reaction, especially among younger people.[31] The series appeared at the end of a decade that had seen the denouements and emotional voids caused by frustrated attempts at social change, including a challenge from the side of committed terrorists. Its reflection in the 1977 film *Deutschland im Herbst* (Germany in autumn) exposed the mood of hysteria and fear that penetrated everyday life in West Germany. When Michael Rutschky, a cultural critic, defined the emotional voids as *Erfahrungshunger,* a craving for experience and emotional immersion, he pointed to the fact that many of the rebels of 1968 had previously engaged in the generational accusation of their parents as Nazis or collaborators.[32]

The harrowing story of the Jewish middle-class family Weiss in the TV series *Holocaust* provided an opportunity to distinguish, sympathize, and identify with the individual victims of Nazi society, the structures of which had continued to shape family life after 1945. Only the publication of the *Diary of Anne Frank* had given a similar reference for a personal engagement with the issue of the persecution of Jews. But unlike in the 1950s, when the story of the victim Anne Frank lacked a projective dimension for personal application, the TV series produced a sense of affiliation with the victims which a sizable segment of the second generation, clued into the language of terror and pain, acted out, most dramatically toward the rapidly escalating anxieties vis-à-vis the nuclear threats in the early 1980s.[33]

As a symbol for the barbarism that bourgeois society had allowed to happen, Auschwitz was painted on a large canvas together with other symbols of capitalist inhumanity, most prominently the Vietnam War and the imperialistic exploitation of the Third World, and increasingly, awed by the nuclear confrontation of the superpowers in the early 1980s, with Hiroshima and the dangers of a nuclear Holocaust, as it was called. The fact that the psychological fallout from the renewed escalation of the Cold War was particularly heavy among Germans—both in the West and the East—drew international attention but seldom led to a deeper exploration of the psychological predicament for the apocalyptic susceptibility.[34] The protest movement against NATO's double-track decision to station intermediate-range missiles on German territory engaged in a campaign of nuclear anxiety and victimhood that surpassed all fear tactics of the peace movement in other countries. Accusing Reagan's America of triggering a new phase of superpower confrontation, German protesters—about three hundred thousand at a rally in Bonn in 1981—conjured Germany as the sure victim of the nuclear deterrents on both sides. In both German states, they elicited an unusually broad response to their appeal to hidden fears of catastrophe and destruction, a response which, in its intense identification with the victimization by the atomic bomb—Hiroshima—reflected the urge to measure up to another victimization that had taken place much closer to home. The rather self-righteous buildup of victimhood in the early 1980s—"we are more the victims than others because we live at the front line of the nuclear Holocaust" was one of the sayings—seems to betray the intensity with which a generation that felt trapped by the devastating legacy of the war generation was working through unsettled guilt feelings. Hiroshima and, after 1986, Chernobyl, provided the emotional catalysts for reliving the victimhood of Jews in an identification that was to provide both absolution and a new self-consciousness, even self-esteem in the universal world of victimhood. The demonstrators of the massive campaign against building the Runway west at the Frankfurt Airport are reported to have shouted toward the police: "The Jews were gassed in the gas chambers, we in the street."[35]

It would take more than a short essay to sort out the different components of this mixture of aggression and projected victimhood, which also contained traces of anti-Semitism. A whole chapter would have to be devoted to the aggressive stance of the German—and European—Left against Israel in the 1970s.[36] The public use of Auschwitz for the politics of Angst in the escalating nuclear confrontation after 1980 was a reflection of deeper psychological struggles that created a sense of urgency and foreboding. Without its emotional drama neither the Bitburg episode[37] nor President Richard von Weizsäcker's plea at the fortieth anniversary of the end of World War II in 1985[38] would have become such landmarks in the official efforts to come to terms with the Nazi past. When, shortly thereafter, the historians began their dispute (the *Historikerstreit*) about "normalizing" German history—by contextualizing Auschwitz with other genocides and mass terror—they were obviously less motivated by new scholarly discoveries than by the desire of conservative colleagues to encode the persecution of Jews in new, more acceptable ways. Aftershocks of the emotional earthquake of the early 1980s unsettled the German public during the Gulf War in 1991, when public opinion split over the rejection of war and the need to side with Israel against the Arab aggressor.

NO GERMAN CULTURE OF MOURNING?

Was this confused but energetic immersion into the experience of victimhood just an "acting out" in the Freudian sense, or did it advance to a "working through" as part of remembering? An acting out it was, whether in the Freudian sense or not. The difference from the repressive mood of the war generation from whom the Mitscherlichs had expected signs of mourning could not have been bigger. A whole wave of memory literature about the fathers *(Väterliteratur)* by authors like Christoph Meckel, Peter Härtling, and Ruth Rehmann in the late 1970s portrayed the moral and emotional immobilization of the war generation and left no doubts as to how much the mental code of stoic endurance through war, death, cruelty, and hardship had stifled the emotional growth of the second generation. "Even the deaths of those whom they held most dear were to be accepted without grieving," stated Michael Schneider in an incisive essay on the generational difference. Schneider asserted:

> If the generation of the fathers had manically defended itself against sorrow, melancholy, depression, and all the emotional problems which went along with it, the present generation is made up of little else. The earlier generation forced itself to "stick in there no matter what may come," first during the Third Reich and then in the subsequent period of reconstruction. The ability of their children to tolerate frustration in their political undertakings as well as their personal relationships seems to have sunk to an all-time low—they were able to hold their collective outburst of 1968 together for little more than two or three years, and they are now despairing of their own "principle of hope" when they have only just discovered it.[39]

Schneider's juxtaposition might be somewhat schematic, yet it helps locate the therapeutic code within the different generational experiences. Since the focus of this essay is on the German attitudes toward the Holocaust and not on the Freudian agenda itself, its broader perspective can help define the intergenerational dialectic. This perspective registers not only the dynamics of the emotional rebellion of the second generation but also the fact that the mental self-immobilization of the war generation is more directly affected by other psychological reactions than a mere Freudian agenda might perceive.

There can be no dispute that the main motivation for silence in the period of "psychic numbing" was the determination to suppress feelings of guilt and responsibility. More specifically, the insistence upon not having known much about the deportation of Jews, whether accurate or not, which surfaced much before 1945, reflected the strategy of trying to remain ignorant as much as possible in order to salve one's conscience.[40] But there was a factor that the Mitscherlichs seem to have unduly ignored. Although their decision to link the inability to mourn the loss of Hitler with the inability to mourn the victims of National Socialism[41] was never fully convincing, the authors seemed to have reason for this conjunction, as it supported the notion that a culture of mourning constitutes a prerequisite for remembering and working through a catastrophic loss. What they left undiscussed, however, defines an important current in German social, cultural, and emotional history since World War I: the fact that Germans were deeply drawn into a culture of mourning *before* 1945. This involvement stemmed from the lost First World War and was magnified by the Nazis and their cult of the dead, culminating in the propaganda featuring Stalingrad as the greatest sacrifice of life for the nation. This cult, devoid of psychoanalytical theory yet full of psychotherapeutic strategies and practices, became effective under war conditions, though it eventually led to the powerful realization that not only the battle for Stalingrad but the whole war lacked any redeeming qualities.

In his study of the war dead, *Fallen Soldiers: Reshaping the Memory of the World Wars,* George Mosse has shown the immense social investment in the public display of mourning everywhere in Europe, calling the war cemeteries sacred spaces of a new "civic religion."[42] Having learned to manipulate a therapeutic response to the violence they created,[43] the Nazi leadership decided to apply to the disaster in Stalingrad a cathartic corrective on the German population. Göring said at a Wehrmacht rally on January 30, 1943, when the battle of Stalingrad was practically over, "One day the history of our own times will read that 'should you come to Germany, then report that you have seen us fighting in Stalingrad as the law, the law of national safety, commanded.' . . . [I]t is ultimately a matter of indifference to the soldier whether he fights and dies in Stalingrad or Rzhev, in the deserts of Africa or the snows of Norway."[44] In his propaganda, Goebbels did his utmost to give meaning to the disaster. "His campaign reached an emotional intensity that exceeded even the victory celebrations of the summer and fall of 1941," as Jay Baird stated in his analysis of the myth of Stalingrad.[45] The radio broadcast of the special announcement of the fall of Stalingrad opened with solemn marches, followed by drumrolls and three stanzas of one of the saddest German war songs, "Ich hatt' einen Kameraden." Then came the announcement, followed by the German, Italian, and Croat national anthems. Three minutes of silence ended with Beethoven's Fifth Symphony, and a three-day period of mourning was ordered.

In the Nazi effort to squeeze out of the act of mourning a catalytic effect for the morale of the German population, Stalingrad became the crucial event, though not as planned. The therapeutic intent of the Stalingrad myth was to take everybody through the war to the bitter end, thereby evoking in the survivors the feeling of obligation and determination. When, shortly thereafter, Hitler erased the topic of Stalingrad, where a whole army had vanished from public view and the population was left only with rumors which fanned its worst fears, it became obvious that this kind of mourning had only thinly disguised the complete senselessness of the loss. It was long before the end of the war that most Germans learned to discard obvious acts of mourning, designed to recover a sense of meaningfulness, as purely ritualistic.

One might add that not only the numbed silence regarding the experience of war and death but also the concentration on the existential moment—the present—as the only moment of accountability had its origins long before 1945, confirming Walter Benjamin's dictum about the survivors of the battlefields of

World War I, who had "grown silent—not richer, but poorer in communicable experience."[46] In his novel *Stalingrad,* considered by many contemporaries the best novel about World War II in Europe, Theodor Plievier clearly did not want to restate Erich Maria Remarque's therapeutic narrative of the war to end all wars, *All Quiet on the Western Front.* Instead Plievier settled on a statement about the senselessness of the battle and the war in general. His sober epic account with its overwhelming details from the Russian winter influenced the disillusioned war literature of the 1950s, although it did not prevent the rise and frequent dominance of the self-pitying tone with which Wolfgang Borchert and Heinrich Böll shaped the literary image of the German soldier as a victim.

Self-pity was not limited to the writers, however. It became the reigning mode after the end of the war. Rejecting a cult of mourning does not mean to forgo self-pity. Everyone turned into a victim, preferably by the Nazis, and this included the Nazis themselves. Bestowing the qualification of victim to most of the Germans brought together the deserving as well as the undeserving and helped prolong the indifference to the Jews that had been systemic before 1945. As World War II had drawn a great percentage of the civil population into the deadly warfare, the practice of counting the actions against the Jews as part of war was continued long after the killing machine of Auschwitz and other death camps had been revealed as a particular if not the crucial project of the Nazis. Even if special consideration was extended to the Jewish victims, German victims were brought into the picture. When the Bundestag debated the final shape of the treaty with Israel, initiatives were put on the agenda to also address the problems of Germans fleeing from East Germany and of those expelled from eastern Europe.[47] The Cold War enabled German atrocities in Eastern Europe to be subsumed under warfare, at least in the eyes of large segments of the population. The suffering and elimination of the Jews in the eastern camps receded into an increasingly shadowy perception of the war.

Still, while self-pity abounded, a culture of mourning did not emerge, could not emerge, unlike the aftermath of World War I. In view of the atrocities perpetrated by Germans, the strictures were manifold, both emotional and political, individual and collective. Neither the demise of millions of Germans on their flight from the East in 1945 nor the loss of six hundred thousand civilians in air raids[48] became catalysts for big national campaigns of remembrance. Their legacy shifted mainly to the domain of the legislature and the social administration. The same is true for other war-related disasters, in particular the rape of almost two million women by soldiers of the Allied forces in 1945. The rapes were completely extinguished from public memory.[49] Michael Schneider's assessment of the emotional immobilization of the war generation helps us understand the extent to which the silence represented both avoidance and a kind of adjustment to mass death within the predicament of family and bourgeois life that had begun long before 1945.[50] But there is still more to be rediscovered and brought back into the discourses of loss, pain, and mourning of the following generations.

TOWARD AESTHETIC REPRESENTATION

Speaking about a code—a system of symbols used to send messages, as the definition goes—runs the risk of implying that the mediation supersedes the reality of an event. But this is more or less what has happened in recent decades. The mediation of Auschwitz increasingly *became* the reality of the event, as was confirmed in the worldwide appreciation for Steven Spielberg's movie *Schindler's List* in 1993. The most incisive moment for asserting the importance of a new understanding came when the TV series *Holocaust* led to the preponderance of the term *Holocaust* over the words *Auschwitz* and *Judenvernichtung*. Different from the sacrificial connotation of *Holocaust,* the word *Auschwitz* always retained its link to the locality of mass death in eastern Europe. The same holds true for the word *Judenvernichtung,* which Omer Bartov called the definitive German term, "since it describes the Event with unadorned clarity, not to say brutality."[51] Using the term *Holocaust* enabled the Germans to encode the organized elimination of Jews by its former government as a verbal and therefore mental unit which projects an inner telos beyond the catastrophic implosion of innumerable scenes of inhumanity. As the real, yet unfathomable event becomes the Holocaust, its representational identity provides an ever-renewable presence within which identification with the victims can be instant. Psychic intensity dominates over documentary recovery of history—even in the instruction in schools.[52] It provides more accessible exposure and has been embraced by the media and popular culture.[53] The aesthetics of devotional distance for which Adorno articulated the most poignant agenda remained a domain of high culture, at times even defined it.

When Saul Friedländer, in his widely discussed *Reflections of Nazism: Essay on Kitsch and Death,* defined "a new discourse" about Nazism that emerged in the 1970s, he located its base in the "psychological dimension," which stimulated the "aesthetic reelaboration" in the films by Marcel Ophuels *(The Sorrow and the Pity),* Hans-Jürgen Syberberg *(Hitler—ein Film aus Deutschland),* Rainer Werner Fassbinder *(Lili Marleen),* and Luchino Visconti *(The Damned);* the novel *The Ogre* by Michel Tournier; and other works.[54] Friedländer's analysis of the new encoding of Nazism, superseding established ideological, political, and economic arguments, illuminates the representational turn in the 1970s:

> It seems logical. . . to suppose, a priori, that a new discourse on Nazism will develop at the same level of phantasms, images, and emotions. More

than ideological categories, it is a matter of rediscovering the durability of these deep-seated images, the structure of these phantasms common to both right and left.[55]

Although the therapeutic reelaboration aims at working through earlier life experiences, it shares with the aesthetic reelaboration the cathartic use of images and phantasms. Friedländer's reflections illuminate the effects of the *Erfahrungshunger,* as Michael Rutschky called the craving for life experience in the 1970s. These effects entail emotional and aesthetic encounters with fascism that include, often hidden or masked, those with the Holocaust. In his endeavor to explain the conjoining of Kitsch and death, Friedländer reverts, without mentioning Freud, to an insight in *Civilization and Its Discontent:*

> Modern society and bourgeois order are perceived both as an accomplishment and as an unbearable yoke. Hence this constant coming and going between the need for submission and the reveries of total destruction, between love of harmony and the phantasms of apocalypse, between the enchantment of Good Friday and the twilight of the gods.[56]

These tensions stimulate aesthetic elaborations but require answers that involve our whole psychological makeup. Or so Freud would intimate. The breakthrough of therapeutic language in dealing with Auschwitz can be traced to emotional needs, free-floating feelings of guilt, a craving for victimhood, suppressed anti-Semitism, nuclear Angst, and a sense of working-through a repressed past. Its manifold expressions often touch upon the aesthetic code which Friedländer analyzed. Anselm Kiefer's ascent to world renown as a painter in the 1980s was clearly based on his ability to endow his oversized landscapes with a distinctly German flavor of transgression and affliction.

Speaking about the fading of the therapeutic approach cannot conclude without the realization that the notion of therapy implies the expectation of healing. While codes of understanding and communication fade and are superseded by other codes, the therapeutic process aims at a transformation, if not a closure. The Freudian notion of working through, instrumental for the subject of this chapter, generates expectations of completion for which aesthetic works have become more and more important as signposts.[57] Aesthetic works, redesigning and reemploying phantasms, images, and emotions both from the victims' and the perpetrators' sides, take the place of living memories, transposing redemptive projections into the realm of the aesthetic. As the sphere of representation still fosters spiritual innovation in this culture of memento, it assures more resistance, though often trivial and pretentious, against forgetting than the upkeep of memorials which will be on the agenda of future generations. For a short while in the 1990s, it seemed as if the concept of German culture refashioned itself in reference to Auschwitz, drawing on the emotional and moral intensity of this legacy above and beyond the endeavors to create new cultures in East and West after World War II. The recoding of the legacy of Auschwitz in cultural terms did not express a lessening of interest but rather a shift toward public representation.

And yet, the strength of the expectation of closure and healing should not be underestimated. It can easily be mixed up with the desire among Germans to "close" the case of the persecution of Jews. This happened when Martin Walser, in his Peace Prize speech at the Frankfurt Book Fair of 1998, complained about the fact that Auschwitz was still "instrumentalized" as "a permanent exhibit of our shame."[58] His frustration might not have been so pointed if he had not engaged earlier with such intensity in the topics of guilt and moral indifference. Having done in the 1960s more than most German writers of his generation to admonish his audience to face Auschwitz,[59] Walser seems to have vented, with equal energies, his frustration about the fact that his plight has not led to redemption. There has been an assumption that Germans of the second generation can "repair." Many had an unwritten agenda for redemption, if not of the parents and the country then at least of themselves. In the 1990s it became clear that there is no restitution of an earlier normality,[60] or a closure concerning the encounter with Auschwitz.

NOTES

1. Alexander and Margarete Mitscherlich, *The Inability to Mourn: Principles of Collective Behavior* (New York: Grove Press, 1975); originally published under the title *Die Unfähigkeit zu trauern: Grundlagen kollektiven Verhaltens* (Munich: Piper, 1967).

2. Tilman Moser, "Die Unfähigkeit zu trauern: Hält die Diagnose einer Überprüfung stand? Zur psychischen Verarbeitung des Holocaust in der Bundesrepublik," *Psyche* 46 (1992): 405.

3. Geoffrey Cocks, *Psychotherapy in the Third Reich: The Göring Institute* (New York: Oxford University Press, 1995).

4. *The Collective Silence: German Identity and the Legacy of Shame,* ed. Barbara Heimannsberg and Christoph J. Schmidt (San Francisco: Jossey-Bass, 1993). The term *silence* has become a signpost both of respect and negligence in a variety of discourses—linguistic, aesthetic, psychological, moral, and political—on the Holocaust. Ernestine Schlant, in her study, *The Language of Silence: West German Literature and the Holocaust* (New York: Routledge, 1999), uses it as a metaphor of failure on the part of postwar German writers like Böll, Grass, and Andersch. Schlant's approach was strongly criticized by Jeffrey Herf ("Eloquent Absences," *The New Republic,* August 2, 1999, 46–49) and Robert Holub ("The Memories of Silence and the Silence of Memories," *German Politics and Society* 18 [2000]: 105–23).

5. Jeffrey Herf, *Divided Memory: The Nazi Past in the Two Germanies* (Cambridge, Mass.: Harvard University Press: 1997). An incisive overview in Helmut König, "Das Erbe der Diktatur: Der Nationalsozialismus im politischen Bewußtsein der Bundesrepublik," *Leviathan* 24 (1996): 163–80.

On the official language see Helmut Dubiel, *Niemand ist frei von der Geschichte: Die nationalsozialistische Herrschaft in den Debatten des Bundestages* (Munich: Hanser, 1999).

6. Jörg Drews, "Das Tabu über Aggressivität und Kritik: Zu einer verborgenen Kontinuität der deutschen Literatur vor und nach 1945," in *"Gift, das du unbewußt eintrinkst . . ." Der Nationalsozialismus und die deutsche Sprache,* ed. Werner Bohleber and Jörg Drews (Bielefeld: Aisthesis, 1991), 114–31.

7. Jean Améry, *Jenseits von Schuld und Sühne: Bewältigungsversuche eines Überwältigten,* new ed. (Stuttgart: Klett-Cotta, 1977), 15.

8. A thorough study of the phenomenon of latent anti-Semitism in the Federal Republic in Jürgen Bellers, "Moralkommunikation und Kommunikationsmoral: Über Kommunikationslatenzen, Antisemitismus und politisches System," in *Antisemitismus in der politischen Kultur nach 1945,* ed. Werner Bergmann and Rainer Erb (Opladen: Westdeutscher Verlag, 1990), 278–91. See also the comprehensive study by Werner Bergmann and Rainer Erb, *Anti-Semitism in Germany: The Post-Nazi Epoch since 1945* (New Brunswick, N.J.: Transactions, 1997).

9. Sibylle Hübner-Funk, "Jugend als Symbol des politischen Neubeginns: Strategien zur Bannung der rassistischen Vergangenheit," in *Antisemitismus in der politischen Kultur,* ed. Werner Bergmann and Rainer Erb (Opladen: Westdeutscher Verlag, 1990), 218–35.

10. Exemplary is the radio manuscript by Wolfgang Jäger et al., *Unsere jüdischen Mitbürger: Ein Funkmanuskript* (Munich: Juventa, 1958).

11. Theodor W. Adorno, "Kulturkritik und Gesellschaft," in *Prismen* (Frankfurt: Suhrkamp, 1955), 31.

12. Theodor W. Adorno, "Offener Brief an Rolf Hochhuth," *Frankfurter Allgemeine Zeitung* no. 132, June 10, 1967, "Bilder und Zeiten," p. 2.

13. Theodor W. Adorno, "Erziehung nach Auschwitz," in *Zum Bildungsbegriff der Gegenwart,* ed. Theodor W. Adorno, Wilhelm R. Gaede et al. (Frankfurt: Diesterweg, 1967), 112.

14. Alf Lüdtke, "'Coming to Terms with the Past': Illusions of Remembering, Ways of Forgetting Nazism in West Germany," *Journal of Modern History* 65 (1993): 551.

15. Philip Rieff, *The Triumph of the Therapeutic: Uses of Faith after Freud* (Chicago: University of Chicago Press, 1966).

16. Richard Sennett, *The Fall of Public Man* (New York: Knopf, 1974).

17. See Friedrich Knilli, "Die Judendarstellung in deutschen Medien," in *Antisemitismus nach dem Holocaust: Bestandsaufnahme und Erscheinungsformen in deutschsprachigen Ländern,* ed. Alphons Silbermann and Julius H. Schoeps (Cologne: Wissenschaft und Politik, 1986), 115–32 ("Holocaust als Modewort," 123–32).

18. Michael Geyer and Miriam Hansen, "German-Jewish Memory and National Consciousness," in *Holocaust Remembrance: The Shapes of Memory,* ed. Geoffrey Hartman (London: Basil Blackwell, 1994), 175–90.

19. Daniel Jonah Goldhagen, *Hitler's Willing Executioners: Ordinary Germans and the Holocaust* (New York: Knopf, 1996).

20. Helmut Dubiel, "Über moralische Souveränität," *Merkur* 48 (1994): 889.

21. Michael S. Roth, ed., *Freud: Conflict and Culture* (New York: Knopf, 1998).

22. *Erinnern, Wiederholen, Durcharbeiten: Zur Psycho-Analyse deutscher Wenden,* ed. Brigitte Rauschenbach (Berlin: Aufbau Taschenbuch, 1992). See also Margarete Mitscherlich-Nielsen, "Die Unfähigkeit zu trauern in Ost- und Westdeutschland: Was Trauerarbeit heißen könnte," *Psyche* 46 (1992): 406–18; Karola Brede and Alfred Krovoza, "Die deutsche Vereinigung unter dem Einfluß einer unerledigten psychosozialen Vorgeschichte," *Psyche* 46 (1992): 419–46.

23. Günter Grass, "Don't Reunify Germany," *New York Times,* January 7, 1990, op-ed page.

24. Richard Brickner, *Is Germany Incurable?* (Philadelphia: Lippincott, 1943), 29 f. See the panel discussion responding to Brickner: "What Shall We Do with Germany?" *Saturday Review of*

Literature 29 (May 29, 1943): 4–10. See also Michaela Hönicke, "'Know Your Enemy': American Wartime Images of Germany, 1942–1943," in *Enemy Images in American History*, ed. Ragnhild Fiebig-von Hase and Ursula Lehmkuhl (Providence, R.I.: Berghahn, 1997), 231–78.

25. Theodore Abel, "Is a Psychiatric Interpretation of the German Enigma Necessary?" *American Sociological Review* 10 (1945): 457–64.

26. Helmut König, "Was leistet die Psychoanalyse für die Erklärung gesellschaftlicher Verhältnisse?—Über Alexander Mitscherlich," *Leviathan* 13 (1985): 219–37.

27. Anita Eckstaedt, *Nationalsozialismus in der "zweiten Generation": Psychoanalyse von Hörigkeitsverhältnissen* (Frankfurt: Suhrkamp, 1989), 11.

28. Eckstaedt; see also Moser, "Die Unfähigkeit zu trauern," 402; and Ilse Grubrich-Simitis, "Vom Konkretismus zur Metaphorik: Gedanken zur psychoanalytischen Arbeit mit Nachkommen der Holocaust-Generation–anläßlich einer Neuerscheinung," *Psyche* 38 (1984): 1–28.

29. See Robert M. Prince, *The Legacy of the Holocaust: Psychohistorical Themes in the Second Generation* (Ann Arbor: UMI Research, 1985). A lively guide to the differences between Israeli and German perceptions of mourning can be found in the documentation of a conference at Hebrew University's Sigmund Freud Center in 1988: *Persistent Shadows of the Holocaust: The Meaning to Those Not Directly Affected*, ed. Rafael Moses (Madison, Conn.: International Universities Press, 1993).

30. Harold Marcuse, "The Revival of Holocaust Awareness in West Germany, Israel, and the United States," in *1968: The World Transformed*, ed. Carole Fink, Philipp Gassert, and Detlef Junker (Cambridge: Cambridge University Press, 1998), 421–38.

31. *Im Kreuzfeuer: Der Fernsehfilm "Holocaust." Eine Nation ist betroffen*, ed. Peter Märthesheimer and Ivo Frenzel (Frankfurt: Fischer Taschenbuch, 1979).

32. Michael Rutschky, *Erfahrungshunger: Ein Essay über die siebziger Jahre* (Cologne: Kiepenheuer & Witsch, 1980).

33. In his insightful report on the 1984 congress of the Deutsche Gesellschaft für Psychotherapie, Psychosomatik und Tiefenpsychologie, Tilman Moser analyzes the current obsession both with the nuclear and the "real" Holocaust: "Ängste und Bomben: Psychoanalytischer Kongreß und das Gleichgewicht des Schreckens," *Frankfurter Allgemeine Zeitung*, November 5, 1984.

34. Dieter E. Zimmer, "Deine Angst und meine Angst: Den Schrecken vor atomarer Vernichtung hat uns die Natur nicht beigebracht," *Die Zeit*, U.S. ed., no. 47 (November 20, 1981): 16–17. See Ilona Stölken-Fitschen, *Atombombe und Geistesgeschichte: Eine Studie der fünfziger Jahre aus deutscher Sicht* (Baden-Baden: Nomos, 1995), 298–92; Michael Salewski, ed., *Das Zeitalter der Bombe: Die Geschichte der atomaren Bedrohung von Hiroshima bis heute* (Munich: Beck, 1995).

35. Ruth Waldeck, *"Heikel bis heute": Frauen und Nationalsozialismus: Der Opfermythos in Christa Wolf's "Kindheitsmuster"* (Frankfurt: Brandes & Apsel, 1992), 140.

36. Martin W. Kloke, *Israel und die deutsche Linke: Zur Geschichte eines schwierigen Verhältnisses* (Frankfurt: Suhrkamp, 1990); Andrei S. Markovits and Beth Simone Noveck, "West Germany," in *The World Reacts to the Holocaust*, ed. David S. Wyman (Baltimore: Johns Hopkins University Press, 1996), 426–28.

37. Geoffrey Hartman, ed., *Bitburg in Moral and Political Perspective* (Bloomington: Indiana University Press, 1986).

38. Richard von Weizsäcker, "The 8th of May 1945—Forty Years After," in *A Voice from Germany: Speeches* (New York: Weidenfeld & Nicolson, 1987), 43–60.

39. Michael Schneider, "Fathers and Sons, Retrospectively: The Damaged Relationship Between Two Generations," *New German Critique*, no. 31 (winter 1984): 30, 50.

40. David Bankier, *The Germans and the Final Solution: Public Opinion under Nazism* (Oxford: Blackwell, 1992), 156.

41. Mitscherlich, *The Inability to Mourn*, 23 f.

42. George Mosse, *Fallen Soldiers: Reshaping the Memory of the World Wars* (New York: Oxford University Press, 1989), 7.

43. Frank Trommler, "The Therapeutic Response: Continuities from World War I to National Socialism," in *War, Violence and the Modern Condition,* ed. Bernd Hüppauf (Berlin: de Gruyter, 1997), 65–76.

44. Quoted by Jay W. Baird, "The Myth of Stalingrad," *Journal of Contemporary History* 4 (1969): 197.

45. Ibid., 198.

46. Walter Benjamin, *Illuminations: Essays and Reflections* (New York: Schocken, 1968), 84.

47. Robert G. Moeller, "War Stories: The Search for a Usable Past in the Federal Republic of Germany," *American Historical Review* 101 (1996): 1017.

48. See W. G. Sebald, *Luftkrieg und Literatur* (Munich: Hanser, 1999), 11.

49. See the special issue of *October* (no. 72, spring 1995) under the title "Berlin 1945: War and Rape: 'Liberators Take Liberties.'"

50. For an extensive discussion see Michael Geyer, "Das Stigma der Gewalt und das Problem der nationalen Identität in Deutschland," in *Von der Aufgabe der Freiheit: Politische Verantwortung und bürgerliche Gesellschaft im 19. und 20. Jahrhundert. Festschrift für Hans Mommsen,* ed. Christian Jansen, Lutz Niethammer, and Bernd Weisbrod (Berlin: Akademie, 1995), 673–98.

51. Omer Bartov, *Murder in Our Midst: The Holocaust, Industrial Killing, and Representation* (New York: Oxford University Press, 1996), 58.

52. Matthias Heyl, "Education after Auschwitz: Teaching the Holocaust in Germany," in *New Perspectives on the Holocaust: A Guide for Teachers and Students,* ed. Rochelle L. Millen (New York: New York University Press, 1996), 275–86.

53. Alvin H. Rosenfeld, "Another Revisionism: Popular Culture and the Changing Image of the Holocaust," in *Bitburg in Moral and Political Perspective,* ed. Geoffrey Hartman (Bloomington: Indiana University Press, 1986), 90–102.

54. Saul Friedländer, *Reflections of Nazism: An Essay on Kitsch and Death* (New York: Harper & Row, 1984), 13, 14.

55. Ibid., 14 f.

56. Ibid., 135.

57. See Eric L. Santner, *Stranded Objects: Mourning, Memory, and Film in Postwar Germany* (Ithaca, N.Y.: Cornell University Press, 1990); and Manuel Köppen and Klaus R. Scherpe, eds., *Bilder des Holocaust: Literatur—Film—Bildende Kunst* (Cologne: Böhlau, 1997).

58. Martin Walser, "Erfahrungen beim Verfassen einer Sonntagsrede," in *Die Walser-Bubis-Debatte: Eine Dokumentation,* ed. Frank Schirrmacher (Frankfurt am Main: Suhrkamp, 1999), 7–17.

59. See, in addition to Martin Walser's plays on the Nazi legacy in the early 1960s, *Eiche und Angora* and *Der schwarze Schwan,* his comments on the Auschwitz Trial in "Unser Auschwitz," in Walser, *Heimatkunde* (Frankfurt: Suhrkamp, 1968), 7–23.

60. Hans Mommsen, "The Legacy of the Holocaust and German National Identity," Leo Baeck Memorial Lecture 42 (New York: Leo Baeck Institute, 1999), 15.

Eight

AGENTS, CONTEXTS, RESPONSIBILITIES: THE MASSACRE AT BUDY

Debórah Dwork

In the midst of a heated discussion about the importance of gender as a factor in historical analysis of the Holocaust, the perspicacious historian Marion Kaplan turned in frustration to the equally sharp historian Steve Aschheim.

"Steve! If you had been one of the Jews hauled out of the cattle cars at the railroad siding in Birkenau, would you prefer to have been a woman or a man?"

"I would not have wanted to be there at all," he replied.[1]

Aschheim was correct, or course. No one would have wanted to be there. But, as a historian, Kaplan had gone further. Her aim was to challenge the boundaries of analysis and, as far as Aschheim and many others that day were concerned, both to think the unthinkable and to articulate the unspeakable. Aschheim's central point was that the Jewish identity of the victims was of paramount and singular importance. It superseded and overwhelmed all other factors; indeed, to focus on any other characteristic was tantamount to, or a genre of, denial of the essence of the Holocaust. Kaplan's point, with which I agreed, was that focusing on individual characteristics of the victims, such as age, social class, degree of religious observance, political affiliation, or gender, augmented our understanding of the murderous process we call the Holocaust.

For my part, I wondered how Aschheim had come, inadvertently, to adopt the

Germans' view of the Jews: the only thing that mattered about these human be-ings was that they were "Jews." How was it that a fine historian would reduce the whole of each victimized person to one salient characteristic? Is it appropriate—indeed, is it even useful—to see the victims solely as the Germans did? I certainly was not interested in such an enterprise. Indeed, the purpose of my own work was to explore and analyze the interior and exterior daily lives of Jewish children during the Holocaust; of the people who sought to rescue them; of the people—mostly German and mostly male—who, step by step, established and enlarged Auschwitz until it became the epicenter of the Judeocide; of the refugees from Nazi Europe and the displaced persons thereafter.[2] If the goal of historical en-quiry is nuanced understanding, I did not find the flattening of the victims ("Jews"), or the rescuers ("Righteous Gentiles"), or the perpetrators ("Nazis") helpful.

Significantly, the historians who balked at gendered analyses were not dis-turbed by the consideration of age. Evidently, age is perceived as a neutral factor of demarcation; no one questions or is troubled by it. But age was not the only important marker in the lives of the European Jews: culture, class, gender, and so on also figured into their experiences. From the Nazi German perspective, all Jews in occupied Europe were slated for death. But the months and years on the road to that end were not experienced by the Jews themselves in an identical fashion. For many, the road itself was not identical. The lives of Jewish girls and boys, and women and men were colored and were shaped by their gender, just as they were colored and shaped by their age, culture, degree of religious obser-vance, or political affiliation. This is obvious and this is clear.

What is not so obvious and not so clear is the ways in which interpretations of events also were—and are—colored and shaped by gendered suppositions and ideas. This chapter is thus rooted in a triple interest: the daily lives of Jewish women during the war, the history of Auschwitz, and the way we think about and write history.

Helen Tichauer-Spitzer was one of the first twenty thousand Slovakian Jews to be deported from her homeland in 1942; half, Helen among them, were sent to Auschwitz-Birkenau, the rest were shipped to Majdanek. "The order came four weeks prior to the end of March," Helen recalled. "End of February. They printed large placards which were pasted on kiosks. No written invitation. They announced that Jewish girls, unmarried, I think it was fifteen or sixteen through forty-five or fifty, were ordered to assemble on a certain date. It was the 21st of March, I remember, on a Monday" [sic].[3]

Helen understood that nothing good would come of this, but "the order said that if you don't report, your parents will be taken instead. So it was a little bit of a tricky business. Nobody wanted to sacrifice their parents. If I would have undertaken to escape to the neighboring countries, the parents would be taken instead."[4]

Helen, however, seemed to have another option. She was a sign writer, and her "employer, who was German, decided to ask for an exemption because there was a shortage of manpower in the profession." The employer was successful; the exemption "was signed; it was ready." But " it was that bloody Monday which was the turning point in my life. I had to leave for the collection point early in the morning, before office time, so I could not go to my employer and collect the permission. I still had to leave because if I wouldn't have reported at the gathering point, they would have picked up my parents. It was a very tricky business. It was bad luck. One day difference and I could have stayed."[5]

Helen reported to "the gathering point, an empty ammunition factory near the railway station," where she was kept until Saturday morning. When another 999 people had been assembled, the Slovak Hlinka guards loaded them onto a train, squeezing them into boxcars. "The journey took one day, one night, and late in the afternoon of the next day we arrived. We arrived on a Sunday." The train stopped "in an open field before the [Auschwitz] railway station. We had to leave everything behind. They marched us to the main gate. I went through the *Arbeit macht frei* gate."[6]

Helen Spitzer had not been deported to be murdered in Auschwitz. In March 1942, Belzec had just gone into operation, and Sobibor would follow a month later. These were planned sites to actualize Judeocide, and the Jews transported to these facilities for death were doomed from the moment they were picked up for transport. Helen and her ten thousand compatriots were not slated for immediate death, however. It was their fate to be shipped to Auschwitz to achieve another Nazi objective: ethnic cleansing. Ethnic cleansing was a major program of the Nazi state. From the moment the National Socialists came to power, they pursued a policy of "homecoming" (as they saw it) for ethnic Germans. It was their aim to bring *Volksdeutsche* who had been living outside the borders of Germany, primarily in the countries of eastern Europe, back to the greater Reich, while simultaneously deporting "undesirables" such as Poles and Jews. The German-Soviet division of Poland in September 1939 gave them an opportunity to realize those goals. The *Volksdeutsche* in the east who would have come under the jurisdiction of the Soviet Union were, with Russian cooperation, to be repatriated in the west and resettled on the newly gained land in Poland. Within eighteen months a total of some 490,640 ethnic Germans were relocated to greater Germany. The great majority of these *Volksdeutsche* were farmers, and they were given the farms of Poles deported to the General Government.[7]

One of the resettlement areas was the area around Auschwitz, which was incorporated into the Greater Reich after the Germans conquered Poland in September 1939. Deportation of the Polish population just south of Auschwitz began in September 1940, and resettlement of the ethnic Germans continued until June 1941.[8]

But the ethnic Germans needed more than land to prevail; their success depended on the practical support they would receive. They had to be educated about local conditions and provided with livestock. Heinrich Himmler, Reich commissioner for the consolidation of the German nation as well as head of the SS empire, suggested the creation of estates to provide training for the farmers and to house nurseries. It was his idea to use the already existing concentration camp at Auschwitz, originally established to incarcerate recalcitrant Poles, to house a large agricultural support center. Indeed, Himmler decided that the agricultural support center would employ most of the camp's projected population of ten thousand Polish inmates. The metamorphosis of the camp into an agricultural estate worked by slaves caught his fancy.[9]

Himmler's ambitions for the camp did not stop there. From month to month, from December 1940 until July 1942, his plans for Auschwitz became increasingly grand. Not only would he create a German agricultural utopian community; he would recreate Auschwitz as a German town, building schools, theaters, sports complexes, and a solid German town hall, which is still used today. To actualize this elaborate urban project, Himmler needed even more slaves, and the projected inmate population increased to one hundred thousand. A new sector of the camp was to be opened near the village of Brzezinka, or Birkenau, to accommodate them.[10]

Initially, Soviet prisoners of war were designated to be those slave workers. After Germany invaded the Soviet Union in June 1941, Himmler offered to take Russian prisoners of war off the army's hands, and the generals accepted gratefully. In October, ten thousand POWs were shipped to Auschwitz to begin construction of the Birkenau camp, but as the Germans provided them with neither food nor shelter, almost all the men had died of starvation, disease, or exposure by February 1942. Himmler was desperate. There was a lot of work to do in Auschwitz, and no more Soviets would be coming his way. Reich Marshall Hermann Goering had gained control over all prisoners of war, and on January 8 he announced that the Russians would be assigned to the war industry. Himmler had to look elsewhere, and his eye fell on the Jews. There was no place for Jews in the German utopia he envisioned, but he could not build it without them. A group of Jews who could be assembled and moved quickly had to be secured.[11]

The Jews of Hitler's client state of Slovakia fitted the bill. As the historian Yehuda Bauer has explained, in 1940 the German government had compelled the rulers of their client state of Slovakia, Monsignor Josef Tiso and Professor Vojtech Tuka, to agree to send 120,000 Slovak workers to the labor-strapped Reich. The Slovaks regretted this arrangement and dragged their feet. In the late summer of 1941 the Germans demanded the immediate transfer of 20,000 workers. Asked if they would take 20,000 Slovak Jews, the Germans declined.

Tiso and Tuka continued to hold out. In the hope that the Germans would take Jews instead of Christians, they concentrated the 90,000 Slovakian Jews in large labor camps and ghettos. In January 1942 they again offered the German Labor Ministry 20,000 strong, young Jews for work in Germany. By then, Himmler needed slave laborers in the east, and the Germans accepted: 10,000 were to be sent to Auschwitz and 10,000 to Majdanek.[12]

Helen Spitzer's transport of Slovak Jewish women was destined for Birkenau, but there had been a delay in the Germans' building schedule and far fewer barracks had been constructed than they had planned. Birkenau officially had been in operation since the beginning of March, when the remaining Soviet prisoners of war, a group of German criminals, and 1,200 sick male inmates from the lazarett, had been moved to the area designated for the women. The transfer of the women to Birkenau had to wait; in the meantime they were packed into ten specially walled-off barracks in the base camp at Auschwitz.

"They were not prepared for us," Tichauer-Spitzer recalls. "Everything went in such a hurry. They were so quick on the trigger. When we arrived, they just pushed us into a barrack, and the next day they shaved us and put us into some old Russian uniforms." Great as had been the Germans' rush to deport the Jews, "they didn't know what to do with us."[13]

She was right. A few days before her transport arrived at Auschwitz, a trainload of 999 female prisoners from the concentration camp at Ravensbrück and a small number of female SS supervisors pulled into the station. The supervisors were sent from Ravensbrück to Auschwitz to set up the women's camp; some of the prisoners were to be camp functionaries and the rest had been dispatched to relieve overcrowding at Ravensbrück.[14]

The situation at Auschwitz was worse. "Once the Jewish transports from Slovakia began to arrive, it was crammed to the roof within a matter of days," Kommandant Rudolf Höss explained in his self-pitying postwar autobiography. "Wash-houses and latrines were sufficient, at the most, for a third of the number of inmates that the camp contained."[15]

Conditions did not improve when the women moved to Birkenau that August. "Everything was much more difficult, harsher and more depressing for the women, since general living conditions in the women's camp were incomparably worse," Höss acknowledged. "Furthermore, the disastrous overcrowding and its consequences, which existed from the very beginning, prevented any proper order being established in the women's camp" (75–76).

"Proper order" was important to Höss, and in his autobiography he particularly blamed the women supervisors for his failure as Kommandant to have achieved that goal. "To have put these swarming ant-heaps into proper order would have required more than the few female supervisors allotted me from Ravensbrück. And I must emphasize once again that the women I was sent were not the best" (80).

Kommandant Höss and SS Chief Himmler disagreed about the employment of women to run the women's camp. Himmler had petit bourgeois and vaguely chivalric notions about women, which colored his views even of Jewish women prisoners, who could be flogged only with his personal and specific permission (77 n. 88). He believed in a gendered separation of tasks and functions; his SS was a male organization and he never was comfortable with women in it. Indeed, strictly speaking they were not in it at all: the German women guards who came from Ravensbrück were SS manqué; they belonged to a parallel and paraorganization without the rights and privileges of their male counterparts, and their sole function was to be guards in concentration camps.

Himmler's ideology clashed with Höss's strict hierarchical subordination of women to men. Himmler, however, was the Reichsführer SS, and as Höss acknowledged, the boss "wished a women's camp to be commanded by a woman." But Höss had no use for the women authorities. The first overseer of the women's camp, Johanna Langefeld, "was in no way capable of coping with the situation, yet she refused to accept any instructions given her by the commander of the protective custody [i.e., main] camp." The rest of the staff "had been thoroughly spoiled at Ravensbrück. . . . They [had been] given the best of accommodation and were paid a salary they never could have earned elsewhere. . . . Now posted to Auschwitz . . . most of them wanted to run away to the quiet comforts and easy life of Ravensbrück" (80–81). As for the "'green' [criminal] female prisoners, . . . they far surpassed their male equivalents in toughness, squalor, vindictiveness and depravity" (76).

Höss tried to subordinate Langefeld to the male *Lagerführer* of the base camp. Langefeld, however, was not easily intimidated and challenged his authority to do this. She was supported by Himmler, who ordered Höss "to detail an SS officer to act as her assistant," to which he complained, "But which of my officers would be willing to take his orders from a woman?" (81)

It is not clear whether Höss could not tolerate tough women, brutal women, women with authority, or women he thought were incompetent. But that they were incompetent as well as brutal and tough is corroborated by Helen Spitzer, who, from her position in the camp office until January 1945, had the opportunity to observe the administration closely.

Within the context of Auschwitz, Helen Spitzer had a sinecure. She had an inside job, work she still describes as "interesting," and access to both material goods and the arbiters of power. It quickly became clear to her that the women supervisors wanted to appear capable and efficient, and that they were particularly interested in making a good impression on their male colleagues. The slave workers in the camp office provided the German women officers with the means to do that. The prisoners' ledgers, bookkeeping, maps, models, and daily accounts were valued by their overseers, and they were protected from the worst of Birkenau in turn.[16]

Few were so well protected. Most women prisoners were assigned to in-camp labor squads as well as to the labor demanded by the agriculture experiment station projects. Men, by contrast, were detailed to construction and industrial work. Indeed, as the women arrived, they took over the former tasks from the men, who were then reassigned to the latter. Clearly, at least initially, the Germans assigned tasks by gender: women were best suited to the infrastructural housekeeping tasks of the camp and agricultural work, while men were fit to build and for the factories. All of it was lethal, but these jobs were not on the same route to death.

~

Agricultural work at Auschwitz was not bucolic. The concentration camp was situated on a swampy corner of land wedged between the Vistula and the Sola. The ground altitude was little higher than the rivers, so the region flooded regularly. Water (rain, melting snow, floodwaters) could not drain into the rivers, nor could it seep into the earth; the soil was impervious marl, two hundred feet thick. If this land were to be transformed into an agricultural estate, drainage posed a tremendous problem. A soil engineer, Professor Zunker, examined the site and submitted a thirty-three-page report suggesting major hydrologic improvements of the Vistula and the Sola to prevent flooding. He also recommended reconstructing the lake-sized fishponds in the southern part of the area, cleaning up the existing drainage channels and digging new ones, and laying a massive network of 3.6 million drainage pipes in 3,000 acres of future farmland. Considering the number of pipes needed, Zunker noted that it would be cheaper to purchase a pipe factory than to buy them from regular suppliers. A more detailed program of improvement was drafted which concentrated first on the improvement of the fishponds by removing the muck on the bottom, the fertilization of adjacent fields with that same muck, and cleaning and digging drainage canals.[17]

Zunker's plan was adopted, and the program that was to demand the labor of tens of thousands of prisoners and claim the lives of thousands began. There was no earth-moving equipment, and every day for four years squads of inmates were sent out to excavate the heavy clay. On starvation rations and beaten by the kapos, they dug for twelve hours at a time without rest. This was women's work in Auschwitz. As soon as women prisoners began to arrive in the early spring of 1942, they were assigned to the agricultural estate squads. It was their job to actualize the projects Zunker had recommended: to construct and maintain the riverbanks, build roads, dredge the fishponds, clear tree stumps from crop fields, and dig drainage ditches. The then–fifteen year old Kitty Hart-Felix was on one of the early transports of women. Born in Bielsko (Bielitz), Poland, she and her mother had entered the Reich illegally on forged papers, to work as Catholic Poles. Ultimately betrayed, they were shipped to Auschwitz (ironically within fifteen miles of their hometown), and Kitty was detailed to a road repair unit. "We were divided into work parties of about two hundred and marched out to the sound of the band. . . . For miles we marched. An hour, two hours, seeing nothing but the vast stretch of the camp until we came to fields and deserted farmhouses; all the little villages and farms in the region had been evacuated." Without resting, the girls were put to work carting stones for a road.

> I stared. Lifting any one of them would be beyond me, let alone carrying it any distance. *"Schneller, du Arschloch."* The kapo gave me a jab in the back. I stooped and tried to lift a stone: it wouldn't budge. As the other girls tugged away and stones from the top of the mound began to crash down, I looked for the smallest. But they were all enormous. With an effort I got one up into my arms and tottered away with it. After three trips, I was finished. My back felt as if it was breaking and I had a pain in my stomach. Not the ache of a twisted muscle, but the sickening wrench of diarrhoea. My guts were going to drop out. And they did—or at any rate, a filthy mess ran down my legs. That was another of the things you had to get used to if you worked so many hours a day and were beaten so often. And beaten up I was. As soon as I faltered, an SS woman with a dog came racing up towards me.[18]

The women died or were killed, but the work went on. Magda Somogyi was deported from her small town in Hungary to Auschwitz in June 1944. It was more than two years after Kitty Hart-Felix had arrived, but she, too, was assigned to a road-building detail. And she, too, was beaten. "I was in Auschwitz and we were working on the road. Once I dropped a great stone because it was so heavy. I couldn't carry it, and it fell down. The SS came to me and he whipped me. From this time, every day when I began to work, first he whipped me and then I could go to work. He told me, 'You understand? You will learn that you do not need to drop the stone.' He was right. I didn't drop the stone any more. I could carry it."[19]

Magda and her seventeen-year-old sister were thought to be twins, and they were sent to special barracks where such siblings were subjected to medical experimentation. Kitty went on to other agricultural labor details, drainage ditch digging among them. By then it was late summer, and fearfully hot. "We were issued with heavy spades. I leaned on mine, got my foot on it, and tried to push it into the ground. All I achieved was a slight scratch on the iron-hard surface. It was impossible to cut through the solid crust, let alone dig any soil out. None of us had the physical strength any more for that sort of task." By the end of the day, "many of the girls had collapsed; scores were unconscious on the ground as the whistles blew for our return to camp, and the rest of us, in not much better shape, had to drag them along or improvise stretchers from building material on the edge of the men's work site." Those who could not stand on their own two feet for the evening roll call "ran the risk of being declared unfit for further work and taken away. You didn't ask where. Those who were dead were piled up in heaps ready for collection by cart or, if there were a lot of them, by tip-up lorry."[20]

The agricultural work details continued to operate until the very end of the history of the concentration camp. Shortly before Auschwitz was evacuated in January 1945 and the forced march of the sixty thousand remaining prisoners into Germany began, Hannah Kent-Sztarkman, who had turned fifteen in October, was sent out on a riverbank detail. "It was winter and they [the Germans] decided that they wanted to even up the banks of the Vistula River. They sent a bunch of us women to work on the banks. We were dressed completely inappropriately. We didn't have any warm clothes and the Polish winters are cold. We didn't have shoes." She and the other women stood in the icy water all day and she developed frostbite, the sequelae of which she suffers from still.[21]

Himmler's agricultural estate project was carried on with the naked strength of the mostly women slave laborers. His bucolic fantasy engendered a brutality that exceeded the conditions in the sand- and gravel-pit industrial work assigned to men. The women simply had no machinery of any kind to help them. It was lethal work. Many died, and nearly no one survived without permanent injury.

~

Helen Spitzer soon realized that she could use her influence in the camp office to help friends and acquaintances obtain what were considered "easier" work details. Assignment to the poultry farms at the subcamp of Harmense, the plant-growing station at Rajsko, and the agricultural farm at Budy were thought to be lifesaving.[22]

But at Auschwitz, nothing was certain. One night early in October 1942, the German women kapos, or maybe the kapos together with the German male guards, massacred some ninety Jewish women at Budy. Höss's account is surprisingly laconic. "The Budy bloodbath is still before my eyes. I find it incredible that human beings could ever turn into such beasts. The way the 'greens' knocked the French Jewesses about, tearing them to pieces, killing them with axes, and throttling them—it was simply gruesome."[23]

Pery Broad, an SS lieutenant arrested immediately after the war by the British, gave his captors a much more detailed and slightly different account. According to Broad, the tensions between the male and female power hierarchies engendered the murders. "The SS men, who did their duty as guards in the camp, used to instigate the German women prisoners with functions to maltreat the Jewish women. . . . If the former did not comply, they were threatened with being . . . 'shot while escaping.'. . . The result of that unbearable state of things is that the German women always were in a state of fear lest the tormented Jewish women take vengeance on them for their terrible lot. But the Jewish women, who mostly belonged to intellectual circles, e.g. some had formerly been students at the Sorbonne or artists, never even thought of getting down to the level of the vulgar German women prostitutes and of planning revenge, though it would have been understandable if they did so."[24]

The women were domiciled in the local school, and that evening a German woman saw a Jewish woman "going upstairs to the sleeping quarters. The German woman thought she held a stone in her hand, but that, of course, was her hysterical imagination only. At the gate below a sentry was standing guard. As everybody knew, he was the [German] woman's lover. Leaning out from the window, she cried for help, saying she had been hit by the Jewess. All guards on duty immediately ran upstairs and together with the depraved women prisoners they began to hit the Jewish women prisoners indiscriminately. . . . The German woman, who had instigated the butchering, stayed behind in the bedroom with her lover. It may have been what she intended with her design. The 'rebellion' was meanwhile mastered with bludgeons, gun butts and shots. Even an axe had been used. . . . Even when all the women lay on the ground, the fiends, drunk with blood, kept hitting the helpless victims again and again. They wanted, above all, to kill everybody, so as to destroy all witnesses of their atrocities."[25]

Disgusted as Höss may have been by the wanton brutality, he, too, wanted to silence the remaining witnesses. After he inspected the scene early the next morning, the wounded women were shot. When women who had managed to hide emerged later in the day, they were interrogated and then killed by an injection of phenol in the heart. "The criminal investigators did a lot of photographing of the spot," Broad reported. Only one copy of each photograph was later developed in the darkroom, under strict supervision. The plates had to be destroyed in the presence of the commandant and the photos were put at his disposal."[26] Finally, six German women prisoners, including the guard's paramour, who had participated in the murders also were killed. "6 women from the Budy mutiny got [phenol] injections," a camp physician, Johann Paul Kremer, noted in his diary on 24 October 1942. Interrogated in 1947 about his role in this action, Kremer explained that he "was detached to be present at the execution in order to ascertain the death as doctor."[27] Significantly, the guard himself got off with an admonishment.

Helen Tichauer-Spitzer provides us with yet a third account. Budy, she says, "was maybe the worst experience of my life. Camps like Budy, Harmense, Rajsko, were known as camps that would never be affected by selections. So what have we done in the camp office knowing that? We have helped to transfer people, friends, relatives to those camps. I talked some of the girls into going; friends, schoolmates. We were 100 per cent sure nothing would happen, that it was a chance to survive."

After the massacre, Tichauer-Spitzer claims that she and her colleagues in the camp office organized the demise of the rest of the women kapos. "We blamed them with impossible lies of sins they committed, and they were put in the strafkommando [penal squad]. That was all we could do in the camp office. We mentioned to the SS woman in charge, 'Look, she [a Budy kapo] did that, that, and that.' And for that they put you for two, three months in the strafkommando. In the strafkommando they were sometimes killed because it was very, very heavy work. . . . The women who committed the massacre did not survive. We made sure they would not survive, I can tell you that. That is all we could do to repay our anger."[28]

—

It is probable that we will never know what happened at Budy or to the German women kapos. And so the history we tell, the story we construct, reflects our assumptions and prejudices. The massacre is a mirror of the way we think about and write history, and the role gender plays in those intellectual processes. Let us examine the accounts I have given more closely. Which aspects of whose version should we credit, and why? First, why did the German male administrators kill six German women kapos? If the administration's goal was to hush up either the "revolt" or the massacre or both, they would have had to execute all the German women kapos as well as the German male guards. And this they did not do. Furthermore, brutality by German kapos towards Jewish prisoners was the norm. Clearly, another boundary had been transgressed, and perhaps that was the nature of the violence. In other words, the German women acted too violently; it was wanton, uncontrolled brutality, and this Höss could not tolerate. As we have seen, Höss was very specific in his autobiography about the role he wanted women to have in the camp hierarchy: they were to be subordinate to the men. Perhaps the ruthless cruelty and brute physical violence of the German women kapos was simply too independent and therefore too threatening to his control of the camp.

While we can only speculate as to why Höss had six of the German women kapos executed, we know why Helen Spitzer wanted to organize the punishment of the rest. She was enraged, she was in mourning, she felt responsible, she felt, she said, "guilty." But did she and the rest of the women in the office have the means to effect their goals? Or is the whole notion of Jewish women slaves influencing the German female kommandantur a revenge fantasy?

As with so much regarding Budy, we will never know. It is clear, however, that slaves can wield a certain kind of power. It is internecine, subterranean, and manipulative; not straightforward or direct. But it is power. The Jewish office workers were important to the German women rulers. The latter depended on the former. Indeed, it is precisely because Helen Spitzer was so important to Langefeld and Mandel, and because they relied on her, that she was not summarily replaced by someone else and that she survived. In a very, very limited context, Spitzer had a professional (and that is her word) relationship with her bosses. It is her contention that once such a professional relationship was established, she and the other Jewish women similarly situated had some semblance of standing with the German female officers. They could ask for things, like underpants. And when they mentioned infractions by the German women kapos from Budy of rules the hierarchy held sacred, the kommandantur took note.

Our tendency, however, is to discredit Helen Tichauer-Spitzer's account. It is difficult to believe that Jewish women prisoners would have had the power to influence the fate of German women kapos, while it is all too believable that someone—especially someone who feels "guilty"—would have constructed a more satisfying conclusion to the story through which she could experience the pleasure of reparation and revenge. But we should beware. None of the German women kapos at Budy has been seen and identified since the war.

Finally, let us turn our attention to the massacred Jewish women at Budy. Neither Höss, nor Broad, nor Tichauer-Spitzer believed that the intellectual Jewish women may have intended to harm the German women kapos that night. Höss did not even mention any intention of physical retaliation by Jewish women against the German kapos. Broad dismissed the idea as a figment of "the hysterical imagination" of the German woman kapo. For Helen Tichauer-Spitzer, the whole idea was merely an excuse adduced by the Germans. "There was no reason for the women [to have revolted]. . . . It was a good camp," she explained.

Furthermore, not one of them believed that those intellectual Jewish women would have considered, or were capable of, revolt. For Broad it was a question of social class: Sorbonne students and artists do not "go down to the level" of vulgar prostitutes. In a way, Helen Tichauer agreed: "There were no women among them who were somehow inclined to rebel."[29]

Are they correct? Their accounts read Jewish intellectual women prisoners as incapable of armed (a stone) revolutionary activity. Is that right? These women were young, and the massacre occurred in the autumn of 1942, not 1944. The prisoners had been deported to Auschwitz at most six months earlier, and they may still have been healthy. They were in Budy, not Birkenau, and that may have given them the margin they needed even to *consider* action. And if indeed they were Sorbonne students, artists, intellectuals, the Left Bank was alive with political activity. Perhaps these women were trained to think politically, to unite, to plan, to act. For all we know, the French Jewish women of Budy belonged to well-run and well-organized Communist cells. In another context, the concomitant attributes "woman," "Jewish," "intellectual," "Sorbonne student" certainly would lead an investigator to consider the possibility of radical political activism.

Context is key not only to what happened in the past but to our interpretation of what happened in the past. We are prepared to accept, to comprehend, political activism and resistance in the long-term ghettos of eastern Europe, but we cannot quite believe it possible in Auschwitz. We readily see the Jewish ghetto inhabitants as individuals: they are recognizable to us as people, individual people, with their own personalities, physical characteristics, occupations, family structures, relationships. But when the same people are transported to Auschwitz, their individuality is erased *for us*. We lose our ability to see the distinguishing characteristics, to hold on to the particulars of their different lives, to remember that each was a separate entity. The German view prevails. The Jewish inmates become an undifferentiated mass.

The outcome has determined our perception of the course. We forget that in October 1942 there were gas chambers in Auschwitz, but the crematoria of the Holocaust were still under construction. By October 1942, Auschwitz was a murderous place; masses of Jews were being killed in two peasant cottages adapted for that purpose and known as Bunker I and Bunker II. But Auschwitz had not yet undergone the final transformation into a camp dedicated primarily to genocide, with industrial facilities for that purpose. Knowing what is to come shapes our interpretation of the moment before it happens.

A paradox underlies every historical narrative: while in everyday life each moment unfolds with no certainty of outcome, "history" is based on a known conclusion that charges an otherwise tedious chronicle with portent and pregnancy. In the case of Auschwitz, this certainly is true: the end is always there, sometimes not quite visible, but ever present. The end gives value, meaning, and significance. Every bit of information cannot but be an annunciation of the end to come. Whether we want it or not, the final misery of Auschwitz dominates our understanding of its history before that last evil occurred.

For us, *Auschwitz* is synonymous with the industrialization of murder, both as fact and metaphor. Perhaps it is that image of efficient factorylike killing procedures, the Auschwitz of 1943 and 1944 with crematoria II, III, IV, and V, that has shaped our analysis of the massacre at Budy in October 1942. In a one-line private diary entry, the only contemporary account we have, the physician Johann Kremer called it a "mutiny." Maybe *mutiny* meant "breakout," and why is it impossible that those Jewish intellectual women may have devised a breakout plan? Three months earlier, a Polish woman had escaped from Budy, and the camp still was not well guarded. Broad specifically noted that "the single barbed wire fence" at night was neither loaded with electricity nor sufficiently illumined.[30] And the alleged incident was at night.

Was it not in the Germans' best interest to suppress the very idea of an attempted revolt, and to quell the notion that Jewish intellectual women are capable of violence or concerted action, thus rendering the Jewish women even more powerless?

~

I think it is possible that the German woman was right. Perhaps the Jewish woman had a stone in her hand. Perhaps the women's plan counted on the guard on duty: sex would keep both the kapo and the guard busy. Perhaps the stone was to be used as a weapon in case of misadventure. In short, perhaps the Jewish women prisoners at Budy did plan to break out.

We may never know what happened at Budy, and it may not matter. What matters, and matters very much, is that our exploration of these events challenges us to face our own prejudices and assumptions. For fifty years, everyone who wrote about the Budy massacre accepted Höss's and Broad's account. Jewish women intellectuals were passive and were victims. No one entertained the idea that they may have been young, energetic, vibrant, committed to organized activity—and desperate. Real women, in fact. But the history of such violent episodes can push us to make an imaginative leap, to eschew paper cutouts and cardboard figures.

In the end, Marion Kaplan was right: the individuality of each victim is important. Historical exploration and analysis of the Holocaust that takes into account a whole range of characteristics such as age, gender, social class, culture, and occupation augments our understanding of the Judeocide, just as it has enriched our knowledge about other historical events and eras.

And Steve Aschheim was right, too, because the people who had power, who were in the position to make decisions that affected the very lives of their victims, did not see them as individuals. The murder system itself was based on stereotype. The inmates at Budy were not in a nice café in Paris, but in a genocidal situation controlled by men who had insane and fixed ideas.

These are two different histories: the history of who the women really were, and the history of how the Germans saw these women. The massacre at Budy illuminates how little we know about the women, and how dominant the German legacy has been. It shows, too, that when the individuality of the victims collided with the stereotype the Germans held, as may have been the case at Budy, the history we write about that tragic event or heroic episode is both a challenge and an opportunity.

NOTES

1. Discussion at the first international workshop "Women and/in the Holocaust," Hebrew University, Jerusalem, 1995.

2. See, inter alia, Deborah Dwork, *Children With A Star* (New Haven, Conn.: Yale University Press, 1991); Dwork and Robert Jan van Pelt, *Auschwitz, 1270 to the Present* (New York: W. W. Norton, 1996); Dwork, "Lamed-Vovniks of Twentieth-Century Europe: Participants in Jewish Child Rescue," in *Resistance against the Third Reich, 1933–1990,* ed. Michael Geyer and John Boyer (Chicago: University of Chicago Press, 1994), 89–118; and Dwork, "Custody and Care of Jewish Children in the Post-War Netherlands: Ethnic Identity and Cultural Hegemony," in *Lessons and Legacies, Volume III: Memory, Memorialization, and Denial,* ed. Peter Hayes (Evanston, Ill.: Northwestern University Press, 1999), 109–37, 274–78.

3. Helen Tichauer-Spitzer, oral history recorded by Deborah Dwork and Robert Jan van Pelt, New York, N.Y., April 20, 1995, transcript, pp. 24–25. Ms. Tichauer's memory is not quite correct in that March 21, 1942, was a Saturday. Her memory does correlate with the timing of deportation from Slovakia, however. According to Yehuda Bauer, deportations began on March 26. Thus, Ms. Tichauer's recollection of assembly on the twenty-first followed by deportation one week later on March 28 is in accordance with Bauer's dates. See Yehuda Bauer, *Jew for Sale? Nazi-Jewish Negotiations, 1933–1945* (New Haven, Conn.: Yale University Press, 1994), 69.

4. Oral history of Helen Tichauer-Spitzer, 25.

5. Ibid., 25–26.

6. Ibid., 27–28.

7. See chapter 5, "A Paradise of Blood and Soil," in Dwork and van Pelt, *Auschwitz,* 127–59. See also Robert Lewis Koehl, *RKFVD: German Resettlement and Population Policy, 1939–1945: A History of the Reich Commission for the Strengthening of Germandom* (Cambridge, Mass.: Harvard University Press, 1957); and Götz Aly and Susanne Heim, *Vordenker der Vernichtung. Auschwitz und die Pläne für eine neue europäische Ordnung* (Frankfurt: Fischer Taschenbuch Verlag, 1994).

8. Dwork and van Pelt, *Auschwitz,* 181–88.

9. Ibid., 188–90.

10. Ibid.; see chapter 7, "IG Farben" and chapter 8, "Birkenau."

11. Ibid., 262, 271–75.

12. Bauer, *Jews for Sale?* 62–70.

13. Oral history of Helen Tichauer-Spitzer, 28.

14. Imtraud Heike, ". . . da es sich ja lediglich um die Bewachung der Häftlinge handelt . . ." in *Frauen in Konzentrationslagern: Bergen-Belsen, Ravensbrück,* ed. Claus Füllberg-Stolberg et al. (Bre-

men: Edition Temmen, 1994), 221–39. See also Rudolf Höss, "Autobiography of Rudolf Höss," in *KL Auschwitz Seen by the SS: Höss, Broad, Kremer,* ed. Jadwiga Bezwinska and Danuta Czech (N.Y.: Howard Fertig, 1984), 76 n. 87.

15. Bezwinska and Czech, *KL Auschwitz,* 79–80.

16. Oral history of Helen Tichauer-Spitzer, 9.

17. Dwork and van Pelt, *Auschwitz,* 191–92.

18. Kitty Hart, *Return to Auschwitz: The Remarkable Story of a Girl Who Survived the Holocaust* (London: Sidgwick and Jackson, 1981), 70.

19. Magda Somogyi, oral history recorded by Debórah Dwork, Budapest, Hungary, July 19, 1987, transcript p. 9.

20. Hart, *Return to Auschwitz,* 73, 76.

21. Hannah Kent-Sztarkman, oral history recorded by Debórah Dwork, Stamford, Conn., December 13, 1995, transcript pp. 22f, 37; and July 15, 1995, transcript pp. 15–16.

22. Oral history of Helen Tichauer-Spitzer, 19–20.

23. Höss, *Autobiography,* 77.

24. Pery Broad, "Reminiscences of Pery Broad," in *KL Auschwitz Seen by the SS: Höss, Broad, Kremer,* ed. Jadwiga Bezwinska and Danuta Czech (N.Y.: Howard Fertig, 1984), 166.

25. Broad, "Reminiscences," 167.

26. Ibid.

27. Johann Paul Kremer, "Diary of Johann Paul Kremer," in *KL Auschwitz Seen by the SS: Höss, Broad, Kremer,* ed. Jadwiga Bezwinska and Danuta Czech (N.Y.: Howard Fertig, 1984), 226 (text and nn. 85, 86).

28. Oral history of Helen Tichauer-Spitzer, 20.

29. Ibid., 21.

30. Broad, "Reminiscences," 164.

Part Four

TRAUMA AND
THE LIMITS OF
REPRESENTATION

Nine

NEW SOUNDINGS IN HOLOCAUST LITERATURE: A SURPLUS OF MEMORY

Froma Zeitlin

Imaginative efforts in the area of Holocaust studies are always surrounded by a whiff of suspicion, if not potential scandal. There is a continual risk involved in confronting that abyss in history through literary or other artistic means. The risk lies not just in the danger of disapproval from the historians themselves, who generally claim the high ground in guarding the truthfulness and facticity of their subject, but from all those who police these borders, lest this devastating event in any way be exploited or appropriated, domesticated or trivialized, falsified or aestheticized—in a word, desanctified. As Ernst van Alphen has recently observed, it is only when the topic of the Holocaust is at stake that the value and propriety of such imaginative discourses or images are called in for radical questioning, particularly when it comes to the introduction of "narrative elements that relate to Holocaust 'reality.'"[1] At best, as another critic notes, fiction is thought to function "as a weaker kind of testimony when compared with history, or at worst, a misleading, dangerous confusion of verisimilitude with that 'reality,' and a consequent falling off of moral seriousness."[2]

At the same time, this is not the whole tale. Historians have become far more conscious of the discursive nature of their craft, of the representative modes of rhetorical style and techniques of emplotment and narrative, which they use in constructing a narrative. Of late, they even go so far as to insist on including the subject position of the writer and his or her own role as a "witness," whether in the case of Saul Friedländer, who belongs to the survivor generation and can therefore "partake at one and the same time in the memory *and* the present perceptions of this past," or of James Young, who speaks of "received history" in the sense of becoming a "vicarious witness" by his own implication in the lives and memories of those who preceded him.[3] Then, too, the seemingly unbridgeable divide between history and memory has also been challenged by the recognition that the history of the Holocaust, above all, must include the voices of the victims (however partial and, at times, inaccurate their testimony may be). Finally, it is time to acknowledge that the canonical status achieved by certain memoir texts (and images), such as the work of Primo Levi or Tadeusz Borowski, is not because they offer some transparent window through which "truth" and "reality" in any absolute sense may be guaranteed. If these and other "classics" like them continue to claim readers' attention, they do so because their modes of telling— structure, language, narrative strategies, and sensibility—belong as well to literature.[4]

Nevertheless, despite the advances made by these various approaches and refinements of categories of thinking—which bear far more elaboration than I am able to provide in this essay—the dilemmas (and suspicions) of representation, especially of avowedly literary works, remain. As the last witnesses are dying out, there has been a rush to testimony by aging survivors, to leave a tangible record behind, whether in print or in oral form, for oneself, for one's vanished families and towns, and for those who have come and will come after. And likewise, the intractable pressure of the event on those who were not there, those "witnesses by adoption," as Geoffrey Hartman has called them, or "second-generation witnesses," has lured considerable talent to take on the burdens of memory, shaped to their own creative needs in the context of here and now, and to produce an ever growing body of imaginative and sometimes startling new work.[5] This phenomenon of post-Holocaust literature has attracted considerable interest of late and it is one, I feel certain, which has by no means reached its conclusion.[6]

The original mandate for this essay was to consider "the responsibilities of memory and the possibilities of new futures," a charge that already, to my mind, implicitly suggested the indispensable role that the imagination must play, when the last eyewitnesses are gone and when the Holocaust inevitably passes into history as "a trauma both remembered and not remembered, transmitted and not transmitted."[7] Even now, Anne Michaels, whose *Fugitive Pieces* will be one of the works I later discuss,[8] has said that for her "the challenge was to get beyond the facts of history, and to experience in words those events I did not live through or witness personally, but that I have been able to absorb. . . . My goal was to investigate and understand it, not just be influenced by it, but to get beyond it and grasp it."[9] Michael Berg, the German protagonist of Bernhard Schlink's novel *The Reader,* another work I will include, never attains this goal, which, despite all his efforts, eludes him to the end. But the unsatisfied desire that rules this work in more ways than one is the driving force behind the entire enterprise.[10]

I stress the word *desire,* taking my cue from a brilliant essay by Hans Kellner entitled "'Never Again' Is Now." In remarking on an incommensurable gulf between the urge to commemorate the past and the inadequacy of the means to do so in the present, Kellner attempts to explain why such efforts are so problematic:

> Both fictional and historical representations are dreamlike in that they express some sort of desire, in all the complexity of that term. The pressing need to represent the Holocaust in poetry, novels, films, drama, music, and history must come from a desire to repeat in the imagination happenings and events that horrify and fascinate. We only represent what we desire. The desire to represent the Holocaust, however, is not a desire to repeat it as an event, nor necessarily a desire to repeat the form-giving pleasure of representation itself; rather, it is a desire to repeat the Holocaust in a suitably altered form to meet complex, often contradictory, sets of present needs. It is the power of these needs, often unrecognized and elusive, that drives the process, and so . . . creates the problem. Once we acknowledge the reality of need and desire in representations of the past, we are open to the tacit contrast of the weight of the event represented and the weight of present desires. It is the overwhelming sense of imbalance between the Holocaust and any interest in it that leads to the quest for limits to representation, which is actually a reproach to the consuming power of discursive desire. . . . Guilt arises at every turn, whether turned upon a missing enemy or upon the audience or upon representation.[11]

Kellner's aim is to insist that historical writing, too, is subject to the same constraints as literature and the arts. "To be brought to life, or at least to a simulacrum of life that makes possible academic or even popular publication, the material will have to be reshaped, and this, in turn, means revision."[12] If we take his term *revision* in its more radical etymological sense, of "re-vision" as seeing again under new eyes, since "familiarity has made it difficult to see" what "before had been keenly felt," it is the role, above all, of the mind's eye to keep interest alive in new and disturbing ways. Yet even in the most innovative works of literature, certain persistent themes or common trends can be found. These

deserve attention as indications of recent responses that answer to the social interests and needs of a contemporary audience, more than a half a century after
the event.

In a previous essay, "The Vicarious Witness: Belated Memory and Authorial
Presence in Recent Holocaust Literature," I focused on the presence of the author in the text (or film) as a mediating figure who "dramatizes the work of recollection and, by so doing, emphasizes the process itself of reconstructing the
past as filtered through the consciousness (and complicity) of a belated witness
in the fusion of then and now."[13] Starting from Claude Lanzmann's *Shoah* and Art
Spiegelman's *Maus* as influential paradigms, I explored two other, little-known
works (one in French and one in Polish),[14] which I argued go still further in "reconstructing memory" at second or third hand. Both these authors resort to the
uses of fiction, particularly in the invention of literary personae, in order, paradoxically, to arrive at a deeper knowledge of the Holocaust. Above all, I claimed
that, for all their differences, both works "foregrounded the process—the vocation—of writing as the essential means of creating that authorial presence, one
that involved the reader throughout in the anguish, guilt, necessity, doubts and
contradictions, but also the remedial nature of the task."[15]

This time I want to turn to other, more recent, fictional works from diverse
sources: one from Canada, one from Germany, and the third from Switzerland.
Translated into numerous languages, they have captured public interest as striking efforts to reengage in provocative ways the emotional and cognitive issues
that inhabit the inner landscapes of haunted memory, reflecting the pervasive
grip that the traumatic past continues to hold upon present lives and identities—for their characters, and, by extension, for us. To cite Geoffrey Hartman
once again, "after" is by no means "beyond."[16] "How many centuries before the
spirit forgets the body?" asks one of the narrators in the three books I will discuss. "How many years pass before the difference between murder and death
erodes?"[17]

In addition to Anne Michaels's *Fugitive Pieces* and Bernhard Schlink's *The
Reader,* I include Binjamin Wilkomirski's *Fragments: Memories of a Wartime Childhood* as a work of fiction as well.[18] This harrowing story, published in German in
1995 and in English in 1996 (as well as in other languages), shattered its readers with the piercing shards of a child's fragmentary recollections of unadulter-
ated trauma and the confusing horror of his experiences, both during and even
after the war, when he was adopted by a Swiss couple but still continued to inhabit a private concentrationary universe, with predictably awful results. Until
1998, the book was taken as a small masterpiece because the child's-eye view,
deprived of any adult interpretation, cast the atrocities he witnessed and en-
dured in his body and his soul into a still harsher and more unbearable light. It

now seems certain, however, that the author was an impostor—in reality, an illegitimate Swiss child—and his recovered memories if not a deliberate fraud, then the product of a hallucinated mind and a sadly confused identity. The circumstances surrounding the author of *Fragments* have taken on a surrealistic dimension in an adopted child's persistent conviction, despite incontrovertible evidence, that his true self is other than official records show it to be. For some, this work is evidence of the abuse which so-called recovered memory has engendered; for others, the scandal surrounding Wilkomirski's now discredited memoirs has cast a long shadow on personal testimony in general, even from authentic witnesses. The case all the more raises doubts for historians, who are so often uneasy with representations of the Holocaust in any form, other than in the approved ways. The issue is decidedly a serious one; it has compromised the respected line between genuine memoirs and imagined fiction in the author's self-representation and would seem to have abjured those very "responsibilities of memory" that depend on the good faith of the author. Given its truth claims as a memoir, the work cannot simply be taken as fiction, because it abrogates an implicit contract between reader and author. It cannot be taken as a hybridized form, one which may for literary reasons elide the difference between genres. But for all its mimetic obfuscations and self-deluded invention of a memory that is not his, the merits of the work still remain, in my opinion, even if it may never escape the stigma which is now attached to it. Those merits reside in a ferocious vision, a powerful narrative, an accumulation of indelible images, and the unforgettable way in which a small child's voice is deployed in an unfeeling adult world, during the war and thereafter. Even as pseudomemoir, *Fragments* gains a certain symbolic value, pressing the limits of both recollection and representation, once we renounce Wilkomirski's narrator as a "legitimate object of identification" and "turn attention" instead "to those formal techniques that proved so effective in creating the illusion of authenticity."[19] On these grounds alone (although there are others), it deserves a place, I would argue, in the current context as a product of its time, especially given its setting in Switzerland and recent challenges to Swiss political myths regarding their actions during and after the Shoah and their own willed amnesia.[20]

Each of these works approaches the subject of the Holocaust through first-person male narrators, and as we discover sooner or later in these nonlinear narratives, the events of the past, recollected from the perspective of time over a long duration, have in no way lessened their grip on the present. Quite the contrary. The past incessantly resurfaces into consciousness in both direct and oblique ways with all the urgency of an obsession that disrupts chronology and casts a shadow over all subsequent experience.[21] Despite their quite radical difference in styles, techniques, and even purposes, the texture of memory is shown as elliptical, often fragmentary, tantalizingly elusive, inscribed on the body, and favoring nonverbal signals in the recording of sensations, such as sight, touch, smell, sound. "I learned to tolerate images rising in me like bruises," says one of these narrators.[22] All look back to early experience, two of them as children, one in adolescence; and the stories they recount, in stressing the nonknown and the not fully understood, gesture in some measure toward the incomprehensibility, the disorientation, the opacity of the event, even now—or, all the more so—after so many years. But paradoxically, such techniques rely on a reader's already acquired knowledge to decipher the allusions and fill in the gaps, and in so doing to look once again at the known under a newfound shock of awareness. It is therefore not surprising that these self-enclosed works should have the sense, at times, of an oneiric, dreamlike quality, and indeed, each reports a recurrent dream or dreams as a sign of disturbed consciousness, of a repetition compulsion that signifies the continuing invasion of an unresolved past into present time, with disabling results. Let us begin with an account of these three dreams.

FIRST DREAM

The peaceful calm of that first sleep in the new children's home was shattered by a nightmare. It would repeat itself mercilessly in the years that followed, image by image, detail by detail, night by night, like an unstoppable copying machine.

I was in half darkness, and the only child on earth. No other human being, no grass, no water, nothing. Just a great desert of stone and sand.

In the middle of the world, a cone shaped mountain loomed up against the dark sky. Its peak was capped with a black, metallic, glinting ominous helmet. At the foot of the mountain was a hut with a sort of canopy. Under it were a lot of coal cars on rails. Some of the cars were full of dead people; their arms and legs stuck out over the edges. A narrow rail track ran up the peak and in under the helmet, into a gaping jawbone with filthy brown teeth. The cars cycled uphill, disappearing into the jaw under the helmet, then cycled back down again, empty.

All over the plain around the mountain, hordes of biting insects suddenly came crawling out of the ground. Thicker and thicker . . . the plain looked like a sea of evil creatures.

The bugs crawled over me. Ants, lice, beetles. . . . My skin began to itch and burn. I knew I was their last meal on earth. Where could I go to save myself? I saw that the only places they avoided were the iron cars. . . . But it was no use fleeing to one of the cars. They travelled as unstoppably and regularly as clockwork up the mountain and tipped their contents into the awful gullet under the helmet. Jumping onto one of cars would only postpone the end.

I awoke with a sense of despair and the absolute certainty that there was no way out. Any relief is not real, it's the last false hope before the inevitable arrival of death. And I knew it would be both slow and agonizing.[23]

SECOND DREAM

They waited until I was asleep, then they roused themselves, exhausted as swimmers, grey between the empty trees. Their hair in tufts, open sores where ears used to be, grubs twisting from their chests. The grotesque remains of incomplete lives, the embodied complexity of desires eternally denied. They floated until they grew heavier and began to walk, heaving into humanness; until they grew more human than phantoms and through their effort began to sweat. Their strain poured from my skin, until I woke dripping with their deaths. Daydreams of sickening repetition—a trivial gesture remembered endlessly. . . .

I tried to remember ordinary details, the sheet music beside my sister, Bella's bed, her dresses. What my father's workshop looked like. But in nightmares, the real picture wouldn't hold still enough for me to look, everything melting. Or I remembered the name of a classmate but not his face. A piece of clothing but not its color.

When I woke, my anguish was specific: the possibility that it was as painful for them to be remembered as it was for me to remember them; that I was haunting my parents and Bella with my calling, startling them awake in their black beds. . . .

Never trust biographies. Too many events in a man's life are invisible. Unknown to others as our dreams. . . . And nothing releases the dreamer; not death in the dream, not waking.[24]

THIRD DREAM

The building on Bahnhofstrasse is no longer there. I don't know when or why it was torn down. I was away from my hometown for many years. . . . I had been aware of this building since I was a little boy. It dominated the whole row. . . . Inside I imagined a stairwell with plaster moldings, mirrors, and an oriental runner held down with highly polished brass rods. I assumed that grand people would live in such a grand building. But because the building had darkened with the passing of the years and the smoke of the trains, I imagined that the grand inhabitants would be just as somber, and somehow peculiar—deaf or dumb or hunchbacked or lame.

In later years, I dreamed about the building again and again. The dreams were similar, variations on one dream and on one theme. I'm walking through a strange town and I see the house. It's one in a row of buildings in a district I don't know. I go on, confused, because the house is familiar but its surroundings are not. Then I realize that I've seen the house before. I'm not picturing Bahnhof-strasse in my hometown, but another city, or another country. For example, in my dream I'm in Rome, see the house, and realize I've seen it already in Bern. This dream recognition comforts me . . . like encountering an old friend by chance in a strange place. I turn around, walk back to the house, and climb the steps. I want to go in. I turn the door handle.

If I see the house somewhere in the country, the dream is more long-drawn-out, or I remember its details better. I'm driving a car. I see the house on the right and keep going, confused at first only by the fact that such an obviously urban building is standing there in the middle of the countryside. Then I realize that this is not the first time I've seen it, and I'm doubly confused. When I remember where I've seen it before, I turn around and drive back. . . . The road is always empty. I'm afraid I'll be late and drive faster. Then I see it. . . . The house is no darker than it was on Bahnhofstrasse, but the windows are so dusty that you can't see anything inside the rooms, not even the curtains; it looks blind.

I stop on the side of the road and walk over to the entrance. There's nobody about, not a sound to be heard, not even a distant engine, a gust of wind, a bird. The world is dead. I go up the steps and turn the knob.

But I do not open the door. I wake up knowing simply that I took hold of the knob and turned it. Then the whole dream comes back to me, and I know that I've dreamed it before.[25]

~

The first dream of the mountain and trains is from Wilkomirski's *Fragments,* which, as mentioned above, purports to issue from the recovered memory of a Jewish child, hardly more than a toddler when the Nazi violence began. Born in Riga, it is claimed, he undergoes a series of horrific experiences, including the camps, and ends up transferred from a children's home in Cracow to Switzer-land, where he was adopted by a couple who urged him to forget what happened to him, to think of prior events as merely "a bad dream" (123).

Now his traumatic past reawakens, and he sees "a rubble field of isolated images and events. Shards of memory with hard knife-sharp edges, which still cut flesh if touched today. Mostly a chaotic jumble, with very little chronological fit. . . . If I'm going to write about it, I have to give up on the ordering logic of grown ups; it would only distort what happened." He survived; although the "plan was for him and all the other children to die," they are alive. "We're the living contradiction to logic and order" (4–5).

His terrible dream is not difficult to decipher: the desolated spot, the solitary

child, the ravening maw of the personified machine that takes in the endlessly advancing trains filled with bodies, trains which return empty and begin the journey again and again. His terror, his aloneness, and the death that is merely post-
poned are vividly portrayed. Above all, the panic of trauma is inscribed, like the
metaphor for his memories, in assaults upon the body, which recall the lice-
infested atmosphere of the camps, whose miseries offer an alternative almost
as horrifying as the death awaiting the victims inexorably dispatched to their
anonymous end.

The second dream comes from Michaels's *Fugitive Pieces,* a remarkably complex account of another child, Jakob Beer, seven years old, who is hidden in a
closet when the enemy arrives at his home in a Polish town.[26] "The burst door.
Wood ripped from the hinges, cracking like ice under the shouts. Noises never
heard before, torn from my father's mouth. Then silence. My mother had been
sewing a button on my shirt. She kept her buttons in a chipped saucer. I heard the
rim of the saucer in circles on the floor. I heard the spray of buttons, little white
teeth" (10). The parents are dead; his beloved older sister, Bella, however, simply
disappears. Emerging from the peat bog to which he had fled, he is miraculously
saved by Athos, a Greek geologist, who has been excavating a centuries-old
buried town, Biskupin, in the vicinity. Athos smuggles him out and takes him to
Greece, to the island of Zakynthos. There he spends four years of the war in his
benefactor's isolated house, mostly in hiding once again, since the Germans come
there, too, in search of Jews. Even so, he gains from Athos a remarkable education in science, history, literature, and much else. After the war, he follows
Athos to Toronto, when the latter accepts a university post in geography. There
he grows up, becomes a poet and a translator, and finds happiness finally in a late
second marriage, which is tragically cut off when both are killed in a random
auto accident on an Athens street. He had been writing his memoirs in Athos's
family house on another Greek island, Idhra. These are eventually found by Ben,
a younger acquaintance from Toronto, himself a child of survivors who, in escape
from his own troubled life, has come to Greece to search for the lost work of a
man he had admired, but whose life had barely touched his own.

For Wilkomirski's child, whose fractured memories recall only the crushing
brutality to which he was subjected and the loss, each time, of any transient nur-
turant or helpful figure in his life, whether an adult or another child (Motti, an
older brother; Jankl, a friend in the camp; or Mila, from the Cracow orphanage),
life, both during and after, is lived in a bewildering haze of lonely and mistrust-
ful exclusion. His recollections are unbearably vivid, but he cannot make sense
of them. He suffers from guilt for having betrayed a younger child in the camps
in an incident that led to the little one's death. He suffers later, when asked to address the strange new woman in his life as "mother," thinking that he is betraying

the "mother" he only recollects as an almost lifeless gray form in the camp barracks to whom he was taken once by a guard. And in perhaps the most terrifying
moment of the book, he describes the sight of dead mothers, whose heaving bel-
lies contained not infants but rats gnawing inside them, and wonders whether he
is "a human child or a rat child, or . . . both at once." He recalls the shock of the
gaze, "kneeling in the mud with his mouth open, and I can't close it. . . . There
are no feelings left" (86–87).

For Jakob, however, quite the opposite is true. Surrounded by love, first from
his family at home, then from his savior and guardian, Athos, and later from two
other couples who cherish him as well (one in Greece, one in Toronto), he continues to suffer, we might say, from an unbearable grief of overattachment. "To
survive was to escape fate. But if you escape your fate, whose life do you then step
into?" (48) As the one dream I recounted shows, the dead are always with him,
in sleep as in waking, especially his adored older sister, Bella. At times, he says,
he hears "her breathing or singing next to me in the dark, half terrified that my
ear was pressed against the thin wall between the living and the dead, that the vi-
brating membrane between them was so fragile" (31).

Wilkomirski's child, who was confronted everywhere with unspeakable horror in the visual assaults of atrocity—as, for example, the sight one morning of
blue babies, who had gnawed their frozen fingers down to the white bones—can
declare finally at one of the worst moments, "I'm just an eye, taking in what it
sees, giving nothing back" (87). But the obsession that drives Jakob is precisely
the fact that he was hidden away, first in the closet, then in the peat bog, and
again on Zakynthos. "I did not witness the most important events of my life,"
he mourns. "My deepest story must be told by a blind man, a prisoner of sound.
From behind a wall, from underground. From the corner of a small house on a
small island that juts like a bone from the skin of the sea" (17). Worst of all is the
uncertainty about Bella's fate, the fruitless search to learn what happened to her.
"Night after night, I endlessly follow Bella's path from the front door of my parents' house. In order to give her death a place. This becomes my task. I collect
facts, trying to reconstruct events in minute detail. Because Bella might have died
anywhere along that route. In the street, in the train, in the barracks" (139).
Jakob's life story is constructed between two poles—the duty to remember, to
keep faith with the dead, and the need to separate from them, to accept the reality of the split between absence and presence, then and now, in a lyrical (but almost clinical) example of Freud's theories on mourning and melancholia. For all
the care that is lavished upon him by Athos, the father substitute, and for all the
maternal affection he receives from women (wives of Athos's friends or of his
own), Bella's haunting image prevents him from embracing the present with any
joy. This holds true especially in his relationship with his first wife, Alex, whose

exuberant and unconventional love of life, her love for music like Bella's, only drives him further into his conviction that he is betraying those whom he has lost.

Despite the enormous differences between these two works, both are marked by their creation of an interior mindscape wherein the past continually erupts into the present, triggered, often unexpectedly, by fleeting sensory signals or some small occurrence in an endless variety of repetitive, fragmentary recollections and associative images. For Jakob, "every moment is two moments," an "overheard word fastened to a melody," a gesture, an object, a smell (138, 109); and where recollection fails because memory is absent, his imagination takes over to fill the gaps of what might have, must have, happened—whether in the immediate scenes of his childhood home or in his eventual knowledge of the fate that befell all of European Jewry. In Wilkomirski's case, however, this layering of different points of time is born out of confusion and ignorance, with no firm line drawn between his experiences during and after the war. If anything, the world seems even more dangerous in his new surroundings, because now everything is "hidden and disguised. . . . They've taken off their uniforms . . . but they can still kill" (150–51). It's only a matter of time, especially since the adaptive survival strategies he had learned in the camps now bring him only ridicule, and his self-taught capacity to make sense of experience entraps him further in a web of misunderstanding.

In what is perhaps the most humiliating moment of the book, he interprets a picture of William Tell as an SS man shooting at a child. Yet there is something seriously wrong with the picture, he realizes, since "only grown ups get shot . . . or they go into the gas. The children get thrown in the fire, or killed by hand— mostly that is" (129–30). His Swiss teacher's furious reaction to this "drivel" now reminds him of a vicious block warden he once knew, her red sweater evoking images of fire and blood, and the jeers of the other children alienate him further. "And anyway—SS men don't shoot apples—that's just stupid." Once he's killed the hungry child, Tell will eat it himself. The teacher must be lying, and even if the other children believe her, he doesn't. She doesn't punish him, but the other children fall upon him after school, and their fury bewilders him: "Why do they fight me? They're children too" (133).

For this orphan, the dream he has earlier reported even finally turns into what he thinks is reality, when at the age of ten or twelve he goes on a group outing to the mountains and sees the ski lift that takes children up the mountain on hooks attached to ropes, run by an immense iron wheel, that disappear finally into a yawning black hole upon arrival. The death machine, he thinks. The grave's inside the mountain, agrees another child, who is the only other one to have understood from her experience what he, too, knows. But this is a girl he will see only this one time and never again (140–42). Life has once more withdrawn the possibility of an enduring connection, one that might be constructed on shared memories, however terrible they might be, and the comforting presence of an other who speaks his language. Society has turned its back on him. This is the cruelest blow of all, and the stark depiction of this breach between the despair of the lost child from "over there" and an unfeeling, at best indifferent, Swiss environment of obtuse conformity is one of the most compelling features of the book.

The narrators of both works come eventually to learn the wider historical facts as they mature, but this knowledge is not truly a solace for either. Jakob learns that "history and memory share events; that is, they share time and space," but "one, history is amoral: events occurred, and the other, memory is moral, what we consciously remember is what our conscience remembers. . . . History is the *Totenbuch,* The Book of the Dead, kept by the administrators of the camps. Memory is the *Memorbücher,* the names of those to be mourned, read aloud in the synagogue. . . . I seek out the horror which, like history itself, can't be stanched. I read everything I can. My eagerness for details is offensive" (138). This knowledge leads him to fashion that itinerary for Bella cited above, but also to broaden his empathy with all those victims in contemplating their collective destinies, whether from "Kielce or Brno or Grodno . . . or Lvov or Berlin," and to suffer all the more. "I couldn't turn my anguish from the precise moment of death. I was focused on that historical split second: the tableau of the haunting trinity—perpetrator, victim, witness" (139–40).

Wilkomirski's narrator is already a senior in high school when he learns about the Nazi system and World War II, absorbing his lessons with a passion but keeping it secret from his foster parents, for whom the subject was taboo. "I wanted to know everything. I wanted to absorb every detail and understand every connection. I hoped I would find answers for the pictures that came from my broken childhood memory some nights to stop me going to sleep and to give me terrifying nightmares. I wanted to know what other people had gone through back then and compare it with my own earliest memories. . . . But the longer I spent at it . . . the more elusive the answer—in the sense of what actually happened—became." The question that now haunts him has haunted so many other survivors: Why me and not others? Why me, when I was so unworthy and had a bad conscience over my betrayals and desertions? (147–48) Worst of all, it is only when the teacher shows a documentary film about the Nazi period and the camps that he learns about liberation by the Allies. He sees happy faces as the tanks roll in; embraces, cheering, food being handed out. But he never was liberated; he just ran away from the camp, and people on the outside only jeered: "We thought Hitler had gassed the lot of you." "Nobody," he cries out in anger, "ever told me the war was over, that the old times and their evil games and rules were over and I could go forward without fear or threat into a new time and a new world." And still struggling fiercely with himself to hold on to the one reality he knew and understood, he is forced to admit "perhaps it's true—somehow I missed my own liberation" (149, 151).

Jakob, in his maturity, undergoes a belated epiphany. On a winter afternoon in Greece, he suddenly comes to realize that "to remain with the dead is to abandon them." All the years, he says, "I felt Bella entreating me, filled with her loneliness, I was mistaken. I have misunderstood her signals. Like other ghosts, she whispers, not for me to join her, but so that, when I'm close enough, she can push me back into the world" (170). Wilkomirski's narrator also undergoes a transformation when he grows up, but it is one far more radical, in that to establish his identity and certainty of being, he searches for a voice that would be his, looks to others to help him clarify the fragments of memory he carries and arrange them in a more coherent order. He writes "these fragments of memory," he says, "to explore both myself and my earliest childhood." And like so many other survivors before him, "it may also have been an attempt to set myself free" (155). In writing, in telling, he would find the liberation he had missed at the end of the war. Several years ago, this would have been the message, enhanced by his stated desire to help others like himself to find empathetic listeners and to assuage his feelings of estrangement by retrieving an authentic self. But now we know that Wilkomirski is not what and who he says he is. Yet it is perhaps all the more astonishing that he could imagine so intensely an identity and a set of memories that he truly believes in—and, even more incredible, that he has managed to produce a text that corresponds to what clinical experience has discovered about some child survivors, for whom "a smell, a sound, an image evoke fragments of images or emotions, more compelling than current reality, fragments to which all experiences of pain, anger, fear, shame, and powerlessness have attached themselves."[27]

As a Canadian psychiatrist has recently observed:

The most pervasive preoccupation of child survivors is the continuing struggle with memory, whether there is too much or too little. . . . For a child survivor today, an even more vexing problem is the intrusion of fragments of memory—most are emotionally powerful and painful but make no sense. They seem to become more frequent with time and are triggered by thousands of subtle or not so subtle events. . . . As children they were encouraged not to tell, but to lead normal lives and forget the past. . . . Some are able to protect themselves by splitting time into past, present, and future. . . . The interviewer can assist in sequencing fragments of memory, sometimes even filling in gaps with historical information and other data. Fragments of memory which made no sense had often been experienced as "crazy" and never shared with anyone. . . . To achieve relief for symptomatic child survivors, the knowledgeable thera-pist elicits memories, assists in their integration, makes sense of the se-quence and encourages the child survivor to write their story, publish it, tape, or teach it.[28]

Wilkomirski's case, for some, is only one more instance of the problems associ-ated with recent efforts towards recovering memories of childhood trauma. In many instances, these techniques have proved destructive, resulting in false or mistaken accusations and casting doubt on the reliability of childhood memory in general. While it is true that childhood amnesia is a common occurrence, re-cent work on child survivors of the Holocaust often confirms the findings of the psychologist whose work I have quoted above.[29] Although it might be argued that Wilkomirski might have had access to this data, taking the facts he needed from his historical research and structuring his narrative accordingly, as a "constructed formal analogue of traumatic recall,"[30] the actual results certainly exceed any sense of mimetic exactness or mechanical falsification.[31]

From a psychological standpoint, no doubt, parallels of another kind in the clinical literature could be found to validate the symptoms of Jakob Beer's psy-chic life and the wounded sense of self as depicted so vividly (and poetically) in Anne Michaels's novel.[32] Images and metaphors seem to rise, unbidden, out of the text from some secret inner space like a kind of vibrant "soul-music" that cap-tures the subtle intensities of sadness, love, guilt, and longing.[33] Nothing in Holo-caust literature comes close to the richness and density of the huge imagination at work here: the intricate symmetries, the bold interlayering of art and science, nature and poetry, history and music, as well as the expansion of horizons—both temporally and spatially, in height as in depth, in geology as in geography— which no brief summary can hope to convey.[34] Throughout a single note plays with infinite variations: What is the meaning of death? What happens to the dead when the memory of them is still lodged in the living, acutely present, and they reside in a twilight space between ghost and flesh? From the child who emerges from his entombment in the Polish peat bog to the buried memories of his loved ones which continually resurface, the work of mourning is a continual excavation of sorts, one that is matched by Athos's profession. "Athos was an expert in buried and abandoned places. His cosmology became mine. I grew into it natu-rally. In this way, our tasks became the same" (49). Furthermore, "because Athos's love was paleobotany, because his heroes were rock and wood as well as human, I learned not only the history of men but the history of earth. . . . I learned the power we give to stones to hold human time" (32). It cannot be by chance that Michaela, his second wife, the soul mate he finds late in life, is an ar-chaeologist, who unearths lost evidence of the past from the ground.[35]

The child of *Fragments* has been displaced from a home he remembers only in a few disconnected images and follows an odyssey through the camps to postwar Poland and eventually to Switzerland, where he feels even more isolated and estranged. "I couldn't pull the two worlds together. . . . I could only get away from this unbearable strange present by going back to the world and images of my past. Yes, they were almost as unbearable, but they were familiar, at least I understood their rules" (68). Displacement is an even more pervasive theme in the case of Jakob, another adopted orphan, who leaves Poland for Greece and later migrates to Canada, but returns to Greece on several visits. He, too, inhabits several worlds, in mind as in experience. Literally, of course, his trajectory has taken him to different continents, different cultures. But his mind, too, can shuttle between the ever present memories of his home and the wider realm that Athos's scientific lessons had taught him to inhabit, "one big as the globe and expansive as time" (29). The broader perspective objectifies the world in nature as a way of opening up unknown vistas and explorations that are the antidote to Jakob's solitary communion with his dead. But its islands and rocks, its weather systems and currents, its lands and seas, also supply a source of subjective identification that consoles and at the same time revives personal sorrow. "It is no metaphor to feel the influence of the dead in the world, just as it is no metaphor to hear the radiocarbon chronometer, the Geiger counter amplifying the faint breathing of rock, fifty thousand years old (like the faint thump from behind the womb wall)" (53). Nature does not forget. Landscape is personified; it can be wounded by destructive upheavals, in war or through natural disasters, such as earthquake or hurricane; and it, too, solicits grief and empathy. Landscape is also the familiar terrain of home. "What is a man, who has no landscape? Nothing but mirrors and tides. . . . Try to be buried in ground that will remember you" (76, 78).

Jakob's profession as a poet turns the "power of language to destroy, omit, obliterate" into the power to restore (79). His two volumes are appropriately named *Groundworks* and *What Have You Done to Time,* and his efforts as a translator mediate his geographical wanderings in a linguistic amalgam of the various cultural strands woven into the texture of his life. Unlike the poet, he says, who "moves from life to language, the translator moves from language to life; both, like the immigrant, try to identify the invisible, what's between the lines, the mysterious implications" (109). By contrast, Wilkomirski's child begins his narrative with the despairing sense of no authentic language. "I have no mother tongue, nor a father tongue either. . . . The languages I learned later on were never mine. . . . They were only imitations of other people's speech" (4–5).

The theme of the child is not a new one in imaginative literature of atrocity. Quite the contrary. A number of the most memorable books engage the child's point of view with devastating effects. Jerzy Kosinski's *Painted Bird* comes first to

mind as an analogy to *Fragments* in the portrait of a brutalized child who attempts
to make sense of a vicious world and comes of age in the most desperate of conditions.[36] But one can also point to a good deal of the work of Aharon Appelfeld,
himself a child survivor, including *Tzili* and the *Age of Wonders,* or to Louis Begley's *Wartime Lies,* among many other examples.[37] Moreover, the focus on the
child, the most vulnerable of all victims, not only sharpens the impact of attempted genocide but also allows for the special perspective of that mysterious
inner world of a child's consciousness, one that when encompassed within adult
narrative, especially from hindsight, promotes a double vision.[38] At this juncture
in time, the last witnesses are indeed the survivor children, in whom interest has
really surfaced only in recent years. Previously, they were thought to be too
young to remember, and their experiences were discounted by comparison to
the sufferings of adults.[39] Nor is the next generation exempt, as we become
aware of the legacy of trauma to children of survivors and their own role now in
witnessing, captured so powerfully in Art Spiegelman's *Maus* or in the fictional
work of their contemporaries, such as the figure of Momik in David Grossman's
remarkable novel, *See: Under Love.*[40]

Fugitive Pieces insists on the continuities, intersections, and reciprocities between first and second generations. Athos's flight from the buried prehistoric
city, Biskupin, with the child he rescued was also the means, as it happened, of
his own rescue from the fate of his other colleagues, who shortly thereafter were
either murdered by the Nazis or sent to the camps. The premature death of his
beloved wife, Helen, as we later learn, helps him all the more to engage with
Jakob's loss. More important, the last part of the book is given over to the figure
of Ben, a meteorologist by profession, the child of survivors in Canada, who carries the burdens of his parents' wounded lives. Himself wounded, he uncannily
replicates in part the unhappy sequencing of Jakob's still unresolved hauntings
from the past and shares the older man's engrossment in both music and science.
His marriage, like Jakob's first one, is in jeopardy, and he, too, writes books. In
Ben's case, these are efforts to link the random catastrophic effects of extreme
weather to the events of both history and biography, not unlike the lessons Jakob
had absorbed about science, the self, and the world. For him, a weather map is
"like a musical score; when you read it, you are reading time. . . . One could
chart a life in terms of pressure zones, fronts, oceanic influences" (122).

But in contrast with Jakob, the memories that haunt him are not his own, and
he is caught in a larger history that oppresses him at every turn. Ben has difficulty
understanding his parents, who, typical of survivors, are overprotective (his
mother) or overly perfectionist (his father), and he is impatient with the anxieties
that rule their lives. His father, a music teacher, lives in dread of drawing attention to himself, whether in initially refusing rescue from a flooded house or in ap-

plying for his pension. Yet while he insists that his son—named only generically, Ben (in Hebrew, the word for *son*)—learn about the Holocaust through books and especially through searing photographic images, he and Ben's mother, like so many other survivors, harbor dark secrets of their own which they are never able to reveal to him.

It was Ben, let us note, who, after Jakob's death, goes to Greece to search for the other man's lost memoirs. At the outset of the novel, we are told that "during the Second World War, countless manuscripts—diaries, memoirs, eyewitness accounts—were lost or destroyed. Some of these narratives were deliberately hidden—buried in back gardens, tucked into walls and under floors—by those who did not live to retrieve them. Other stories are concealed in memory, neither written nor spoken. Still others are recovered, by circumstances alone" (1). Ben was lucky in his quest. But in finding Jakob's missing notebooks (the text we have been reading all along), Ben does more than unearth the sought-after object, does more than serve as the custodian and transmitter of Jakob's memories in keeping faith with the dead. He becomes the spiritual or adoptive heir to Jakob's own experience, now for his own transformation, so that he can come to terms with the reasons for his failure to love his wife, Naomi, and hope to recover that relationship, now that his parents are gone.

Whereas Wilkomirski's child has no genealogy he can call his own (the deepest source of his estrangement), *Fugitive Pieces* suggests that it is the transfer of affection to others not related by blood that can bring some closure to the act of mourning and authorize the sense of an individual identity. If adoption counts more than biology, then Ben can overcome his fatalistic conviction that "my parents' past is mine molecularly" (280). Marriage, too, introduces an other into the family circle to disrupt or mediate between kin. Even more, it is the intertwining of stories and destinies—Athos with Jakob, Jakob with Ben—that enlarges the field of sympathy and endows these relationships with restorative power, even as Naomi was able to love her in-laws to Ben's initial consternation and envy. Having now read Jakob's memoirs and inspected the shortcomings of his own life, which include his betrayal of Naomi on the island with an American woman appropriately named Petra,[41] Ben can finally conclude: "In the hotel room the night before I leave Greece, I know the elation of ordinary sorrow. At last my unhappiness is my own" (292).

Ben had learned his parents' deepest secret only after his father's death, when he discovers a photograph, dated June 1941, of a happy couple with two children, whom he realizes were ones his parents had loved and lost and of whose existence he had never known. For the author, anyone born after the war is in Ben's position, "not precisely but philosophically," and hence this is one reason he is so crucial to the entire story. Michaels's aim finally, as she has said, was "to look at how events we don't live through ourselves shape us and what invisible connection there is between history and personal life."[42] In her redemptive vision, which depends on finding love and in crossing the bridge to empathy and understanding, the longing for children of one's own is finally the sign of accepting that bridge between history and personal life, as it has been for so many other survivors. The note Ben finds in Jakob and Michaela's bedroom after their death reads simply, "if a boy, Bela, if a girl, Bella" (278–79; cf. 195).

From Wilkomirski's account as a purported primary eyewitness, himself subjected to the effects of atrocity and deprivation; to Jakob's story, still of the first generation, but one who did not witness the events that shaped his life; and from Ben, the survivors' child, who is compelled to imagine what took place before he was born, we move to my third and last example, whose dream we have already heard but have not yet attended. He, too, belongs to the second generation, and yet, in a still more daring experiment with Holocaust memory, he comes from the other side—that of the perpetrators. Bernard Schlink's short, enigmatic novel *The Reader* (Der Vorleser) is a story of brief happiness, pain, loss, ambivalence, and psychic numbing that exemplifies in another way Michaels's insistence on searching for the "invisible connection . . . between history and personal life." Recollected from a distance of a number of years, Schlink's narrator, too, is preoccupied with the relations of the present to the past, of his own story to the larger one that surrounds it. "The tectonic layers of our lives rest so tightly one on top of the other that we always come up against earlier events in later ones, not as matter that has been fully formed and pushed aside, but absolutely present and alive. I understand this. Nevertheless, I sometimes find it hard to bear" (217–18).

Written primarily for a German audience, the book is even more provocative than the other two in the questions it raises, both personal and political, and the answers it does *not* give—at least not to our satisfaction. The work concerns a fifteen-year-old adolescent growing up in a German town during the 1950s who accidentally enters into a clandestine relationship with an older woman a bit more than twice his age. This relationship, oddly enough, is conducted not just through sex but also through her insistence that he read aloud to her in intimate literary sessions. Difference in class as well as in age adds a further dimension to their story. The boy, Michael Berg, knows virtually nothing of her life; she is now a streetcar conductor, while he is the child of a professor of philosophy who has resumed his career after losing his position during the war for delivering a lecture on Spinoza. An aloof and distant father, he presides over a household crammed with books and abstract ideas. As the power relationships shift between Michael and Hanna, she is at first dominant, often unreasonable, and even cruel in sudden anger or cold withdrawal, although in this strange liaison, he later also seems to gain the upper hand. But then, tempted back into the world of his peers—he fails at one crucial point to acknowledge her—he "disavows" her, he thinks, and she disappears, leaving him feeling both guilt and humiliation, both anger and abjectness at what he thinks was his betrayal of her.

In the second part of the book, when after a number of years he is now a law student, Michael encounters Hanna in a courtroom. He learns she was a guard in a Nazi concentration camp, on trial for her part in a terrible event at the end of the war, when a church containing women prisoners was bombed and caught fire. The women burned to death because the doors were locked and the guards had the key. That is, all perished except two, a mother and daughter, whose account brought the case to light and was the primary evidence that brought Hanna and her companions to trial during the 1960s. In the course of the proceedings, the narrator discovers another secret, which he deduces from Hanna's courtroom behavior—she does not know how to read. The fact of her illiteracy and her desperate desire to conceal it had organized the whole course of her life. It led her finally to stumble into her role as an SS guard, we are told, rather than betray her shame when offered a promotion in the factory position she was holding at the time. It is also the reason she had disappeared from Michael's life under similar circumstances in her job as a streetcar conductor, not because, as he thought, he had failed to acknowledge her presence in the company of his friends on the last occasion they crossed paths.

While Hanna is in prison serving a lengthy sentence, Michael marries briefly and has a child, but then he drifts off. After eight years have gone by, he begins to send Hanna homemade tape recordings of books and continues to do so for ten more years, though he never goes to see her. He keeps the relationship entirely impersonal. He never asks for any information or reveals anything about himself, nor does he answer the notes she now occasionally sends. He just records the author, title, and text of the book in question, including his own work when he starts to write himself, although we have no idea of its contents. Called upon by the prison warden at the time of her expected release, he once again comes face to face with her, now an aging and unattractive woman who no longer matches the image he has retained of their previous life together. He discovers she has finally learned to read; her prison cell is stacked with books on the Holocaust, among other works. In the end, she commits suicide, leaving him feeling just as confused as before. Even ten years later, the narrator still confesses: "I was tormented by the old questions of whether I had denied and betrayed her, whether I owed her something, whether I was guilty for having loved her. And sometimes if I was responsible for her death. And sometimes I was in a rage at her and at what she had done to me. Until finally the rage faded and the questions ceased to matter. Whatever I had done or not done, whatever she had done or not to me—it was the path my life had taken" (216).

But Hanna had also left a legacy. In her will, she asked Michael to give her meager funds, including money she had kept in a little lavender tin box, to the daughter who had survived the fire in the church, now living in New York, for whatever purpose she should choose. This last encounter is as disturbing in its own way as the rest of the book. The journey takes him to the United States, and for the first time he actually confronts a victim of the Holocaust, who quickly and matter-of-factly punctures any of his illusions. She will not accept Hanna's money. "Using it for something to do with the Holocaust would really seem like an absolution to me, and that is something I neither wish nor care to grant" (214). He can donate it to any Jewish organization he wishes. Although the daughter wryly remarks that "illiteracy, it has to be admitted, is hardly a Jewish problem," he eventually finds one called the Jewish League Against Illiteracy (for as she had remarked with equal irony, "if there are organizations for something, then there are Jewish organizations for it" [215]).

However, the daughter wants to keep the little tin. It reminds her of the one remaining childhood treasure in which she had kept her few mementoes. She had brought it to the camp, but it was stolen from her. "The tin itself, and what could be done with it, were worth a lot" there (214). This one small detail—the history of a commonplace object, souvenir of the daughter's prewar childhood, keepsake of the concentration camp guard—gestures ironically (and painfully) to a whole history of the failed relationship between Germany and its Jews, who shared the same culture, down to love of the same trivial objects. For however Hanna had atoned in prison for the atrocities she committed, her possessions remained intact, while the daughter's cherished token disappeared into the brutal economy of the camps, valued as never before.

This jolt from the outside world, a reality testing of sorts, is in its own way also disconcerting. The daughter's reaction indicates an unbridgeable gap between victim and perpetrator. There is no question of forgiveness, if that was what Michael had hoped. But she also astutely divines (the only one to do so) not only the erotic nature of his relationship with Hanna but also its destructive influence on the subsequent emotional failures of his life. Did she know, asks the daughter, what she had done to you? He can give no answer to that question, although he is convinced that Hanna came "to know what she did in the camps" (213). Does the daughter then see Michael as a victim, too, one who has also suffered from Hanna's disregard for human life? Does her cutting verdict, even if not acknowledged by him in this scene, reinforce the uneasy parallels between Holocaust victim and perpetrator in their erotic liaison, parallels which in his account keep shifting from one side to the other?

The Reader is and is not a parable of the haunted relationships between German children and their parents in the aftermath of the war. Alienated from his own peers, failed in his subsequent marriage, and uncertain of his own feelings,

Michael reflects on the course of his life when he speaks of the impulse that led him to undertake the relationship with Hanna: "I don't know why I did it. But today I can recognize that events back then were part of a life long pattern in which thinking and doing have either come together or failed to come together—I think, I reach a conclusion, I turn the conclusion into a decision, and then discover that acting on the decision is something else entirely, and that doing so may proceed from the decision, but then again it may not. Often enough . . . I have done things I had not decided to do. Something goes into action" (20). The problem is that he can neither identify with the past, though he is bound to it by his relationship with Hanna; nor can he fully enter into the world of his own generation, which he finds too smug and judgmental. "I envied the students who by then had dissociated themselves from their parents and thus from the entire generation of perpetrators, voyeurs, and willfully blind, accommodators and acceptors, thereby overcoming perhaps not their shame, but at least their suffering because of that shame. . . . But then how could one feel guilt and shame, and at the same time parade one's self righteousness. . . . Was their dissociation mere rhetoric . . . to drown out the fact that their love for their parents made them irrevocably complicit in their crimes?" These thoughts, he tells us, "did not come until later and even then brought no comfort. How could it be a comfort that the pain I went through because of my love for Hanna was, in a way, the fate of my generation, a German fate, and that it was only more difficult for me to evade, to manage, than for others. All the same, it would have been good for me back then to be able to feel I was part of my generation" (171).

Like so much else in this cryptic and maddeningly spare text, the dream, too, is susceptible of varying interpretations. The grand house about which Michael continues to dream, long after it is torn down, is the apartment house where Hanna lived. Its dominant size on the block, his previous imaginings of its rich interior but also of its now ugly and deformed inhabitants, suggest that the building stands for the generation that preceded him and the bourgeois elegance of a prewar era. But the discrepancy between outside and inside must also stand for Hanna herself, now that her past is known, even as she is the all too intimate emblem of that generation. The house is familiar because he recognizes it wherever he sees it in the dream. He takes comfort in it like a long-lost friend, but its displacement onto other towns and other landscapes is also deeply unsettling. What is more, whether he finds the house in the city or the country, the dream ends with his hand on the doorknob. He turns the knob but never enters the house. The dream is not exactly a nightmare but nevertheless the symptom of a malaise he never loses. His relationship to the house, an inanimate object, takes the place of contact with persons. He is always alone: the road he follows is deserted, and the world around him is dead and lifeless, not unlike the dream images of Wilkomirski's solitary child. After Hanna, he was never able to establish a satisfying intimate relationship. But since his recurrent dream, it is presumed, begins after his affair is over, the dream reflects his further inability to situate that intimacy in the context of what the building has come to represent. It reverts to the earlier image he had conceived of the house, when he passed it as a child, but he also knows that in reality it no longer even exists, having been torn down some years before. It is the memory of it that now remains uncomfortably alive, and with its dusty, opaque exterior, it turns a blind eye to his unarticulated desire.

A significant element of the dream recurs in another context. Reflecting on the unreality of the Holocaust in his own mind, Michael determines to confront the past by "direct observation" and so decides to visit the nearest concentration camp, Struthof (Natzweiler) in Alsace. When he was growing up, before the popular culture of television and film had stimulated the imagination to "supplement and embellish" what had previously been merely registered, it was difficult to get beyond the "few images derived from Allied photographs and the testimony of survivors," which "flashed on the mind again and again, until they froze into clichés" (148). His tour of the camp, however, leaves no tangible psychological impression, despite the fact that he dutifully examines the topography of the now deserted camp, with its barracks, crematorium, cells, and memorial, which he visits more than once. All was in vain, "and I had a feeling of the most dreadful, shameful failure" (154). At the time, he noticed, too, a "small house opposite a restaurant that had a sign on it indicating it had been a gas chamber. It was painted white, had doors and windows framed in sandstone, and could have been a barn or a shed or servants' living quarters." This building, too, was closed, and "I didn't remember if I had gone inside it on my first visit. I didn't get out of the car. I sat for a while with the motor running, and looked. Then I drove on" (155). We note that in his typically vague way Michael cannot reconstruct the exact scene in his mind, neither on the first visit nor the second. But the essential point is perhaps an unspoken analogy between this house, labeled a gas chamber, and the building in the dream that was formerly the site of his assignations with Hanna. Both are constructed of sandstone, both are incongruous in their present settings, one of which he never enters and the other he cannot recall whether he did or not.

Yet the only vivid aspect of his life was his relationship with Hanna. Like Jakob in *Fugitive Pieces,* Schlink's protagonist is attached to an older female figure who obsesses him, and she, too, like Bella, intervenes in his consciousness to forestall happiness with another. Also like Jakob, he recalls the smallest gestures, the voice, the hair, the scent. Oddly enough, Michael translates his psychological disorientation into a figurative sort of homelessness, as though he himself were a refugee, like Jakob. The *Odyssey* was his favorite book in school, but now that he has become a student of legal history, he interprets it "not as a story of home-coming," as he had once thought, but rather a "story of motion, both purposeful and purposeless, successful and futile" (181–82). In fact, Homer's epic is the first work he tapes and sends to Hanna in prison. And much later, on his first trip to the United States, en route to the home of the daughter who survived the church fire, he dreams of Hanna and himself in a house there together, realizing even within the dream that time and space are both impossibly distorted. "I woke up and knew that Hanna was dead. I also knew that my desire had fixed on her without her being its object. It was the desire to come home" (211). In this belated dream, home itself, wherever it might be, is *unheimlich,* and the displaced building that appeared in his recurrent dreams is even more so.

In Michael's case, the intertwining of the public and private, his hopelessly compromised feelings towards Hanna, and the moral complexities and misunderstandings on both sides alternately baffle and exasperate the reader, as do the varying interpretations that can be given to the acts of reading, both symbolic and literal, within the text. The angle of vision keeps shifting with shifts in mood; the narrator, whose claustrophobic viewpoint dominates the text, remains entirely within himself, so we must depend entirely on what he says, even if tempted, as most of us are, to intuit or supplement what he leaves out. As Joyce Hackett acutely observes, "Depending on how you read it, Michael as narrator is either reliable or unreliable; Schlink is either advancing the apologist position that in Nazi Germany there was no visible line—or chillingly depicting the problem, which is that Michael's complicitous love for Hanna makes him unable to draw it."[43]

It would be easy to reach a negative conclusion about this work as some have done, including one well-known Jewish author who has voiced her indignant rejection of a book that would desecrate the Holocaust by equating illiteracy with exoneration of terrible crimes.[44] If this were so, however, the opposite equation should also hold true. Yet, as we know, one of the most serious affronts to our notion of civilization has been the knowledge that the heritage of German culture, with its history of achievement in music, literature, and philosophy, did not avail to stem the tide of a barbaric ideology. Quite the contrary. Goethe's famous oak, as often noted, stood outside the gates of Buchenwald. SS personnel in the camps waxed ecstatic over concerts of Beethoven performed by inmate musicians. Within the book itself, all the classic texts that Michael reads to Hanna, both during their affair and later in prison, may "testify to a great and fundamental confidence in bourgeois culture" (185), but they have hardly equipped him to deal with the moral issues that plague him or given him courage and insight into the management of his own life.[45]

At her trial, Hanna is remembered for having selected young and delicate girls as her favorites until they were deported with the rest of the victims. The girls' task, it turned out, despite Hanna's strict demand for secrecy, was to read aloud to her, night after night (116). Whatever they might have read to her certainly made no difference in her subsequent behavior as a guard that night in the church. The other inmates, in any case, had assumed an erotic interest that exploited the weakest among them, and while this conjecture is never confirmed, it also cannot be ruled out altogether. The book as a whole, after all, is governed by two kinds of desires: the erotic passion between the boy and Hanna and Hanna's passion for knowledge, education, and culture, which established a relationship that oddly combined the acts of lovemaking and of reading aloud.[46]

At the trial, Michael is as puzzled as we are by Hanna's illiteracy as the key to all her actions. "I could understand she was ashamed at not being able to read or write, and would rather drive me away than expose herself. I was no stranger to shame as the cause of behavior that was deviant or defensive, secretive or misleading or hurtful. But could Hanna's shame at being illiterate be sufficient reason for her behavior at the trial or in the camp? . . . If Hanna's motive was fear of exposure—why opt for the horrible exposure as a criminal over the harmless exposure as an illiterate?" (133) What he wants to know most of all was whether her actions were motivated by evil intent or by the reflexive defense of her secret shame, and after much anguished reasoning, he comes down in favor of the latter, especially with regard to her recruitment. "She had decided against a promotion at Siemens, and fell into a job as a guard" (133). In his eyes, everything followed from that point and was borne out by what happened at the trial. Yet he turns that anguish, too, against himself: "However, the fact that I had not driven her away did not change the fact that I had betrayed her. So I was still guilty. And if I was not guilty because one cannot be guilty of betraying a criminal, then I was guilty of having loved a criminal" (134). Nevertheless, the end of the book suggests that during the long years of imprisonment, Hanna had come to an understanding of her moral responsibility and could acknowledge her guilt, in part because of the trial and to a greater extent because she was able to educate herself through reading historical accounts and memoirs of the Holocaust. Surely, there is a distinction between a passive reception of culture (being read to) and an active engagement with it (reading for and by oneself). In prison, Hanna may still be a listener to the tapes sent by Michael, but now she can also *choose* what to read—and this may make all the difference.[47] Nevertheless, certain irreducible problems remain.

If "illiteracy in the story," as Eva Hoffman comments, "stands not only for the deficiency of book-learning, but also for an inability to decipher the world and the attendant helplessness," then "owing to her insulation, Hanna gets caught in a situation she has not chosen, and whose wider context, meanings, and implications she cannot grasp." But as a "notional explanation" for Hanna's behavior, Hoffman continues, the problem is the representation of Hanna's character altogether, which although "filtered through the narrator's vision and voice . . . her wartime past . . . is presented so sparsely, and at such a speculative remove, that the force of her ignorance in that situation is never persuasively shown."[48]

The connection between literacy and morality is by no means self-evident. In fact, it is worth mentioning in this context another work in which the issue of literacy is also at stake, but functions in quite an opposite way. This is Claude Lelouch's epic film, *Les Misérables* (1995), which recasts Victor Hugo's classic into a twentieth-century version of France under Nazi occupation and translates the figure of Jean Valjean into an illiterate truck driver and former boxer, Henri Fortin. On the run from the threat of a false imprisonment, Fortin finds himself heroically striving to save the various members of a Jewish family, also on the run, especially the young daughter, who is a stand-in for Cosette. Relentlessly pursued by a latter-day Javert, he follows the dictates of his conscience on more than one occasion. The only reward he asks is that his passengers on these and other trips read aloud to him Hugo's novel, since again and again he has been told that it bears an uncanny resemblance to the course of his own life. Just as bookish in its own way as *The Reader,* the film, according to a quasi-romantic ideology, may also support the desire for literacy and all it is meant to signify. But what motivates the protagonist's behavior is the simple and unequivocal morality of a "natural man" who does the right thing because he cannot do otherwise.

There are other disquieting aspects to *The Reader* which have scarcely been mentioned. Since it was written, after all, for a German audience, we, for our part, may view some unexamined problems quite differently. Michael's original motive for attending the trial of the camp guards had nothing to do with Hanna, whom he did not know would be one of the defendants. As a law student, he was a member of a seminar on the question of retroactive justice, led by an old professor who had returned from exile but remained an outsider in legal circles. The issue they were investigating was meritorious: how to judge the violation of statutes against murder already on the books but enforced quite differently in the Nazi era, particularly in the case of mass extermination. Well and good. The defense of only having "followed orders" is well known in all such trials, and the conflict between the demands of personal morality and state-sponsored crime in obedience to orders is hardly a trivial one. But it is also the nature of courtroom proceedings to raise another problem, one that in the success or failure of legal maneuvers may prove to separate law from the administration of justice. Hanna has an incompetent lawyer (in whom at any rate she does not confide) and her bewildered candor only further antagonizes the judge, ensuring that of all the defendants she is the one who will be made to take the largest share of blame. Her fellow guards accuse her of having written the damning report, a charge she cannot contest, since she would have had to admit that she could not read or write. But the verdict of the trial that "unfairly" inculpates Hanna more than she "deserves" only emphasizes all the more, from our point of view, the incommensurable gap between any legal procedure altogether, with its witnesses, evidence, and courtroom protocols, and the nature and extent of the horrific crimes committed.[49]

This is not to say that Michael Berg minimizes the horror of those crimes, nor does he overlook the obnoxious behavior of the lawyers, "with their rhetorical legalistic pugnacity, jabbing pedantry, or loud, calculated truculence." (101) But in observing the general numbness that eventually took hold of the spectators, faced with the continual "intrusion of horror into daily life," he goes on to attribute the same numbness to "perpetrators and victims" as well as to "judges and lay members of the court . . . who had to deal with these events." It is not easy to sort out this double equation, namely which is worse: the inclusion of spectators and court functionaries as sharing the same psychological response as those who experienced these events, or the similarity between prisoners and their persecutors? In the latter case, he quickly disavows any equivalence. He knows well the difference between "enduring suffering and imposing it on others" and makes it clear, if somewhat half-heartedly, that "when I likened perpetrators, victims, the dead, the living, survivors, and their descendants to each other, I didn't feel good about it and I still don't" (103).

What exercises him most, however, is the dilemma of his own generation: "What should it do with the knowledge of the horrors of the extermination of the Jews?" There is no place for comprehension, comparisons, or discussion, because that would turn the Holocaust into an object of discussion. Silence is their only recourse. "To what purpose," he asks, and ends with the cry: "But that some few would be convicted and punished while we of the second generation were silenced by revulsion, shame, and guilt—was that all there was to it now?" (104) Above all, he uses the occasion to indict the first generation when he has Hanna confront the judge and ask him point blank: under the same circumstances in the panic of the fire in the church, "what would *you* have done?" The judge's reply is abstract and evasive and hardly did "justice," says the narrator (with what we hope is a certain irony), "to the seriousness of her question. . . . She had wanted to know what she should have done in her particular situation, not that there are things that are not done" (112; cf. 128).[50]

A second, perhaps more disturbing omission occurs in the scene with Michael's father, equally of the judge's generation. Having divined Hanna's secret, Michael finds himself in an acute moral predicament. Should he intervene and tell the judge now what he knew, a fact which might help her case ("she was guilty, but not as guilty as she appeared"), or simply remain silent and not "barter her self-image for a few years in prison" (137–38)? He goes to his father, the professor of moral philosophy who had written books on Kant and Hegel, to ask his advice. I introduce this scene here because it brings us back to the issue of the meaning of culture, education, and a library of books, and also because the generic difficulty of such a decision is one that forces readers, too, perhaps for the only time in the book, to situate themselves in the place of the other. What would we have done? What would we do now if faced with such a choice in any far less loaded situation?[51] Michael frames the question only in the abstract, even though his father assumes the matter has something to do with the trial. Under normal circumstances, his father's reply is commendable. "It is not the future happiness of a person that is in question." Rather, "he instructed me about the individual, about freedom and dignity, about the human being as subject and the fact that one may not turn him into an object" (141). While Michael's first reaction was relief that he did not have to act (his usual tendency), his father's further advice was to speak with the person directly in an effort at persuasion, a step Michael could certainly not take.

One of the main purposes of the scene is to highlight the relationship between a son and his remote parent, who was never available to him as a child. Michael had to make an appointment to see the professor, as though he were one of his father's students. His father, we may recall, had been relieved of his professorial post during the Nazi regime for having delivered a lecture on Spinoza. Still, his son had placed him, too, under "a sentence of shame," as did all his peers with their parents, "even if the only charge we could bring was that after 1945 they had tolerated the perpetrators in their midst" (92). At any rate, the outcome of their awkward conversation does nothing to resolve the embarrassment they share in each other's presence. Once again the personal and the political intersect with unresolved ambivalence. But for readers on the other side, the father's advice requires at least the intimation of an ironic undercurrent. Under the influence of Kant and Hegel, how could a professor of philosophy, after 1945, speak of the dignity and freedom of the individual without a single trace of self-reflection? How could one speak authoritatively of not treating a person as an object, when an entire political culture had dehumanized an entire group of persons, even and especially before sending them to their deaths? All the more so under the present circumstances of a trial, which the father must have known revolved around the criminal culpability for just such a series of acts, in the camps and on the death marches?[52] Like the judge, the father, too, takes refuge in abstractions rather than face a genuine issue with courage and some self-reflective humility.[53]

In the long run, what may disturb readers most is the humanization of the perpetrator in the person of Hanna, and Michael's conflicted and lasting attachment to her. While most of us have gotten beyond the comforting idea that those who participated in the Holocaust were somehow set apart from their fellow human beings by some innate depravity or ideological fanaticism, Schlink compels us to confront the uncomfortable reality of ordinary personhood through the lens of his tormented narrator, even though he stops short of giving us a fully realized portrait. Many others, like Hanna, also drifted into the orbit of the camps out of weakness, ignorance, or just happenstance, and, once there, were enlisted into the entire operation and remained with it.[54] While Michael cannot fully accuse his parents—as a number of his friends could theirs and with good reason—he views his love affair in somewhat the same light. "The finger I pointed at her turned back to me. I had loved her. Even more, I had chosen her. I tried to tell myself I had known nothing of what she had done. . . . I tried to talk myself into the state of innocence in which children love their parents. But love of our parents is the only love for which we are not responsible." Although perhaps we are responsible, he adds (170–71).

On the personal level, Michael Berg's story follows a familiar literary scenario. A boy comes of age through an affair with an older woman, a situation which in literature equates adulthood with profound loss and eventual disenchantment, if not a tragic outcome.[55] In this case, Michael never completes his mourning. He never gets beyond his choice of a love object, whom he had no right to love, twice over—for its transparent Oedipal overtones as for the terrible history she carries. One of the activities they share is joint bathing—a species of purificatory rituals for her, a maternal function for him? Schlink's achievement, for all its flaws, is to confuse all the issues without supplying any simple resolutions to the messy accidents of life, on the one hand, or to the horrors of history, on the other. The forbidden erotic merges with and to some extent is paired with the tormented political. Given the social taboo on an affair such as his, Michael has his own alienating secret which he cannot divulge to his family or peers, and Hanna has hers. He feels at times like the victim; at others, he comes close to accusing himself of being a perpetrator. The past is embedded in the body of a woman, whose scent suffuses him with longing and whose power over him remains to haunt his life over these many years, especially in those memories which he would both dispel and revive, a story he thinks was sad but happy. To the end his ambivalence remains, even in the version he finally writes:

> Soon after her death, I decided to write the story of me and Hanna. Since then I've done it many times in my head, a little differently each time, with new images, and new strands of action and thought. Thus there are many different stories in addition to the one I have written. The guaran-

tee that the written one is the right one lies in the fact that I wrote it and not the other versions. (216)

Is this confession merely a postmodern gesture to the indeterminacy of any recollected account? Or is it yet another instance of Michael's own retreat from life, his own apologetic, as it were, for the style of the entire book? He may be the consummate reader, but as a writer he reserves the right to keep us, his readers, at a disconcerting remove. Interestingly enough, there is one book he reads outside his literary canon. This is the survivor daughter's memoir, which he evaluates in a way that quite uncannily mirrors the effect of his own narrative. The memoir had not yet been translated into German, and so he had to read the book in English, which caused him some difficulty. "As always, the alien language, unmastered and struggled over, created a strange concatenation of distance and immediacy." The book itself "remained as alien as the language itself." Later he reads it again, this time in his own language, and realizes that "it is the book that creates distance. It does not invite one to identify with it and makes no one sympathetic, neither the mother nor the daughter, nor those who shared their fate in various camps." Nor does it give a clear enough picture of the oppressors, their names, their faces and shapes, "for the reader to be able to relate to them, to judge their acts for better or for worse. It exudes the very numbness I tried to describe before" (118–19). Yet he admires its powers of analysis and observation as well as the fact that the author had not only survived but was able to "give literary form" to her experiences. While her account is the closest the narrator can come to at least knowing the facts of the events for which Hanna and the other guards were put on trial, he still cannot find the empathy and understanding to make the experience part of his internal life, not unlike the problems he has with recounting his own story in full.

Nothing could be further from Wilkomirski's pseudomemoir, whose narrator, equally alienated from his German-speaking environment, overidentifies with the victims of the Holocaust, to the extent that he has imagined himself to be one of them. Nothing could be further, either, from the premises of *Fugitive Pieces,* in which one man's memoirs are the catalyst for another's self-understanding and, more broadly, suggest a way for memory to continue from one generation to the next. Yet even so, *The Reader,* despite (or because of) its inability to overcome its solipsistic uncertainties, also tells us something important about the workings of memory: its disruptive effects on consciousness as well as on narrative, together with the recording of thoughts, images, and experiences so long after the fact.

The Reader illustrates the problematization of memory itself, the feature that finally unifies these three very different works, along with efforts to relieve—but also to relive—the effects of traumatic experience through the act of writing it-self. If anything, there is what could be called "a surplus of memory" underlying present experience, ready to resurface into uncanny repetition or painful con-trast. The fragmented, at times disjointed jumble of Wilkomirski's images; the poetic density of Jakob Beer's (or Ben's) layered recollections; and Schlink's el-liptical challenge to both history and memory each in its own way uses style as well as content to probe the effects of the Holocaust on present-day comprehen-sion, with a renewed intensity that borders on fixation. For Wilkomirski and Michaels, their voices also correspond to contemporary preoccupations with childhood trauma and vexing questions of fragmentary and incomplete (or even recovered) memory, whose aftereffects of loss and grief are deepened by the gaps in their knowledge and perceptions. Feelings of guilt and shame, along with self-accusations of betraying others, are repeated refrains in all three texts. These powerful emotions are typical for survivors, but they have special resonance in *The Reader.* The novel engages both political and personal issues and involves the collective relations between first and second generations, parents and children, but even more so, the love affair between Michael and Hanna. What is perhaps most interesting (and problematic) is Hanna's moral journey from *shame* at her il-literacy as the major influence in her life to her subsequent acceptance of *guilt* (and responsibility) for what she has done, while Michael remains trapped in his own equivocations, to the extent of audaciously usurping the categories of vic-tim and perpetrator in his private erotic sphere.[56]

The last common feature to be addressed is the intersection between the pol-itics and poetics of memory, which gives two of these works greater depth and relevance—one perhaps accidentally, the other already of long duration. It is deeply ironic that the publication of *Fragments,* the work, long in the making, of a Swiss author, with its indictment of his heartless society, should have coin-cided with the scandal involving the Swiss banks' concealment of Holocaust vic-tims' assets for so many years. It was even less predictable, of course, that the subsequent revelation of his real identity would complicate, in the eyes of some, the political revelations that have compelled the Swiss to subject their national myths to serious scrutiny. Even more to the point with regard to *The Reader* is Germany's continuing engagement with "overcoming the past" as a still active dialectic between a yearning for "normalization," for *Vergangenheitsbewältigung,* and the impossibility of yet achieving it, even now with the third generation and thereafter. "At what moment does wood become stone, peat become coal, lime-stone become marble?" asks Jakob Beer of *Fugitive Pieces* (104). The answer is surely not yet, if ever, especially when recent efforts at "ethnic cleansing" in Europe seem to have taken the Holocaust as its model. It remains to be seen, of course, whether these fictional works will endure beyond a predictable time span, but the questions they raise, the techniques they use, and the traces they themselves leave in the mind, long after a first reading, suggest that at the current time they might be considered evidence of what I have called "new soundings" in Holocaust literature.[57]

NOTES

1. Ernst van Alphen, *Caught by History: Holocaust Effects in Contemporary Art, Literature, and Theory* (Stanford, Calif.: Stanford University Press 1997), 4.

2. Sara Horowitz, "Auto/Biography and Fiction after Auschwitz: Probing the Boundaries of Second-Generation Aesthetics," in *Breaking Crystal: Writing and Memory After Auschwitz,* ed. Efraim Sicher (Urbana: University of Illinois Press, 1998), 283.

3. James Young, "Between History and Memory: The Uncanny Voices of the Historian and Survivor," *History & Memory* 9 (1997): 51; and James Young, "Towards a Received History of the Holocaust," *History and Theory* 36 (1997): 35.

4. Primo Levi, *Survival in Auschwitz,* trans. Stuart Woolf (New York: Collier, 1959); and Tadeusz Borowski, *This Way for the Gas, Ladies and Gentlemen,* trans. Barbara Vedder (New York: Penguin Books, 1976).

5. Geoffrey Hartman, *The Longest Shadow: In the Aftermath of the Holocaust* (Bloomington: University of Indiana Press, 1997), 8. I have found the following discussions most useful on all these issues: Horowitz, "Auto/Biography," 276–94; Sara Horowitz, *Voicing the Void* (Albany: State University of New York Press 1997), 1–32; Efraim Sicher, "The Burden of Memory: The Writing of the Post-Holocaust Generation," in Sicher, *Breaking Crystal,* 19–88; and Sem Dresden, *Persecution, Extermination, Literature,* trans. H. G. Schogt (Toronto: University of Toronto Press, 1995). Van Alphen, *Caught by History,* offers the fullest exploration of the supposed divide between fact and fiction, as between history and representation. The two pioneering books of Sidra Ezrahi, *By Words Alone: The Holocaust in Literature* (Chicago. University of Chicago Press, 1980), and James Young, *Writing and Rewriting the Holocaust: Narrative and the Consequences of Interpretation* (Bloomington: University of Indiana Press, 1988), remain of fundamental value, along with their subsequent writings.

6. See, for example, Efraim Sicher, "The Future of the Past: Countermemory and Postmemory in Contemporary Post-Holocaust Narratives," *History & Memory* 12 (2000): 56–91; James Berger, *After the End: Representations of Post-Apocalypse* (Minneapolis: University of Minnesota Press, 1999); Sue Vice, *Holocaust Fiction* (London: Routledge, 2000); and Michael Rothberg, *Traumatic Realism: The Demands of Holocaust Representation* (Minneapolis: University of Minnesota Press, 2000). All these were published after this essay was written.

7. Horowitz, "Auto/Biography," 278.

8. Anne Michaels, *Fugitive Pieces* (Toronto: McClelland & Stewart, 1996).

9. Nicholas A. Basbanes, "Interview with Ann Michaels," from *George Jr.: Internet Monthly* (June 1997) <http://www.georgejr.com/jun97/michaels.html>.

10. Bernhard Schlink, *The Reader,* trans. Carol Brown Janeway (New York: Pantheon, 1997), 104. "What should our second generation have done? . . . We should not believe we can comprehend the incomprehensible, we may not compare the incomparable, we may not inquire because to inquire is to make the horrors an object of discussion, even if the horrors themselves are not questioned, instead of accepting them as something in the face of which we can only fall silent in revulsion, shame, and guilt? To what purpose. . . . But that some few would be convicted and

punished while we of the second generation were silenced by revulsion, shame, and guilt—was that all there was to it now?"

11. Hans Kellner, "'Never Again' Is Now," *History and Theory* 33 (1994): 128.

12. Ibid.

13. Froma I. Zeitlin, "The Vicarious Witness: Belated Memory and Authorial Presence in Recent Holocaust Literature," *History & Memory* 10 (1998): 5–42. A revised version was published in *Shaping Losses: Cultural Memory and the Holocaust,* ed. Julia Epstein and Lori Hope Lefkovitz. (Urbana: University of Illinois Press, 2001), 128–60.

14. Henri Raczymow, *Un cri sans voix* (Paris: Gallimard, 1985); trans. Dori Katz under the title *Writing the Book of Esther* (New York: Holmes & Meier, 1995); and Jaroslaw Rymkiewicz, *Umschlagplatz* (Paris: Instytut Literacki, 1988); trans. Nina Taylor under the title *The Final Station: Umschlagplatz* (New York: Farrar, Straus, Giroux, 1994).

15. Zeitlin, "Vicarious Witness," 15.

16. Hartman, "Longest Shadow," 6.

17. Michaels, *Fugitive Pieces,* 53.

18. Binjamin Wilkomirski, *Bruchstücke: Aus einer Kindheit 1939–1948* (Frankfurt am Main: Suhrkamp, 1995); trans. Carol Brown Janeway under the title *Fragments: Memories of a Wartime Childhood* (New York: Schocken, 1996).

19. J. J. Lang, "Bernhard Schlink's *Der Vorleser* and Binjamin Wilkomirski's *Bruchstücke*: Best-Selling Responses to the Holocaust," in *German-Language Literature Today: International and Popular?* ed. Arthur Williams and Stuart Parkes (Lang: Bern, 2000), 62–63. I disagree, however, with his claim that the commercial success of *Fragments* was due merely to the fact that "the harrowing account of a traumatic childhood [is a] commodified genre that lends itself to easy, uncritical consumption" (64).

20. The author, whose real name is Bruno Doesseker, was born in 1941, not in 1939 as claimed, although I will use his "other" name throughout this essay. For the analysis of the Wilkomirski case, see Elena Lappin, "The Man with Two Heads," *Granta* 66 (1999): 9–65; Philip Gourevitch, "The Memory Thief," *The New Yorker,* June 14, 1999, 48–68; and above all, the exhaustive study of Stefan Maechler, *The Wilkomirski Affair: A Study in Biographical Truth,* trans. John E. Woods (New York: Random House, 2001). His work was commissioned by German publisher Suhrkamp, which had withdrawn the original "memoir" from circulation (*Fragments* is now included at the end of Maechler's book). In addition to Maechler's brilliant detective work and thorough exposition of virtually every relevant issue, see, too, Susan Suleiman, "Problems of Memory and Factuality in Recent Holocaust Memoirs," *Poetics Today* 21 (2000): 543–59. See now Blake Eskin, *A Life in Pieces: The Making and Unmaking of Binjamin Wilkomirski* (New York: Norton, 2002). This journalistic account covers a good deal of the same ground as Maechler (and may well be indebted to it), but without its range and depth. Its primary interest lies in Eskin's personal access to Wilkomirski. This was his mother's family's original name (before it was Americanized to Wilbur) and its members came from Riga, the same birthplace claimed by Doesseker. Only a few of Wilkomirski's detractors would insist that he knowingly perpetrated a hoax. Rather, as Maechler, *The Wilkomirski Affair,* says, "Wilkomirski did not decide to construct a character and devise a story with which to deceive the world. His present-day identity arose over the course of four decades, unplanned and improvised, with new experiences and necessities constantly woven into it and contradictions arising from a lack of any plan smoothed over, though over time with less and less success." Moreover, Wilkomirski's original intention, as he insists, was never to seek publication but to write down his "experiences" for himself and his children. I am grateful to Sidra Ezrahi, Marianne Hirsch, and Susan Suleiman for sharing their strong opinions on the Wilkomirski affair.

21. Each narrator emphasizes the temporal distance from the events he recounts: thirty years for Schlink, more than fifty years for Michaels, and at least forty-five years for Wilkomirski.

22. Michaels, *Fugitive Pieces,* 19.

23. Wilkomirski, *Fragments,* 38–39; cf. 123. Subsequent page references are given in the text.

24. Michaels, *Fugitive Pieces,* 24–25, 141. Subsequent page references are given in the text.

25. Schlink, *The Reader,* 6–9. I have abbreviated the much longer account of the narrator's dream. Subsequent page references are given in the text.

26. The year is given in the book as 1937, but, judging from the chronology of the work, it must be 1940.

27. L. van Ravesteijn, "Gelaagdheid van herinneringen" (Layering of memories), *Tijdschrift boor Psychotherapie* 5 (1976): 195, quoted in translation from the following website on traumatic amnesia and memory among Holocaust survivors: <http://www.sidran.org/refs/ref1.html>.

28. R. Krell, "Child Survivors of the Holocaust: Strategies of Adaptation," *Canadian Journal of Psychiatry* 38 (1993): 384–89.

29. Judith Kestenberg was a pioneer in this field. See in particular the following volumes she coedited: Judith Kestenberg and Eva Fogelman, eds., *Children during the Nazi Reign: Psychological Perspective on the Interview Process* (Westport, Conn.: Praeger, 1994); Judith Kestenberg and Ira Brenner, eds., *The Last Witness: The Child Survivor of the Holocaust* (Washington, D.C.: American Psychiatric Press, 1996); and Judith Kestenberg and Charlotte Kahn, eds., *Children Surviving Persecution : An International Study of Trauma and Healing* (Westport, Conn.: Praeger, 1998).

30. Lang, "Best-Selling Responses," 59.

31. On the pros and cons of the "recovered memory syndrome," see the discussion in Maechler, *The Wilkomirski Affair,* 246–62, about Wilkomirski's experiences, especially as a very young foster child in an abusive situation, and later, in his therapy. In this essay, I have not introduced the variety of theories about traumatic experience, its manifestations, representations, etc. These are often burdened by extravagant and facile claims, including those pertaining to so-called traumatized readers and the hyperventilated insistence on the unique "unrepresentability" of Holocaust experience. Studies of trauma, especially with regard to the Holocaust, have lately become very popular in some academic circles, and any responsible discussion would require a lengthy excursus, which space does not permit here. A major exception is Mary Jacobus's treatment of Wilkomirski's memoir: "Border Crossings: Traumatic Reading and Holocaust Memory," in *Psychoanalysis and the Scene of Reading* (Oxford: Oxford University Press, 1999), 124–62.

32. D. M. R. Bentley, "Anne Michaels' *Fugitive Pieces,*" *Canadian Poetry* 41 (1997): 9, applies insights from Freud's "Mourning and Melancholia." He sees Jakob's incorporation of his sister in his ego "as an idealized specter and a source of prolonged melancholy" as a result of "a sense of uncertainty and feeling of profound 'shame.'" By contrast, the traumatic loss of his parents is at least known and is "therefore conducive to introjection and successful mourning." Ann Parry, "'. . . To Give . . . Death a Place': Rejecting the 'Ineffability' of the Holocaust: The Work of Gillian Rose and Anne Michaels," *Journal of European Studies* 30, no. 4 (2000): 353–68, looks at Michaels in the light of Rose's revisionist theories about mourning.

33. This aspect is well treated by Méira Cook, "At the Membrane of Language and Silence: Metaphor and Memory in *Fugitive Pieces,*" *Canadian Literature* 164 (2000): 12–33.

34. In addition to Bentley and Cook, I have found some interesting observations in the essays by Adrienne Kertzer, "*Fugitive Pieces:* Listening as a Holocaust Survivor's Child," *English Studies in Canada* 26, no. 2 (2000): 193–217; and Annick Hillger, "'Afterbirth of Earth': Messianic Materialism in Anne Michaels' *Fugitive Pieces,*" *Canadian Literature* 160 (1999): 28–41. Each in its own way traces some of the important influences and allusions in Michaels's work, such as the Zohar, quantum mechanics, chaos theory, Darwin, and even Heidegger. See, too, Nicola King, "Holocaust, Memory, Representation: Georges Perec's *W or The Memory of Childhood* and Anne Michaels' *Fugitive Pieces,*" in *Memory, Narrative, Identity: Remembering the Self* (Edinburgh: Edinburgh University Press, 2000), 119–49; and Susan Gubar, "Empathic Identification in Anne Michaels's *Fugitive Pieces:*

Masculinity and Poetry after Auschwitz," *Signs: Journal of Women in Culture and Society* 28, no. 1 (2002): 249–77.

35. And, as many have pointed out, her name indicates that she is the "alter-ego" of Michaels herself.

36. Virtually every critic, including Maechler, *The Wilkomirski Affair,* 242–43, has pointed to analogues between Wilkomirski's work and that of Jerzy Kosinski, *The Painted Bird* (Boston: Houghton Mifflin, 1965), and surmise that Wilkomirski was influenced by it in his own account. In fact, the parallels in detail are actually very minor, while the differences in style and substance are huge. But from another point of view, the case of Kosinski is instructive. At times the author declared his story was autobiographical, at other times that it was not. Nonetheless, unlike the imagined terrains, whether city, country, or Nazi camps, in Wilkomirski's account, Kosinski as a child actually lived during the war, hidden with his family, in the remote part of rural Poland where the book takes place. Yet if Kosinski himself has been stigmatized by his self-misrepresentation, the book has not lost its enduring place in the canon of Holocaust literature.

37. Aharon Appelfeld, *The Age of Wonders,* trans. Dalya Bilu (Boston: Godine, 1981); Aharon Appelfeld, *Tzili: The Story of a Life,* trans. Dalya Bilu (New York: Dutton, 1983); and Louis Begley, *Wartime Lies* (New York. Knopf, 1991).

38. See, for example, Naomi Sokoloff, *Imagining the Child in Jewish Fiction* (Baltimore: Johns Hopkins University Press, 1992); and Andrea Reiter, "The Holocaust Seen through the Eyes of Children," in *Narrating the Holocaust,* trans. P. Camiller (London: Continuum, 2000), 230–41, esp. 237–40 on Wilkomirski.

39. With the exception of Azriel Eisenberg, *The Lost Generation: Children in the Holocaust* (New York: Pilgrim Press, 1982), note the recent dates of other examples: Debórah Dwork, *Children with a Star: Jewish Youth in Nazi Europe* (New Haven, Conn.: Yale University Press. 1991); André Stein, *Hidden Children: Forgotten Survivors of the Holocaust* (Toronto: Penguin, 1994); Laurel Holliday, ed., *Children in the Holocaust and World War II: Their Secret Diaries* (New York: Pocket Books, 1995); Brigitte Pimpl and Erhard Roy, eds., *Was für eine Welt: Jüdische Kindheit und Jugend in Europa 1933–1945: ein Lesebuch.* (Constance: Hartung-Gorre,1995); Maria Ochberg-Marianska and Noe Grüss, eds., *The Children Accuse,* trans. Bill Johnston (London: Valentine Mitchell, 1996); Henryk Grynberg, *Children of Zion,* trans. Jacqueline Mitchell (Evanston: Northwestern University Press, 1997); and Wiktoria Sliwowska, ed., *The Last Eyewitnesses: Children of the Holocaust Speak,* trans. Julian and Fay Bussgang (Evanston: Northwestern University Press, 1998). Three remarkable children's memoirs bear special mention: Magda Denes, *Castles Burning: A Child's Life in War* (New York: Norton, 1997): Cordelia Edvardson, *Burned Child Seeks the Fire,* trans. Joel Agee (Boston: Beacon, 1997); and Imre Kertész, *Fateless,* trans C. C. Wilson and K. M. Wilson (Evanston: Northwestern University Press, 1992).

40. Art Spiegelman, *Maus,* 2 vols. (New York: Pantheon, 1986, 1991); David Grossman, *See Under Love,* trans. Betsy Rosenberg (New York. Farrar, Straus, Giroux, 1989).

41. *Petra* means "stone." *Naomi,* on the other hand, recalls the loving relationship of daughter-in-law and mother-in-law in the Book of Ruth, although in reverse. Ironically, the event that brings Ben's affair with Petra to an end (the willful disorder she creates in the house) is the catalyst that also brings Jakob's lost memoirs to light. Her vandalism of the "shrine" that is Jakob's house is a violent form of excavation that associates her with the Nazis' desecration of Biskupin at the beginning of the novel and is the antitype to Michaela's vocation as an archaeologist. As so often in Michaels, the same image or activity bears a generic ambivalence.

42. Mary Ann Grossman, interview with Ann Michaels, (St. Paul, Minn.) *Pioneer Planet,* August 23, 1998.

43. Joyce Hackett, "Half Lives," *London Magazine* 39, nos. 5–6 (1999): 53.

44. The author in question is Cynthia Ozick, "The Rights of History and the Rights of the Imagination," in *Quarrel and Quandary* (New York: Knopf, 2000), 108–19. For a recent ferocious review,

see Ruth Franklin, "Immorality Play," *The New Republic,* October 15, 2001, 54 ff. See, too, for example, Lang, "Best Selling Responses"; Ian Sansom, "Doubts about *The Reader,*" *Salmagundi* 124–25 (fall 1999-winter 2000): 3–16; and Ernestine Schlant, *The Language of Silence: West German Literature and the Holocaust* (New York: Routledge, 1999), 209–35.

45. One might compare the more subtle uses of the vast and eclectic library of Athos in *Fugitive Pieces,* 28, which contained such items as "books on zoology, on the history of glass, on Japanese scroll painting, on gibbons, icons, insects, Greek independence, botany, paleontology, biographies of all sorts, and, of course, poetry in more than one language."

46. The English title, *The Reader,* cannot capture the exact nuance of the German, *Der Vorleser,* which means "the one who reads aloud or recites." Hence, the book is fittingly about Michael Berg and not Hanna, who learned to read for herself from the tapes he had sent to the prison by laboriously matching voice to printed word.

47. I owe this last observation to Anson Rabinbach.

48. Eva Hoffman, review of Bernhard Schlink, *The Reader, The New Republic,* March 28, 1998, 33–36. Berg learns the few facts of her biography early on (39): she was born and raised in a German-speaking community in Rumania, came to Berlin at the age of sixteen, worked at a factory job, and entered the army at twenty-one. He might have explained her illiteracy with reference to the fact that she was not educated in Germany proper; likewise, he could have invoked her youth and inexperience as mitigating factors. But he never does either.

49. We might be reminded of Ida Fink's searing playlet, "The Table," in *A Scrap of Time and Other Stories,* trans. Madeline Levine and Francine Prose (New York: Pantheon, 1987), which implicitly confronts this very issue. It, too, stages a Holocaust trial, this time one of SS officers, who conducted a massacre of Jews in a town square. The lawyers' insistence that the survivors provide eyewitness exactitude down to the smallest details (especially the dimensions and placement of the table at which the officers sat) succeeds finally in undermining the entire case against the defendants.

50. Hackett ("Half Lives," 54) comments: "The issue is not what anyone *should* do or would do but what, if one wishes to retain an intact moral self, one ought never to do."

51. Cf. Schlink, *The Reader,* 138.

52. Michael Berg does, in fact, go to see the judge, so we fully expect him to reveal the truth ("I couldn't make myself visit Hanna. But neither could I endure doing nothing" [158]). Yet in a scene even more baffling than so many others, we realize only afterwards (and several re-readings) that he ultimately said nothing, but gives no reason for his decision.

53. In a recent interview with Schlink by Steven Erlanger, "Postwar German Writer: A Bard of a Generation," *New York Times,* January 19, 2002, sec. A, p. 4. Schlink defends Michael's decision "to protect . . . her *Lebenslügen,* her life's lies, which are only hers to reveal." And Schlink continues: "We're not entitled to destroy them. . . . We cannot know better what is best for the other person. It's a paternalistic approach I think is wrong." If the irony of the scene still seems to have escaped him, the author-narrator might have indicated at least the contrast between the circumstances of then and now.

54. These are the uncomfortable findings, for example, of Henry Friedlander, *The Origins of Nazi Genocide: From Euthanasia to the Final Solution* (Chapel Hill: University of North Carolina, 1995), which studied the sociological profiles of the personnel in the euthanasia program, many of whom went on to staff the death camps. Robert Lifton's well-known study, *The Nazi Doctors: Medical Killing and the Psychology of Genocide* (New York: Basic Books, 1986), also disallows any easy answers.

55. The French in particular seem to like this theme; the most famous example is Raymond Rodriguet's novel, *Diable au Corps* (Paris: Grasset, 1923). One might think as well of authors such as Colette, Françoise Sagan, and Marguerite Duras. Robert Anderson's play, *Tea and Sympathy* (New York: Random House, 1953; film version dir. Vincente Minnelli, 1956), belongs to this genre. But

the most compelling case is a powerful Swedish film, *Torment* (dir. Alf Sjöberg, 1944), featuring Ingmar Bergman's first screenplay.

56. Unlike Wilkomirski and Jakob Beer, who while growing up were desperate to read everything they could find on the Holocaust to enlarge their own sphere of reference, Michael Berg, for all his prowess as a reader, cannot seem to take this route to confront head on the deeds of the perpetrators—his legacy, his nation's history. Ironically, Hanna's little library in her prison cell includes some quite standard Holocaust books, suggesting that her self-education through reading led finally to self-knowledge and hence to acknowledgment of guilt. Reading, in this sense, takes on quite a different valence, not as the means to the acquisition of culture, broadly speaking, but as a major source of information. But cf. the quotation in n. 10 above.

57. My thanks to Marianne Hirsch, Daniel Medelsohn, Sidra Ezrahi, Susan Gubar, and Stanley Corngold for their astute comments and suggestions. This essay was completed several years ago. I have added references to the new bibliography which has appeared since then.

Ten

HOLOCAUST TESTIMONIES: ATTENDING TO THE VICTIM'S VOICE

Dominick LaCapra

The interest in testimonies has been on the rise in the course of the last twenty years or so. Claude Lanzmann's *Shoah* of 1985 was not only a significant film; it also heralded the turn to survivor videos, a turn that helps to place Lanzmann's film in a broader context and enables a more informed and critical response to it, notably with reference to problems of interviewing and representation.[1]

The interviewer in survivor testimonies is in a position comparable to that of the oral historian. And one important role for testimonies is to supplement more standard documentary sources in history. But they may at times be of limited value when used narrowly to derive facts about events in the past. Historians who see testimonies as sources of facts or information about the past are justifiably concerned about their reliability. Less justifiably, they are at times prone to dismiss an interest in them. The importance of testimonies becomes more apparent when they are related to the way they provide something other than purely documentary knowledge. Testimonies are significant in the attempt to understand experience and its aftermath, including the role of memory and its lapses, in coming to terms with—or denying and repressing—the past. Moreover, the interviewer in an exchange with the survivor or witness generally does not seek purely documentary knowledge of the past. His or her manifest implication in an affectively charged relationship to the survivor or witness and the special, stress-ful demands this relationship places on inquiry may have more general implica-tions for historical research, especially with respect to highly sensitive, emo-tionally laden, and evaluatively significant issues—issues quite prominent in (but of course not confined to) Holocaust studies. One issue that is raised in accentu-ated form by the study of survivor videos is how to represent and, more gener-ally, come to terms with affect in those who have been victimized and trauma-tized by their experiences, a problem that involves the tense relation between procedures of objective reconstruction of the past and empathic response, espe-cially in the case of victims and survivors.

The psychoanalyst and interviewer for the Yale Fortunoff collection of sur-vivor videos, Dori Laub, tells the following story:

> A woman in her late sixties was narrating her Auschwitz experience to in-terviewers from the Video Archive for Holocaust Testimonies at Yale. . . . She was relating her memories as an eyewitness of the Auschwitz uprising; a sudden intensity, passion and color were infused into the narrative. She was fully there. "All of a sudden," she said, "we saw four chimneys going up in flames, exploding. The flames shot into the sky, people were running. It was unbelievable." There was a silence in the room, a fixed silence against which the woman's words reverberated loudly, as though carrying along an echo of the jubilant sounds exploding from behind barbed wires, a stam-pede of people breaking loose, screams, shots, battle cries, explosions.[2]

Laub continues:

> Many months later, a conference of historians, psychoanalysts, and artists, gathered to reflect on the relation of education to the Holocaust, watched the videotaped testimony of the woman, in an attempt to better under-stand the era. A lively debate ensued. The testimony was not accurate, his-torians claimed. The number of chimneys was misrepresented. Histori-cally, only one chimney was blown up, not all four. Since the memory of the testifying woman turned out to be, in this way, fallible, one could not accept—nor give credence to—her whole account of events. It was ut-terly important to remain accurate, lest the revisionists in history discredit everything. (59–60)

Referring to himself, Laub comments that

> a psychoanalyst who had been one of the interviewers of this woman, pro-foundly disagreed. "The woman was testifying," he insisted, "not to the number of chimneys blown up, but to something else, more radical, more

crucial: the reality of an unimaginable occurrence. One chimney blown up in Auschwitz was as incredible as four. The number mattered less than the fact of the occurrence. The event itself was almost inconceivable. The woman testified to an event that broke the all compelling frame of Auschwitz, where Jewish armed revolts just did not happen, and had no place. She testified to the breakage of a framework. That was historical truth." (60)

Lest one leap immediately to the conclusion that there was a confusion of tongues in this interchange between "the historians" and "a psychoanalyst" or even a differend based on two utterly incompatible visions of the truth, one may offer a different interpretation. The woman testified to and, to some extent, re-lived her experience of events. At a certain intense point in her narrative, as Laub puts it, "she was there"—or so it seems. In one important sense, her testimony is not open to criticism as evidence of her experience as she now recalls and re-lives it. How that testimony relates to an accurate empirical reconstruction of events involved in her account, such as the number of chimneys exploded or set aflame at Auschwitz, is a distinguishable question. What she relives of the past, as if it were happening now in the present, may, to a greater or lesser extent, be (or not be) an accurate enactment, reconstruction, or representation of what actually occurred in the past. It may involve distortion, disguise, and other permutations relating to processes of imaginative transformation and narrative shaping perhaps as well as repression, denial, dissociation, and foreclosure. But these issues have a bearing only on certain aspects of her account and could not invalidate it in its entirety. Moreover, one may well argue that the woman testifies not only to her personal experience but to something larger, having social significance: the breaking of what Laub terms an "all compelling frame." The ability to break this compelling frame, if only retrospectively by talking about it in a certain way, is an indication that the woman is not simply reliving or compulsively acting out the past but to some extent working it over and possibly working it through. The performativity of her narration is complex insofar as it extends over analytically distinguishable but existentially intertwined processes of acting out, working over, and working through—processes that of course have many subtle intermediaries and combined or hybridized forms.

The response of the woman in Laub's story prompts one to raise the question of traumatic memory and its relation to memory both in the ordinary sense of the word and in its more critical sense insofar as it is tested and, within limits, controlled by historical research. In traumatic memory the event somehow registers and may actually be relived in the present, at times in a compulsively repetitive manner. It may not be subject to controlled, conscious recall. But it returns in nightmares, flashbacks, anxiety-attacks, and other forms of intrusively repetitive behavior characteristic of an all-compelling frame. Traumatic memory (at least in Freud's account) may involve belated temporality and a period of latency between a real or fantasized early event and a later one that somehow recalls it and triggers renewed repression or foreclosure and intrusive behavior. But when the past is uncontrollably relived, it is as if there were no difference between it and the present. Whether or not the past is reenacted or repeated in its precise literality, one feels as if one were back there reliving the event, and distance between here and there, then and now collapses. To use Heidegger's term, one might perhaps refer to traumatic *Dasein* as experientially being back there, anxiously reliving in its immediacy something that was a shattering experience for which one was not prepared—for which one did not have, in Freud's term, *Angstbereitschaft* (the readiness to feel anxiety). Traumatic *Dasein* haunts or possesses the self, is acted out or compulsively repeated, and may not be adequately symbolized or accessible in language, at least in any critically mediated, controlled, self-reflexive manner. Words may be uttered but seem to repeat what was said then and function as speech acts wherein speech itself is possessed or haunted by the past and acts as a reenactment or an acting out. When the past becomes accessible to recall in memory, and when language functions to provide some measure of conscious control, critical distance, and perspective, one has begun the arduous process of working over and through the trauma in a fashion that may never bring full transcendence of acting out (or being haunted by revenants and reliving the past in its shattering intensity) but which may enable processes of judgment and at least limited liability and ethically responsible agency. These processes are crucial for laying ghosts to rest, distancing oneself from haunting revenants, renewing an interest in life, and being able to engage memory in more critically tested senses.

In memory as an aspect of working through the past, one is *both* back there *and* here at the same time, and one is able to distinguish between (not dichotomize) the two. In other words, one remembers—perhaps to some extent still compulsively reliving or being possessed by—what happened then without losing a sense of existing and acting now. This duality (or double inscription) of being is essential for memory as a component of working over and through problems. At least in one operative dimension of the self, one can say to oneself or to others: "I remember what it was like back then, but I am here now, and there is a difference between the two." This is not moralistically to blame someone tragically possessed by the past and reliving its suffering to such an extent that present life and the assumption of its responsibilities become impossible. Nor is it to assert the possibility of total mastery or full dialectical overcoming of the past in a redemptive narrative or a speculative *Aufhebung* and *Versöhnung*—a stereotypically

Hegelian overcoming and reconciliation—wherein all wounds are healed without leaving scars and full ego identity is achieved. Indeed severely traumatized people may have different dimensions of the self engaged in acting out, working over, and working through, which may not, to a greater or lesser extent, effectively communicate with one another.

The process of working over and through the past is itself repeated and subject to remission, but it counteracts the compulsively repetitive, full reliving of the traumatizing past and the feeling that one is simply back there in which "there" involves an experiential identity between here and there, now and then. It also enables ethically responsible behavior, including consideration for others, which may not be available to someone insofar as he or she is in an impossible situation (as were certain inmates of concentration and death camps) or compulsively reliving a traumatic past. Moreover, it is conceivable that in working through problems, memory may assimilate the results of critical testing and integrate accurate information as a validated component of the way the past is recalled, especially as memory is disseminated in the public sphere. Indeed one of the ways history is not merely professional or a matter of research is that it undertakes to create a critically tested, accurate memory as its contribution to a cognitively and ethically responsible public sphere. Memory of this sort is important for an attempt to acknowledge and relate to the past in a manner that helps to make possible a legitimate democratic polity in the present and future.

I have broached the perplexing question of how to represent and relate to limit events. Traumatic limit events pose challenges to both reconstruction or representation and dialogic exchange. Jean-François Lyotard and others (Saul Friedländer, for example) have theorized this problem in terms of the unrepresentable excess of extreme events that call for discursive and affective responses that are never adequate to them.[3] This is, I think, an important point even if one would want to signal its dangers and qualify it in certain ways. In videos one has the embodied voices of witnesses and survivors who typically have been overwhelmed by the excess of traumatizing events and the experience of them. Those interviewed are both living archives and more or other than living archives. Viewing these videos has effects on people. The sound of the voices, the often agonized looks on the faces have a powerful, at times an overwhelming, effect, and the impression may remain with the viewer long after the actual event. Different people are able to view these videos for variable but limited periods before they shut down and are unable to take more. (In using videos in teaching, I have found that about one hour is a general limit for students.) There is, moreover, the ethically induced feeling that one may not be responding with sufficient empathy, a reaction that increases the anxiety one feels both because of the evident, often overwhelming pain of the survivor recalling and even returning to the position of helpless victim and because of one's own helplessness in doing anything about what is being recounted or relived.[4]

Despite its significance, the notion that traumatic limit events involve and convey an unrepresentable, anxiety-producing excess may have two questionable consequences, even if one does not go to the hyperbolic point of identifying that excess with the "real" or with the idea that, in traumatic memory, the event is repeated in its incomprehensible, unreadable literality. First, an exclusive emphasis or fixation on unrepresentable excess may divert attention from what may indeed be represented or reconstructed with respect to traumatizing limit events, which should be done as accurately as possible. The latter includes the daily life of victims, a problem to which Saul Friedländer's *Nazi Germany and the Jews* is dedicated. As Friedländer says in his introduction:

> At each stage in the description of the evolving Nazi policies and the attitudes of German and European societies as they impinge on the evolution of those policies, the fate, the attitudes, and sometimes the initiatives of the victims are given major importance. Indeed, their voices are essential if we are to attain an understanding of this past. For it is their voices that reveal what was known and what *could* be known; theirs were the only voices that conveyed both the clarity of insight and the total blindness of human beings confronted with an entirely new and utterly horrifying reality. The constant presence of the victims in this book, while historically essential in itself, is also meant to put the Nazis' actions into full perspective.[5]

A second dubious consequence of the notion of an unrepresentable excess in traumatic limit events is that it may lead to a construction of these events in terms of an insufficiently differentiated, rashly generalized, hyperbolic aesthetic of the sublime or even a (positive or negative) sacralization of the event which may prompt a foreclosure, denigration, or inadequate account not only of representation but of the difficult issue of ethically responsible agency both then and now. One may perhaps detect such a hyperbolic appeal to the sublime and the unrepresentable in Lyotard himself.[6] I have speculated that the sublime may itself be construed as a secular displacement of the sacred in the form of a radically transcendent, inaccessible, unrepresentable other (including the alterity of radical evil). The typical response it evokes is silent awe. I have also argued that one important tendency in modern thought and practice has been the attempt to link the traumatic to—or even convert it into—the sublime by transvaluing it and making it the basis for an elevating, supra-ethical, even elated or quasi-transcendental test of the self or the group. Such an attempt took a particular form in certain Nazis themselves, involving the ability to perpetrate and endure scenes of unheard-of devastation and horror. Here one may briefly recall Himmler's 1943 Posen speech to upper-level SS officers—in important ways a proof text of Nazi ideology and of an important dimension of modern thought more generally, particularly with respect to the fascination with excess and unheard-of transgression. In that speech, Himmler asserted that Nazis remained decent in the face of a geometrically increasing expanse of corpses and that their ability to combine these antinomic features—decency (in Kantian terms, the morally beautiful and uncontaminated), on the one hand, and a seeming mathematical sublime, on the other—is what made them hard.

Moreover, I have suggested that the notion of a negative sublime—one in which the negativity perhaps always involved in sublimity becomes particularly accentuated—is applicable to dimensions of the Shoah, notably to the Nazi quest for redemption or regeneration through an extremely violent, distorted sacrificial process involving quasi-ritual anxiety about contamination and the redemptive quest for purification of the *Volksgemeinschaft* from putatively contaminating presences.[7] The possible role of a Nazi sublime should be understood as one factor (not a total explanation) of Nazi ideology and practice, especially with respect to fanatically committed Nazis such as Hitler, Himmler, and Goebbels as well as many upper-level SS officers who were prime movers of the Holocaust. (It probably did not apply, at least typically, to middle- and lower-level functionaries or to such groups as police battalions of "ordinary" men motivated by "ordinary" forces such as obedience to orders, peer pressure, and the desire to conform.) Its possible role nonetheless attests to the importance of distinguishing between the different modalities of the sublime and of being as careful as possible about its invocation, especially with respect to a dubiously homogenizing and possibly evasive use of it in one's own voice to apply to the Holocaust as an undifferentiated scene of excess and unimaginable horror.

Despite its clear and present dangers, the value of the notion of an unrepresentable excess is to foreground the problem of the possibilities and limits of both representation and dialogic exchange in responding to—or coming to terms with—events of the Shoah (as well as other limit events in history). And it simultaneously raises the question of the relations between research, memory, and what limits them.

A goal of historical understanding is, as I have intimated, to develop not only a professionally validated public record of past events but also a critically tested, empirically accurate, accessible memory of significant events which becomes part of the public sphere. A related goal at the horizon of memory work is to assist in the effort to restore to victims (at least symbolically or even posthumously) the dignity perpetrators took from them—a restorative effort in which historical discourse is itself engaged to some extent in processes of mourning and attempts at proper burial (important forms of working through the past). This process of memory work is related to—but not identical with—research, and it is bound up with the problem of trauma and the challenges it poses to memory in the sense of critically tested recall or recollection. Research is of course crucial, and, in an important sense, it is broader than memory; it involves elements that are not committed to memory either by the collectivity or by the individual, including the historian. But one may contend that the past is significant in its bearing on the present and future to the extent that it makes contact with problems of memory. It is what is allowed or made to enter into publicly accessible memory—not historical research in general—which enables the past to be available for both uses and abuses, and the precise manner in which it becomes available (or is suppressed, distorted, or blocked) is of the utmost importance.[8]

Accurate memory of the past may or may not be necessary for an individual "cure" (if one can indeed provide an acceptable definition of this medicalized notion which it may be best to avoid, at least in historical and critical-theoretical work). But one may argue that such memory—including memory that confronts the traumatic dimensions of history—is ethically desirable in coming to terms with the past both for the individual and for the collectivity. It is bound up with one's self-understanding and with the nature of a public sphere, including the way a collectivity comes to represent its past in its relation to its present and future. One may also argue that accurate memory concerning events that play a crucial part in a collective past is an important component of a legitimate polity.[9] Moreover, accurate, critically tested memory work is related to the kind of active forgetting of the past, or letting bygones be bygones, which (to the extent it is possible) is both earned through collective effort and desirable in group relations—not simply a matter of political expediency. (In this sense, active forgetting is of course a complement of—not an alternative to—remembering and memory work.) In this context, an extremely difficult problem is how to respond to—and give an account of—traumatic limit events and their effects in people's lives in different genres and areas of study.

Any answer to this question is problematic and contains—in the dual sense of "includes" and "holds or hems in"—paradoxes, because trauma invites distortion, disrupts genres or bounded areas, and threatens to collapse distinctions. The problem here is how one tries to inscribe and bind trauma and attendant anxiety in different genres or disciplinary areas in spite of the fact that no genre or discipline "owns" trauma as a problem or can provide definitive boundaries for it. I think the anxiety attendant on trauma and related to a questioning of clear-cut definitions of genres or disciplines should in important ways remain active and not be denied or repressed. It is, for example, what motivates a certain hesitancy (what in Thomas Mann's *Doctor Faustus* is expressed in terms of the narrator's or writer's trembling hand) in putting forth a general method or even a limited interpretation of a problem, and it also inhibits unqualified rejection or avoidance of analyses or interpretations with which one does not agree. But all distinctions, while being subjected to pressure and recognized as more or less problematic in their relation to phenomena, should not be conflated with binary oppositions and blurred or collapsed. Nor should the notion of trauma be rashly generalized or the difference between trauma victim and historian or secondary witness—or, for that matter, between traumatization and victim-hood—be elided.[10]

In testimonies the survivor as witness often relives traumatic events and is possessed by the past. These are the most difficult parts of testimony for the survivor, the interviewer, and the viewer of testimonies. Response is a pressing issue, and one may feel inadequate or be confused about how to respond and how to put that response into words. One question is whether one can and should develop what might be called an ethics of response for secondary witnesses—interviewers, oral historians, and commentators. Such an ethics would at least become a force or consideration in a larger force field. Here it is important to recognize that a historian or other academic, however attentive and empathetic a listener he or she may be, may not assume the voice of the victim. In addition, the academic (as academic) is not—and is not entitled simply to identify with—a therapist working in intimate contact with survivors or other traumatized people. Reading texts, working on archival material, or viewing videos is not tantamount to such contact. Moreover, with respect to the interviewer or oral historian, one may argue that it is dubious to try to induce the survivor to relive trauma and in a sense be revictimized before the camera even if one's motive is to empathize or even to identify fully with the victim and transmit the experience to the viewer. (Such an attempt to take the survivor back—figuratively and at times even literally—to the scene of victimization and traumatization is evident in Claude Lanzmann as interviewer in *Shoah,* and at times it leads to intrusive questioning.)

More generally, one may question the desire to identify fully with, and relive the experience of, the victim in however vicarious a fashion. The force of this desire may both occlude the problem of agency in one's own life and desensitize one to the problem and process of attempting to move, however incompletely, from victim to survivor and agent in survivors themselves. This arduous process, which bears on the afterlife of victims as survivors, warrants extensive study. It is not a concern in Lanzmann's *Shoah* or even in Lawrence Langer's *Holocaust Testimonies,* both of which are concerned with victims as victims, not as survivors or agents.[11] Also dubious is a response to which Lanzmann and Langer are decidedly (I think justifiably) opposed: one that circumvents, denies, or represses the trauma that called it into existence, for example, through unqualified objectification, formal analysis, or harmonizing—indeed redemptive narrative through which one derives from the suffering of others something career enhancing, "spiritually" uplifting, or identity forming for oneself or one's group.[12]

Unqualified objectification and narrative harmonization as well as unmediated identification are particularly questionable when they occur in areas of political and social life, including the classroom. Without positing a simple binary opposition, I would suggest that excessive objectification, purely formal analysis, and narrative harmonization (including what Eric Santner has termed *narrative fetishism*) may be more likely when one uses printed sources or conducts archival research.[13] In partial contrast, videos may present in an especially powerful form the temptation of extreme identification.[14]

Objectivity is a goal of professional historiography related to the attempt to represent the past as accurately as possible. One may reformulate and defend this goal in postpositivistic terms by *both* questioning the idea of a fully transparent, unproblematic representation of the way things in the past "really were" and recognizing the need to come to terms with one's transferential implication in the object of study by critically mediating projective inclinations, undertaking meticulous research, and being open to the way one's findings may bring into question or even contradict one's initial hypotheses or assumptions. One may also distinguish objectivity from excessive objectification that restricts historiography to narrowly empirical and analytic techniques and denies or downplays the significance of the problems of subject position and voice in coming to terms with the implication and response of the historian with respect to the object of study (including the voices of others). Simultaneously, one may recognize the need for objectification within limits both for research and for the protection of the researcher, especially in areas in which traumatic suffering is marked and the tendency to identify fully with the victim may be compelling.

Pronounced, if not excessive, objectification is at times present in even so unquestionably important and groundbreaking a work as Raul Hilberg's *Destruction of the European Jews,* and it is exacerbated by the fact that Hilberg, in his painstaking analysis of the Nazi "machinery of destruction," tended not to employ the testimony of victims and based his study largely on documents left by perpetrators. In Hilberg an objectifying methodology induces (or at least is conjoined with) what may be an insensitivity to the plight of members of Jewish Councils, whom Hilberg discusses in a distanced and harshly critical way, largely oblivious to the double binds or impossible situations in which Nazi policy placed these councils.[15] In marked contrast, Daniel Goldhagen, while relying on printed sources, has instantiated the possibility of extreme identification with Jewish victims (as Goldhagen understands—or rather imagines—them in their relation to perpetrators) accompanied by an inability to employ evidence to test rather than simply illustrate extremely questionable hypotheses and assumptions. (One such assumption is the idea that "the long-incubating, pervasive, virulent, racist, eliminationist antisemitism of German culture," indeed "the ubiquity of eliminationist antisemitism" in Germany, was the sole significant motivational factor for perpetrators in the Holocaust).[16]

Still, even when one resists going to Goldhagen's extreme, videos may present in an especially forceful manner the temptation of a primarily participatory, identificatory response. In the first of her chapters in *Testimony,* Shoshana Felman recounts how her class at Yale faced radical disorientation and the threat of breakdown, both socially and as individuals, after viewing Holocaust videos. She tells of how she became "a witness to the shock communicated by the subject-matter; the narrative of how the subject-matter was unwittingly *enacted,* set in motion in the class, and how testimony turned out to be at once more critically surprising and more critically important than anyone could have foreseen."[17] Coupled with reading literary texts, the viewing of testimonies "carried the class beyond a limit that [she] could foresee"—something that took her "completely by surprise. The class itself broke out into a crisis" (47). After consulting with Dori Laub, they "concluded that what was called for was for [her] to reassume authority as the teacher of the class, and bring the students back into significance" (48).

One may question whether taking up an authoritative role that brings students "back into significance" is tantamount to working through problems. As I have intimated, one may also raise doubts about an academic's tendency to identify with a therapist in intimate contact with traumatized people as well as about the identification of a class with trauma victims and survivors—tendencies that may induce the reader's identification with one or the other subject position. In any case, the extreme traumatization of a class through a process of unchecked identification with victims would obviously not be a criterion of success in the use of survivor videos. And it would be preferable to avoid or at least counteract such traumatization—or its histrionic simulacrum—rather than to seek means of assuaging it once it had been set in motion.

The broader question is the role of empathy in understanding, including historical understanding, and its complex relations to objectification and dialogic exchange. Empathy is an affective component of understanding, and it is difficult to control. Certain professional identifications or research strategies may attempt to marginalize or even eliminate (perhaps blind one to) its role along with affective response in general. But empathy is bound up with a transferential relation to the past, and it is arguably an affective aspect of understanding which both limits objectification and exposes the self to involvement or implication in the past, its actors, and its victims. As I have already tried to argue, desirable empathy involves not full identification but what might be termed empathic unsettlement in the face of traumatic limit events, their perpetrators, and their victims.

Empathic unsettlement may of course take different forms, and it may at times result in secondary or muted trauma as well as objectionable self-dramatization in someone responding to the experience of victims. It is plausible to think secondary trauma is likely in the case of those who treat traumatized victims or even in the case of interviewers who work closely with victims and survivors. But it may be hyperbolic to argue that all those who come into contact with certain material, such as Holocaust videos, undergo at some level secondary or muted trauma. And one may justifiably be wary of the overextension of the concept of trauma, even though any idea of strictly mastering its use and defining its range may be self-defeating. But it is blatantly obvious that there is a major difference between the experience of camp inmates or Holocaust survivors and that of the viewer of testimony videos. Still, even the viewing of videos may have different subjective effects on different people, including recurrent nightmares, and the possibility of secondary trauma cannot be discounted.

Without implying a rash generalization of trauma, empathic unsettlement should, in my judgment, affect the mode of representation in different, nonlegislated ways, but still in a fashion that inhibits or prevents extreme objectification and harmonizing narratives. Indeed it is related to the performative dimension of an account, and, despite the ways performativity may lend itself to abuse, the problem of performative engagement with unsettling phenomena is important in an exchange with the past. One's own unsettled response to another's unsettlement can never be entirely under control, but it may be affected by one's active awareness of, and need to come to terms with, certain problems related to one's implication in, or transferential relation to, charged, value-related events and those involved in them. In addition, the attempt to give an account of traumatic limit events should have nonformulaic effects on one's mode of representation even independent of all considerations concerning one's actual experience or degree of empathy. In other words, one may maintain that there is something inappropriate about modes of representation which in their very style or manner of address tend to overly objectify, smooth over, or obliterate the nature and impact of the events they treat.[18] Still, one need not go to the extreme of dissociating affect or empathy from intellectual, cognitive, and stylistic or rhetorical concerns, and one may ask whether empathy is on some level necessary for understanding (however limited or self-questioning that understanding may be). With respect to perpetrators, one may justifiably resist empathy in the sense of feeling or understanding that may serve to validate or excuse certain acts. In fact one may feel antipathy or hatred. But one may nonetheless argue that one should recognize and imaginatively apprehend that certain forms of behavior (that of the *Einsatz-gruppen* or of camp guards, for example) may be possible for oneself in certain circumstances, however much the events in question beggar the imagination. One may even suggest that recognition is necessary for being better able to resist even reduced analogues of such behavior as they present themselves as possibilities in one's own life.[19]

The foregoing argument does not mean that one can provide a how-to book that stipulates formulaically the manner in which historians or others should respond with "proper" empathy and enable that response to affect their writing or mode of representation. In fact a primary commitment to objectification and empirical-analytic methods in historiography may confront anyone trying to create a problematic space for empathic response (a space that in no sense excludes careful research and critical, contextual analysis) with a double bind or dilemma. On the one hand, one may be asked for concrete procedures, analogous to those employed in empirical-analytic research, which could be taught and followed as rules of historical method. But how could one, with respect to empathy, provide anything analogous to procedures for footnoting references or authenticating sources? On the other hand, any such procedures or rules— more plausibly, any suggestions one puts forward—might bring the charge that they could readily be mechanized and abused. The double bind is a reason it is difficult to acknowledge affective response within a disciplinary framework that, in any case, may be constitutively informed by an attempt to exclude or marginalize affectivity and attendant anxiety. It may also be taken to indicate that one cannot—and should not even attempt to—provide procedures or rules concerning the proper use or correct "dosage" of affect or empathy. Rather the problem is how an attentiveness to certain issues may lead to better self-understanding and to a sensitivity or openness to responses that generate necessary tensions in one's account. This attentiveness creates, in Nietzsche's term, a *Schwergewicht,* or stressful weight, in inquiry; and it indicates how history in its own way poses problems of writing or signification which cannot be reduced to writing up the results of research.

In literature and art (of course including film), one may observe the role of a practice that has perhaps been especially pronounced since the Shoah but may also be found earlier, notably in testimonial art: experimental, gripping, and risky symbolic emulation of trauma in what might be called traumatized or posttraumatic writing ("writing" in the broad sense that extends to all signification or inscription). This markedly performative kind of writing may be risky— at least insofar as it is not automatized and assimilated in mimetic fashion as an all-purpose methodology that predictably privileges excess, incalculability, the transgression of limits, (self-)shattering, unbound or associative play, and so forth. But, even in its riskier and less predictable forms, it is a *relatively* safe haven compared with actual traumatization. It may even be a means of bearing witness to, enacting, and, to some extent, working over and through trauma whether personally experienced, transmitted from intimates, or sensed in one's larger social and cultural setting. Indeed such writing, with significant variations, has been prevalent since the end of the nineteenth century in figures as different as Nietzsche, Mallarmé, Virginia Woolf, Blanchot, Kafka, Celan, Beckett, Foucault, and Derrida. One crucial form it takes—notably in figures such as Blanchot, Kafka, Celan, and Beckett—is what might perhaps be seen as a writing of terrorized disempowerment as close as possible to the experience of traumatized victims without presuming to be identical to it.

It is debatable whether such writing has a place in literary criticism and the kind of philosophy which is close to it and to literature itself.[20] I would defend its role in criticism that emulates its object, but I would not see it as the only or even the preferred path for literary criticism or for its interaction with philosophy and literature. It is an extremely demanding and easily mishandled limit form of the attempt to bring criticism into close proximity or dialogue with art and prevent it from aspiring to the status of a masterful metalanguage; but the active attempt to distance oneself from this pretension to full mastery may take other forms that include a role for historical analysis and the elucidation, not only the emulation, of experimental literary texts or other artworks. Emulative writing becomes especially open to question when it takes an unmodulated orphic, cryptic, indirect, allusive form that may render or transmit the disorientation of trauma but provide too little a basis for attempts to work it through even in symbolic terms.

Still, some of the most powerful and thought-provoking recent criticism is that which opens itself to the reinscription or emulation of disorienting, disruptive, posttraumatic movements in the most powerful and engaging literary texts or works of art. One may at times sense such movements in Cathy Caruth's writing. One remarkable use of the term *precisely,* along with *paradoxically,* in her writing comes precisely when the thought is least precise and most perplexing, perhaps at times disoriented—but in thought-provoking ways that give a "feel" for traumatic experience. In this sense, *precisely* may be invoked more or less unconsciously as a compellingly repeated marker or trace of posttraumatic effects that may not be sufficiently worked through. Shoshana Felman uses the terms *paradoxically* and *paradoxically enough* so repeatedly that their meaning and force are almost evacuated—or perhaps they come to function as apotropaic devices that both conjure up and conjure away the unsettling effects of paradox. Still, her last chapter in *Testimony,* in which she discusses Lanzmann's *Shoah,* is quite different from her first chapter, in which she somewhat self-dramatizingly is anxious about the effects of trauma in a class. In her discussion of *Shoah* she writes in a fragmented, lyrical, participatory style that helps to evoke the movement and almost compulsive power of the film, although her approach may entail certain sacrifices in the critical analysis of Lanzmann's masterpiece.[21]

In historiography the attempt at, or effect of, bearing witness to or even "emulating" trauma (if that is the right term) in an extremely exposed and experimental style would be questionable to the extent that it overwhelmed the demands of accurate reconstruction and critical analysis instead of tensely interacting with and, to some extent, raising questions for those demands. One important text in which such a style at times seems to undercut the historical nature of the analysis is Foucault's *Folie et déraison: Histoire de la folie à l'âge classique.*[22] In it Foucault does not quote or even summarize the voices of radical disorientation or unreason but rather allows them to—or is open to the manner in which they—agitate or infiltrate his own tortured, evocative discourse—a discourse that may exhilarate the reader or threaten to make him or her mad (in both senses of the word).[23] I would in general argue that in history there is a crucial role for empathic unsettlement as an aspect of understanding which stylistically upsets the narrative voice and counteracts harmonizing narration or unqualified objectification yet allows for a tense interplay between critical, necessarily objectifying reconstruction and affective response to the voices of victims. I would even entertain the possibility of carefully framed movements in which the historian attempts more risk laden, experimental overtures in an attempt to come to terms with limit events.

A larger question here is the complex relation of acting out, reliving, or emulatively enacting (or exposing oneself to) trauma and working it over as well as possibly working it through in a manner that never fully transcends or masters it but allows for survival, a measure of agency, and ethical responsibility—a question that bears in significantly different ways on people occupying significantly different and internally differentiated subject positions, such as victim, witness, therapist, "imaginative" writer or artist, and secondary witness or historian. In an attempt to address this extremely complex and difficult question, there may be limited justifications for various responses short of full identification and unqualified objectification. The problem that clearly deserves further reflection is the nature of actual and desirable responses in different genres, practices, and disciplines, including the status of mixed or hybridized genres and the possibility of playing different roles or exploring different approaches in a given text or "performance."

Survivor testimony, including the interviewing process, is in certain ways a new, necessarily problematic genre-in-the-making with implications for oral history, particularly in especially sensitive areas of research. Historians have not yet worked out altogether acceptable ways of "using" testimonies, and their task is further complicated by the at times marked differences between the conditions and experiences of victims as well as their responses to them. As one limited but significant instance of the diversity of responses to limit events within the group of Jewish victims and survivors alone, one may briefly mention the cases of Helen K. and Leon S. in the Yale Fortunoff collection.[24]

Helen K. seems to see the world in secular terms. She stresses the role of resistance and the manner in which her desire to defeat Hitler in his will to kill her was a force in her survival. Discussing her father's disappearance in the Warsaw ghetto, she speculates on the basis of little evidence that he was picked up by a German patrol. She never allows herself to entertain the possibility that he abandoned the family: this disturbing thought—which can only be suggested by the viewer—is not allowed to enter her mind. Her mother was captured (first thought killed) during the Warsaw ghetto uprising when Germans invaded the house in which they were hiding (a house that also contained the bunker of Resistance leader Mordechai Anielewicz). She later is surprised to find her mother in Majdanek and spends six or eight impossible weeks with the weak and debilitated woman until the mother is "selected" for death. In the tightly packed cattle car in which Helen K. and her thirteen-year-old brother are deported after the fall of the Warsaw ghetto, the brother, suffering from lack of oxygen, dies in her arms. At this point, she tells us, she said to herself: "I'm going to live. I must be the only one survivor from my family. I'm going to live. I made up my mind I'm going to defy Hitler. I'm not going to give in. Because he wants me to die, I'm going to live. I was going to just be very, very strong." She recounts other difficult experiences in Majdanek and Auschwitz and concludes by saying: "I don't know. I don't know if it was worth it. I don't know if it was worth it—because, you know, when I was in concentration camp and even after I said: 'You know, after the war people will learn, they will know. They will . . . they will see. We, we'll learn.' But did we really learn anything? I don't know."

In contrast with Helen K., Leon S. is a gaunt, spectral presence and often speaks in an excruciating, halting manner in which each word, like a fragile monument, is separated by a gap from the following word. He saw his grandmother, upon asking for help from a German, shot before his eyes. His closest friend, who helped him through the camp experience, later committed suicide. Leon S. becomes religious after his harrowing experiences and says of his belief: "There is God. Despite the terrible things that happened to us, I couldn't deny the existence. I would never." Of his behavior and attitude toward Germans, he observes: "I could say I didn't raise my hand. I didn't hit a single German. And this may come as a surprise to you. I don't hate them." He adds: "You cannot blame the whole people for something that was done by a group of people." Helen K. and Leon S. may share certain sentiments, and both undergo moments of breakdown or extreme disempowerment in which they seem to relive in anguish the past that haunts and at times possesses them. But they are very different people with different ways of coming to terms with that past.

Even when one comes to question the inclination of some historians to exclude or marginalize survivor testimonies as unreliable sources of history, one may still be at sea with respect to the proper use of testimonies.[25] The questions I have raised do not settle this issue. At most they explore options and possibilities, especially with respect to the relation between objectifying reconstruction or representation and what escapes it or is not encompassed by it, including the historian's own implication in, or transferential relation to, the past, having strongly affective and evaluative dimensions, and his or her conscious and unconscious exchange with that past and those living through it. The attempt to come to terms with survivor videos poses an important challenge to history in that it forces a question to which we may at best provide essentially contested answers: how to represent trauma and to give a place in historiography to the voices of victims and survivors.

NOTES

An earlier version of this essay was published in Dominick LaCapra, *Writing History, Writing Trauma* (Baltimore: Johns Hopkins University Press, 2001), 86–113. Copyright © 2000. The Johns Hopkins University Press. Reprinted with permission of The Johns Hopkins University Press.

1. On this problem, see my *History and Memory after Auschwitz* (Ithaca, N.Y.: Cornell University Press, 1998), chap. 4.

2. Shoshana Felman and Dori Laub, M.D., *Testimony: Crises of Witnessing in Literature, Psychoanalysis, and History* (New York: Routledge, 1992), 59.

3. See Jean-François Lyotard, *The Differend: Phrases in Dispute,* trans. George Van Den Abbeele (1983; Minneapolis: University of Minnesota Press, 1988); and Saul Friedländer, *Memory, History, and the Extermination of the Jews of Europe* (Bloomington: Indiana University Press, 1993).

4. It is important to note that the person being interviewed was not *simply* a victim in the past, but that victimhood may well have been an especially difficult, disempowering, and incapacitating aspect of the past which may at times be relived or acted out in the present. Testifying itself, in its dialogic relation to attentive, empathic listeners, is a way of effecting, at least in part, a passage from the position of victim compulsively reliving the past to that of survivor and agent in the present.

5. Saul Friedländer, *Nazi Germany and the Jews,* vol. 1, *The Years of Persecution, 1933–1939* (New York: HarperCollins, 1997), 2.

6. See Jean-François Lyotard, *Differend: Phrases in Dispute and Heidegger and "the jews,"* trans. Andreas Michel and Mark S. Roberts, with a foreword by David Carroll (1988; Minneapolis: University of Minnesota Press, 1990). One may also find a hyperbolic appeal to a "thematic" of the traumatic and the sublime, in different ways, in Shoshana Felman, Lawrence Langer, Claude Lanzmann, Hayden White, and Elie Wiesel.

7. See my *Representing the Holocaust: History, Theory, Trauma* (Ithaca, N.Y.: Cornell University Press, 1994), esp. 100–110. See also *History and Memory after Auschwitz,* 27–30.

8. How one remembers the Shoah is of obvious importance in Israel, Germany, and the United States, as well as elsewhere, and memory will of course have different personal, collective, cultural, and political functions in its different modes and sites.

9. This is the kind of point Jürgen Habermas made concerning Germany during the 1986 *Historikerstreit*. One may ask whether the point is slighted in Habermas's defense, ten years later, of Daniel Jonah Goldhagen's *Hitler's Willing Executioners: Ordinary Germans and the Final Solution* (New York: Alfred A. Knopf, 1996). On this question, see chapter 4 of *Writing History, Writing Trauma* (Baltimore: Johns Hopkins University Press, 2001). The problem of a collectivity's relation to its past is also at issue in contemporary Israel in the debate over post-Zionist historiography in the work of Benny Morris and others. For Habermas's contributions to the Historians' Debate, see his *New Conservatism: Cultural Criticism and the Historians' Debate,* ed. and trans. Shierry Weber Nicholsen, intro. Richard Wolin (Cambridge, Mass.: MIT Press, 1989). For a comparison of the German Historians' Debate and the debate in Israel over post-Zionist historiography, see José Brunner, "Pride and Memory: Nationalism, Narcissism and the Historians' Debates in Germany and Israel," *History & Memory* 9 (1997): 256–300. Brunner does not note that the stage that may well follow the post-Zionist debate in Israel may bring out elements shared by (but concealed by the heated debate over) so-called Zionist and post-Zionist historiography, notably a focus (if not a fixation) on Israel, a very restricted interest in comparative history, a limitation of research on the Holocaust largely to Israeli responses, and the absence of any rereading or reinterpreting of the Diaspora (which tended to be presented negatively in Zionist historiography and is marginalized in post-Zionist historiography, which focuses, understandably enough, on Israeli-Arab relations).

10. One may also contest the idea that one of the roles played by the historian is that of secondary witness. One may argue that the historian is limited to objective modes of understanding involving only empirical inquiry, observation, analysis, and commentary. It is probably less contestable to argue that the interviewer is a secondary witness in bearing witness both to the witness and to the object of testimony conveyed by the witness. This status implies an affective bond with the witness which Dori Laub describes as follows: "Bearing witness to a trauma is, in fact, a process that includes the listener. For the testimonial process to take place, there needs to be a bonding, the intimate and total presence of an *other*—in the position of one who hears" (*Testimony,* 70). This statement is dubious even for the interviewer, indeed for the interviewer-cum-therapist whose presence, however intimate, is never total and who may not undergo secondary traumatization. In any event, it is implausible for the historian or other commentator. At most one may argue that the historian is a secondary witness through empathy or compassion that nonetheless respects the otherness of the other and does not pretend to full and intimate presence of either self or other, much less to bonding (mis)understood as fusion or identification. To the extent that one denies the role of transference and rejects an affective component in understanding, notably in the form of empathy (or what I term empathic unsettlement), one will also resist the notion that one role played by the historian is that of secondary witness, even when that witnessing is situated at a respectful distance from the experience of the victim and not necessarily tantamount to secondary traumatization.

11. Claude Lanzmann, *Shoah: The Complete Text of the Acclaimed Holocaust Film* (New York: Da Capo Press, 1995); Lawrence Langer: *Holocaust Testimonies: The Ruins of Memory* (New Haven, Conn.: Yale University Press, 1991).

12. This is a temptation both in professional historiography and in the media, for example, in a film such as *Schindler's List*. It may of course also be a feature of political uses of the Holocaust as symbolic capital or in identity-building group formation and nationalism.

13. For Eric Santner's incisive analysis of narrative fetishism, see his "History beyond the Pleasure Principle: Some Thoughts on the Representation of Trauma," in *Probing the Limits of Representation: Nazism and the "Final Solution,"* ed. Saul Friedländer (Cambridge, Mass.: Harvard University Press, 1992), 143–54.

14. Of course the opposite tendencies are also possible, for example, simply shutting down emotionally when viewing testimonies. But I think the dangers I stress occur in some important, influential works, for example, Lawrence Langer's *Holocaust Testimonies,* Lanzmann's *Shoah,* and Shoshana Felman and Dori Laub's *Testimony.* Moreover, shutting down may be a defense against the threat of identification.

15. Raul Hilberg, *Destruction of the European Jews* (New York: Holmes & Meier, 1985). On Jewish Councils and the double binds in which Nazi policy placed their members, see Isaiah Trunk, *Judenrat: The Jewish Councils in Eastern Europe under Nazi Occupation,* intro. by Jacob Robinson and new intro. by Steven T. Katz (1972; Lincoln: University of Nebraska Press, 1996). The basic factor Hilberg stresses is a putative centuries-old habitus or "coping mechanism" inducing passivity and nonresistance in Jews. He even unselfconsciously repeats the comparison of Jews with lemmings he attributes to the commander of the two death camps, Franz Stangl (299)—and is close to blaming the victim when he concludes that "the Jewish victims, caught in the straightjacket of their history, plunged themselves physically and psychologically into catastrophe" (305).

16. Goldhagen, *Hitler's Willing Executioners,* 419, 435. See the responses in *Unwilling Germans? The Goldhagen Debate,* ed. Robert R. Shandley (Minneapolis: University of Minnesota Press, 1998); and Norman G. Finkelstein and Ruth Bettina Birn, *A Nation on Trial: The Goldhagen Thesis and Historical Truth* (New York: Henry Holt and Company, 1998). See also my comments in *History and Memory after Auschwitz.* Finkelstein provides an often convincing, detailed refutation of Goldhagen. But one of Finkelstein's own more dubious tendencies is to postulate a tendentious "disciplinary division between holocaust scholarship—primarily a branch of European history—and Holocaust literature—primarily a branch of Jewish studies"—a division that presumably was "mutually respected" before the publication of Goldhagen's book (which represents the extreme of a "Holocaust literature" or "Jewish studies" approach for Finkelstein). Finkelstein tends to associate objectivity with Holocaust scholarship (the epitome of which is Raul Hilberg's *Destruction of the European Jews*) and sentimentalizing empathy with Holocaust literature—a category that includes not only Elie Wiesel but (along with Lucy Dawidowicz) Yehuda Bauer and Dan Diner (88 n.). Finkelstein also misleadingly states: "Arno Mayer's main blasphemy was emphasizing the salience of anti-Bolshevism alongside anti-Semitism in Nazi ideology" (90 n.). By contrast Mayer subordinated anti-Semitism to anti-Bolshevism in Nazi ideology and practice, even going to the extreme of terming "the war against the Jews . . . a graft or parasite upon the eastern campaign, which always remained its host, even or especially when it became mired in Russia." See *Why Did the Heavens Not Darken? The "Final Solution" in History* (New York: Pantheon, 1988), 270; and my discussion of this book in *Representing the Holocaust,* chap. 2.

17. Felman and Laub, *Testimony,* 7.

18. The so-called normalization of the Holocaust would presumably entail stylistic normalization in its representation as well. While one may argue that historiography of the Holocaust requires the use of professional techniques in authenticating documents, providing footnotes, validating empirical assertions, and so forth, one may still object to the full normalization of Holocaust historiography if it involves a simple reliance on conventional style and standard operating procedures. But, as I have intimated, it would also be questionable to use an undifferentiated "experimental" style (often associated with the sublime) for all aspects of the Shoah. For pertinent discussions of problems of representation, see Ernst van Alphen, *Caught by History: Holocaust Effects in Contemporary Art, Literature, and Theory* (Stanford, Calif.: Stanford University Press, 1997); Geoffrey Hartman, *The Longest Shadow: In the Aftermath of the Holocaust* (Bloomington: Indiana University Press, 1996); Michael Roth, *The Ironist's Cage* (New York: Columbia University Press, 1995); and James E. Young, *The Texture of Memory: Holocaust Memorials and Meaning* (New Haven, Conn.: Yale University Press, 1993).

19. These points are of course contestable and difficult to demonstrate with any degree of adequacy. The minimal desirable function they serve is to inhibit demonization of the other and facile

self-certainty or self-righteousness. Moreover, the idea that one should recognize and imaginatively apprehend that certain extreme forms of behavior may be possible for oneself in certain circumstances does not mean that one is prone to, or even capable of, such behavior, although one can
never tell how one would respond in a certain situation until one is indeed in that situation. Still,
speculations about what one can or cannot imaginatively apprehend do not imply the desirability
of trying to run various scenarios of atrocity by one's mind, and such speculations may be particularly pointless in view of the way limit events, such as those of the Holocaust, may disempower the
imagination or exceed its ability to conjure up situations.

20. Jürgen Habermas, in his hostile reaction to Derrida's way of effecting an interaction between philosophy and literature, does not address this problem in writing, although it would seem
germane to his concerns. See *The Philosophical Discourse of Modernity,* trans. Frederick Lawrence
(1985; Cambridge, Mass.: MIT Press, 1987), 161–210.

21. Bessell A. van der Kolk's neurophysiological theory of trauma has been especially important for Cathy Caruth. Van der Kolk argues that there is a registration of the traumatic event in its
literality as a neural pathway—what in his later work becomes an imprint, engraving, icon, or
image in the amygdala of the right side of the brain, which is not accessible to symbolization or
verbalization. Hence the traumatic event as experience would be inscribed as a literal pathway or
image that is in itself incomprehensible or unreadable—one that is read belatedly *(nachträglich)*
not because of repression or disavowal but because of literal dissociation from language centers
in the left side of the brain. This view is not limited to neuroscientific claims, however. Quoting
van der Kolk and Onno van der Hart, Caruth asks whether "the possibility of integration into
memory and the consciousness of history thus raises the question 'whether it is not a sacrilege of
the traumatic experience to play with the reality of the past'" (Caruth, ed., *Trauma: Explorations
in Memory* [Baltimore: Johns Hopkins University Press, 1995], 154). For van der Kolk, the initially inaccessible traumatic imprint may in time be addressed or represented in language as the
"translation" between the right and left sides of the brain is achieved. The verbalization of the traumatic imprint and the perhaps "sacrilegious" variations played on it may be necessary for a traumatized person's recovery or "cure." (One example van der Kolk gives of variation or flexibility is
imagining "a flower growing in the assignment place in Auschwitz" [Caruth, ed., *Trauma,* 178].
Roberto Benigni's film, *Life Is Beautiful,* might be seen as a dubious analogue of this idea in that it
is an event in the public sphere which both presents a questionable image of concentration camps
and, especially in its "magical realist" or even fairy-tale treatment of camp life, may well prove
offensive to survivors.)

Caruth builds on and extends van der Kolk's argument, often combining it with Freudian
views. Indeed her version of trauma theory, as well as Shoshana Felman's, may itself be interpreted
as an intricate displacement and disguise of the de Manian variant of deconstruction. (See also
Cathy Caruth, *Unclaimed Experience: Trauma, Narrative, and History* [Baltimore: Johns Hopkins University Press, 1996]). In this view (close to Lacan's) the real or the literal is traumatic, inaccessible,
and inherently incomprehensible or unrepresentable; it can only be represented or addressed indirectly in figurative or allegorical terms that necessarily distort and betray it. I would speculate
that the further displacement (as well as distortion and disguise) involved here may be with respect
to a variant of religion in which the Hidden God is radically transcendent, inscrutable (or unreadable) and, in a secular context, dead, unavailable, lost, or barred. All representations of such an absolute are sacrilegious or prohibited. In this context, trauma may itself be sacralized as a catastrophic revelation or, in more secular terms, be transvalued as the radical other or the sublime.
This compelling frame of reference is also at play in other figures, including Claude Lanzmann in
his commentaries on, and role in, *Shoah.* The difficulty is that this frame of reference may either
foreclose any attempt to work through problems or immediately conflate the latter with a necessarily pollyanna or redemptive dialectical *Aufhebung.* By contrast, one may conceive of working

through as a limited *process* of integration or introjection of the past which may never fully transcend the acting-out of trauma or achieve full integration and closure. At best it effects more or less viable compromise formations.

Van der Kolk himself seems at times to allow for a very optimistic idea of "complete recovery" through full integration of traumatic memory in a "life history" and the "whole" of a personality (*Trauma: Explorations in Memory*, 176)—a view perhaps facilitated by his resistance to the notion of a dynamic unconscious that exerts pressure and creates conflict in the self. Van der Kolk also tends to believe that "traumatic memories cannot be both dissociated and repressed" (169). He associates dissociation (which he accepts) with "a horizontally layered model of mind" in which the dissociated forms "an alternate stream of consciousness," while he links repression (which he rejects in cases of trauma) to "a vertically layered model of the mind" in which "what is repressed is pushed downward, into the unconscious" (168). Van der Kolk nonetheless refers to the dissociated as subconscious and as not accessible to consciousness but maintains that it is not repressed or subject to conflictual forces related to forbidden wishes or desires. One might of course object that a dissociated "memory" may indeed be associated with or attached to repressed and forbidden desires (for example, the desire for the death of a parent), and such an association would make even more traumatic and conflict-ridden an actual occurrence (for example, the death of the mother in a case van der Kolk discusses—that of Janet's patient Irène, in which the mother's death was associated with abusive behavior towards Irène on the part of her father).

Van der Kolk might himself be seen as transferentially repeating or acting out the processes he studies in that he splits or dissociates repression from dissociation and resists any notion of their connection. Moreover, his notion of the lodging of the traumatic memory in one half of the brain which is inaccessible to the other half could be seen as a questionable yet convenient literalization of the lateral model of dissociation, which "explains" why there is dissociation without repression or other unconscious forces. Distortion would arise not from repression but by the very attempt to "translate" what is literally incomprehensible (or unreadable) into language. In any case, it should be evident that what is experienced as the exact repetition of the traumatic "memory" (or scene) does not entail that the repetition is the exact or literal replication of the empirical event itself. Moreover, it should be stressed that van der Kolk's notion of the exact literality of the imprint or icon of trauma is related to his rejection of unconscious processes such as repression with the distortion and disguises it brings about. Whatever one makes of his neuroscientific claims (that may rely on an overly functionally specific model of the brain in which the amygdala becomes something like a neurophysiological analogue of the Kantian noumenal sphere), one may find many of van der Kolk's observations concerning trauma and memory to be insightful; and both Caruth and Felman are amenable to a sympathetic, if still partly symptomatic, reading wherein one may try to bring out how, despite—perhaps at times because of—their critical shortfalls, they each, in their affectively charged modes of writing, convey something of the "feel" and pathos of the experience of trauma.

22. Michel Foucault, *Folie et déraison: Histoire de la folie à l'âge classique* (Paris: Gallimard, 1961). For an extensive analysis of this important text, see my *History and Reading: Tocqueville, Foucault, French Studies* (Toronto: University of Toronto Press, 2001), chap. 3.

23. Another way of making this point is to say that, at his most disorienting, Foucault in *Folie et déraison* does not so much speak about (or even for) the mad as to—and at times with—the voices of unreason in something close to a free indirect style. I would further note that the operationalized adaptation of Foucault in historiography that provides genealogies of concepts or an objectifying account of disciplines, as in the important work of Jan Goldstein or Ruth Leys, tends to downplay severely, eliminate, or deny this dimension of Foucault's writing.

24. Fortunoff Video Archive Tape A-35 and Fortunoff Video Archive Tape A-25, Yale University. Any further discussion of survivor videos would have to include an analysis of problems in

interviewing and filming, including the role of seemingly insensitive or dubious questions and the reliance on techniques such as zoom shots or close-ups apparently to intensify emotion that is already overwhelming—hence in a manner that is unnecessary at best and offensively intrusive at worst. Still, the power of testimonies is that they often transcend such stumbling blocks or sinadequacies.

The differences in experiences and responses multiply when one adds other groups of victims such as political prisoners, Jehovah's Witnesses, Slavs, homosexuals, and "Gypsies." A related point is that it can be misleading to study victims in isolation from other—at times intricately related or even partially overlapping—subject positions and groups such as perpetrators, collaborators, bystanders, and resisters. In my judgment, the historian should not simply identify with any single participant subject position or group but try to work out varying modes of proximity and distance in the effort to understand each one as well as the relations among them. The historian might even attempt to work out ways of getting beyond the grid that locks participant positions or groups together in theory and practice.

25. I noted Raul Hilberg's tendency not to employ survivor testimonies. Although he continues to emphasize, at times excessively, the role of a machinery of destruction in all aspects of the Shoah, Hilberg's later approach to testimonies and, more generally, to the problem of interpreting the behavior of victims (notably that of members of Jewish Councils) is somewhat more nuanced than in *The Destruction of the European Jews.* See especially his *Perpetrators Victims Bystanders: The Jewish Catastrophe 1933–1945* (New York: HarperCollins, 1992); his contributions to *Writing and the Holocaust,* ed. Berel Lang (New York: Holmes & Meier, 1988), esp. 274; and his "The Ghetto as a Form of Government: An Analysis of Isaiah Trunk's *Judenrat,*" in *The Holocaust as Historical Experience,* ed. Yehuda Bauer and Nathan Rotenstreich (New York: Holmes & Meier, 1981), 155–71. See also the important discussion and the comments of Isaiah Trunk at the end of the last book. Trunk asserts: "I agree with most of what [Hilberg] said about the Jewish Councils; I disagree only with his characterization of the ghettos and the Councils as a 'self-destructive machinery.' Here he comes close to Hannah Arendt's absurd supposition that without the Councils annihilation would not have been so total" (268).

Despite her proximity to the perspective of victims (as she understands it), Lucy Dawidowicz stresses the importance of corroborating eyewitness accounts through other documentary sources and gives survivor testimonies a rather limited supplementary importance "to fill out, augment, and enrich the substantive sources for the history of the Holocaust" (*The Holocaust and the Historians* [Cambridge, Mass.: Harvard University Press, 1981], 128). Yehuda Bauer quotes and integrates into his narrative, without comment, limited selections from survivor written narratives and testimonies, both restricting their role and lending them a distinctive authority (*A History of the Holocaust* [New York: Franklin Watts, 1982], chap. 9). Lawrence Langer (not a professional historian) goes to the opposite, comparably questionable extreme from the early Hilberg in explicitly and emphatically privileging survivor oral testimonies as a locus of authenticity while downplaying the significance of survivor writings (*Holocaust Testimonies: The Ruins of Memory* [New Haven, Conn.: Yale University Press, 1991]): "Beyond dispute in oral testimony is that every word spoken falls direct from the lips of the witness" (210 n.). Indeed for Langer "oral testimony is distinguished by the absence of literary mediation" (57). Langer, however, also makes this thought-provoking comment: "Though we have the option of rejecting such testimony as a form of history, we also face the challenge of enlarging our notion of what history may be, what the Holocaust has made of it, and how it urges us to reconsider the relation of past to present (in a less hopeful way, to be sure), and of both to the tentative future" (p. 109). (Langer returns to these and related questions in his *Preempting the Holocaust* [New Haven, Conn.: Yale University Press, 1998].)

See also the insightful analysis of Marianne Hirsch (a literary critic), who extends the investigation of testimonies and witnessing into the study of photographs and their relation to narrative

(*Family Frames: Photography, Narrative, and Postmemory* [Cambridge, Mass.: Harvard University Press, 1997]). She proposes the notion of postmemory for the memory of later generations not directly implicated in events: "Postmemory characterizes the experience of those who grow up dominated by narratives that preceded their birth, whose own belated stories are evacuated by the stories of the previous generation shaped by traumatic events that can be neither understood nor recreated. I have developed this notion in relation to children of Holocaust survivors, but I believe it may usefully describe other second generation memories of cultural or collective traumatic events and experiences" (22).

Eleven

HOLOCAUST AND HOPE

Geoffrey Hartman

> Thinking and the death camps are opposed . . . thought entails as much a moral hope (that it may be triumphant, mastering its object, dissolving the difficulties, containing and elucidating the conundrum) as it is the investment of skill and dispassion in a methodic procedure. The death camps are a reality which, by their very nature, obliterate thought and the humane program of thinking.
> —Arthur A. Cohen[1]

> One cannot write the history of Jewish hope without a parallel history of Jewish despair.
> —Yosef Yerushalmi[2]

What are we to think when Jorge Semprun changes the title of his book on the aftereffects of his experience in Buchenwald from *Writing or Death* to *Writing or Life*?[3] Was it hope that fluttered up from the depth of Pandora's box, or was it the knowledge that writing is a form of life after death for survivors of the Shoah? I would like to say something of hope about hope, which I might do more effectively if hope could be separated from its opposites: not only from despair but also from muteness and suicidal grief, and above all from the fear of coldness, of becoming insensible to new life—its sorrow or joy. "Sometimes," Semprun tells us, and many survivors say the same, "I felt certain that there hadn't really been any return, that I hadn't really come back. . . . I was nothing other than a conscious residue of all that death."[4]

It could be considered hopeful that, despite the pain, so many are dealing with the Holocaust antiworld. Beyond the eyewitnesses themselves and the exemplary writings of, among others, Primo Levi, Elie Wiesel, Imre Kertesz, Charlotte Delbo, Ida Fink, Robert Antelme, Dan Pagis, Yitzhak Katznelson, and Paul Celan, there is a second-generation witness, there is a third-generation witness, there are what may be called witnesses by adoption; above all, and in spite of taboos and cautions, there exists a growing attempt via literature, history, film, video testimony, monuments, and art to focus on the madness of genocide.

Moreover, there does exist a tradition of comfort, if not exactly of hope. God and the Shechinah weep, they mourn, they go into exile with Israel. But those who quote such texts do so hesitantly, to show that they persist from the time of the destruction of the First and Second Temples, not that they would reconcile us to the Holocaust. And Christian theologians, insofar as they have broken their silence, and acknowledged the role of religious anti-Semitism, realize that the plea for reconciliation remains precarious.[5] So Wilhelm Marquardt concedes, in one of those many waves of self-confrontation Germany has gone through, this time after the mediocre and yet—in Germany—effective TV serial *Holocaust:* "How could anyone of us be at peace with himself, who must be shunned like a fearful abnormality *[Abscheu]* by the victims. It would be an important Christian task to learn how one can keep living as a human being, when one is shunned by other humans."[6]

I limit myself to a literature that rarely suggests a redemptive value in what it continues to value: writing and language as such. This literature respects a reversal in the status of the victim, but honors no myths. As an early article by Robert Antelme discloses, the concentration camp inmate, immediately following liberation, was asked to be the same person as before this experience, or to get on with life as if nothing had happened.[7] (In some cases the deportees were even greeted with suspicion, as tainted personalities who may have survived because of their collaboration.) The reversal of status that came about was due partly to the Eichmann trial and partly to the persistent writings and activities of Elie Wiesel, who viewed survivors as embodying the duty of remembrance and compelling the world to see Auschwitz as a rupture in history amounting to a second origin, as defining in its way as Sinai.[8]

Early postwar witness accounts from East Germany that glorify communist and worker resistance are not always, moreover, without justification. Even as the Nazi terror turned against the Jews, it also targeted whoever might have become a base for political resistance, in particular German social democrats and communists. Yet the only general myth or "grand narrative" we find in addition to a "chaos narrative"[9]—fragmented, wounded, plural memories that need stitching up—is that of *Überleben,* of surviving in order to tell the story and becoming by sheer act of will an Ahasver, or, as in the Book of Job, the "I alone have escaped to tell thee."

I do not feel confident enough to speculate on what may have nourished hope during the Holocaust itself, or whether such hope contributed to survival. Certainly, for some like David Weis Halivni, the Jewish learning tradition was so powerful that the recovery of a single page of Talmud, rescued from a guard who had wrapped his meal in it, seemed a miraculous event.[10] And Roberto Benigni's controversial movie, *Life Is Beautiful,* carries to the point of absurdity an insight already expressed in Jurek Becker's *Jacob the Liar,* where the hero, claiming to have access to a clandestine radio, lifts the morale of the ghetto by inventing broadcasts that keep hope in liberation alive. The logic of *Life Is Beautiful* pits the desperate make-believe of a father against the unbelievable inhumanity of the events he reinterprets. The very absurdity of the father's wager, that the death camp is simply a challenge, a game he and his son must win, even as it offends us in this context, even as it flouts historical possibility and artistic probability, not only prolongs a lifesaving vision of innocence[11] but recalls the precarious habit of euphemism, without which ordinary life, too, is not bearable.

Yet when the full extent of the disaster became known, what diminished hope was, in addition to the fact that such a genocide had been systematically carried out, the realization how thoroughly the German public had been brainwashed, how everyday speech and the media had been debased by a massive, state-sponsored propaganda. Heinrich Mann would diagnose the literary situation as early as 1934. "Everything is prefabricated, paid for, distorted" [Alles gestellt, alles bestellt, alles verstellt].[12] The interpretive spin that produces the humor and pathos of *Life Is Beautiful* was totally reversed, during the Nazi era, into a boundless malignity. Victor Klemperer, in notebooks that scrupulously record, like the philologist he was, what he calls LTI, the Language of the Third Reich,[13] shows how thoroughly both public and private discourses were contaminated during the thousand year Empire's twelve years. Leo Spitzer, the émigré scholar, wrote as follows after the war to a former associate: "The pain that a continuous self-purification should have brought with it, would have been so severe that you must have gone mad."[14]

State control of the media was total in Nazi Germany: thought was besieged, day in, day out, by a mixture of exalted and criminal ideas. After the war, therefore, liberation meant more than restoring freedom of speech. The subjection of the populace had been too great: its belief in Hitler, but also in the Nordic myth, seemed in retrospect a kind of trance or intoxication (*Rausch* is the word often used by commentators who lived through this period);[15] and, when it was over, when the war was lost, there seemed to be no basis for discussing what had happened.[16] For language itself had fallen under a spell and would have to be liberated.

Not only the material and psychic powers of Germany were exhausted but also its cultural heritage—squandered by a shameless appropriation. This heritage with its honorable words had shrunk so much through Nazi misuse that, according to Elisabeth Langgässer, the writer could no longer live in the German language as a natural home. It became "a remnant, a last primal rock formation identical with the writer, who suffered this fearful contraction as a trial of its °indestructibility."[17]

I do not want my emphasis to be misunderstood. The corruption of language is a topic central to modernism, and is often alleged against modernism itself—before postmodernism made it seem like an archaic scruple. Even Heidegger's revision of philosophical language is involved. Premonitions during the rise of totalitarianism (both of the Right and the Left) revealed their full ethical implications only after the war. We should recognize, George Orwell wrote in "Politics and the English Language," his well-known essay of 1964, "that the present political chaos is connected with the decay of language, and that one can probably bring about some improvement by starting at the verbal end. . . . Political language . . . is designed to make lies sound truthful and murder respectable."[18]

~

I wish to go a step beyond this modernist concern to focus on the generic impact of the Holocaust on the way we consider language, especially literary language. The writer I will mainly take up is Maurice Blanchot, influenced by Emmanuel Levinas, yet an original thinker and one of those responsible for a distinctive mode of writing that has remained enigmatic to many. Blanchot came to realize that language had to be reoriented, that the breach of civilized speech that occurred, even among intellectuals and professionals, whose behavior can only be called a culpable self-disenfranchisement (the German *Entmündung* captures that meaning),[19] should lead to a new consciousness of words as the most responsible of human gifts. I see Blanchot's work as an extended *procès verbal* directed against those who reduce language's social, imaginative, and intellectual character to instrumentalized phrases.

French was less corrupted, in this respect, than German; the French literary heritage had not been, on the whole, drawn into the *Kulturkampf* and betrayed. Even someone as virulently anti-Semitic as Charles Maurras remained an enemy of Germany and protected the French classical heritage. Blanchot's task, therefore, was a prosaic one; but his analysis of the gift of speech, of its everyday power of contestation—and also his extreme skepticism concerning that power—led him to stylistic experiments, not as daring as those of Paul Celan yet exemplary in their own way.

One of the difficulties in reading Blanchot is easy to describe. Because, according to him, words speak across a distance without eliminating it and preserve, in this way, the individuality or otherness of interlocutors, including their right to withdraw from political engagement, his scenarios, in fiction as in criticism, stage a relentless, as if endless, conversation, with little reliance on psychological characterization, myth, or plot. The plot, in fact, seems to be language itself, or the passion of writing trapped in what Octavio Paz once called a "vertigo of the inbetween." Yet even if we tolerate Blanchot's at once ascetic and intensely verbose procedure, a doubt remains: will this "entretien infini," this endless conversation, make sense, when the desire to make sense—outraged so often as we recall the Holocaust—is at the heart of what is contested?

Blanchot's word-consciousness does not fall from heaven; it has historical and cultural specificity. Let me mention only its political prehistory rather than its complex literary sources. Blanchot was, for a time, an "enragé" who contributed before the war to right-wing journals prone to anti-Semitism, especially after Léon Blum became France's prime minister. He mysteriously stopped his militant journalism around the time of Munich in 1938 and turned almost completely to literature and literary theory. Associated later with Vichy's "La Jeune France," he eventually resigned and also refused a leading role in the revived *Nouvelle Révue Française* during France's era of collaboration. He nevertheless contributed a nonpolitical literary chronicle to the Vichy-supported *Journal des débats* as late as August 1944. It was learning about the camps through Robert Antelme, author of *L'espèce humaine,* that seems to have been decisive. The story of Antelme's rebirth after his near-death in the camps, together with his reaffirmation of an irreducible humanity and the significance of words outside a power context, will never leave Blanchot.[20]

To value Blanchot's antirhetorical view of language, we must also understand that the question of our speech—of what we can say about the Shoah—has not become less difficult since 1945. Ingeborg Bachmann, in her burdened account (burdened by literary tradition as well as the Shoah) of what she saw ten years after the end of the war in the Ghetto of Rome on the Day of Atonement, affords, if only for a moment, a glimpse of life being renewed. She describes a child that must have been born shortly after liberation calling to the musicians *"Spiel weiter!"* [Keep on playing], not realizing what that phrase meant in the camps.[21] This kind of innocence, with the passage of time, is complicated by the guilt of increased, ever-increasing knowledge: we are fast reaching the point—given the proliferation of books, films, and discourses, and aware that despite them genocidal acts continue—where a fatigue enters, one that makes us doubt the human species itself, or the very commandment to remember—to transmit the bad news we compulsively investigate.

In such an atmosphere even the concept of testimony, of bearing witness, whether by the victimized or those who wish to show companionship with them, is in danger of becoming a benevolent and impotent cliché. The pathos of Mallarmé's "La chair est triste, hélas, et j'ai lu tous les livres" [roughly: The body is sad, alas, and I've had it with books] seems, all of a sudden, understated. There is compassion fatigue, as it has been called, but also a reading fatigue, especially among those sensitive to language, who fear that no word-concept is adequate or will escape erosion and controversy.

"Think of any key concept in the vocabulary of civilized discourse," Terrence Des Pres has written, "and immediately, if its sounding board is the Holocaust, you are in trouble."[22] Such terms as *extreme experience, trauma, terror, disaster, catastrophe, uniqueness,* even *Holocaust* or *Shoah,* are unable to support the work of reflection and self-reflection that tries to understand, to really "grasp," this democidal century—a "grasping" that would ordinarily lead to dedicated personal conviction and political action.[23] Instead, the impasse between the garrulity of trying to say as much as possible and the near-silence of choosing one's words in such a way that others will not despair or be consumed by grief affects every attempt at writing. This happens not only as we confront the Shoah but when, facing renewed atrocities, and not wishing to reject language or abandon life to unreason, we salvage rationality by representing philosophy, literature, and history writing as forms of remedial action.

It is precisely this defense against grief that no longer works—insofar as it makes too hopeful a claim. How can the most rational of our desires be substantiated, that there should be a link between speaking, or expression generally, and progress? In the past, there were those who believed a doctrine *because* it was absurd: now we have reached a similar stage with the hope we still invest in the effectiveness of reasonable words.

Even commentators like Lawrence Langer, who are eloquent against the presumption that from the Holocaust a specific historical or moral lesson could emerge, cannot entirely forgo the language of hope. Langer wants his essays to contribute to "the incessant anxious dialogue" (an endless conversation?) "about how our civilization may absorb into its reasonable hopes for the future the disabling outburst of unreason we name the Holocaust."[24] The radical character of Blanchot's project—after a certain date—is to find an alternative to the language of historical hope, Hegel's legacy to this day,[25] and which we all, Langer included, seem to need.

Blanchot's critique is not directed against historical meanings as such, only against their overestimation. He attacks the confusion that makes the study of history in general—not just of the Holocaust—a source of definitive meanings whose influence could integrate a catastrophic past. That we live in the best of all possible worlds is an idea that died long ago with Voltaire's *Candide:* after the Holocaust the question becomes what better world is still possible. In Blanchot, writing, so often associated with action or trying to be justified as an act, begins to accept itself as a passion story, the place where Sarah Kofman's proposition about wording the Holocaust is realized: "Talk one must—without having the power."[26]

Blanchot, however, while rejecting any systematic effort to derive lessons from history, does not give up on finding a rationale for art. He modifies the position taken by Theodor Adorno's famous essay "Engagement."[27] Adorno wanted to shield the Holocaust from profanation, doubting art's capacity to present it without a meretricious stylization; Blanchot is concerned rather with defending art by setting its "passive" integrity against attempts to discredit it once more after so radical a shock. He argues that writers who, as citizens, are ideologically engaged cannot thereby engage literature, too, that is, subdue it to a mimetic-realistic or instrumentalist end—however worthy that end may be. If anything, literature takes back from politics pursued as a religion the power of naming. Poetry, in particular, does not add meaning to catastrophe: on the contrary, in the presence of poetic words meanings withdraw—with the result that words become more opaque and material, more thinglike, and often fascinate *qua* verbal images.[28] Blanchot once defined the word as "a janus-faced monster, verbal reality which has a material presence and a signification which is an ideal absence."[29]

Yet Blanchot does worry about the unresolved intersection of ethical and aesthetic. Though he insists that writers should not sacrifice their vocation, there may have to be a "détournement," a diversion to politics of the critic's or artist's acquired authority. This must be temporary, however, and for a specific cause, all the more so since war and violence as political means often turn into ends and displace that cause.[30] Blanchot, moreover, when it comes to the relation between words and world, adapts a key notion from Levinas, that of exteriority.

~

Exteriority points to what cannot be internalized; it serves to reject a Hegelian type of mediation in which everything becomes knowable, hence meaningful. Hegel's dialectic is viewed as a form of knowledge lust. But exteriority also points to an external world that is aesthetic in the sense of phenomenal: a world of immediate perception, of colors, sounds, and shapes. The medium of the verbal, says Blanchot, "dreams of unifying itself to objects of which it would have the weight, the color, the heavy and dormant aspect."[31] The word artist is not fundamentally different in this from the painter who acknowledges that colors and shapes exist which seem irreducible to verbal or ethical schemes of meaning. Both arts are driven by "un *moi* insatiable du *non moi*" [a self, hungering insatiably for a nonself].[32]

The effort to appease this hunger leads, however, to a violence of its own—when we substitute words for things or subdue the life in words to purely realistic ends. Blanchot's early novel *Thomas L'Obscur* describes the revenge of words that turn the tables on the artist and attack him with a devouring intimacy. They are suddenly glimpsed as living beings, even vampires who desire to become real through a transfusion of his essence. "He was seized, kneaded by intelligible hands, bitten by a vital tooth; he entered with his living body into the anonymous shapes of words, giving his substance to them, establishing their relationships, offering his being to the word 'be.'"[33]

Thus even words have an otherness to be respected. Words keep things "in the difficulty of what it is to be" (Wallace Stevens). "The one who encounters *l'Autrui* [the other-in-his-otherness]," Blanchot writes in the spirit of Levinas, "can only relate to him by deadly violence, or by the welcoming gift of the word."[34] Blanchot's "infinite conversation," then, is not an escape from reality into words but the result of an uncompromising choice: words or violence. Yet words themselves, as I have said, are always shadowed by an intrinsic violence, by their difference from things, their breach with phenomenality. This breach, internal to speech and even more to writing, leads to a dangerous undertow that tempts the writer back into the more organic sphere of embodied and especially politically sanctioned meaning.

The writer, then, must be doubly wary: of words as well as the world. Speech, nevertheless, remains the place where we can best meet in understanding and amity, despite the otherness of the other and the pull toward a speechless violence. "Speech invites man to no longer identify with his power."[35] The opposite happened in Nazism, where the word became exclusively a power instrument, as also at times in Blanchot's prewar phase, in which his journalism turned to a rhetoric of revolutionary or oppositional violence.

━

Let me focus more sharply on the moral point made by both Blanchot and Levinas. Hegel's *Phenomenology* had argued that increase of knowledge leads to increase of being, while absolute knowledge, the end of humanity's journey, is nothing less than a fullness in which being and meaning coincide.[36] Levinas rejects, like Blanchot, Hegel's reason-of-history. Hegel's dialectical view of the way history moves legitimized the political realm through the key concepts of nation and cultural progress. But when that realm of public action and discourse devours privacy, it becomes simply a more potent form of oppression. So Czeslaw Milosz's *Captive Mind* is a powerful reminder of how ideals that enforce an interpretation in the name of politics *(raison d'état)* engender an all-encompassing hypocrisy as invasive as the voice-over of propaganda newsreels. This hypocrisy, a pathological form of theatre, kills all hope of humor and dialogue, appropriating the past and coercing the future by ideology.

As the expression of a post-Holocaust morality, Blanchot's literary theory is allergic to any such totalizing move. His most dramatic application of this refusal of ideology affects the meaning of death. We consider it tragic when meaning disappears from death, and heroic when there is an effort to give meaning to that meaninglessness. Hence the link, in so much thinking, between Holocaust death and martyrdom. Blanchot is among those who question this tragic-heroic link. The Holocaust not only took from its victims the possibility of an authentic, dignified, or beautiful death; the death of that death, as it has been called, takes from us, even now, the conviction that this epoch is over, or that a previous innocence can be restored. Edith Wyschogrod says that a primordial mode of being-in-the-world, described by phenomenology as a "life-world," suppressed in the camps' universe of death, continues to be part of humanity's collective experience. *"Once the death-world has existed it continues to exist, in the mode of eternity as it were, for it becomes part of the sediment of an irrevocable past."*[37]

Blanchot, possessed by a parallel intuition, defines the Holocaust as an absolute event in which history itself burns up (that is, the Hegelian concept of history), so that "the movement of meaning was ruined."[38] The emphasis here falls on "movement": there is a disorienting finality to the Holocaust which leads to dejection rather than hope, because no dialectical and sublimating move seems possible.[39]

Making sense of Auschwitz, then, is something impermanent, a simple, repetitive moment of hope, a shimmer unattached to fulfillment. Daniel Libeskind, the architect, has talked of a "Hope-Incision." Though the seductiveness of writing may remain linked to our ability to face the Shoah (to work it through with the help of language), writing worthy of its name is never a power play using a prophetic or historical determinism as its instrument. Blanchot rejects Hegel's "imposture of completed meaning" [l'imposture du Sens achevé] and also reverses Christian triumphalism. "Judaism," he asserts, "is the sole thought that does not mediate."[40] His watchword becomes "Watch over [i.e. safeguard] absent meaning."[41]

~

There is, nevertheless, one oddly redemptive feature in art as such. Kant, watching in his own way over absent meaning, had emphasized the irreducibility of the aesthetic judgment to a concept: what is perceived and enjoyed aesthetically is disinterested, in the sense that a specific teleological meaning cannot be discerned. Blanchot, focusing on art, emphasizes the persistence of formal elements: stylistic repetitions that illuminate the antiexpressive, inertial features of literary language, and generally its "non-sense" or resistance to change and novelty as sources of meaning.[42] Touching back to poetry as well as philosophy, to Mallarmé's hyperbolic "Governments change; versification remains," as well as Hegelian reflections on how language participates in a "labor of the negative," he refuses to declare that literature is on the way to a "new order" of words. He accepts the hazard that gave us the words we have, whose spirituality has been tainted, and whose relation to existence is, in a strong pun of Derrida's, "hauntological."

Thus the formalism of literary language persists, though shaken by the Shoah—and that it persists, that it outlives that event, resilient as grass and flowers covering the killing fields, is scandalous. "The glory of a 'narrative voice,'" Blanchot asserts, prevails whatever the content of our speech. Artistic words always turn wounds into pearls, and thus language and thought will be, after a disaster, as they were before, "exterior" to each other.[43]

How does this insight affect Blanchot's own style? His *Writing of the Disaster,* published in 1980, is not so much a book as a series of fragments. The prose fragment has become a genre by now; points of comparison are Pascal's *Pensées* on the one hand, and Romantic experiments on the other. Also Kafka's parables. We encounter a restless style that allows very little closure. Some will say Blanchot's style doesn't add up, which is precisely its difference from Hegel's totalizing manner.[44] Others might quote Adorno's axiom, that the fragmentary is the intervention of death in the work.

In Blanchot, writing is linked to "disaster" in the etymological sense; and Judaism provides the prototype by its monotheistic displacement of the stars as deities. Yet writing as star-breaking cannot be systematized, since that would recuperate the negative and convert it, as Hegel did, to a motor for transcendence.[45] Blanchot, then, seeks a different spiritual language ("une langue autre"), one that is neither theological nor a displacement of the theological. The older idiom has been irreversibly tainted by fascism's "spiritual revolution" and inflammatory rhetoric.

Does Blanchot achieve this "other language"? He at least describes what guarantees its possibility. It will be marked by a contemplative streak, the "désinter-essé du désastre"—a phrase suggesting that the disaster brings with it a special detachment,[46] one so much part of the disaster that it frees us from it as an obsessive, singular object of concern. The writer's anguish comes, however, precisely from this intellectual freedom: he is torn apart, Blanchot says in an early essay, "by the harmony of his images, by the air of happiness radiating from what he writes. He experiences this contradiction as the unavoidably oppressive aspect of the exaltation that he finds in that writing, an exaltation that crowns his disgust."[47]

~

It helps to contrast with Blanchot's disorienting style the forceful, Old-World simplicity of writers like Améry, Levi, Wiesel, Fink, Chalamov, Klima, and Kertesz, who continue to respect the formula of "new wine in old bottles." They do not problematize the recession of words or the "abyss" between words and thought: the collapse of faith in the progressively greater truth capacity of language. Ernst Simon, in an essay "The New Midrash," sought to show how, after 1933, Martin Buber and others developed a *"Binnensprache,"* Aesopian words of resistance based on aggadic midrash.[48] Poets, too, like Sutzkever and Radnoti, mobilize the strength of traditional forms, even if Radnoti, who revives the eclogue, feels compelled to ask: "Is there still a land, tell me, where this verse form has meaning?"[49] The poets who continue to write do so in a no-man's land. Radnoti's despair is clear from a poem excavated with his corpse:

> I lived on this earth in an age
> When poets too were silent: waiting in hope
> For the great Prophet to rise and speak again—
> Since no-one could give voice to a fit curse
> But Isaiah himself, scholar of terrible words.[50]

While Blanchot, conscious that the Shoah has modified narrative competence or intellectualizing arrogance in only minor ways, struggles with language against it, against the seductiveness of narrativity and voice, Radnoti and Primo Levi do not display that obsessive focus. When Levi quotes a passage from Dante's *Hell* in the hell of Auschwitz, he preserves rather than estranges the literary moment.[51] The concern of both Radnoti and Levi is to speak without cursing.

Yet the radical direction taken by Blanchot is paradoxically sustained by them. For if any redemptive structuring of time or language is a passing hope, then literature after Auschwitz will not be essentially different from literature before Auschwitz, despite our anguished consciousness. The terrible beauty born in the wake of the Holocaust is terrible and beautiful because of a sameness, a repetition, an invincibly pastoral or contemplative element. Both types of art, of willing and of defiant consent to traditional literary forms, strengthen Adorno's comment: "The world grown dark makes the irrationality of art rational: art, itself the radically darkened."[52] It is this rationality of art, despite a hopelessness that afflicts us after the Holocaust, which I have tried to epitomize in this essay.

EPILOGUE (250 YEARS AFTER GOETHE'S BIRTH)

> Only for the sake of those who have no hope is hope given us.
> —Walter Benjamin, "Goethe's *Wahlverwandschaften*"

Imagine, now, that Goethe, from his place in the literary firmament, saw what happened between 1933 and 1945: the murderous assault of the Nazi regime on the Jews, as well as on others scorned as ethnically inferior, asocial, or unworthy of life, an assault in the very name of culture, of a pure Aryan culture. I do not conjure up a Goethe looking down from heaven because his temperament was Olympian but because he understood the relation between the extremes of happiness and unhappiness, the danger of exaltation together with the fall from sublimity into a disenchantment that must lead to incurable melancholy or savage revenge. "Es fürchte die Goetter / Das Menschengeschlecht" [Mankind must fear (coming near) the gods]: the opening of Iphigenia's "Parzenlied," her hymn to the Fates in *Iphigenia in Tauris,* is but one of Goethe's warnings against identifying with *"Herrscher"* mania. Precisely such deification inspired the leaders of a self-styled master race and attracted an enormous number of fanatics and fellow travelers.

Perhaps you will object to my fantasy because whatever it was that Goethe intuited was exceeded by the enormity of the Holocaust to such an extent that he would have been unable to fathom it, or because the Goethean response, in a poem like Iphigenia's hymn, can no longer go to the heart of the matter. Part of me agrees with that assessment. Goethe, who wrote, "there are unbeautiful, terrifying things in nature, with which literature, however skillfully it may treat them, ought neither to concern nor to reconcile itself," and who, though recognizing Kleist's genius, was also repelled by it, may not be—if anyone can be—an adequate witness. But as we pass from generation to generation, and by now the third after the Shoah has come of age, it is impossible to omit from the cause of hope the country from which the destruction originally arose.

As the ravage of genocide is repeated in other parts of the world, it is human nature itself we confront. No god out of the machine can help, as in Aeschylus or Euripides, though an invention like that is prompted by the impasse in human affairs between amnesty and the retaliatory demands of justice. But if we anticipate a lifting of despair, and therefore seek to *study* (I can find no better word) the possibility of hope, it has to come from a renewed understanding of language or art, including Germany's contribution.

It is relatively easy to honor—I do not say to comprehend—Paul Celan, but does the art of a Goethe still move us, can such art prevail despite the Nazi disaster? Reading Goethe today, must we overlook what began to happen only a hundred years after his death? Can we enjoy his wisdom and virtuosity only by confining him to his historical corner, blinkering the inspiration of a creator who is as important to German literature as Shakespeare is to English?

I realize that even Shakespeare's place is no longer entirely secure. Yet his dramas have proved to be more adaptable to a contemporary world that has "supp'd full of horrors." Akhmatova still invokes him, thinking of Londoners during the Blitz: "Time is writing Shakespeare's twenty-fourth drama." But, she adds, "not this, not this, not this, / this even we aren't capable of reading."[53]

What terror and trauma Goethe knew are not portrayed with the visual force and super-realism of Shakespearean tragedy. For those devoted to literature, however, it may be as important to justify art through Goethe as through Shakespeare. It is precisely because of his reticence, or "klassische Dämpfung," as Leo Spitzer named it—the fact that in *Iphigenia* he evokes catastrophe from the distance of ballad and oral tradition ("Vor meinen Ohren tönt das alte Lied," says Iphigenia, "The ancient song comes to my ears")—that my looking to Goethe may be relevant. What might he have said, obliged to star in a "Prologue in Heaven" like the one introducing his own *Faust*? That *Iphigenia in Tauris* tries to undo a spell ascribed to the Fates, even if it originated in human nature. The Holocaust institutes once again a break in civilization *(Zivilisationsbruch)* and unleashes a horrendous chain of consequences. This time it is irreducible to the story of an eponymous family on which so much of ancient Greek tragedy is based, the story of Tantalus, Pelops, and his family feud. Yet Goethe, too, seeks to exorcize the Furies, even if his play is almost entirely a learned rumor, a belated pandect of classical themes, and therefore (like Greek tragedy itself) as much recitation as dramatic action. It is, in effect, as pointed in its moral urgency as anything in Shakespeare.

The audience in Berlin which saw *Iphigenia* staged in 1998 was, I am sure, sensitive to its topical appeal, since the play raises the issue of hospitality to foreigners. Was it only, though, my ears that responded to the pathos of the sister's refusal to save her brother and herself, before making sure that Tauris would abolish human sacrifice? I cannot vouch for the audience around me, but I thought of the curse the Holocaust had brought upon Germany when she speaks the following words:

Soll dieser Fluch denn ewig walten? Soll
Nie dies Geschlecht mit einem neuen Segen
Sich wieder heben?

[Must this curse then last for ever? Can
this people never be reestablished
through a new blessing?][54]

NOTES

"Epilogue (250 Years after Goethe's Birth)" from Geoffrey Hartman, *Scars of the Spirit: The Struggle against Inauthenticity* (New York: Palgrave, 2002). Copyright © Geoffrey Hartman. Reprinted with permission of Palgrave Macmillan.

1. Arthur A. Cohen, "Thinking the Tremendum: Some Theological Implications of the Death Camps." *The Leo Baeck Memorial Lecture,* no. 18 (1974): 3.

2. Yosef Yerushalmi, "Un champ à Anathot: vers une histoire de l'espoir juif," in *Mémoire et histoire: Données et débats,* ed. Jean Halpérin and Georges Lévitte (Paris: Denoël, 1986).

3. Issued in English translation as *Literature or Life* (1997).

4. Jorge Semprun, *Literature or Life*, trans. Linda Coverdale (New York: Viking, 1997). See for the French edition *L'ecriture ou la vie Paris* (Paris: Gallimard, 1994): "La certitude qu'il n'y avait pas vraiment eu de retour, que je n'en etais pas vraiment revenu" (126) and "Je n'etais rien d'autre, pour l'essentiel, qu'un residu conscient de toute cette mort" (131).

5. See Albert Friedlander, in Friedrich-Wilhelm Marquardt and Albert Friedlander, *Das Schweigen der Christen und die Menschlichkeit Gottes: Gläubige Existenz nach Auschwitz* (Munich: Kaiser Tractate, 1980), 46–49. The most compelling remarks on Jewish-Christian relations after the Holocaust remain for me those of Emil Fackenheim in *The Jewish Return to History: Reflections in the Age of Auschwitz and a New Jerusalem* (New York: Schocken Books, 1978), 32–40.

6. Marquardt and Friedlander, *Das Schweigen der Christen und die Menschlichkeit Gottes*, 12. In this there is a double meaning, intended or not: Christians cannot learn this lesson unless they identify with what happened to the Jews, their "shunning." Dostoievsky's Ivan Karamozov tries to sustain his faith despite the "tears of humanity with which the earth is soaked from its crust to the center." But it is impossible for Jews to accept his vision of reconciliation, even if it echoes the Book of Job and other biblical sources. "I want to see with my own eyes the hind lie down with the lion and the victim rise up and embrace his murderer."

7. Robert Antelme, "Témoignage du camp et poésie," in *Le Patriote résistant*, no. 3, 15 May 1948; reprinted in *Robert Antelme: Textes inédits Sur L'espèce humaine Essais et témoignages* (Paris: Gallimard, 1966), 44–48. Fifty years later Lawrence Langer, in *Preempting the Holocaust* (New Haven, Conn.: Yale University Press, 1998), x, will strongly acknowledge what he calls "the legacy of permanent disruption" caused by the survivors' experience.

8. On this, consult Annette Wieviorka, *L'ère du témoin* (Paris: Plon, 1998), 172–75. Primo Levi's influence, in this respect, began to be felt in America and Europe somewhat later.

9. See Arthur W. Frank, *The Wounded Storyteller: Body, Illness and Ethics* (Chicago: University of Chicago Press, 1995), chap. 5. Lawrence Langer coins the striking phrase the "legacy of unheroic memory" in *Holocaust Testimonies: The Ruins of Memory* (New Haven, Conn.: Yale University Press, 1992), 205.

10. David Halivni, *The Sword and the Book: A Life of Learning in the Shadow of Destruction* (New York: Farrar, Straus & Giroux, 1996).

11. In this respect, *Life Is Beautiful* is one of many films in which "the survival of a child, even a single one, signifies a resistance to the brutal facts, a ray of hope for the future." See Froma I. Zeitlin, "The Vicarious Witness," *History & Memory* 10 (1998): 32. It has not been noted, however, that there is an affinity between the father-child relationship in *Life Is Beautiful* and an entirely different film that is a classic of postwar Italian cinema: Vittorio da Sico's *Bicycle Thief.*

12. Heinrich Mann, "Das weiss eigentlich jeder," reprinted in *Heinrich Mann Das Führer Prinzip/ Arnold Zweig Der Typus Hitler: Texte zur Kritik der NS-Diktatur* (Berlin: Aufbau Taschenbuch Verlag, 1993), 19.

13. Now partly available in translation. Victor Klemperer, *I Will Bear Witness: A Diary of the Nazi Years, 1933–1941,* trans. Martin Chalmers (New York: Random House, 1998).

14. "Das Leiden, das eine fortwährende Selbstreinigung mit sich hätte bringen müssen, wäre ja so stark gewesen, dass Sie hätten den Verstand verlieren müssen." He adds: "Das ist es ja gerade, was uns Emigranten so unverständlich ist! Wie die Menschen in Deutschland nicht den Verstand verloren haben." The letter is addressed to Hugo Friedrich. Cited by O. G. Oexle, "Zweierlei Kultur. Zur Erinnerungskultur deutscher Geisteswissenschaftler nach 1945," in *Rechtshistorisches Journal,* Hersg. Dieter Simon (Frankfurt am Main, 1997), 16:383. See also Elisabeth Langgässer, "Schriftsteller unter der Hitlerdiktatur," *Erster Deutscher Schriftsteller-kongress 4.-8. Oktober 1947,* Herausgegeben von Ursula Reinhold, Dieter Schlenstedt, and Horst Tannenberger (Berlin: Aufbau-Verlag, 1997), 136–41. I should add the following thought. That an ambitious and ruthless regime should conspire with the aggressive side of human nature, and idealize war and the removal of the shame of a prior defeat, is not surprising: imperialism and militarism, which coex-

isted with a high degree of personal and artistic culture in Rome, continued to appeal to a later European elite. Nazi ideology, often under the auspices of the SS, resurrected the *völkisch* myth of a Nordic race whose ancient Aryan rites and *Herrenvolk* character had supposedly been suppressed by the Romans. (It became, thus, a perverse kind of high culture.) Added to this myth was a biological *Rassenlehre* that made the extrusion and killing of the so-called antirace of Jews appear not only legal but normal. Citizen was alienated from citizen; years before the Final Solution murderous acts took place with immunity in the camps that sprung up immediately after the transfer of power in 1933; and the fear of Jewish contamination—based on an insidious form of blood libel—was deliberately propagated.

15. See, e.g., a book written beginning 1946 by the theologian Martin Dibelius but only recently published: *Selbstbesinnung des Deutschen,* ed. Friedrich Wilhelm Graf (Tübingen: Mohr Siebeck, 1947), 2–4.

16. Cf. D. Bar-On, *Legacy of Silence: Encounters with Children of the Third Reich* (Cambridge, Mass.: Harvard University Press, 1989). The "black box" of unopened memory also contained many personal disasters suffered by the German populace: see, e.g., Elisabeth Domansky, "A Lost War: World War II in Postwar German Memory," in *Thinking about the Holocaust: After Half a Century,* ed. Alvin H. Rosenfeld (Bloomington: Indiana University Press, 1997), 233–71. The Mitscherlichs, well-known German psychiatrists, diagnosed an incapacity to mourn; that incapacity involved verbal as well as psychic impotence.

17. Langgässer, "Schriftsteller unter der Hitlerdiktatur," 137. One must acknowledge, at the same time, the fact to which Karl Kraus is the most outspoken witness, of a more general debasement of language, not only in Germany but in the West before (and after) Hitler. George Steiner's admonitions are well known; see also Cohen, "Thinking the Tremendum," and my remarks below on the language-consciousness of modernism.

18. George Orwell, *Shooting an Elephant* (New York: Harcourt, Brace, and Company, 1950), 92.

19. On the role of academics, in addition to Max Weinreich's classic *Hitler's Professors,* see Oexle, "Zweierlei Kultur," 16:359–91.

20. After the war, Blanchot emerged as a political activist principally during the Algerian crisis (when he joined the famous Declaration of the 121) and the student turmoil of 1968. An "essai biographique" of Blanchot has finally been published: see Christophe Bident, *Maurice Blanchot: Partenaire Invisible* (Paris: Champs Vallon: 1998). Philippe Mesnard has focused on Blanchot's complicated incursion into and withdrawals from politics in *Maurice Blanchot: le sujet de l'engagement* (Paris: L'Harmattan, 1996). For a remarkable account of Antelme and his rescue—an account that takes as its point of departure the *explication de texte* of a letter Antelme wrote to the author in June 1945 about his recuperation and dealings with speech—see Dionys Mascolo, *Autour d'un effort de mémoire: Sur un lettre de Robert Antelme* (Paris: Maurice Nadeau, 1987). Also, for Blanchot's most direct statements on Antelme, see *Robert Antelme: Textes inédits,* 72–87. Blanchot met Antelme through Mascolo circa 1958: see his "For Friendship," *Oxford Literary Review* 22 (2000): 28–29.

21. "und der die Geige spielt, ist ganz weiß geworden und setzt einen Takt lang aus" [and he who plays the violin turns pale and misses the beat for a long time]. The complexity vis-à-vis the Shoah of this description in Ingeborg Bachmann's "Was ich in Rom sah und hörte" (1955) is carefully demonstrated by Sigrid Weigel, who recovers for us Gershom Scholem's poem of 1967 referring to this scene in Bachmann's sketches, a poem that contests a messianic allusion—and the possibility of messianic hope after the Shoah—which is probably not there. See Weigel, "Gershom Scholem und Ingeborg Bachmann. Ein Dialog über Messianismus und Ghetto," *Zeitschrift für deutsche Philologie* 115 (1996): 608–16. The literary burden is that of walker-tourist-flâneur, from Schiller's "Spaziergang" through Rilke's *Malte Laurids Brigge* to Walter Benjamin. The "Spiel weiter" may recall Celan's "Totesfuge."

22. Terrence Des Pres, *Writing into the World: Essays: 1973–1987* (New York: Viking, 1991), 27.

23. See Catherine Coquio, "L'extrême, le génocide, l'expérience concentrationnaire," *Critique* 600 (1997): 339–64; Michael A. Bernstein, "Homage to the Extreme: The Shoah and the Rhetoric of Catastrophe," *Times Literary Supplement,* March 6, 1998, 6–8; and Tzvetan Todorov, *Les abus de la mémoire* (Paris: arléa, 1998). See also the report by Dominique Dhombres in *Le Monde* of 11 July 1998 (pp. 1, 12), on a conference in Lisbon organized by the Calouste-Gulbenkian Foundation. Under the headline "Malaise dans la culture européenne," Dhombres quotes George Steiner on this crisis as a language crisis from the First World War on. René Girard, also participating, sees another crisis, one that actually unifies European and world culture: a troubling major focus on the victim.

24. Lawrence L. Langer, *Preempting the Holocaust* (New Haven, Conn.: Yale University Press, 1998), xix.

25. History yields not simply an explanatory cause but a justification, in the sense in which Yosef Yerushalmi writes (though of the *Wissenschaft des Judentums* rather than specifically of Hegel): "history becomes what it had never been before—the faith of fallen Jews. For the first time history, not a sacred text, becomes the arbiter of Judaism. Virtually all nineteenth-century Jewish ideologies, from Reform to Zionism, would feel a need to appeal to history for validation." *Zakhor: Jewish History and Jewish Memory* (Seattle: University of Washington Press, 1982), 86.

26. Or, "without being able to" [sans pouvoir]. See Sarah Kofman, *Paroles suffoquées* (Paris: Galilé, 1997), 16: "Parler—il le faut—*sans pouvoir:* sans que le langage trop puissant, souverain, ne vienne maîtriser la situation la plus aporétique, l'impouvoir absolu et la détresse même, ne vienne l'enfermer dans la clarté et le bonheur du jour?"

27. Blanchot takes up the issue of the engagement of the intellectual in *Les intellectuels en question: ébauche d'une réflexion* (Paris: Fourbis, 1996), with relevant remarks on Sartre on pages 57–58.

28. This echoes Mallarmé's famous "la fleur, l'absente de tous les bouquets." The point at which this withdrawal touches words themselves points to the difference between Blanchot's spirituality and that of Judaism. In the latter, meanings may withdraw into the text, but the text (as Scripture) is always maintained. Yet his essay on Jabès conflates "cette écriture qui est la difficulté du poète," the one who wants to find the *mot juste,* and "la justice difficile, celle de la loi juive, la parole inscrite avec laquelle on ne joue pas, et qui est esprit parce qu'elle est le fardeau et la fatigue de la lettre." Maurice Blanchot, *L'amitié* (Paris: Gallimard, 1971), 252.

29. Maurice Blanchot, *La part du feu* (Paris: Gallimard, 1948), 328. My translation.

30. Blanchot, *Les intellectuels en question,* 56–59.

31. Blanchot, *La part du feu,* 45. Levinas's attitude toward this phenomenal exteriority is very intricate, however: Derrida has exposed its complexity or ambivalence in his essay on Levinas, "Violence and Metaphysics," in *Writing and Difference* (Chicago: University of Chicago Press, 1978). Exteriority in the sense in which it is opposed to Hegel's phenomenological perspective owes something to Heidegger's concept of Existence as a standing-outside-of (ec-sistence) and endurance (punning on the German *ausstehen*) of this outsiderness.

32. The phrase comes from Baudelaire's description of Constantin Guys in his essay "The Painter of Modern Life."

33. Maurice Blanchot, *Thomas the Obscure: New Version,* trans. Robert Lamberton (New York: David Lewis, 1973), 26.

34. Maurice Blanchot, *L'entretien infini* (Paris: Gallimard, 1969), 189. My translation. I should add that Levinas does not seem to share Blanchot's view of art which he says gratifies like politics "the essential violence of action." See Emmanuel Levinas, *Totality and Infinity. An Essay on Exteriority,* trans. Alphonso Lingis (Pittsburgh: Dusquene University Press, 1969), 298.

35. "la parole, celle qui invite l'homme à ne plus identifier avec son pouvoir." Blanchot, *L'amitié,* 253.

36. This is the context in which we should read Levinas's protest against Hegel, that moral knowledge is "other than being and beyond essence." See Levinas's book of that title and, for a summary, *Éthique et Infini: dialogues avec Philippe Nemo* (Paris: Fayard, 1982). Other Levinas quotations come from "Ethics as First Philosophy," in *The Levinas Reader,* ed. Sean Hand (Oxford: Basil Blackwell, 1989), 75–87. Cf. Blanchot's many remarks on passivity and the "discourse of passivity" in *The Writings of the Disaster,* 17–20. In how far Levinas and Blanchot are influenced by Kojève's famous proposition that "history" in the Hegelian sense is complete, that we are "beyond essence" in that sense, cannot be discussed here.

37. Edith Wyschogrod, "Concentration Camps and the End of the Life-World," in *Echoes from the Holocaust: Philosophical Reflections on a Dark Time,* ed. Alan Rosenberg and Gerald E. Myers (Philadelphia: Temple University Press, 1988), 335 (author's emphasis).

38. Blanchot, *L'écriture du désastre,* 180: "L'holocauste, l'événement absolu de l'histoire, historiquement daté, cette toute-brûlure où toute l'histoire s'est embrasée, où le mouvement du sens s'est abîmé."

39. See also Michael Rothberg's development of this insight as it surfaces in both the fictional and discursive work of Maurice Blanchot, in *Traumatic Realism: The Demands of Holocaust Representation* (Minneapolis: University of Minnesota Press, 2000), 85 ff. Blanchot, as I have mentioned, hints at various times that with Auschwitz history has come to an end, in the sense that Kojève talked about Hegel's end of history. It is, to invert the Kantian formula, a "fin sans finalité." Negativity remains—part of the sequelae of the Holocaust—but cannot operate as a dialectical machine producing new meanings.

40. Blanchot, *L'écriture du désastre,* 104.

41. My summary is based mainly on *L'écriture du désastre.* "Veiller sur le sens absent" is on p. 72, and the remark on "imposture" on p. 79, in a discussion of the relation between Hegel, meaning, and system, pp. 79–80. *Veiller,* the French for "to watch over," is also the word for watching at the bedside of a dying person, looking for a sign of that person's salvation, of whether he makes a "good end." Blanchot's "wake" inverts this religious watching, without forgetting Pascal's "Il ne faut plus dormir."

42. Unlike many modernists between the wars, who were attracted to the idea of a "conservative revolution," he does not seek to "make it new," or break through to an antibourgeois or archaic stratum. Ezra Pound and Gottfried Benn are obvious examples, though the latter moved away from his *Schwärmerei* for the Nazi regime.

43. See Blanchot's "Postface" to *Vicious Circles: Two Fictions & "After the Fact"* (Barrytown, N.Y.: Stationhill Press, 1985), 68. Also on passivity, *L'écriture du désastre,* 28 ff.

44. Yet, interestingly enough, Hegel as the least fragmentary of writers is not absent. Blanchot's description of Hegel's prose, "l'asperité d'un style sans repos" [the asperity of a style that cannot find rest], fits Blanchot, too. The phrase is applied to Hegel in *L'écriture du désastre,* insofar as Hegel is conscious of the impossibility of a totalizing closure. It is not till *L'écriture du désastre,* however, that the conventional, monologic prose of Blanchot's essays and reviews comes closer to the style of his *récits.* In Derrida, the prose of the essay and the prose of fiction cohabit differently.

45. Blanchot comes very close, also, with his antisystematic bent, to Walter Benjamin's concept of the "expressionless," depicted in Benjamin's essay on Goethe's *Elective Affinities* as both an interruption and perpetuation of the semblance *(Schein)* of the harmonious and beautiful. "Das Ausdruckslose" is at the base of a work's completion *as* fragments of the truth. It "zerschlägt was in allem schönen Schein als die Erbschaft des Chaos noch überdauert: die falsche, irrende Totalität— die absolute." Further, "Dieses erst vollendet das Werk, welches es zum Stückwerk zerschlägt, zum Fragmente der wahren Welt, zum Torso eines Symbols." See Walter Benjamin, *Illuminationen: Ausgewählte Schriften* (Frankfurt am Main: Suhrkamp, 1961), 127.

46. The smile of the Rheims angel in Antelme's description comes to mind. See *Robert Antelme: Textes inédits,* 15–16.

47. Maurice Blanchot, "From Dread to Language," originally in *Faux pas* (1943); trans. Lydia Davis in *The Gaze of Orpheus,* ed. P. Adams Sitney (New York: Station Hill, 1981), 4.

48. Ernst Simon, "Der neue Midrash," in *Aufbau im Untergang: Jüdische Erwachsenenbildung im nationalsozialistischen Deutschland als geistiger Widerstand* (Tübingen: C. B. Mohr, 1959), chap. 4.

49. Miklos Radnoti, "The Seventh Eclogue."

50. Miklos Radnoti, "Fragments," trans. Clive Wilmer and George Gömöri, in *Poetry of the Second World War,* ed. Desmond Graham (London: Pimlico, 1998), 17.

51. See Primo Levi, "The Canto of Ulysses," in *Survival in Auschwitz.*

52. Theodor Adorno, "Die Verdunklung der Welt macht die Irrationalität der Kunst rational: die radikal verdunkelte," in *Aesthetische Theorie* (Frankfurt a/M.: Suhrkamp, 1970), 35. When Paul Celan, in a famous pronouncement, says that, after the Holocaust, and "despite a thousand eclipses *[Finsternisse]* language remained," he is refusing, despite an increasingly radical poetic practice, to reject the culture, even if suborned, of the mother tongue.

53. Anna Akhmatova, in Graham, *Poetry of the Second World War,* 62.

54. Emil Fackenheim said the following about Goethe in 1976: "It is not certain how long the world will be inspired by the wisest German. But we must live with the grim certainty that the shadow of the most depraved German [Hitler] will never cease to haunt it." *The Jewish Return to History,* 261.

Twelve

LAMENT'S HOPE

Paul Mendes-Flohr

In the grim shadows cast upon our civilization by the Holocaust, Geoffrey Hartman (chapter 11) has spoken to us "about and of hope." Focusing on the burden assumed by language to contain disaster and *pari pasu* also hope, his finely tuned discussion of this paradoxical capacity of the spoken and written word is appropriately humble, even muted. I shall allow myself to be a bit more bold in reflecting upon the concept of hope, and offer some tentative comments about the nature and possibility of hope in the wake of the Holocaust.

The concept of hope—its epistemological and phenomenological contours—may be illuminated by an epigram coined by my Jerusalem colleague, R. J. Zwi Werblowsky: "Optimism is a natural vice; Hope is a supernatural virtue."[1] This somewhat whimsical allusion to St. Augustine's theological elaboration of the notion of grace comes to underscore that optimism and hope are not identical. The former, optimism, is emphatically an emotional disposition; it is a function of mood and feelings—emotions which are, of course, notoriously mercurial. Optimism—or the lack thereof—may also be a result of sober assessment of reality. Hope, on the other hand, is a form of knowledge, divinely dispensed and etched in our graced souls, indeed, very being. Thus one may be bereft of optimism and yet have hope.

The late marxist philosopher Ernst Bloch elaborated this insight in his writings on the "spirit of utopia" and what he called "das Prinzip Hoffnung." For Bloch, an avowed atheist, the source of hope is not a divine dispensation; hope is not, as Augustine would have it, a supernatural virtue. Rather, Bloch held, it inheres in the very structure of being; it is ontologically grounded. The human being's instinctive refusal to acquiesce to the present social and political realities as absolute pushes the mind, fanned by dreams and fantasies of alternative realities, to behold the future, the not-yet being *(das noch-nicht Sein)* and the ought of the world.[2] This glimpse of the *das noch-nicht Sein* generates hope. Hope, then, is not simply an emotional state; it has a two-fold epistemic role, for it allows one to perceive the present as not absolute and thereby also points to the promise of existence borne by a vision of a happier, more just future. As knowledge of the possibilities that lie beyond the temporal horizon, if but adumbrations of what might be, hope serves to differentiate the present from the promise of the future:

> As long as the past and future of things seemed to coalesce [undifferenti-ated], . . . the process between the primeval accident *(Urzufall)* and God can only with difficulty reach a new metaphysical phase. Only when the trajectory of time no longer lives in the merely perceptible *(sinnlich)* shadow of an eternal present will the night of existence *(Dasein)* be illuminated by existence's now apprehended past and future.[3]

The future illuminated by hope has a unique countenance that marks it radically, indeed ontically apart from the past and present. Hope therefore grants us what Bloch somewhat gnomically celebrates as an "unhappy certainty"[4] that the present is not absolute. As such, hope engenders a *Glückdifferenz*,[5] that is, an epistemic dissonance engendered between one's perception of present reality and the soul's intimation of a happier—a politically and socially more just—future. But Bloch was quick to add that hope remains vacuous if it does not inform our interpersonal life and political judgments. If hope does not contain a genuine future, that is, if it is not borne by a commitment to realize in the here-and-now that future, "it is merely wishful thinking, hocus-pocus."[6]

Bloch's initial mentor in the metaphysics—and politics—of hope was Hermann Cohen,[7] the neo-Kantian philosopher who also contributed decisively to the renewal of creative Jewish thought in the twentieth century. Cohen associated hope with the teachings of Israel's prophets and their insistent discontent with existent realities of the world. By probing the alternative reality promised by the future, prophetic hope obliges us to be restlessly impatient with the imperfections of the present. Hope commands us to remember the forlorn, the disinherited, to remember all those who weep, and to include them in our vision of the Promised Land.[8] This is the prophetic imperative of hope: Hope is nurtured by a sacred discontent with the woes of the world, our own sorrow but also and preeminently that of the other. We—not our ancestors of yore alone—were slaves in Egypt. We are the impoverished, we all are the victims of crazed hatreds; we are the dwellers of the slums, the dispossessed, the residents of refugee camps; we are battered women and abused children. We all are the disinherited, past and present. And the deeper our anguish, the stronger our hope. Prophetic hope demands of us an unabashed Weltschmerz.

If I may extrapolate from Bloch's and Cohen's reflections on the prophetic dialectics of hope, I should like to address the question of hope and the Holocaust. As Jews—as human beings in general—we are all to regard ourselves as survivors of Auschwitz, and to live our lives with all the burdens of survival. These burdens are first and foremost to mourn, to rend our garments with grief as we recall the victims of Auschwitz, those six million human beings exterminated for the scandal of being born of Jewish parents (not to speak of countless other individuals—homosexuals, mentally impaired, Gypsies—who were condemned to elimination because of putative ontological defects). To forget, to proceed with our lives without the tears of remembrance would be to vitiate and void hope. Historical amnesia—as labile as optimism—is the enemy of hope, hope as a vision and political ethos.

As an anguished identification with the victims of Hitler's satanic fury, remembrance is a multivalent moral duty. In the first instance, as Paul Ricoeur points out, we remember lest we allow forgetfulness to kill the victims twice over.[9] "We owe a debt to the victims of Auschwitz. And the tiniest way of paying our debt is to tell and to retell what happened at Auschwitz" (3). The story of what took place in those dark chambers of inhumanity, the brute tale itself, unadorned by extraneous ideological and metaphysical commentary, not only rescues the victims and their cruel death from the threat of oblivion, it "prevents their life stories from becoming banal" (4). We are morally beholden to remember—to relate the tale of Nazi barbarity—without an attendant demand for an explanation, theological, historical, or otherwise. Remembrance refuses to understand, for to understand means to tame the inherently incomprehensible; understanding seeks to cauterize an inconsolable loss with the balm of explanation. Explanation perforce renders the Holocaust—as all senseless horror—banal. And the danger of banality, as Ricoeur admonishingly notes, "may be greater today than the danger of sheer forgetfulness" (ibid.). Scholarly reconstruction and explanation threaten to overshadow and transfigure the mourner's lament. "Historians, sociologists, and economists may claim to explain the tragedy so thoroughly that it becomes merely one case of barbarism among others." Even more distressing, Ricoeur continues, "an allegedly full explanation may make the event appear as necessary, to the extent that the causes—which are either economical, political, psychological, or religious—would be held to exhaust the meaning of the event" (ibid.).

The mourner seeks no explanation. Her lament is a protest both against evil and its explanation. Her lament refuses to allow the scandal of Auschwitz to be contained by explanation. The mourner's cry pierces and transcends language, the cradle of explanation. Lament thus, paradoxically, also bears hope, for in decrying what is—was—it implicitly but insistently affirms what ought to be. Resolutely refusing to accept the decree of fate, hope is borne by an unmitigated outrage, not by explanation.

In the Jewish tradition lamentation is intimately linked with hope. The fast of Tish'ah be-Av, which commemorates the destruction of both Temples—and all other calamities that befell the Jewish people throughout its millennial journey—is said to be the day on which the Messiah is born.[10] On Tish'ah be-Av, pious Jews mourn the loss of the Temple and all the horrors since visited upon the Children of Israel by fasting, placing ashes on their heads, desisting from all creaturely comforts and pleasures, and reciting in the synagogues the Book of Lamentations—in some communities also the entire Book of Job—and singing dirges *(kinot)*. It is a day of ritual weeping—and of eschatological hope. The day concludes with the prayer *u-Va le-Zion Go'el:* "And there shall come for Zion a Redeemer. . . ." On the night following Tish'ah be-Av, inspired by kabbalistic custom, the community gathers and joyously recites the Blessing on the New Moon, for as the moon is renewed, so Israel is to be renewed.

It is said the moderns have forgotten how to mourn, and, in consonance, have jettisoned the practice of ritual weeping nurtured by various religious traditions.[11] Indeed, despite the proliferation of Holocaust memorials and assemblies of remembrance, little cultural space has been provided for commemorative lamentation.[12] Indicatively, instead of assigning Holocaust remembrance to Tish'ah be-Av, where according to traditional prescription it would belong, the Israeli parliament designated a date in the secular calendar, namely, the day before the celebrations marking Israeli Independence. Hence the commemoration of the Holocaust—which world Jewry has by and large adopted—is linked with the reestablished Jewish political sovereignty in the ancient homeland as the answer to Jewry's interminable suffering in the lands of exile. Not insignificantly, the full name of the national day of remembrance is *Yom ha-Shoa ve'Gevurah,* Remembrance Day of the Holocaust and Heroism—the latter noun acknowledging Jewish armed resistance to the Nazis. *Gevurah*—which in Hebrew is etymologically derived from the root word for man *(gever),* so the term bears the inflection of manliness—resonates the defiant and proud cry, "Never Again." Never again will Jews be haplessly victimized by the gentiles. These intonations allow for neither focused lamentation nor the hope of which Geoffrey Hartman speaks.

The need to ground the remembrance of the Holocaust in the memory of the desperate, indeed heroic armed resistance of Jewish men and women, such as in the Warsaw Ghetto uprising, is from a national and psychological perspective palpable and incontrovertible.[13] But the insistence of affiliating commemoration with heroism—manly heroism, even when shared in by brave women—may also have something to do with secularization and modern European sensibilities. It has been noted that with the Renaissance and the concomitant reconfiguration of Europe's class structure there slowly crystallized well-defined bourgeois codes of public comportment, in which excessive public expressions of emotion, especially weeping, were regarded as improper, "unmanly," tears being relegated to the lachrymose domain of women and children.[14] Accordingly, after having learned of his father's murder, Richard in Shakespeare's *Henry the Sixth, Part 3* exclaims:

> I cannot weep; for all my body's moisture
> Scarce serves to quench my furnace-burning heart;
> Nor can my tongue unload my heart's great burthen,
> For self-same wind that I should speak withal
> Is kindling coals that fires all my breast,
> And burns me up with flames that tears would quench.
> To weep is to make less the depth of grief:
> Tears then for babes; blows and revenge for me. (2.1.79–86)[15]

This gender-inflected code of emotional control also influenced the way European culture would view commemorative lamentation. Hence, caught between the primordial cadences of Jewish tradition and practice and the dictates of modern secular sensibility, Jews are uncertain how to commemorate and express the awful pain wrought by Auschwitz.

The quandary is poignantly illustrated by what may be labeled the scandal of weeping Israeli soldiers. During Israel's undeclared war in Lebanon against the Hezbollah, hundreds of Israeli soldiers were killed. With the ever increasing numbers of deaths, the myth of the *sabra*—said to be hard on the outside, and soft inside—broke. At the funerals, they would openly cry with grief at the loss of their fallen comrades. The custodians of the national ethos were outraged.

In the Israeli parliament, the Knesset, it was debated whether the weeping soldiers should be reprimanded for their public display of unmanly behavior; the army leadership undertook a program to instruct its ranks to exercise greater self-control. There were, of course, many in Israel—including politicians and ranking army personnel—who identified with these young soldiers who dared to weep.[16]

Perhaps we should learn to follow their lead and learn anew to lament and thereby express outrage at a senseless fate[17]—and therefore to hope.

NOTES

1. Orally communicated.

2. Ernst Bloch, "Man as Possibility," in Bloch, *The Future of Hope*, ed. Walter H. Capps (Philadelphia: Fortress Press, 1970), 64.

3. Bloch, *Kritische Erörterung über Rickert und das Problem der modernen Erkennistheorie* (Ludwigshafen am Rhein: Baur'sche Buchdruckerei, 1909), 64 f.

4. Ibid., 48.

5. Ibid.

6. Bloch, "Man as Possibility," 67.

7. See Bloch's dissertation, *Kritische Erörterung über Rickert,* last chapter. On Bloch's indebtedness to Cohen, see my *Divided Passions: Jewish Intellectuals and the Experience of Modernity* (Detroit: Wayne State University Press, 1991), 376 f.

8. On Hermann Cohen's doctrine of hope, see the collection of his essays: Cohen, *Reason and Hope,* ed. and trans. Eva Jospe (New York: Norton, 1971), passim.

9. Paul Ricoeur, "The Memory of Suffering." *Criterion* [Publication of the Divinity School, University of Chicago] (spring 1989): 2–4.

10. See Midrash Rabba 1:51.

11. See Gary L. Ebersole, "The Function of Ritual Weeping Revisited: Affective Expression and Moral Discourse," *History of Religions* 39, no. 3 (February 2000): 211–46; and Peter Homans, ed., *Symbolic Loss: The Ambiguity of Mourning and Memory at Century's End* (Charlottesville: University of Virginia Press, 2000), especially the editor's comprehensive introduction, "The Decline of Mourning Practices in the Modern West: A Short Sketch," 1–40. For extensive historical treatments of the same theme, see also Philippe Ariès, *The Hour of Our Death,* trans. Helen Weaver (New York: Oxford University Press, 1977); Michel Vovelle, *La Mort en l'Occident de 1300 à nos jours* (Paris: Gallimard, 1983); and Joachim Whaley, ed., *Mirrors of Mortality: Studies in the Social History of Death* (New York: St. Martin's Press, 1981).

12. Commemorative lamentation should be distinguished from private weeping, which is, indeed, often evoked by visits to Holocaust memorial and museums. The latter is an expression of grief and is personal, the former—commemorative or ritual lamentation allows for a communal process of symbolic and cultural mourning. The distinction I am suggesting parallels that made by Freud in his essay, "Mourning and Melancholia," in *The Standard Edition of the Complete Psychological Works of Sigmund Freud,* ed. James Strachey (London: Hogarth Press, 1957), 14:243–60. Also see Homans's observations that whereas grief is an emotion (Freud's melancholia), mourning is "a grief-infused symbolic action." Op. cit. (see note 16, above), pp. 7ff.

13. In recent years, especially among the second and third "post-Holocaust" generation, there has been growing resentment against the linkage of commemoration with heroism, for, in their view, it implicitly cast the shame on the vast majority of Jews who did go to slaughter as sheep. Moreover, it is claimed, the alleged shame renders weeping and genuine mourning difficult. This is the explicit message of the highly controversial autobiographical film of 1988 by Yehuda Poliker, an Israeli-born son of Greek Jewish survivors of Auschwitz, *Biglal ha-Milchamah ha-Hi* (Because of that war). On the cultural significance of Poliker's film, see Martina Urban, *Erinnerungskultur und Erinnerung als Arbeit. Neustrukturierung der Identität der post-Shoah Generation in der Bundesrepublik Deutschland und in Israel* (Jerusalem: Franz Rosenzweig Research Center, 1994), Discussion Paper no. 10.

14. Ebersole, "The Function of Ritual Weeping Revisited," 228–30. Cf. Various studies "have convincingly shown that in the Renaissance the popularity and proliferation of manuals on manners, which instructed bourgeois readers on how to act like persons of class, signaled an expanded awareness that the social self could be consciously fashioned" (228).

15. Cited in ibid., 230.

16. The affair of the weeping soldiers is discussed in the collection of essays by Nahum Barnea, *Yorim u- vokhim* (They shoot and they cry) (Tel Aviv: Zemorah, Bitan, Moran, 1981), passim.

17. There is, perhaps, a significant difference between personal loss and the commemoration of what Peter Homans aptly calls symbolic loss (see note 16), certainly of the nature of the Holocaust. Whereas the mourning of personal loss ideally entails a "working-through" and thus ultimately a reconciliation with the loss, commemoration of a loss that has the moral and political dimensions of the order of the Holocaust does not—I dare say, should not—allow for such closure. It would, indeed, be an immeasurable moral obscenity to reconcile oneself to the Holocaust—or *mutatis mutandis* any other barbarity resulting in the massive violation of human dignity and death. Secured in the liturgical calendar, ritual weeping serves to prevent the disgrace of closure, and hence sustains hope-against-hope that humanity will one day enter paradise. Until then, hope obliges us to resist resignation and concomitantly to resist evil.

Acknowledgments

This volume has its origins in a conference, held at the University of Chicago in November 1998, that was organized around the central clusters of debates that have—after more than fifty years of reflection—come to shape scholarly thinking about the Holocaust. The conference as well as the present volume was largely made possible through the passion and generosity of Harriet and Rick Meyer, whose support of the Committee on Jewish Studies at the university has been unflagging. The conference was conceived over the course of many hours of discussion—really a series of seminars—conducted by Moishe Postone, Eric Santner, Michael Geyer, and Michael Fishbane. We thank not only the scholars whose much revised contributions appear in this volume but also those who took part in the conference but did not publish in this collection: Peter Hayes, Ulrich Herbert, Marion Kaplan, David Levin, Michael Geyer, and Sander Gilman. Alan Thomas of the University of Chicago Press has our deep gratitude for shepherding the collection through the long process of its emergence as a real book. We also thank the three readers whose critical reflections on the manuscript helped in its final revisions. We are especially grateful to Spencer Leonard for the careful work he has done over the entire course of this project.

Contributors

Omer Bartov is the John P. Birkelund Distinguished Professor of European History at Brown University. He is the author of several books, most recently *Murder in Our Midst: The Holocaust, Industrial Killing, and Representation* (1996); *Mirrors of Destruction: War, Genocide, and Modern Identity* (2000); and *Germany's War and the Holocaust: Disputed Histories* (2003). He is also the editor or coeditor of *The Holocaust: Origins, Implementation, Aftermath* (2000); *In God's Name: Genocide and Religion in the Twentieth Century* (2001, with Phyllis Mack); and *The Crimes of War: Guilt and Denial in the Twentieth Century* (2002, with Atina Grossmann and Mary Nolan).

Dan Diner is professor of modern history at the Hebrew University of Jerusalem, director of the Simon Dubnow Institute for Jewish History and Culture at Leipzig University, and a member of the Saxon Academy of Sciences, Leipzig. His most recent books include *Das Jahrhundert verstehen* (1999); *Beyond the Conceivable: Studies on Germany, Nazism, and the Holocaust* (2000); and *Feindbild Amerika: Über die Beständigkeit eines Ressentiments* (2002).

Debórah Dwork is Rose Professor of Holocaust History and the founding director of the Strassler Family Center for Holocaust and Genocide Studies at Clark University. She is the author of *Children with a Star* (1990) and coauthor, with Robert Jan Van Pelt, of *Auschwitz, 1270 to the Present* (1996) and *Holocaust* (2002).

Saul Friedländer is 1939 Club Professor of History at the University of California, Los Angeles and Maxwell Cummings Emeritus Professor of History at Tel Aviv University. Friedländer publishes widely on the history of Nazism and the Holocaust; his most recent book is *Nazi Germany and the Jews,* volume 1, *The Years of Persecution, 1933–1939* (1997). He was awarded a MacArthur Fellowship in 1999 and was elected to the American Academy of Arts and Sciences in 2000.

Geoffrey Hartman is Sterling Professor (Emeritus) of English and Comparative Literature at Yale and a founder as well as project director of its Fortunoff Archive for Holocaust Testimonies. He is also a distinguished visiting professor of the humanities at the New School University. His most recent publications are

The Longest Shadow: In the Aftermath of the Holocaust (1996); *A Critic's Journey: Literary Essays* (1999); and *Scars of the Spirit: The Struggle against Inauthenticity* (2002). He is a member of the American Academy of Arts and Sciences and a Corresponding Fellow of the British Academy.

Dominick LaCapra is professor of history, Bryce and Edith M. Bowmar Professor of Humanistic Studies, and director of the Society for the Humanities at Cornell University. He is also director of the School of Criticism and Theory. LaCapra is the author of numerous books, most recently *History and Reading: Tocqueville, Foucault, French Studies* (2000) and *Writing History, Writing Trauma* (2001).

Paul Mendes-Flohr is a professor of modern Jewish thought at the University of Chicago Divinity School. He also serves as the director of the Franz Rosenzweig Research Center for German-Jewish Literature and Cultural History at the Hebrew University of Jerusalem. He has written *German Jews: A Dual Identity* (1999) and is currently completing two works: a biography of Franz Rosenzweig and a study of post-traditional Jewish identities.

Anson Rabinbach is professor of history and director of the Program in European Cultural Studies at Princeton University. His most recent book is *In the Shadow of Catastrophe: German Intellectuals between Apocalypse and Enlightenment* (1997).

Frank Trommler is professor of German and comparative literature at the University of Pennsylvania. Since 1995 he has been director of the Humanities Program at the American Institute for Contemporary German Studies in Washington. He has published widely in the areas of nineteenth- and twentieth-century German literature, theater, and culture as well as German-American cultural relations, and has a special interest in modernism, Weimar culture, and postwar Germany. Recently he coedited, with Elliott Shore, *The German-American Encounter: Conflict and Cooperation between Two Cultures, 1800–2000* (2001).

Shulamit Volkov, professor of modern history and incumbent of the Konrad Adenauer Chair for Comparative European History at Tel Aviv University, has published books and essays on German social history, German Jewish history, anti-Semitism, and minority history. Her recent publications include *Antisemitismus als kultureller Code* (2000) and *Das jüdische Projekt der Moderne* (2001).

Froma Zeitlin is Charles Ewing Professor of Greek Language and Literature and professor of comparative literature at Princeton University, where she also directs the Program in Jewish Studies. She has published extensively in the field of ancient Greek literature on epic, drama, and prose fiction. Her interest in Holocaust studies stems from courses she has taught for many years. This is her second essay on Holocaust literature.

Index

Adorno, Theodor: aesthetics of devotional distance, 148; on anti-Semitism in the Holocaust, 86–87, 111n. 31; and Auschwitz as "caesura in civilization," 58; on change in approach to Auschwitz, 139; *Dialectic of Enlightenment,* 60–61, 62–63, 86–87, 111n. 31, 112n. 42; on dialect of enlightenment for understanding the Holocaust, 9, 60–61, 62–63; "Engagement," 238; on the fragmentary, 241; on Hitler and German culture, 57; on the Holocaust and art, 242; *Minima Moralia,* 57; on shielding the Holocaust from profanation, 238; on writing poetry after Auschwitz, 139

Agamben, Giorgio, 12

agency: intentionalist-functionalist debate on, 7, 34, 36, 39, 84, 85–86; on part of the victims, 11–12, 165–68

Age of Extremes (Hobsbawm), 79n. 2, 81, 82–83, 107n. 6

Age of Ideology, 8, 19

Age of Wonders (Appelfeld), 188

Ahad Ha'am, 36

Ahasver, 233

Akhmatova, Anna, 243

Aktion Reinhard, 75, 77

Alphen, Ernst van, 173

Aly, Götz, 110n. 25

Améry, Jean, 58, 138, 241

Anders, Günther, 58

Andersch, Alfred, 138

Anderson, Robert, 207n. 55

Anschluss, 75

Antelme, Robert, 232, 233, 236

anti-Semitism: ambiguity of term, 35; as animus, 37–40, 41; and anti-Bolshevism in the Holocaust, 75, 76, 77–78; as anti-modern, 89–90; in anti-Zionism, 101; Bayreuth Circle, 18–19, 42; eliminationist, 8, 31, 35, 37, 39, 140, 219; evaluating its explanatory value, 34–48; fetishism

and, 10, 90–96, 106; Furet on, 107n. 8; in the Holocaust, 8–9, 15–48, 85, 86–87, 95, 138, 219; in immediate origins of "Final Solution," 17–33; as new full-fledged ideology, 35, 39–40, 89; power attributed to Jews by, 89; racial, 18, 19–20; redemptive, 8–9, 18–21, 29, 32, 43; as shaping and shaped by events, 44; and therapeutic language, 149; two models of, 37; why the Jews were singled out, 77, 94; as widespread throughout Europe, 38, 87–88; Zionists on centrality of, 36, 37

Appelfeld, Aharon, 188

"Approaches to the German Problem" (Arendt), 57

Arendt, Hannah: on administrative and technical aspects of the extermination, 3, 86; on anti-Semitism in the Holocaust, 86–87, 111n. 31; "Approaches to the German Problem," 57; "banality of evil," 3; *Eichmann in Jerusalem,* 86, 137; and Heidegger, 59, 60; *The Human Condition,* 60; on Ludwig-Tillich debate, 56–57; on Nazism and Western tradition, 57–58, 59–60; *The Origins of Totalitarianism,* 60, 86, 112n. 42; and spiral model of anti-Semitism, 37; on "the Abyss that opened before us," 64

Armenia, 76

Arrighi, Giovanni, 81, 107n. 7

Aschheim, Steven, 109n. 21, 154–55, 167

Auschwitz: Adorno on writing poetry after, 139; Birkenau, 157, 158; Bunkers I and II, 166; as caesura in civilization for Arendt, 58; as epicenter of the Judeocide, 155; as factory for destroying value, 95; and Frankfurt trials of 1963–65, 99, 137, 139; the Germans never forgiving the Jews for, 100; Habermas on, 7–8; in Hochhuth's *The Deputy,* 139; *Holocaust* becoming-preponderant term for, 148; hydrologic